FULLNESS OF TIME

Titles in The Missiology of Alan R. Tippett Series

The Jesus Documents (2012)

The Ways of the People: A Reader in Missionary Anthropology (2013)

The Road to Bau and *The Autobiography of Joeli Bulu* (2013)

No Continuing City (2013)

FULLNESS OF TIME

ETHNOHISTORY SELECTIONS FROM THE WRITINGS OF ALAN R. TIPPETT

THE MISSIOLOGY OF ALAN R. TIPPETT SERIES
DOUG PRIEST, SERIES EDITOR
DOUG PRIEST, EDITOR

WILLIAM CAREY
LIBRARY

Published by William Carey Library, an imprint of William Carey Publishing
10 W. Dry Creek Circle
Littleton, CO 80120 | www.missionbooks.org

Kelley Wolfe, editor
Brad Koenig, copyeditor
Pourio Lee, cover concept
Josie Leung, designer
Wisnu Sasongko, cover art, courtesy of Overseas Ministries Study Center

William Carey Library is a ministry of Frontier Ventures
Pasadena, CA 91104 | www.frontierventures.org

23 22 21 20 19 Printed for Worldwide Distribution

Cover Photo: "Nativity" by Wisnu Sasongko, 2005.

Library of Congress Cataloging-in-Publication Data

Tippett, Alan R. (Alan Richard), 1911-1988.

[Works. Selections. 2014]

Fullness of time : ethnohistory selections from the writings of Alan R. Tippett / edited by Doug Priest.

    pages cm

ISBN 978-0-87808-477-7

1. Ethnohistory. 2. Ethnology--Research--Methodology. I. Priest, Doug, 1952-, editor of compilation. II. Title.

GN345.2.T56 2014

909'.04--dc23

2013038480

CONTENTS

PART FOUR

PART FIVE

SERIES FOREWORD

Always the creative thinker, Alan Tippett, transplanted to the United States from Australia (never really integrated), is the originator of the concept of cultural fatigue which continues after culture shock has passed. One afternoon he walked the entire midtown business district of Pasadena seeking "a reel of cotton." Returning in despair, what was he asking for? Well, of course, a spool of thread. However, in the field of anthropology, he didn't miss a thing and had a compendious knowledge, especially of the Southern Pacific sphere.

His alert mind took him in many directions, some complete surprises, and from volume to volume in this series you will find very little overlap and much that is rich for contemplation. Thanks to Doug Priest as well as Darrell Whiteman, Charles Kraft, and Greg Parsons for making sure these gems of thought are still available.

Ralph D. Winter
Pasadena, California
May 2009

PREFACE

Alan Tippett held graduate degrees in both history and anthropology. In his autobiography, *No Continuing City*, he commented that he thought his course in ethnohistory at Fuller Theological Seminary was his most original (and enjoyable) teaching. I was fortunate to take that course—twice. The first time was for credit, and the second time to record it for those who could not come to Pasadena.

Tippett often used the phrase "fullness of time" in his lectures and writing, so it is an apt title for this collection of his finest offerings in ethnohistory. However, I toyed with another title, *In and Through Time*, to reflect his use of the distinction between the *diachronic* and *synchronic* analysis of history (see Part Three). I even suggested to Jeff Minard, general manager of William Carey Library, that the series as a whole use this title, with each volume then having its own unique title.

This volume has been needed for the twenty-five years since Tippett's passing. It is unfortunate that an entire generation has missed the opportunity of reading these seminal, instructive, and entertaining entries. Those of us involved in bringing Tippett's materials to publication wish we would have brought the project to fulfillment long ago.

At the time of his death, Tippett had an outline for a text in ethnohistory. He had asked his former student and friend, Darrell Whiteman, to coauthor the text. That outline is included as an appendix. Darrell was kind enough to write the foreword for this book.

I am indebted to Joan Tippett, eldest daughter of Alan and Edna Tippett, for her assistance in the publication of this volume.

Doug Priest
CMF International

FOREWORD

In 1953 the journal *Ethnohistory* was founded as well as the journal *Practical Anthropology*. Perhaps it is just coincidence that the field of ethnohistory matured to the point that it was ready for a journal in the same year that the field of missiological anthropology also found expression in a very innovative journal. The journal *Ethnohistory* is still publishing articles today, but in 1972 *Practical Anthropology* merged into *Missiology: An International Review*, the official journal of the American Society of Missiology. Alan Tippett became its first editor, and I became the fourth editor, serving for thirteen years. This synergistic confluence of missiology and ethnohistory met in Alan Tippett and found expression in his voluminous writing. Now, thanks to the publication of *Fullness of Time*, we are able to discover the range of Tippett's interests and the depth of his insights as he employed ethnohistorical methods to various mission contexts revealing how the gospel related to different cultures and why some missionary methods were more successful than others.

The field of missiological study and mission practice has undergone a significant paradigm shift in my lifetime. The nineteenth and early twentieth century of mission occurred in the context of colonialism when Western superiority was assumed in all things, including our understanding and practice of Christian faith. Authority was in the hands of a few, a paternalistic ethos colored interactions with new believers, and denominational extension more than planting and establishing indigenous churches was the norm. Of course, not all missionaries were colonialist in their mindset or paternalistic and ethnocentric, but unfortunately those who weren't were often in the minority. Today globalization has replaced political colonialism as a dominant force for culture change, but new expressions of economic and ideological colonialism have arisen and are sometimes even more stifling than the old forms of Western imperialism. For example, in too many places Christianity is still perceived as a foreign religion rather than an indigenous way of following Jesus.

Many church leaders in Africa, Asia, and Latin America are discouraged by the fact that it is easier to lead people to make decisions *for* Christ than it is to develop disciples *of* Christ. Why is there such a lack of discipleship, and why do people complain that even though the church in the Global South is growing rapidly, it is often a mile wide and an inch deep in its understanding and practice of faith? Alan Tippett was concerned with this question during his long missionary and missiological career, and he addressed these issues in his writing and teaching. Most of his writing was unpublished, but now with this book and others in the pipeline, Tippett's insights are being made known to a generation of missionaries and missiologists who perhaps have never heard of him.

Alan Tippett was an Australian Methodist missionary posted to Fiji for twenty years as the colonial era was drawing to a close and South Pacific Islanders were gaining their independence from Britain, France, Australia, and the United States. He chafed under many of the colonial structures that were still in place, and he did his best to usher in the postcolonial era of mission. As a missionary in the transition period, Tippett was keenly interested in the dynamics of culture change and the role Christianity had played in bringing about much of that change. He was concerned that the forms of following Jesus should be culturally appropriate to Fijian people and penetrate their Melanesian worldview, bringing about deep transformation and lasting change.

These concerns and interests, together with his natural gifts and graces led Tippett into anthropology and history. Anthropology would give him conceptual tools and practical methods to see how the gospel related to culture. Historiography would help him understand how Christianity had entered the contact situation and brought socioreligious change to Fijian society. This marriage of anthropology and history brought Tippett into the arena of ethnohistory which he discovered was a conceptual and methodological gold mine for understanding the growth or decline of the church over time and how the gospel related to culture. In the discipline of missiology we encounter the methods of ethnohistory in our research when Christian mission, history, and anthropology converge.

Tippett saw himself more as an ethnohistorian in the service of mission and the church than as an anthropologist or historian. Thus his significant anthropological contributions to church growth lore were shaped extensively by his love of ethnohistory as a research methodology. The great potential that ethnohistory has for missiology has not yet been realised. At Asbury Seminary's E. Stanley Jones School of World Mission and Evangelism, I drew on Tippett's legacy to a minor degree when I taught missiological research methods and introduced students to the field of ethnohistory. Today we need lots of case studies on church planting and church growth, and by employing ethnohistorical methods we will better understand how the church has or has not sunk it roots into the culture, reaching the deepest levels of a people's worldview.

To do ethnohistory you need documents, and you need to discover the political, religious, social, and economic context in which the documents have been created. Ethnohistory is one of the ways to chart change over time in cultural complexes and institutions. Primary sources in the form of documents are generally more reliable than secondary sources. Ethnohistory helps us in mission with methodology, data collection, strategic planning, and interpersonal relationships between ethnically diverse members of the body of Christ. The ministry of communicating Christ to the nations needs insights from anthropology and ethnohistory.

For missiologists and other researchers who may not be accustomed to using documents in their studies in order to understand the interaction of gospel and culture and the relationships between mission advocates and indigenous innovators, Tippett gives us five good chapters on the different kinds of documents that exist, where to find them, and how to use them. His chapter on Hawaii using documentary evidence contrasts markedly with James Michener's *Hawaii* (1959) and the even more provocative, stereotypical, and irresponsible movie *Hawaii* (1966), and shows what really happened when New England Protestant missionaries went to Hawaii in 1820.

Tippett's chapters on synchronic and diachronic studies are rich. We enter the world of Fijians or Solomon Islanders and come face to face with how Islanders initially perceived Christianity and how and why they responded as they did, sometimes with full acceptance, but often with modifications and sometimes outright rejection.

I first met Alan Tippett at a conference in 1975 when anthropologists and missiologists with interest in Oceania were interacting together to discuss mission, Christianity, and culture in the Pacific Islands. Shortly afterward I read his classic book *Solomon Islands Christianity* (1967), where he critiqued the paternalistic methods of Methodist missionaries over and against the more culturally sensitive approach of the Anglican Melanesian Mission. For my doctoral dissertation that would later be published as *Melanesians and Missionaries* (1983), Tippett encouraged me to study the Anglican Church of Melanesia, which had evolved from the Melanesian Mission, to discover how Christianity was interpreted and practiced in the Solomon Islands. To carry out this research Tippett introduced me to the field and methods of ethnohistory and instilled in me a great appreciation for the value of documents as primary resources. I had never read so many personal diaries and letters, official and informal reports, as I did to prepare for understanding the contemporary expressions of Christianity in the Solomon Islands.

One of those sets of documents was the personal diaries and letters of Dr. Henry Welchman, a medical doctor with the Melanesian Mission on the island of Santa Ysabel, where my wife and I would carry out our fieldwork in 1977–78. Welchman lived and worked on Ysabel when it was still an island of headhunters suffering from endemic warfare. Because I was soaked in the ethos and world of Dr. Welchman through his personal letters and diaries, I had a historical perspective on how Christianity had first made contact with the islanders of Santa Ysabel. So when I would mention something I had learned from Welchman's diaries to villagers where we were living, it gave me much more credibility than I would have otherwise had. Documents from the past opened doors to the present through which I was able to walk and conduct anthropological research on the impact of Anglican Christianity in the Solomon Islands.

Ethnohistory is not just a combination of anthropology and history, but rather it is a new and creative methodology more than a distinct discipline. Ethnohistory developed out of the discipline of anthropology, not history. So as an anthropologist interested in understanding the impact of Christianity on village life in Melanesia, I had to look at the phenomena through the lens of both time and space. This activity brought me to the methods of ethnohistory, thanks to Alan Tippett's introduction. One of my early publications as a graduate student in anthropology was on the cargo cult–like movement Marching Rule in the Solomon Islands and was published in the journal *Ethnohistory*, and for this research project I relied on documents.

The contact period today is vastly different from the contact period of the Age of Discovery and Exploration and the Colonial Era that followed. But the ethnohistorical methods used to understand what happened when people with the message of Christ came into contact with people without biblical values can still be used today when two billion people in the world have never heard of Jesus, let alone had the opportunity to follow or reject him. *Fullness of Time: Ethnohistory Selections from Alan Tippett* should go a long way in introducing these methods and demonstrating their value for today's mission practice and missiological reflection.

Darrell Whiteman
Vice President and Resident Missiologist
The Mission Society

INTRODUCTION

Towards a Technique for Extracting Anthropological
Data from Oceanic Missionary Records[1]

Introductory Preamble

In 1970 I spent the summer and a term of sabbatical leave visiting the library and archival institutions of the South Pacific, surveying the distribution and quantity of missionary documents available for study purposes. I visited sixteen different repositories and typed up sixty pages of description of the holdings. In the course of this experience I examined scores of private missionary journals and hundreds of letters. It would take a researcher many years to prepare even a simple catalogue of entries, without annotation, to cover the missionary records of the southwest Pacific alone. I came away from the experience with a strong feeling of a huge, untapped anthropological resource, which calls for the serious attention of ethnohistorians.

Although there is a tendency for missionary journals to gravitate to the Turnbull Library in Wellington, New Zealand, and the Mitchell Library in Sydney, Australia, the archives of the missionary societies are more widely distributed, and material in private hands very much so. The present tendency is for the missionary societies, when they hand over their work to indigenous churches, to transfer their archives to a proper archival institution where facilities exist for classification, care, and preservation. This has happened, for instance, both in Sydney and in Suva, Fiji, where the material is housed separately with a reasonable degree of accessibility.

An organisation at Canberra, known as the Pacific Manuscripts Bureau, microfilms records, letters, and journals in private hands. The large number of missionary items that have appeared in their lists points up again the existence of a huge reservoir of material, which is now made accessible to researchers, at least in microfilm form.

However, although the resources certainly exist, and the restrictions on their use are not serious, even so this kind of research is time consuming, and the documents so varied, and so little work has been done on them by anthropologists that there is an urgent need for understanding the precise nature and quality of the documents and for developing adequate techniques for research on them. To this end I am setting down in this paper a few

---

[1]   Paper presented at the annual meeting of the American Society for Ethnohistory (St. Paul, MN, 1974).

tentative guidelines based on my own experience with Oceanic missionary documents, for getting documents located in their proper contexts, and finally commenting on some methods of interpretation with which I have experimented.

The range of suggestions I am able to make, and the principles of context for which I argue, are limited of course by the kind of documents which have come my way. I fully recognise that this is only a beginning, and that others may have had quite different experiences and, indeed, that the contours of ethnohistory itself in the Pacific are still faintly drawn.

Perhaps before attempting to schematise some of my ideas I should consider the question often asked by undergraduate anthropologists—why bother with missionary documents at all?

Why Bother with Missionary Documents?

The notion that missionary records have nothing to say to anthropology because of their bias is a "straw man" or "Aunt Sally" set up to pelt at. Every document has a bias of some kind—even if some are more biased than others. The question to be asked by the thoughtful man is not "Is it biased?" but "What is its bias?" It is only thus that we are able to set one document over against another and see both sides of an issue as it stood between the participants in the islands at the point of time we are researching. Furthermore, no matter how biased one particular missionary may have been, he was nevertheless part of the historic complex of his time and place, and his evidence is part of the total picture. Researchers who refuse to consider this piece of the puzzle because it is intellectually unpleasant to them are probably confusing the missionary's personal religious convictions with bias—two very different things—and thereby demonstrating their own religious bias. Missionaries are individual people and, like anthropologists, they scatter all along the scale of objectivity.

Having made that qualification, I believe there are six good reasons why missionary documents are significant for anthropology. Let me tabulate them:

1. Because of the unexplored wealth of anthropological data still buried in missionary records.
2. Because the data are required for the study of cultural processes through time, especially since the definition of acculturation by Redfield, Linton, and Herskovits (1936).
3. Because the primary observations of customs and structures in Oceania are largely in the missionary records, and there is no way of reconstructing the culture patterns of the contact period other than by using this material.
4. Because the missionary contribution has to be recognised in the writing of any history of anthropology, and this applies especially to linguistics.

5. Because the missionary records are diachronic and describe changes which were and were not effective, and thus they speak to applied anthropology.
6. Because of the unscientific use of missionary data in some twentieth-century ethnography.

The sixth is the one negative reason I have given. It becomes positive if we regard it as a necessary corrective measure. Maybe I should pinpoint this for a moment.

The Shock of Distortion

In 1961 Washburn pointed out that few anthropologists were prepared to give long hours of study to documents, and few historians were prepared to devote years of fieldwork to studying the descendants of the subjects of those documents. He had worked on a study of seventeenth-century Native Americans and found that his historical sources had given the facts correctly but had interpreted them wrongly (1961, 47). He found himself quite agitated and described the experience in terms of "the shock of distortion." I had precisely the same experience when I discovered how far the Fiji historians were away from the truth with respect to Fijian war. They failed to distinguish between the "war of the chiefs" and the local skirmishing behind the social performances with respect to the gradua-tion of warriors (Tippett 1968, 53–66). It was the same again when I read Peter Buck's use of historical data from Tahiti. He was perhaps right in making a cultural point about the conversion of the Tahitians (seeing he was himself a Polynesian), but he was not right in his complete disregard of the historical complex of missionary writing which he had in his possession but only used selectively (Buck 1939, 65–67; Tippett 1971, 221–26, 269).

Both of these cases, from my own experience, represented the misuse of missionary sources. One could write a whole volume on this kind of distortion in anthropological and historical writing—and a series of volumes if one included historical novels. The relevance of ethnohistory as a research method is that it seeks to correct this kind of cross-disci-plinary distortion. More and more, ethnohistory serves this purpose as the contours of its domain are delineated, but its techniques for description and testing still require much expansion and improvement.

Definition of "Missionary Documents"

I would delineate the scope of the term "missionary documents" to include those writ-ten records created by missionaries to Oceania, or by indigenous missionaries to Oceanic areas other than their homeland, or of other leaders involved in the creation of Oceanic church records. I do not include here the biographies of missionaries to Oceania, written in England or America for promotional purposes to the end that Oceanic missions might be sponsored by the home church or sending board.[2] These have an entirely different function and are, for our purposes, "distorted" by selective use. Their value lies in the study of the English church and its missionary policy, not in ethnohistorical reconstruction in Oceania.

We are concerned therefore with those records which were *created in action*—in missionary endeavor itself, in the conversion of the islanders, in the planting of their churches, in the emergence of their new Christian structures—and descriptions of the contact situation. They emerge in the missionary action itself. We are concerned with the personal records of experience, of achievement, of failure, of anxieties, and of planning. We are interested in letters, in journals, in reports, in minutes of meetings, in discussions that were part of the decision-making process of the early island church. We are concerned with missionary notebooks containing accounts of pre-Christian customs and descriptions of institutions like cannibalism, widow strangling, infanticide, folklore, kinship, marriage, and trade patterns. We are interested in the journal entries in which missionaries narrate encounters with these institutions and their ceremonial practitioners. We are interested in their collected vocabularies, translations, and dictionaries. In other words, we are interested in all kinds of documents created in Oceania, by people who lived there, and about things that were going on there. We are looking for the records emanating from missionaries—not the writing about them, but the primary sources they themselves created.

The Missionary Document in Time and Place

Before any techniques can be devised for extracting anthropological data from these missionary records, some attention must be given to the character of those papers, the contexts in which they were created, and the factors which led to modifications in the archival continuum from time to time. In other words, we need to investigate first the *historical* and *cultural* frame of reference or "map" from which our records emerge, and which I will now discuss briefly under four conceptual headings—the relativity of history, the cultural continuum, the continuity of constellations, and the variability of rhythm.

The Relativity of History

Cultural relativity is not confined to the values and systems of different communities on a horizontal level, it may be observed also within any given cultural continuum at different levels of time depth. Sturtevant has made this point with reference to Asia and Africa (1966, 21–22). Thus, to study documents of Fiji, for instance, we could arrange them in a series according to the time level to which they belong. We would discover we had precolonial, colonial, and postcolonial periods, and a good deal could be learned from such an arrangement. The colonial period, however, covers nearly a hundred years, and most

---

2   For example, four biographies of John Hunt have been published, and another exists in manuscript. One of the above is in French, but none of them have the depth and quality of his manuscript journals, of which typescript copies exist.

researchers would want to subdivide it. Missionary records do reflect the sociopolitical strata within that century. The earliest missionary records of the postcolonial level indicate that this period is also stratified. There had been considerable contact before the arrival of any missionaries, and the white adventurers were entrenched in the islands when the missionaries arrived. Western arms and ammunition and liquor were already there in abundance and exchanged for sandalwood or women, and the country was already in a state of dramatic change. I cannot develop this here; I merely make the point that the missionary documents fall into a sequence of historical strata and must never be considered without reference to the levels of their historical context or used to document conditions of other periods than those in which they were created or to which they refer.

Perhaps the easiest way to demonstrate the relativity of history is from semantic change. Supposing one came across the Fijian phrase *luve ni mate*, which literally means "child of the dead," or one might say "an orphan." If the context shows that to be the meaning, the document using it must date to Christian times. If the context shows it to be a term of derision, its time depth must take one back to cannibal times, and the word will be used for a man whose father had been killed by his cannibal enemies and whose death had not been avenged. The son is a "son of the dead" until he has exacted a requital. "The vocabulary of documents," said Marc Bloch, is a "form of evidence" (1964, 168)—here evidence of the relativity of history.

The Cultural Continuum: Spatial and Temporal

At any one of those levels in the historical continuum, a horizontal study may be made. A total diachronic synthesis is a sequence of synchronic analyses: both "spatial and temporal" as Dark puts it (1957, 243). The fantastically large number of extant missionary journals are extremely valuable for these synchronic reconstructions at their respective points of time—provided of course that they speak for that point of time and not another. Thus, for example, the journals of Thomas Williams, John Hunt, Thomas Jaggar, and R. B. Lyth speak for the 1840s, but Fison for the 1860s and 1870s. Fison speaks for the 1840s only when he is reporting an old informant who is speaking about his earlier years. This is valid data but must be seen as "informant recall," not Fison's own "anthropological observation." Hunt and others had informant recall from before the time arms and liquor were first brought to Fiji. But mainly these men were observers of their own period of residence, and herein lies their greatest value.

In 1954 I presented before the Fiji Society a reconstruction of Fijian war from 1839 to 1846 on a basis of the above four journals of the period.[3] I believe these sources to be fair,

---

3   The originals of these journals are distributed as follows: Williams' and Lyth's at the Mitchell Library, Sydney; Hunt's at the Methodist Missionary Society Archives in London; Jaggar's in the Methodist Overseas Missions Collection, housed also at the Mitchell Library. The Fison Papers are scattered, but the largest number of them are with the

factual description without any obvious missionary bias. They provide a synchronic picture from men who had lived through the wars in question.

However, we Westerners have created problems for ourselves also on the horizontal or spatial level. We think of Fiji as if it were a little island, a tiny entity, a total thing for anthropological investigation. It is, of course, an archipelago of some three hundred islands. When the first missionaries arrived, its eight kingdoms were at war, and the eighth was being swallowed up by one of the others. The first missionary translation was being done in four different languages. The coastal people and mountaineers had little dealing with each other, and it was thirty years before penetration began into the mountains. The religious patterns and the physical form of the people suggested several historical migrations to the Group. The eastern islands were more Polynesian than Melanesian. There never was a single Fijian way of life until modern times, when the translation of the Bible and the establishment of colonial government brought unity. Even now the linguistic and customary patterns retain much of their ancient integrity. Now although the early missionaries sailed round the Group and shared their experiences when they got together once a year, the missionary records—journals, letters, and reports—should not normally be identified simply as "Fijian" as if Fiji was one thing.[4]

For example, the writer most used by anthropologists for reconstructions of early Fiji is Thomas Williams (1860), who was in Fiji from 1841–53 and left voluminous records. But I have never seen anyone who, having used him as a database, has pointed out that Williams lived in Lau, Taveuni, and Bua, and in Taveuni he had no mobility. He had no experience whatever of central or western Fiji. Having spent twenty years myself in Viti Levu, the largest and most multiethnic island, and in Kadavu, naturally I view Williams' writing as regional and far from pan-Fijian.

The point is that not only must the missionary source of data be seen at its temporal or historical level, but it also has a spatial or regional context. This often tends to be geographical, but it is more than geographical—it is ethnological and linguistic. Missionary records have to be located, not only with their historical period, but also with their ethnic identification. This becomes more and more apparent in the later period in Fiji after the establishment of Indian indenture, which introduced a new ethnic dimension. Missionaries to the Indians and those to the Fijians, although from the same homeland and the same denomination, nevertheless do demonstrate their regional and ethnic affiliations in their personal values and writings.

---

author of this paper. [The Tippett Collection is housed at St. Mark's National Theological Centre, Canberra, Australia.—Ed.]

4   I raised this question in a review article on two anthropological books which appeared when I was in Fiji. "Anthropological Research and the Fijian People" (1955), dealing with Hocart's *The Northern States of Fiji* (1952) and Roth's *Fijian Way of Life* (1953).

This raises an important question with respect to the evaluation of missionary journals. We have a tendency to quote the opinions of missionaries without indicating the duration of their residence on the field and when they made the statement or evaluation to be cited. When a researcher fails to consider this point, he presupposes that missionary opinion is a static thing, and that is far from the truth. Missionary journals reflect considerable opinion change. Frequently, after a year or so, a missionary passes through a period of culture shock and disillusionment, and thereafter his identification matures and his value judgments are more to be trusted. We badly need a scale of some kind for measuring this quality. To express the time quality of missionary opinion, I find myself using phrases like "soon after he arrived," "after twenty years in the community," or "immediately after such-and-such an experience."

Continuity of Constellations

We must not allow this emphasis on the recognition of the relevance of time and cultural units to blind us to the existence of cultural constellations or clusters, which manifest a continuity through both time and space—the diachronic and synchronic. The fact that there are clusters of cohesive traits or institutions which persist and go on through both time and space, with minor modifications to maintain relevance at each new level, makes it possible for us to study them. Through time, we find evidence of culture change. Through space, we find evidence of cultural diversity. Thus, for example, the researcher studying Lau will find certain basic constellations (social institutions like marriage and burial patterns, clusters of folklore, etc.) mentioned in the writings of David Cargill and again forty years later in those of Lorimer Fison. The continuity is established, but closer examination will reveal numerous minor modifications of the pattern. Here is evidence of culture change going on in the historic levels in one part of the Fijian Group—the windward islands. The motives and drives of Cargill and Fison were similar, and likewise their spiritual beliefs, so it would seem fair to me to compare their writings. Because of the uniformity of motivation and faith, missionary records from Fiji are good material for comparative studies—the variability of the observers being minimal.

Long before it became fashionable to study change, Fison was doing it. He stood at an interesting point of time when the Fiji missionary was distinguishing between "heathen villages" and "Christian villages," and the structures of cannibalism, though on the decline, were still at hand for observation.[5] Fison also had a way with the old men and was a good listener. From these informants he discovered much of the nature of the changes going on. He recorded much on semantic change, for instance. Many words dropped from use altogether. Other clusters continued but acquired new meaning more appropriate to the

---

5   This is brought out well in his correspondence published in *Missionary Notices* in the 1860s and was published by the Australian Wesleyan Missionary Society.

newly accepted Christian values. To give a simple example from Fison's notes (Fison Papers 1867–69), note the word *kusikusima*. Once it expressed the notion of "a desire to eat human flesh." Cannibalism passed, but men still desired to eat "something." The notion was transferred to fish. The word survived for those who felt an urge to eat fish, and still does to our own day, but now the original meaning is completely forgotten. The study of a sequence of missionary journals will often help the anthropologist to detect the configurations that are continuous and where the modifications have been made to maintain their relevance for each historical period and changing sociopolitical values.

Some of these constellations may also be studied horizontally. Many of these are common to all Fiji, again with certain variations according to felt needs in the different localities and environmental diversity. In my study of the Bau/Rewa War in the 1840s, I was fortunate to have access to missionary observations from both sides of the war front. Hunt at Viwa (Bau side), and Jaggar at Rewa, were separated for many months by the war, but both kept journals of the events. These two men, though both very much opposed to war, and especially cannibal war, nevertheless both spoke of "our side" in their descriptions (Tippett 1973, 42–54). This is not the only period of Fijian history for which military data from two sides is available in missionary journals—the 1860s is another.

The Variability of Rhythm

Before I leave the significance of time in missionary records, I recall how the historian Marc Bloch spoke of "the plasticity of history." He pointed out that "human time" was not "clock time" [or to us, "calendar time"]. Human time, he said, has to be measured by the "variability of its rhythm" (1964, 189). Without regard to his context, I want to take that notion of plasticity or variability of rhythm, to distinguish another factor which we must consider.

When I spoke of the periods, or strata, of history in Fiji, I was not thinking in terms of years or decades, which is a mechanical approach uncongenial to the subject, but I was dividing time in terms of variations in patterns of sociopolitical authority which superimposed themselves on the history of two centuries in Fiji, and is therefore a valid basis for classification. But there have been other significant factors through time that have changed the course of Fijian history. There was the phasing out of cannibalism and the phasing in of Christianity. There was the termination of kidnapped labour and the introduction of indentured labour from India. There was the selection of Bauan as the Fijian language, its reduction to writing, and its assumption of the status of *lingua franca*. There was the long period of population decline until 1921, after which the line graph turned upwards again. These were all major stimulants of culture change. They were not single events. They cannot be put down to a single point of time. They are curves, waves, rhythms.

I am certain that none of these Oceanic rhythms could be analyzed properly either historically or anthropologically without the use of missionary journals.

For example, the most refined statistical data on the effect of the measles epidemic
which carried off forty thousand Fijians in the 1870s is found in the Methodist Mission
Archives in Fiji, written in the handwriting of Lorimer Fison, and has been bypassed in the
major textbook which tries to recapture the rhythm of population decline and recovery
(McArthur 1968).

The detection of the presence of these rhythms or themes is possible only by data retrieval, which calls for a technique of documentary criticism, to which we now turn.

Documentary Criticism and Missionary Records

The critical problems which arise in the use of missionary documents fall into two basic
categories: (1) problems of the database, and (2) problems of the researcher.

Problems of the Database

In looking at the missionary archives as a potential database for research, I want to examine the values within the material and the various functions which condition the types of
documents we will meet. Then I shall discuss a couple of methods I have used to extract
the data I want.

Expositional and Scientific Value

Many writers who use the missionary records do so selectively—that is, to find some quote
to validate a point they want to make. This is to abuse the context and integrity of the
document and to impose a present-day purpose on an item created in a completely different kind of situation. A primary source has two genuine values. The simpler is the *scientific
value*—the basic facts that are verified by the document. However, beyond this, we have the
expositional value, or the value of the document for showing how the original participants
themselves thought or felt about the events being discussed. We are not concerned, as
Angell points out (1945, 178–82), with whether that evaluation is true or false, but with the
fact that the participants believed it and that this belief was the basis of their action. Selectivity which disregards the context of a document thereby abuses its integrity. This is bad
in a journalist; it is even worse in an anthropologist. If the researcher is not prepared to
go beyond the scientific value of a document and to work at understanding its expository
value, he has no right to use that material at all.

In *Fijian Material Culture*, which is largely an ethnohistorical study and an attempt to
bring context and function into the study of artifacts, I first classify the artifacts on a basis of the indigenous vocabulary—that is the scientific value of my sources. Then I try to
get beyond these facts and artifacts to the people who created them (the craftsmen) and

who used them (fishermen, sailors, warriors, and so on) and then beyond the people to the institutions and occasions in which they played their roles around the artifacts. I try to re-capture the personal relationships and values the artifacts brought into focus. Thus I seek the expositional value. In one place I give about eight pages to the context and interplay around the turtle-fishing net. It is reconstructed from three major documentary sources, one indigenous and two missionary (Tippett 1968, 121–29).

Or to give another example: no piece of ethnohistorical reconstruction has given me the same satisfaction as that of a feud-and-reconciliation pattern from Choiseul, a large island in the Solomons. It began with the discovery of a piece of factual information about a case of sorcery which brought family retaliation. I picked this up in a source in private hands in Australia (since then microfilmed by Pacific Manuscripts Bureau). From another source, found in New Zealand, came a body of facts about a reconciliation ceremony in the same island, but separated by twenty years. At first I saw no connection, but as I worked through archival material in three countries, it suddenly became apparent that the family feud had developed into a large-scale war that lasted for twenty years. The mere scientific facts in the historical sequence told a story. But as it was pieced together, the charac-ters began to emerge as people and actors, and above all there stood out the figure of the islander who fulfilled the role of mediator, the patterns of his operation, the risks and dangers of the role, and the limitations the society put on his peacemaking actions. Slowly the expositional value of the sequence became apparent, and eventually when the people became Christian this role of the indigenous mediator and the mechanisms for reconcilia-tion conditioned the converts' view of the Christianity they were accepting. You see, there was far more in the documents than the mere table of facts (Tippett 1967).

The Function of the Document

Before citing a document for anthropological purposes, the researcher should establish its *character* and *function*. Helpful in determining the function is to ask first the question—who was the intended reader? If the document is read with this question in mind, the character of its contents may be related to a person. Letters, for example, will be manifestly *private* or *official*, *descriptive* or *promotional*, *polemic* or *confessional*. Each one of these types represents a certain imbalance or bias in the document. No document gives the whole picture—wheth-er it be a letter or a report. One cannot use it or interpret it without first recognising its function in the mind of the writer. The same person may write two very different letters on the same subject, even to the same person, if the functions are different.

Examine two letters of Lorimer Fison, one to the board secretary in Sydney (found in the official file) and the other to his sisters in England (found in his private holograph let-ter book) about the same thing. You will discover that the former is formal and cautious and coldly factual. The latter shows that the writer felt very deeply about the matter under discussion and that he was contemplating an action not at all suggested by the formal letter. It takes the two letters to understand the real situation. Or again, John B. Thurston wrote his report of the Baker Affair in Tonga very formally and made his appraisal with caution. In a private letter to his friend Fison, he described his deeper feelings, his strong impressions for which the verifiable evidence was inadequate for him to take legal action. A letter written by Joseph Waterhouse, to an official, on the matter of the training of Fijian ministry to urge a policy change differs in character from his correspondence with a colleague on the matter, though each within its limited context expressed his feelings (n.d.).

Many of the missionaries in Fiji lived in intense stress situations, like those in the cannibal location in Somosomo, 1839–47, and in unhealthy locations. (The deaths from dysentery in the early years were appalling.) Sometimes a man under great personal stress might react by writing an aggressive or critical letter to a colleague or to the board, only to regret the matter after the boat had taken his epistle beyond his power of retrieval. Then maybe he would write a humble confessional letter in the hope of correcting the situation. The fact that two letters were written makes either one of them only half the story. Only when the two are brought together is the information reliable and this, in turn, throws light on the stress situation itself. A researcher desiring to cite one of these letters is obligated to strive to recover the whole complex, and at least to footnote his quote with a qualification. Not all anthropologists or historians have done this.

Our first obligation to the data is to understand its function and context, but having assured ourselves at this point, the true value of the data now acquires new meaning for us.

The Disappearance and Appearance of Culture Traits

For a number of my Oceania research projects, I have used the ethnohistorical research method known as *upstreaming*, working from the present (and the known) back into the past (and the unknown), arranging my documents in reverse chronology (Fenton 1962). I have used this for research on population decline in the South Pacific, to permit my taking a hard look at Rivers' theory of the psychological factor (1922, 84–113), and also in a study of cannibalism, and again in a diachronic study of Fijian sorcery. The method gave me some high moments of discovery, and I am convinced that in each I have learned things which would never have come to me by any other method.

For example, although it was Christianity and not the colonial administration which disposed of cannibalism, nevertheless the most dramatic period when ceremonial cannibalism was secularised was the period of firearms, the quarter century before the missionaries arrived, when the character of the whole institution was changed. In the population study I was able to identify the precise point where the decline was reversed and dismiss some of the medical reasons given for it. Sorcery stood out as clearly distinct from the pre-Christian theological system, clearer than it had ever been before.

As I went back into the past, I made myself a vocabulary of obsolete words and terms, many of which have never been in the dictionary, and this has provided me with a diachronic measuring tool for reconstructions in Fijian cannibalism and sorcery. I can only say that upstreaming has served me well, but frequently it forces me to experiment with new techniques and models to capitalise on its potential. When I think of what the technique of upstreaming has done for me, and to me, I can join with Marc Bloch and say, "Man spends his time devising techniques of which he afterwards remains a more or less willing prisoner" (1964, 39).

The Ethnolinguistics of Missionary Records

Missionary records provide a superb field for the study of semantic change. I have in my own Fiji notebooks a manuscript of sixty pages describing the impact of Christianity on the Fijian language.[6] The material is classified according to the kinds of semantic and grammatical change. The database for this study was the journals and correspondence of Hunt, Lyth, Williams, and Fison; annual reports of the circuits; minutes of district and teachers' meetings; four different editions of the hymnbook and catechism; two editions of the Fijian Bible and six editions of the New Testament; and eight vernacular works.

The Fijian church passed through four periods of publishing activity: the original period down to the mid-1850s, a second period in the seventies and eighties (the Fison period), the third about the time of World War I and after (Bennett and Deane period), and finally in my own time through the 1950s. Each of these periods had a literary character of its own, and the sequence provides evidence of the continuing process of semantic change going on. Each of these periods had a literary character of its own, and the sequence provides evidence of the continuing process of semantic change going on. A vernacular church newspaper ran from the 1890s to the 1960s, and in this a large part of the material was contributed by Fijians. There are also enough hymns of Fijian composition to permit a serious linguistic paper.

Long before we had heard of ethnopsychology, Lorimer Fison wrote a study of Fijian personality of the cannibal period on the basis of their vocabulary. The manuscript is extant (Fison Papers) but was never published in that form. He used a good deal of it in *Tales from Old Fiji* (1904), which came out a few years before his death. I presented a paper on Fijian proverbs and riddles before the Fiji Society, arranging them on a framework of the social structure (1960). Among other things (not all missionary), I used two published papers of Fison and a missionary dictionary. I am no technical linguist, but I have found the writing of the missionaries ethnolinguistically exciting. Cargill and Hazlewood were

---

6　"The Impact of the Gospel on Language" is accompanied by another study of the reverse effect—"The Impact of the Culture Pattern on the Practice and Belief of the Christian Church." Both are entirely compiled from missionary sources, many of them in the vernacular (Tippett 1958).

skilled linguists, and I doubt if any anthropologist has worked on a Fijian study without being indebted somehow to Hazlewood's grammar and dictionary.[7]

The Triangle of Personal Relationships

Somewhere along the line we need a tool to aid our evaluations and interpretations of the relationships of the participants who interact within a missionary journal. Working on the journal of John Geddie, missionary to Aneiteum, in the New Hebrides,[8] I found it necessary to devise such a tool. The journal itself described a dynamic culture complex over a period of seven years, in which I believed I detected three loci of power in the interaction of its characters. Each of these powers had a number of agents, so to speak. This led me to develop a model to help me fix on any particular relationship I wanted at any time. In the triangle NAM, N represents the native animists, A the foreign adventurers, and M the missionaries. This is the simplest form of the model in which the sides of the triangle represent the personal relationships—NA, AM, or MN, as the case may be. The perimeter of the triangle represents the total configuration. Perhaps this all supports Barzun's claim that "in history no single element is a prime mover, no single kind of clue an explanation of everything else" (1963, 392).

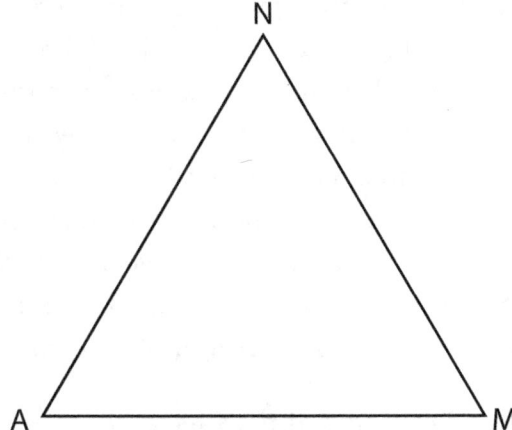

Having fixed my model, I read through the journal again, classifying the data under the heads of NA, AM, or MN relationships. This gave me the database of each different relationship. Although in point of fact one never finds these in isolation like this, it is a useful device for compartmentalising them abstractly for purposes of consideration. I saw that the acceptance of the gospel is not purely an MN issue. People who talk about missionaries converting natives as if no other factors are involved are naively simplistic. When one

---

7   Hazlewood's *Feejeean and English Dictionary* was printed in Fiji at the Mission Press in 1850. He also translated the Old Testament into Fijian. Some of his papers are at the Mitchell Library, Sydney.

8   This journal is handwritten in exercise books. The original is at the Latrobe Library, Melbourne, where my research on this item was done.

identifies the MN interaction, one is continually stopped by the realisation that the native animists are making a "for or against" decision in the light of some factor which is influencing the decision-making process—maybe the foreign adventurers are impinging on the situation somehow.

The model is capable of more sophisticated treatment. For example, the adventurers may be sandalwooders, whalers, or escaped convicts—A1, A2, and A3, and so forth. But the simple form is valid because the native animists classed those three types together, but saw the missionaries as a class on their own (unless one became discouraged, lost faith, and changed camps). This piece of research has been written up in greater detail in *Aspects of Pacific Ethnohistory* (Tippett 1973, 105–25).

The value of this model lies in the way it prevents the researcher from explaining complex phenomena by a single cause. Let me cite a somewhat ludicrous example of this fallacy. Many serious studies have tried to identify the phases of the moon with mental disorders. In World War II, a study in the South Pacific supposedly demonstrated an increase of psychosomatic illness with the fullness of the moon. Unfortunately for the researcher, an equally serious study in the same part of the Pacific showed an increase of Japanese bombing with the same full moons (Webb et al. 1966, 72). Monocausal explanations are always suspect, especially if they are causes given for conversions. In researching the reasons for the conversion of Ratu Cakobau, the "king of the Cannibal Islands," I came up with ten sociopolitical factors which might well be given as reasons. Obviously it was multicausal, but in the last analysis I have a strong feeling, derived from the records, that he was genuinely converted—I mean that the spiritual factor seems to have been the determinative one. One is astonished how competent anthropologists so often grasp on one isolated fact as a reason for the conversion of an animist chief—even Peter Buck at Yale (1939, 65–67) who has a whole people turning Christian because of "a lucky shot." The use of a device like the triangle of personal relationships is a safeguard against oversimplification.

Problems of the Researcher

Not all the problems of research, however, are in the database. Frequently, the most serious problems lie with the researcher himself. This has been so with many anthropologists since the day of salvage anthropology. Let us look at a few of these problems.

Critical and Uncritical Bias

A guide to the historical method produced by the history department of a well-known university distinguishes between *bias* and *subjectivity* (Shafer 1969). The former is judgment without consideration of the evidence, perhaps on the basis of a belief position which precludes critical consideration. The latter, according to this source, is an inescapable human quality, a sense of personal values of which the observer is aware, and which he fully recognises as he critically considers the situation being investigated. Without committing myself at this point to that definition of subjectivity, I recognise the validity of the distinction the writer is making, but would prefer to call them *uncritical* and *critical bias.*

What exercises me, however, about this textbook passage is the manner in which the writer illustrates his point about bias:

> How much communication could exist between Polynesians and early New England missionaries on the "duty" of work, the sin of nakedness, or the beauties of sexual abstinence?

The bias of those missionaries, which I do not deny for one moment, was nevertheless no more serious than the uncritical bias of the man who wrote that oratorical question. If it is not founded on what a Hawaiian newspaper called satirically "the Michener version," it certainly projects present-day misconceptions and feelings back to a situation of 150 years ago. Its presuppositions are quite untested by the missionary documents, or a cultural area analysis of the contact period, or the files of the *Missionary Herald*, which are found in most good libraries in the country. In point of fact, instead of illustrating the bias of the participants in the historical events in Hawaii, it tells us more of the biases of the man using the illustration. Furthermore, it turns out to be not critical bias but a quite uncritical one—reaching a conclusion before fully considering the evidence.

An illustration of that kind should normally presuppose that the user had sufficient familiarity with the missionary sources to form such a critical appraisal. He should be able to document the points he makes. Having read many of the documents myself in this case, I do not believe that he even consulted the primary sources. If he did, he did so selectively, and thus with an uncritical bias. What is probably true is that, if he had really applied his critical faculties to the records, he may well have found plenty of material to illustrate his points—but this would have been a long and tedious road and not a shortcut via a popular novel.

Or again, in order to evaluate the Michener and Melville concepts of the fictional missionary sermons, for example, I read some hundreds of New England missionary sermons, and studied their preaching records in the archives in Hawaii and New England, and made a statistical count of their preaching themes. I found a rigidly structured pattern that did not vary and thematic contents worlds apart from ideas "cooked up" by Michener to make suggestions which cannot be documented. My point here, however, does not concern James Michener but research method. The difference between Michener and, say, Kroeber, is that Kroeber begins his theoretical discussion on cultural fatigue by recognising the historic fact that the religious crisis in Hawaii came before the arrival of the missionaries (1948, 403). Michener, on the other hand, manipulates history to build up a fictional situation for the mood of the audience who will read the book or watch the movie (1966).

To those prepared to work carefully and critically on the records, the rewards are abundant, but there is no place in history or anthropology for presuppositions based on popular notions—unless of course one is wring a paper on "Popular Notions."

The Trap of Generalisation

Before the real information that lies buried in missionary sources can be extracted, the researcher has to appreciate the wide diversity of academic and personality types among the people called missionaries. We are all familiar with the "cop-out" of so many anthropology undergraduates—"The missionaries did this" or "The missionaries did that." Let me say one thing here. In the last decade I have had some five or six hundred missionaries pass through my anthropology classes, and I have never known a more widely diverse group of people. One has to understand this diversity if one wants to draw from the records the missionaries have created. The London Missionary Society missionaries in Tahiti and the Wesleyans in Fiji, for example, not only had different theologies but their terms of employment differed, as did their theory of mission. Some missionaries have gone out under boards which insist in a sound training in anthropology, others have given it no concern at all. Some who have had little training in anthropology have nevertheless developed a fine empathy in their cross-cultural work. Others have never been anything else than ethnocentric Westerners. This means that the records they create are as varied as their personalities. This, by the way, applies equally to medical missionaries, teachers, and administrators. So don't generalise. If the first missionary journal you work on turns out to be a dud, don't judge the others by it. It seems strange that one should even have to make this point in academic circles, but experience shows me that I must.

Another generalisation made about the missionaries is the accusation that they overpainted the situations they confronted for promotional purposes. Frequently, in their biographies produced in England for the English audience, we meet the phrase "too disgusting to mention." I have heard many anthropologists catch on to this and then argue that there was no evidence for it. Some anthropologists still try to "kid themselves" that the noble savage is not a myth. I raise this matter not to argue the case but to make a methodological point.

To those missionaries (who did not write the biographies), the facts of cannibalism and phallic rituals *were* disgusting. But if the critic worked on their journals instead of their biographies, he would have found the evidence in abundance. Certainly the missionaries in Fiji, at least, did not give any phallicism to the public but did record it in their journals. The pre-Christian ceremony for graduating Somosomo youths into manhood are described in the journals of both Hunt and Lyth. Hunt's is the original account and was used by Lyth who, having witnessed it also, added a few details Hunt had overlooked. These accounts provide the Somosomoan text of the phallic liturgy which would never have been tolerated in a biography for English Wesleyans. Fison later on collected a vocabulary of "things too disgusting to mention." I think this gives the lie to the generalisation and points up the danger of speculating on secondary sources where research is called for. Many missionaries had far more material in their notebooks than ever got into print.

Still another generalisation is the notion that in some way the conversion of the islanders was due solely to the Western missionaries. Such a one-sided picture is an anthropological and psychological fallacy, for communication is a two-way process—and that within a context. Howells, in discussing "how a naturally evolved religion fits into the life of a people" ("evolved" rather than "evolving"—does this suggest that island religion of the contact period was static?), goes on to say, "When the missionaries put a stop to something Polynesian . . . etc., etc." (1948, 267–68). Here, it seems to me, he implies a one-sided action. In point of fact, the Polynesians *responded* to missionary advocacy. The acceptors and not the advocates are always in the last analysis the innovators, to use Barnett's terminology (1953). The converts themselves destroyed the pre-Christian paraphernalia (a charge often laid to the missionaries) and did so because of the psychological requirements of religious change within their own worldview. Howells goes on to say, "The people must live by a philosophy (1962, 259)." Precisely! But he does not himself get into the nature of that philosophy. I believe that a deeper research in the primary sources in the Polynesian mission archives would have revealed to him the psychodynamics of iconoclasm associated with Polynesian conversion. The discontinuities in Polynesian religion have to be understood indigenously before the missionary action can be interpreted.

I make no excuse for the outrageous cross-cultural blunders of many missionaries, but I do not generalise about them. At the risk of being accused of generalising myself in the opposite direction, let me list a few insightful anthropological studies on the Pacific produced by missionaries.

In 1947 Dr. Katharine Luomala of the Anthropology Department of the University of Hawaii made a plea for the recognition of the quality of the anthropological data in the records of the missionaries who served in Polynesia (1947, 5–31) and drew her material from 145 sources, almost entirely of missionary origin. No one has yet attempted this kind of thing for Melanesia as far as I know, but it could be done.

No one could ever write a definitive anthropology on Fiji without using Williams (1860), Hunt (1838–48), Lyth (1835–54), Fison (1904), and Deane (1921), or on San Cristoval without reference to Fox (1924), or on Melanesia in general without using George Brown (1908, 1910) and Codrington (1885, 1891), or the Papuan Islands without Bromilow (1929) [though some have tried to do so to their loss], or Samoa without Stair (1897) and George Turner (1884), or the Solomons without Hopkins (1928), or Tahiti without Ellis (1829). These men produced the major Oceanic culture studies of the contact period, and most of them left journals, letters, notebooks, and a variety of memorabilia—and they were all Protestant missionaries.

I haven't even started [mentioning] the Catholics, some of whom left helpful records and monographs.

If we include linguistics in anthropology, we must admit that most of the work on the Pacific languages has been done by missionaries—Hazlewood, Cargill, Moulton, Churchward, and others.[9] They prepared dictionaries and grammars, and translated the Scriptures. Most secular anthropologists have based their researches on these linguistic studies. Malinowski's research, for example, was possible because W. G. Lawes and W. J. Saville had done linguistic research before him on Motu and Mailu (Malinowski 1967, 5, 25).

It would, of course, be quite wrong of me to expect this level of anthropological perception from all the missionaries in the Pacific, but there are many others I might have mentioned. My reason for listing this array of anthropological sophistication is to press my point that we do wrong to generalise as if the missionaries had nothing to offer. The data is certainly there for the person who searches it out.

"Getting into the Act"

If we assume that the researcher has an open mind towards his research documents and recognises that valuable data is there for the finding and understands the historical and cultural frame of reference for pursuing research on Oceanic documents, he still has to get beyond this historical and regional exterior into the inner ethos of the documents themselves. It was a historian (W. K. Hancock) who said that events of "the human-historical world" possess both an *outside* and an *inside*—the former *matter* and the latter *mind*. The events could only be understood by "getting to know the agent inside the act," the "thought inside the deed" (1968, 9).

The researcher has to treat the document as one would a real-life situation, and establish rapport, as it were, with the participants in the record, be it a journal or a complex of letters. One of the most exciting documentary experiences of my life was to spend about ten days at the University of Rochester working over the exchange of correspondence between Lorimer Fison and Lewis Henry Morgan. I finished with a really human picture of two men who had developed a genuine affection for each other, sharing the problems of their respective lives, fighting each other's academic battles, and even exchanging photographs. I felt I was greatly privileged to witness some very personal moments. It was a never-to-be-forgotten experience, perhaps because I was so familiar with Fison, and he became a kind of measuring rod for Morgan.

---

9   Cargill pioneered linguistic studies in Fiji. He had a master's degree in language from Aberdeen. His grammatical and lexical work was the foundation for the other missionaries who followed him. His papers are scattered, but much of his writing was printed in the *Wesleyan Magazine*, as indeed were those of the other missionaries down to the midfifties. Moulton achieved renown as a linguist in Tonga. Hazlewood—see footnote 7. Churchward belongs to this century. He worked on Tongan and Rotuman and produced several grammars and dictionaries.

However, to get into a document from a cross-cultural situation is perhaps a little different. One has to create—or re-create—an unfamiliar ethos out of the past. The people and the institutions recalled are more unexpected. The researcher will discover, for instance, that the features of a missionary journal, created at the time, in the heat of the activity, differ greatly from the biography of the same missionary published for promotional purposes in England. One major difference, for instance, will be the *dramatis personae*. Far more indigenous characters will appear in the journal, and they will play more significant roles. They may not even be mentioned in the biography for Western audiences. The moment one gets into the act in the journal, he discovers a whole new set of dynamic relationships. One sees the indigenous actor, for example, as a decision maker. It squashes once and for all the notion that a handful of missionaries imposed Christian proscriptions and prescriptions on 100,000 indigenes at a point of time. The drama of conversion was never as simple as that. We see the indigene as an actor not a passive victim. Belshaw brought this out in *Changing Melanesia* (1954, 52–53), and Dorothy Shineberg in her study of the sandalwood trade (1967, 214–16). Getting into the act means taking a more critical look at the role of the islander himself in the history of the Pacific. Suddenly the native evangelist becomes a key figure for study and the reinterpretation of history. Then, somewhat belatedly, we realise that a number of these men did actually write their autobiographies. I have seen and read Joeli Bulu's (1871), Jemesa Havea's (n.d.), and Wilisoni Lagi's in Fijian. Bulu's is also in English—translated by Fison (1871b). There are others like Ligeremaluoga's of New Ireland (1932), and also Clement Marau's (1894) to mention two. Here we have event after event through the eyes of islanders—a completely new perspective.[10]

Another exciting discovery that came to me was the acquisition of a whole corpus of letters in the Fijian language, from the Fijian evangelists in Papua and New Guinea, written in the 1890s—two decades before Malinowski went to the area—describing the pre-Christian customs which the Christian Fijians confronted, and many of which had vanished by Malinowski's day. Some of these letters are in archaic Fijian, so that one needs to be familiar with the idiom of the language to interpret them. These letters were written to relatives at home in Fiji and have many personal touches and comments on the stress situations they faced among the headhunters (Tippett 1973, 127–45). A study of the corpus of letters as a whole unit brings to light the fact that a number of dominant culture themes run through them. As the letters were written regularly and described the day-by-day experiences of the Fijian missionaries, one may suggest that we have here a kind of natural random sample, which indicates what Opler has called the dynamic themes of the culture

---

10   The preservation of the writing of Joeli Bulu, Sefanaia Bilivucu, and Jemesa Havea is due to the insight of Fison, and that of Clement Marau due to Codrington. The ties between Codrington and Fison were close. Their correspondence is extant.

(1946, 198). Opler's theoretical frame of reference could be used for a monograph using these letters as a database.

Space and time prevent my continuing with this kind of inventory. These examples must suffice to indicate what I mean by "getting into the act," getting to know the actors in the drama and to feel the atmosphere within which they play their parts. It is here that the investment of time and patience pays its dividends, but both the historical levels and the cultural regions must be appreciated first, and from time to time one may have to prepare his or her own models and measuring tools to meet the situation being investigated.

To recapture an *event*, one needs to remember that every significant event has a time dimension—an antecedent and a consequence. We have here a process with a linear model:

The event has no meaning without a total context, and the researcher had better search in the records for what lies before and after. I worked out this theory with a good deal of archival detail for the event of the murder of Bishop Patteson and found it an exhausting but stimulating exercise which helped me understand the situation better. As I unearthed the facts and put each in its respective compartment on the model, the incident became more and more meaningful (Tippett 1974).

Conclusion

The subject we have before us is large enough for a whole volume rather than a paper. The missionary archives of Oceania are huge reservoirs of untapped information for ethnohistorians prepared to spend the time and effort required to extract it. It calls for a more highly critical methodology, but certainly provides the database for the development of experimental models and the enrichment of ethnohistorical theory. It shows the significance of diachronic and synchronic comparisons, of the need to conceptualise in terms of time and space, the rhythms of change, and the contextuality of events.

I have only touched the surface of one man's adventures in Oceanic ethnohistory. It is like one finding himself in a Fijian canoe on the wide, endless expanse of the Pacific Ocean.

REFERENCES

Angell, Robert. 1945. A critical review of the development of the personal document method in sociology 1920–1940. In *The use of personal documents in history, anthropology and sociology*, ed. Louis Gottschalk, Clyde Kluckhohn, and Robert Angell, 175–232. Bulletin 53. New York: Social Science Research Council.

Barnett, Homer G. 1953. *Innovation: The basis of cultural change.* New York: McGraw-Hill.

Belshaw, Cyril S. 1954. *Changing Melanesia.* Melbourne: Oxford University Press.

Bloch, Marc. 1964. *The historian's craft.* New York: Vintage Books.

Bromilow, W. E. 1929. *Twenty Years among primitive Papuans.* London: Epworth.

Brown, George. 1908. *George Brown: Pioneer missionary and explorer; An autobiography.* London: Hodder & Stoughton.

———. 1910. *Melanesians and Polynesians: Their life histories compared and described.* Trans. Lorimer Fison. London: Wesleyan Mission House.

Brown, Jacques. 1973. Cultural history as a synthesis: Jacques Barzun. In *The varieties of history,* ed. Fritz Stern, 387-402. New York: Vintage Books.

Buck, Peter H. 1939. *Anthropology and religion.* New Haven: Yale University Press.

Bulu, Joeli. 1871. *Joeli Bulu: The autobiography of a native minister in the South Seas.* Trans. Lorimer Fison. London: Wesleyan Mission House.

———. n.d. *Ai Tukutuku ni Noqu Bula.* Unpublished manuscript.

Codrington, R. H. 1885. *The Melanesian languages.* Oxford: Clarendon.

———. 1891. *The Melanesians: Studies in their anthropology and folk-lore.* Oxford: Clarendon.

Dark, Philip. 1957. Methods of synthesis in ethnohistory. *Ethnohistory* 4: 231–78.

Deane, Wallace. 1921. *Fijian society; or The sociology and psychology of the Fijians.* London: Macmillan.

Ellis, William. 1829. *Polynesian researches during a residence of nearly six years in the South Sea Islands &c.* 2 vols. London: Fisher, Son & Jackson.

Fenton, William N. 1962. Ethnohistory and its problems. *Ethnohistory* 9: 1–23.

Fison, Lorimer. 1867–69. Letter book. In Fison papers.

———. 1871a. The Fijian, judged by his own words. Unpublished manuscript. In Fison papers.

———, trans. 1871b. *Joeli Bulu: The autobiography of a native minister in the South Seas.* London: Wesleyan Mission House.

———. 1904. *Tales from Old Fiji.* London: De La More.

Fox, C. E. 1924. *The threshold of the Pacific: Social organization, magic and religion of San Cristoval.* London: Kegan Paul, Trench, Trubner & Co.

Hancock, W. K. 1968. *Attempting history.* Canberra: Australian National University Press.

Havea, Jemesa. n.d. *Ai Tukutuku ni Noqu Bula.* Unpublished manuscript.

Hazlewood, David. 1850. *Feejeean and English dictionary.* Viwa, Fiji: Methodist Mission Press.

Hocart, A. M. 1952. *The northern states of Fiji.* London: Royal Anthropological Society of Great Britain and Ireland.

Hopkins, A. I. 1928. *In the isles of King Solomon.* London: Seeley, Service and Co.

Howells, William. 1962. *The heathens: Primitive man and his religions.* New York: Doubleday.

Hunt, John. 1838–48. Private journals, missionary correspondence.

Jaggar, Thomas. 1838–47. Journal, correspondence.

Kroeber, A. L. 1948. *Anthropology.* New York: Harcourt, Brace & Co.

Lagi, Wilisoni. n.d. *Ai Tukutuku ni Noqu Bula.* Unpublished manuscript.

Ligeremaluoga, Osea. 1932. *The erstwhile savage: An account of the life of Ligeremaluoga.* Trans. Ella Collins. Melbourne: Cheshire.

Luomala, Katharine. 1947. Missionary contributions to Polynesian anthropology. In *Specialized studies in Polynesian anthropology,* ed. Katharine Luomala et al., 5–31. Honolulu: Bishop Museum Bulletin 193.

Lyth, Richard B. 1835–54. Private journals, missionary correspondence.

Malinowski, Bronislaw. 1967. *A diary in the strict sense of the term.* New York: Harcourt, Brace & World.

Marau, Clement. 1894. *The story of a Melanesian deacon.* Trans. R. H. Codrington. London: Society for the Propagation of Christian Knowledge.

McArthur, Norma. 1968. *Island populations of the Pacific.* Canberra: Australian National University Press.

Opler, Morris E. 1946. Themes as dynamic forces in culture. *American Journal of Sociology* 51: 198–206.

Redfield, Robert, R. Linton, and M. Herskovits. 1936. Memorandum on the study of acculturation. *American Anthropologist* 38: 149–52.

Rivers, W. H. R. 1922. The psychological factor. In *Essays on the depopulation of Melanesia,* ed. W. H. R. Rivers, 84–113. Cambridge: Cambridge University Press.

Roth, G. K. 1953. *Fijian way of life.* Melbourne: Oxford University Press.

Shafer, R. J., ed. 1969. *A guide to historical method.* Homewood, IL: Dorsey.

Shineberg, Dorothy. 1967. *They came for sandalwood: A study of the sandalwood trade in the Southwest Pacific 1830-1865.* London: Melbourne University Press.

Stair, J. B. *Old Samoa.* 1897. London: Religious Tract Society.

Sturtevant, William C. 1966. Anthropology, history and ethnohistory. *Ethnohistory* 13: 1–51.

Tippett, Alan R. 1954. *The Christian (Fiji 1835-67).* Auckland: Institute Publishing.

———. 1955. Anthropological research and the Fijian people. *International Review of Missions* 44: 212–19.

———. 1958. The impact of the gospel on language; and The impact of the culture pattern on the practice and relief of the Christian church. Two unpublished manuscripts bound together.

———. 1960. Fijian proverbs, metaphoric idioms and riddles. In *Transaction and proceedings of the Fiji Society,* 65–93.

———. 1967. *Solomon Islands Christianity.* London: Lutterworth.

———. 1968. *Fijian material culture: A study of cultural contact, function and change.* Honolulu: Bishop Museum Press.

———. 1971. *People movements in Southern Polynesia.* Chicago: Moody.

———. 1973. *Aspects of Pacific ethnohistory.* Pasadena: William Carey Library.

———. 1974. The structure and analysis of an event. Unpublished manuscript.

Turner, George. 1884. *Samoa a hundred years ago.* London: Macmillan.

Washburn, W. E. 1961. Ethnohistory: History "in the round." *Ethnohistory* 8: 31–48.

Waterhouse, Joseph. n.d. Missionary correspondence.

Webb, E . J., D. T. Campbell, R. D. Schwartz, and L. Sechrest. 1966. *Unobtrusive measures: Non-reactive research in the social sciences.* Chicago: Rand McNally.

Williams, Thomas. 1839–56. Private journals.

———. 1860. *Fiji and the Fijians.* Vol. 2, *The islands and their inhabitants.* London: Alexander Heylin.

PART ONE

Methods and Models

1

ETHNOHISTORY AS RESEARCH METHODOLOGY[1]

"Ethnohistory," said William N. Fenton, "is a way of getting at certain problems in culture history" (1962, 2). Ethnohistory is neither a discipline in itself nor an interdisciplinary field. It is neither an anthropological view of history, nor a historical view of anthropology. It is a synthesis of methodologies but not merely the sum of the two (Dovring 1960, 75), for there is a precise quality in their symbiotic interrelationship, and this can only come into existence in the research experience itself. Perhaps we should begin with a brief presentation of the anthropological theory which lies behind ethnohistorical method.

Theory of Ethnohistorical Method

Ethnohistory is a technique for considering cultural data *spatially* and *sequentially*. The data itself is organised into *traits* or *elements* and these in turn into spatial patterns which we term *complexes*, and maybe into even larger configurations sometimes called *activities* (Linton 1964, 403; Fenton 1962, 6). This frame of reference permits the study of *function* and *meaning* at various levels.

Any of these configurations may be studied as sequences through time. This sequence we call a *cultural continuum* (Linton 1964, 294–96; Barnett 1942, 30), which Linton points out is "not only a continuum but a continuum in a constant state of change." This process of cultural complexes each in dynamic equilibrium within itself yet moving like a gyroscope through time is the subject of ethnohistorical investigation.

The study of a cohesive but dynamic complex may be made over a wide area spatially *at a point of time*, which for ethnohistorical purposes may be a day, or a decade, or a generation, so that it is within the focus and memory of an informant—this we speak of as a *synchronic* analysis. Or it may be researched as the movement of dynamic change within any cohesive process of the cultural continuum, *through time*. This is called *diachronic* research. These notions came to me through S. F. Nadel's study of social processes, in which methodologically he spoke of "synchronic and diachronic enquiry" (1951, 100).

---

1   Taken from *Aspects of Pacific Ethnohistory* (Pasadena: William Carey Library, 1973), 1–13. Used by permission.

We are struggling with a number of anthropological problems in the study of society, like *continuity* and *change*, and *function* and *meaning*. This is anthropology—the dynamics of cultural change. But, in that change can only be studied through time, it is also history. Ethnohistory is a research methodology for exploring the regions where history phases out into anthropology.

The distinction of diachronic from synchronic research is intended to remind us, as Linton pointed out, that the cultural continuum is never static. Change of some kind is going on all the time. Societies are equipped with mechanisms for stimulating and regulating the speed of change. These changes reflect not only the character and values of a people but also the material culture. To study material culture diachronically is to see the reflection of human development through the generations, just as much as changes in language and customs. Every artifact has meaning only in its context—it relates both to individuals and to society at any given point of time, and if such synchronic analyses are investigated diachronically, we may observe the momentum of culture change throughout a cultural continuum.

There are at least three kinds of cultural reconstruction used in ethnohistorical research. These were defined by Dark as (1) *Cross-sectional* (2) *Institutional* and (3) *Culture Continuum* (1957). In the first type the synthesis is synchronic; in the second it is diachronic and in the third it is both spatial and temporal (synchronic-diachronic).

Each of the patterns of synthesis has been used for effective ethnohistorical reconstructions. Dark takes a number of such research projects or "constellations" and analyses them into subtypes.

In the writer's Fijian research, he has used all three methods of reconstruction. [Some of these studies] are synchronic in that they were the observations in a period of time which could be seen whole in the lifetime of one man. Recently the writer produced a paper for an anthropological society which traced the institution of sorcery from pre-Christian times to the present day with a different body of primary sources for each generation. The book *Fijian Material Culture: A Study in Cultural Context, Function and Change* (Tippett 1968) covers a spatial anthropological study at three or four levels of temporal analysis across Fiji, covering four different institutions—war clubs, canoes and boats, turtle fishing, and house building. This method of synthesis (cultural continuum) brought to light during the research a definite stratum of Tongan influence before the arrival of the white man, and quite independent of the Christian Tongan impact. The existence of this Tongan level in Fiji explains the process of diffusion of Christianity into the Fiji Group. This is a good example of how the study of artifacts may throw light on dynamic and personality factors.

Somehow or other we have to get beyond the merely material artifact. Often when we go to a museum or to some antiquarian's collection we look at meaningless things. They have to have a *context* both in an institution and in a period of history. If we can bring these factors together in a synthesis, the *meaning* immediately becomes apparent. Furthermore, even to members of one society and at one point of time the context will be different as, for example, a beautifully made war club will mean one thing to the craftsman, but something quite different to the warrior. Likewise we have to identify the *generation*. To one warrior the same war club (say, a *bowai*) is a well-balanced weapon, his strength and protection for a particular offensive stroke; but after his death, and when because of his war exploits he has been deified, the club may be the religious shrine for his spirit (*waqawaqa*) to his son, who no longer calls it a *bowai*, but oils it reverently and presents an offering before it before he himself goes to war with another war club, which is a *bowai*, or a *cali*, or a *waka*, or whatever kind of club it happens to be. Here the *meaning* and *function* have changed because the generational context has changed.

So we have a *relativity of contemporaries* and a *relativity of generations*, the former in the synchronic sequences and the latter in the diachronic. The last one especially raises a real problem for museum typologies. Barnett calls the latter the *relativity of needs* (1942, 30), a phrase which came to him as he reconstructed ethnohistorically the experiences of certain American Indians under culture contact. His work could be classed as history as he reconstructed from documents, but he drew also from anthropological data and sought valid generalisations about human behaviour.

Another example of the relativity of generations on an international (rather than personal) level comes from Barnett's research on Palau (Micronesia). Palauan religion, for example, may be studied diachronically as changing under the forces of acculturation through periods of Spanish, German, Japanese, and American domination (1949, 227–40; 1960, 82–84). Diachronic studies of this type are a natural method for Western Pacific research.

Another quite imaginative use of the diachronic approach is the fictionalised reconstruction around an artifact. I remember as a schoolboy reading a British public school story *The Adventures of a Ten-guinea Watch*. Was this perhaps the prototype for Wallace Deane's *The Strange Adventures of a Whale's Tooth*? This is a story for young people, the tale of a whale's tooth (*tabua*), the artifact used in Fijian ceremonial life for making requests for assistance in war, for burning a village, for obtaining a favour, for arranging a marriage, for atonement, for mourning the dead, and so on *ad infinitum*. Deane weaves all these different functions of a real *tabua* into an imaginary story running from pagan whaling days into Christian times. It is a diachronic study of the functional role of a whale's tooth in Fijian ceremonial and an accurate synthesis. This is true ethnohistorical fiction (Deane 1919).

Upstreaming

Another form of ethnohistorical reconstruction is known as *upstreaming*. This term was innovated by Fenton, who describes it as restructuring by direct sequence "against the tide of history going from the known present to the unknown past" (1962, 12). He used it first in a study of suicide, but has made other uses of it since. I used it myself for a reconstruction of Fijian cannibalism. The pattern has two advantages. First, it is easier to go back step by step reconstructing slowly because of the continuity of many cultural features and interpretations. It is easier for me to interpret my father's experiences than those of my great-great-grandfather. So I proceed from father, to grandfather, to great-grandfather, and so on, and thereby eliminate the long-time jump. This gives us a better *historic sense*. Second, one makes most interesting discoveries as he works back through his source material in the reverse chronology, to suddenly find that some significant culture trait disappears. It is like an archaeologist discovering an older form of pottery, or a cruder design, which can only be explained by the invention of the wheel or brush.

Thus one moves from the point of law and order to the war to suppress the cannibalism in the mountain regions (1870s). As one goes back you can trace the spread of cannibalism, and the distribution of Christian and cannibal villages (back to 1854, the conversion of Cakobau the most famous cannibal of all). Before 1854 you find Christianity a really small thing except in Lau. One by one the little Christian groups disappear until 1835 when the Christian mission is no longer there at all. It is like the flood line in Middle East archaeology. But what this "upstreaming" really brings to light is the period from 1835 back to about 1809, when the Fijian wars were under the control of escaped convicts and deserters from sandalwood and whaling ships. Beyond that you are in the period of precontact ceremonial cannibalism. It was the introduction of Western arms and ammunition and renegade whites to service them as gunsmiths and marksmen that cannibalism underwent its dramatic *secularisation*. The religious taboos and controls broke down, and there was a surplus of bodies for the oven, and women and children indulged as they had not done before, and sometimes bodies were eaten without even presentation at the temple. It was a period of secularisation before the missionary arrived. Cannibalism there was as far back as the myths go, for the Fijian gods were cannibal gods, and they required human sacrifices for scores of purposes.

I very much doubt if this stratification could ever have been observed without "upstreaming" through the source material. This helps researchers to "get into the act" themselves, and they are truly exploring as they upstream from the "estuary" to the "source."

An Ethnohistorical Lexicon

A good ethnohistorian must have a wide knowledge of the language of the documents he is studying. This means that he should be able to recognise and date semantic change, and identify dialect words, especially in oral traditions and chants. In doing my studies of Fijian cannibalism, honourable and dishonourable killing, and sorcery, I found I had to

Major Sources for the Study of Fijian Cannibalism	
20th Century	No Cannibalism
4th Period of Acculturation Post Cession Period	Government and Mission Records Memoirs of Government Servants – Brewster, Im Thurn, Thomson Missionary Researcher Deane
3rd Period of Acculturation 1854-74. After Cakobau's Conversion	Missionary Writers, Fison, Langham, Carey, Baker Recorders of Fijian Traditions, Tatawaqa, Toganivalu, Sokiveta, Bulu Official Travellers, Smyth, Seemann Australian Missionary Notices, Letters, Circuit Reports British Consular Records. Transactions Fijian Society
2nd Period of Acculturation 1835-54. Mission Contact Period	Missionary Records, Annual Reports of Circuits (especially Bau 1854) *Wesleyan Magazine* Missionary writings of Joseph Waterhouse and Carey Missionary Journals: Hunt, Jaggar, Lyth, Cross, Cargill, Williams, Lawry Sea Captains, Erskine, Endicott Seamen who resided with Fijians, Jackson, Diapea Beche de mer Trader's wife Mrs. Wallis
Period of Culture Contact c1800-1835	Sea Captains, Wrecked Sailors and Sandalwooders: Siddons, Lockerby. Patterson, Dillon Missionary Journals & Letters: Cross, Cargill, Hunt, Lyth, Waterhouse, Williams, Jaggar, Watsford, Hazelwood
Pre-contact Period Before 1800	First analyses of pre-Christian Religious World View. Cargill, Cross, Hunt, Lyth, Williams Myths and Chants: Hunt, Hazelwood, Quain, Carey, *Transactions of Fijian Society*

Major Sources for Vocabulary of Cannibalism – Hazelwood, Cargill, Hunt, Fison. A. R. Tippett, Aspects of Pacific Ethnohistory (Pasadena: William Carey Library, 1973), 6.

work out my own lexicon of obsolete and modified words, phrases, and symbolic terms and circumlocutions. It stands at about four hundred entries at present and had to be discovered by internal evidence, but once extracted from the documents and put into use as a tool, one knows these subjects could never be properly researched without the lexical key.

Every speaker of Fijian knows, for instance, that *benu* means "rubbish." Not everyone knows that it meant food or body refuse sought by a sorcerer for applying his arts against a victim, or that in another context it meant a widow who escaped from the strangling cord. Or *ai cula*, commonly meaning a fork or needle in acculturated times, might under certain circumstances have represented small wooden pins set in the footprints of the intended victim to make him feel the prick of pain at night, and even to kill him if pushed deeply into the footprints. Or what do we mean by *luvedra ni mate* (children of the dead)? One's guess might be "an orphan." Set in its location of time and context, it indicates men who have not yet avenged the death of their father. Or when does *qa ni vivili* mean a seashell, and when does it indicate the dead body from which the "soul" has fled? Or when is a dead body for the cannibal called "long pig" (*vuaka balavu*), and when a "trussed frog" (*botowa-lai*)? One could go on and on with these terms. Certainly one has to master first a symbolic system. Marc Bloch said that the "vocabulary of documents" is "a form of evidence" (1964, 168). So too is the vocabulary of oral traditions, chants, dirges, and proverbs.

Artifact or "Document"

Lucey (1958, 28) distinguishes between *remains* and *records* and defines the former in this way:

> Remains are tangible evidences of the life of man in society. They are products (artifacts) of man's daily needs and hence are infinite in variety; they were not made with the intent of informing posterity, of man and his activities. The transmission of history was not their primary purpose.

Yet every artifact tells a story of people in society. Just as it is an index to society, so society has to interpret it. Gottschalk says, "A piece of pottery or a coin, an ancient seal or a recent stamp may well be a personal document" (1969, 87). Sometimes an artifact does count in lieu of a document, to signify an agreement.

The Greeks had a custom of two men with a close attachment parting company breaking a small white stone as they separated. If in the fortunes of their descendants two should ever meet again with the evidence of the fitting stones, the personal friendship of their forebears could be taken up as if these descendants were themselves the contracting parties. The stone was an agreement.

The first offer of the Cession of Fiji to Britain was declined on the advice of a military man who feared the cost in men and money of what the missionaries were accomplishing anyway by slow and peaceful means (Smyth 1864, 193, 208). Fiji then turned to the United States. The offer of Cession was made by the presentation of a great whale's tooth—the biggest I have seen. It is currently preserved in the National Archives in Washington, DC, as part of an interesting collection of unusual artifacts which are counted as documents, because they tell of important historical events and have the symbolic meaning of agreements and contracts.

On page 44 of [my] *Fijian Material Culture* (1968), the Fijian mace is illustrated. Originally it was a war club of Ratu Cakobau, who surrendered it to Queen Victoria upon the Cession of the islands to Britain. This club, symbol of the authority of the cannibal king, subsequently became the symbol of law and order under the colonial system. For the people of the kingdom of Bau the surrender of the artifact signified the transfer of the government and was far more meaningful to them than the formal signing of the Deed of Cession, which the Westerners alone fully understood.

But only very few such artifacts have become housed in archives, and many have now lost their meaning, like those in the museums which have no identification of context. We are now in the anthropological area of history. I recall some of the talking points for data collecting of my Fiji days—a turtle skull over the door of a house, a few remains of *tapa* cloth spread over a grave, a row of notches on the handle of a war club (scoring kills), a row of stones each marking a body which ended in a cannibal oven, a weather-eaten whale's tooth at Nakauvadra, petroglyphs on the rock face at Dedevolevu. These are all ethno-historical evidence, but only if we can locate them in their cultural context. Once they interpret *function* and *meaning*, they become evidence. Until then they are raw material for investigation. The stick charts of Micronesia have no evidential value until we identify the waters of the northwest Pacific and the position of the Marshall Islands represented by the shells (i.e., we identify the context), and understand that they are used for navigation and how the Micronesian sailors used them to achieve this purpose. Once their function and meaning are clear, the stick chart is as much a genuine map as any other prepared with the most scientific instruments, and it tells as historically significant a story.

Oral Tradition

Oral tradition has many forms, one of which is *myth*. This requires a book for itself. I mention it merely to distinguish it from that form of oral tradition which is sometimes called protohistory. By this I am eliminating myth at two levels. First, there are the origin myths which frequently assimilate historical characters and events and adapt themselves to political and social changes. If they have any historical value, it is as reflections of the process of change itself. They produce numerous local variations and are often reinterpretations rather than truly origin myths. Second, there are the myths associated with natural formations like peculiarly shaped rocks along the coast. A whole volume could be written on these for the Fijian island of Kadavu alone.

Hocart makes the claim that "custom and myth are inseparable." Myth relates to the serious business of life, is a precedent, and is necessary because it gives ritual its intention (1952, 17, 21).

Oral tradition [is often defined] to mean subrecent traditions identifiable with historical events—floods, eclipses, pestilences, and the first white men's ships [and can be] examine[d] with the hope of identifying some of the local criteria for testing their reliability inherent within the society itself (Sturtevant 1966, 26).

Pacific Research Today

Washburn pointed out that we do ethnohistory a disservice "when we expect it to contain within itself a whole new philosophy." It is a method of approaching problems. "What we can do, however, is to refine and exploit the method" (1961, 33). And for the Pacific this most certainly needs to be done. Ethnologists have appropriated descriptive material from both primary and secondary sources uncritically. Much of the literature on which they depend, posing as history or historical fiction, is itself unreliable. Modern myths emerge even in our own days and are communicated in interviews, to be "swallowed hook, line, and sinker" by gullible researchers—Captain James Cook, Napoleon Bonaparte, and Thomas Baker are passing into Pacific mythology and can be historically studied as part of the mythmaking process itself. And fictitious characters like those of Michener's novel *Hawaii* are emerging as historical people. There never was a time like this when Pacific history so needed to protect itself and so needed anthropological methods to do so (Dening 1966, 32).

I wish to press the point of the great historical and anthropological value of [missionary journals]. Anthropology, in particular, has bypassed these resources, very much to its loss. The exception has been Katharine Luomala, who has written on the subject (1947, 5–31), but much more remains to be said.

One of the most exciting things in Pacific studies in the last decade is the new accessibility of historical documents. One could write a whole article on it were there space. There is the termination of colonial restrictions on the time a document should be regarded as of restricted use. There is the discovery of many journals of traders, missionaries, and other Westerners who lived in the islands and spoke the language. There is the publication of many of these with annotations. There is the availability of many extremely valuable manuscripts on microfilm through such bodies as the Pacific Manuscripts Bureau (including their most valuable listings in *Pambu*). There is the new interest of islanders in their own culture history. There is just so much material available for research that one can hardly expect to cover the material of his own immediate interest.

One is reminded of Butterfield's comment that Lord Acton's development as a historian coincided with the period when European archives were successively opened more to scholars. Ranke also "enjoyed the happiness of these harvest days," and large areas of history were suddenly transformed (Butterfield 1948, 15). With the emergence of young universities in the Pacific, we have hopes of meeting more and more island scholars. Without doubt there are scores of island biographies and cultural histories waiting to be written by ethnohistorians who are themselves islanders.

REFERENCES

Barnett, Homer G. 1942. Culture growth by substitution. *Research Studies in the State College of Washington* 10: 26–30.

———. 1949. *Palauan society: A study of contemporary native life in the Palauan Islands.* Eugene: University of Oregon Publications.

———. 1960. *Being a Palauan.* New York: Holt, Rinehart & Winston.

Bloch, Marc. 1964. *The historian's craft.* Trans. Joseph R. Strayer. New York: Vintage Books.

Butterfield, Herbert. 1948. *Lord Acton.* London: Philip.

Dark, Philip. 1957. Methods of synthesis in ethnohistory. *Ethnohistory* 4: 231–78.

Deane, Wallace. 1919. *The strange adventures of a whale's tooth.* Sydney: Epworth.

Dening, Gregory. 1966. Ethnohistory in Polynesia: The value of ethnohistorical evidence. *The Journal of Pacific History* 1: 23–42.

Dovring, Folke. 1960. *History as a social science: An assay on the nature and purpose of historical studies.* The Hague: Nijhoff.

Fenton, William N. 1962. Ethnohistory and its problems. *Ethnohistory* 9: 1–23.

Gottschalk, Louis. 1969. *Understanding history.* New York: Knopf.

Hocart, A. M. 1952. *The life-giving myth and other essays.* London: Methuen.

Linton, Ralph. 1964. *The study of man.* New York: Appleton-Century-Crofts.

Lucey, Williams Leo. 1958. *History: Methods and interpretation.* Chicago: Loyola University Press.

Luomala, Katharine. 1947. Missionary contributions to Polynesian anthropology. In *Specialized studies in Polynesian anthropology*, ed. Katharine Luomala et al., 5–31. Honolulu: Bishop Museum Bulletin 193.

Nadel, S. F. 1951. *The foundations of social anthropology.* Glencoe, IL: Free Press.

Pambu. 1968–73. Monthly newsletter of the Pacific Manuscripts Bureau, Research School of Pacific Studies, Australian National University, Canberra.

Smyth, W. J. 1864. Report; and Covering letter. In *Ten months in the Fiji Islands*, by Mrs. Smyth. Oxford: John Henry & James Parker.

Sturtevant, William E. 1966. Anthropology, history and ethnohistory. *Ethnohistory* 13, no. 1: 1–51.

Tippett, Alan R. 1968. *Fijian material culture: A study in cultural context, function and change.* Honolulu: Bishop Museum Press.

Washburn, Wilcomb E. 1961. Ethnohistory: History "in the round." *Ethnohistory* 8: 31–48.

2
ETHNOHISTORY[2]

Some of the best ethnohistorical reconstruction studies concern American Indian contexts, but the possibilities of the method have not been ignored in Oceania (Valentine 1960, Keesing 1947,[3] Luomala 1947[4]). The present writer has attempted to use it in several papers with respect to war and magico-religion in Fiji (Tippett 1944, 1954a, 1954b). Recent theoretical statements by American scholars have established several important principles which are relevant also for the South Pacific.

Ethnohistory is a process and a method rather than a rigid discipline, flexible and expansive in both intellectual and organisational outlook (Washburn 1961). The need for such a methodology was stated by Pargellis (1957) as requiring teamwork of ethnologist and historian,[5] the former to seek the patterns of cultural behavior and to ask "why," the latter to chart developments and changes in history. Washburn (1961) pointed out that few anthropologists were prepared to give the long hours required on documentary study, say, of a body of seventeenth-century Indians, and at the same time few historians were prepared to devote years to fieldwork with the descendants of those Indians. Yet both were required. Washburn himself, after much archival research, found that historians who reported facts correctly had wrongly interpreted them. The "shock of this distortion," he confessed, "left a mark on him" (ibid., 47). This is exactly how I felt when my Fijian documentary studies revealed the existence of a "war of the chiefs" and distinguished it from the regular social function of the skirmishing type of warfare. I agree with Washburn's conclusion that ethnohistory adds the dimension of culture history to the strict chronology of history.

The testing and evaluating of sound historical method must be applied to the documents being used (Gottschalk 1945, 10, 38). Oceanic anthropologists have not always done

---

2 Taken from *Fijian Material Culture* (Honolulu: Bishop Museum Press, 1968), 14–18. Used by permission.

3 Keesing's study was a regional breakdown of acculturation in Polynesia, with a bibliography of more than two hundred entries.

4 Luomala's analysis of missionary contributions to anthropology is a breakdown of primary sources within the patterns of archival methodology, and attempts to evaluate their reliability as evidence.

5 Pargellis was not sure that the two could be combined in one person, but Washburn (1961) named Fenton and Ewers as two who had accomplished the synthesis. Perhaps we could add Wallace also.

this. Old documents are not of equal value. The recognition of this fact is one of the important results of laying down principles of ethnohistory (Eggan 1961, 7). The variability of source material has served as a basis for rationalization by some anthropologists for confining their efforts to synchronic studies, in cases where diachronic studies were called for, because documents were available. Lurie (1961, 85–86) argues that source material did not have to be collected by trained anthropologists, provided the person using it applies the same tests that he applies to his field informants. Her point is well made. This brings a great deal of early material listed by Luomala (1947) from Oceania within the orbit of valid data.

Thus it should be possible to locate points of time in our diachronic study at which synchronic studies can be made. Thus I have attempted a synchronic analysis of Fijian warfare at a specific point of time, from 1839 to 1846. Again I have made another in the 1870s in the Viti Levu highlands. These cross-sectional units of data at specific crisis periods in history are of enormous value in the study of culture change.

Although ethnohistory has been regarded as a method and process, it has passed through a period of experimentation and has been applied in various ways. First, there is what Eggan calls the direct historical approach, "by which one went from the present back into the past—as far as possible" (1961, 6). In prewar days it was used in the study of archaeological sites, and is similar to what Fenton calls "up-streaming." He worked back from living communities, testing early descriptions against present-day behavior, and observing changes, and then asking, "Why?" (Pargellis 1957; Fenton 1962).[6]

A second method of using ethnohistory was described by Valentine (1960) in handling an Oceanic field situation in New Britain. He found no time depth among his informants, in the historical sense, but an orientation of precontact (the lost Golden Age), contact (a period of foreign troubles), and the future (a millennium with the restoration of native rule with European power and wealth), and an ignorance of outside historic reference points. As a result, their sequences were confused and locations vague. Valentine left his research and visited Australia to engage in library work and construct a chronological framework as a basis for his ethnology. He concluded that two sets of data were essential, either alone being misleading. He believed that, by integrating the two sets as a contact history, he could then discern the cultural crises in the contact development. In his situation he did the right thing, but was it not that he went to the field in the first place with inadequate historical groundwork?

The third approach (Lurie 1961, 87) is perhaps nearer the truth. Documents should be studied first, we are told, and then, after the field research has been done, one should re-

---

6   Fenton borrowed the term "up-streaming" from Sir Flinders Petrie, who used living cultures for interpreting early sources, following back the sequences against the tide of history. Something similar has been used in physical anthropology, but the process, by Fenton's own admission, has "a built-in fallacy for history." Yet it does provide a tool for testing by means of comparative method. One asks, as one goes upstream, when and where did this change take place, and why?

turn to the documents again. Quite apart from the fact that field situations drive one back to bypassed records, the integration of historical and ethnological data is not merely a matter of splicing two sets of data together. They must be mutually interpretive. This may mean repeated going and coming between archives and field.

We should never regard documentary material merely as a means for discovering a chronology, although we may expect this from it. We seek glimpses into ethnology, linguistics, and other points of reference in culture patterns as well as in time and space. Only at special points do we seek outside references. The value of documentary studies is that they help to (1) recapture lost contexts from the subrecent past, (2) provide cultural data for comparison with present facts, (3) observe and record the changes over time, and (4) seek out the reasons for those changes.

Using the comparative method and working back beyond the frontiers of the ethnographic present leaves one gathering many kinds of data, forming a synthesis which Weltfish calls "the ethnic interpretation of written historical records" (1959, 335). This is very different from Valentine's integration of two sets of data, which, even when integrated, might still be far from a valid reconstruction.

Artifacts and Historical Reconstruction

If artifacts (especially those which are functionally obsolete though physically extant) or their contextual institutions are to be used for comparison with current forms, some effort has to be made to reconstruct total contexts, or at least enough of the contexts to reveal the function of the artifacts within them, and to show whether or not there has been any functional substitute for the obsolete artifacts.[7]

We cannot start with the present and follow upstream in all cases, because Christianity has eradicated some artifacts, such as war clubs. But there are cases where it can be established that some existing artifact is a true functional substitute for an obsolete one. But many obsolete artifacts are now mere museum specimens and, as with Willey's "static moulds" in his Peruvian settlement patterns, one cannot start from living forms or patterns. Therefore I start with the artifact itself and attempt to reconstruct the context in which it originally operated. The degree of attainable success depends on the documents, but some important facts are frequently brought to light, such as the role of the Tongan craftsmen as disintegrators of Fijian social organisation before any white men came to Fiji. Thus Sahlins stated that the "Tongan problem" belongs to the "middle decades of the last

---

7   Sahlins observed, for example, that in the ruins at Navucinamasi, an interior war town (*koro-ni-valu*) on Moala, the platform of the god house (*bure kalou*) had the "same relative location" as the Christian church in the modern villages (1962, 70). The god house is obsolete, but the church is a functional substitute—or is it? This does not hold everywhere as far as the location is concerned, but it may hold for all Moala. I investigate this problem on the level of social structure at Bau, in my house-type case study. Sahlins' observations were based on archaeology. He did not follow it up with any documentary study.

century" (1962, 4), but while it is true that the period was one of Tongan political impact, the social disintegration had been going on for a century.

[Many artifacts] offer scope for the use of ethnohistorical techniques, and to escape the tyranny of morphological typology [one can] commence each case study with an attempted functional typology, which forces one to observe that every artifact had a context of relationships with persons (AB) and institutions (AC) and requires the context (ABC) to give it meaning. Furthermore, the artifacts and relationships are reinforced lexically.

The disappearance of an artifact from the paraphernalia of a group indicates also the disappearance of a role. When a society turns from war to peace and from club law to constitutional rule, not only do war clubs and war canoes vanish, but warriors and navy with them. Craftsmen, creators of club and canoe, seek new roles. Institutions also vanish—war dances, military reviews, hero naming, and so forth. The surviving artifact is sent to a museum. In terms of the symbolic triangle, ABC, the whole triangle disintegrates because roles and institutions have become defunct. The artifact, without a context, is meaningless. AB and AC are no more. If, on the other hand, a new artifact is substituted to perform the same function, the complex, though modified, does retain its entity and integration.

The record of human society in the Pacific has suffered from two forms of iconoclasm. One form destroyed material culture (bitterly attacked by salvage anthropologists without always investigating the reasons ethnohistory could have disclosed). The other form was intellectual, and salvaged material culture by wrestling it from its context and burying it in formal typologies, without recording personal details of the creators or users, functions and contexts, or localities of origin. We must now, at this late hour, turn to ethnohistory and ask how much can be reconstructed.

REFERENCES

Eggan, Fred. 1961. Some anthropological approaches to the understanding of ethnological cultures. *Ethnohistory* 8: 1–11.

Fenton, William N. 1962. Ethnohistory and its problems. *Ethnohistory* 9: 1–23.

Gottschalk, Louis. 1945. The historian and the historical document. In *The use of personal documents in history, anthropology, and sociology*, ed. L. Gottschalk et al., 3–75. New York: Social Science Research Council.

Keesing, Felix M. 1947. Acculturation in Polynesia. In *Specialized studies in Polynesian anthropology*, ed. Katharine Luomale et al., 32–46. Honolulu: Bishop Museum Bulletin 193.

Luomala, Katharine. 1947. Missionary contributions to Polynesian anthropology. In *Specialized studies in Polynesian anthropology*, ed. Katharine Luomala et al., 5–31. Honolulu: Bishop Museum Bulletin 193.

Lurie, Nancy Oestreich. 1961. Ethnohistory: An ethnological point of view. *Ethnohistory* 8: 78–92.

Pargellis, Stanley. 1957. The problem of American Indian history. *Ethnohistory* 4: 111–24.

Sahlins, Marshall D. 1962. *Moala: Culture and nature on a Fijian island.* Ann Arbor: University of Michigan Press.

Tippett, Alan R. 1944. The snake in early Fijian belief. *Transactions and Proceedings of the Fiji Society of Science and Industry* 2, no. 5: 279–96.

———. 1954a. The nature and social function of Fijian war. *Transactions and Proceedings of the Fiji Society* 5, no. 4: 137–55.

———. 1954b. The snake in the magico-religious systems of the Pacific, with special reference to Fiji. *Transactions and Proceedings of the Fiji Society* 5, no. 4: 107–21.

Valentine, C. A. 1960. Uses of ethnohistory in an acculturation study. *Ethnohistory* 7: 1–27.

Washburn, Wilcomb E. 1961. Ethnohistory: History "in the Round." *Ethnohistory* 8: 31–48.

Weltfish, Gene. 1959. The question of ethnic identity: An ethnohistorical approach. *Ethnohistory* 6: 321–46.

3
THE CONTOUR OF ETHNOHISTORY[8]

As soon as we confront the truth that our Lord sent the apostles out *into the world*, we are involved in some kind of encounter with culture. They were "not of the world" (John 17:14, 16), so presumably the sending implied that he was to transmit something supracultural through them. This was at least a peace "given to you as the world could not give" (John 14:27). It was of course his peace, as he had "overcome the world" (John 16:33). But nevertheless the world was the scene of his mission, and throughout history, as the cultural scenes of changing generations and ethnic diffusion demonstrated the diversity of the world into which they were sent, the whole question of cross-cultural communication became inevitably part of Christian mission. The Lord committed his followers to cross-cultural proclamation and witness, and gave them gifts adequate for the task. They were bound to develop methods, strategies, and approaches as the church expanded. Even in the apostolic age, the church confronted ethnic problems and learned to recognise the diversity of culture within the unity of the body (for example, Acts 6:1–7; 15:22–32).

The careless use of the term *ethnohistory* by some missiologists, as if it were merely the sum of history and anthropology, calls for comment. History and anthropology are disciplines, but ethnohistory is a methodology. It recognises its own system of values. It recognises that historical and anthropological techniques have something to offer each other and correct each other's shortcomings. The methodology is symbiotic. I would even go further than this and suggest that it is syngenetic—in other words, something quite new is born through the union. Lynn T. White's article on "History and Horseshoe Nails" is a good example of this. He tells of how his discovery of Kroeber's method for reconstructing history from archaeological artifacts without the use of documents revolutionised his approach to the history of medieval technology (1970, 50). One of the features of the next generation of missiologists will certainly be the development of that currently vague area covered by terms like *ethnohistory, ethnotheology, ethnolinguistics, ethnopsychology,* and *ethnobiblical studies.* If I am still alive at the end of the century, I expect to see a large body of literature along these lines, and I think it will transform the character and quality of

---

8   Taken from "'Contours of Reality' in the History of Mission," *Missiology* 3, no. 4 (1975): 403–12. Used by permission.

missiology in this postcolonial age. These methodologies are probing at the dimension of missiological symbiosis, which pass unnoticed because of the overspecialisation of the traditional disciplines. This, in turn, isolates the latter from the wholeness of human life and endeavor. If we do not develop these interdisciplinary methods, missiology will perish and become no more than a historical experiment of the 1970s and 1980s, an unsuccessful attempt to deal with the anomie of the 1960s.

REFERENCES

White, Lynn T. 1970. History and horseshoe nails. In *The historian's workshop*, ed. L. Perry Curtis 47–64. New York: Knopf.

4
PREAMBLE AND SOURCES[9]

As much as possible I have endeavoured to keep myself out of the picture. We are studying the native Christian. What I think about the form of their faith, or their theology, or
their religious enthusiasm, does not really matter, as long as I can give a true picture of
what they believed, and thought, and did. I have no doubt that readers may not always
react to these things as I have. I leave them to form their own opinions. My work then has
been mainly the assembling of selected material, arrangement of it, and here and there
a simple confirmation that such and such a thing continues to be so to this day as I have
found myself.

The study is almost entirely prepared from primary sources, either published at the
time, or original manuscripts, of which I have been through some thousands. Where
secondary sources are used, these are mostly volumes from which extensive primary material is available in the quotations. On furlough recently I examined material in public
and private libraries in New South Wales, Victoria, South Australia, and Tasmania, but
time was against me. But I have drawn from the Mitchell Library (Sydney), Melbourne
Public Library, and that of the Patterson Street Methodist Church in Launceston for some
important statements made in this monograph—original manuscripts in the former and
original publications in the other two. To these institutions I am deeply indebted. I also
thank the families of several retired missionaries who have helped me. Apart from these,
all my other source material is in the colony of Fiji.

The most valuable source of all in this particular study is that terrific assemblage of
material in the archives of the Methodist Mission in Fiji. I have been wading through this,
off and on, for years. It includes annual reports from the circuits, school reports, baptismal
registers, statistics, reports of committees, minutes of meetings, letter books, and endless bundles of correspondence inwards, and other documents. Most of the official reports
handled at Bishopsgate by Henderson are here also, but these go on and are not terminated
in midfifties. There is, of course, a great deal of repetition in them, but studying these over
the years has given me a sort of background that has become more and more clear as I have

---

9   Taken from *The Christian: Fiji 1835–1867* (Auckland: Institute Printing and Publishing, 1954), 2–3. Used by permission.

proceeded. This picture I have tried to give in this monograph, and though I state many references to specific items in my text, the overall picture is that of the archives as a whole.

I have read statements like this—"For more than 10 years there were few converts. When, however, a few high chiefs were won over, progress was more rapid." I say, when I read statements like that (which comes from the official Colonial Report of Fiji, 1851), I know that sooner or later this monograph will have to be given to the public.

Now, the Mission archival material has some gaps—flood, fire, and hurricane, no doubt, account for them. Fortunately I have been able to find in my own library a good deal of published primary material to fill most of those gaps. The missionaries of the period wrote long letters and reports and kept journals, and most of their material was published in *The Wesleyan Magazine* and *The Wesleyan Juvenile Offering*, and in the later period when this field came under the Methodist Church in Australia the *Wesleyan Missionary Notices* did the same thing. I have these fairly complete, and the few that are missing I have examined in Launceston. In addition to these, my library contains a great many missionary letters, documents, journals, and newspaper cuttings spread out over the last century, and other similar material has been loaned to me from time to time for purposes of study. Any student using this script and studying the references will observe that quite a number are from unpublished sources in my private collection.

Whenever possible I have made use of nonmissionary sources, like Seemann, Erskine, Wilkes, and others, mostly seamen and travellers, but the reader will see at once that the nature of the theme demands a heavy use of mission material.

Some of the original publications used freely are fundamental to the study. Of these I should refer to the following, in particular Calvert's *Fiji and the Fijians*. Calvert came in 1838 and left finally in 1865. He was a great collector of other men's notes. He quoted fully and freely. In 1865 no white man knew more about Fiji than James Calvert. I use both his first and last editions. Waterhouse's *King and People of Fiji* (together with the Bau Annual Reports) cannot be done without for the study of the conversion of Cakobau and the events before and after. Rowe's *Life of Hunt* is indispensable for the study of the Viwa revivals. It was compiled from Hunt's original documents, journals, and letters, and with access to Hunt's widow for any needed confirmations. It quotes freely. With it one should use the Hunt reports in the Mission archives, and his published correspondence in *The Wesleyan Magazine*, and his own publications. Nettleton's *John Hunt* also adds revival material not found elsewhere.

Lawry, Young, Calvert, and others provide native testimonies given at love feasts. In any study of Fijian religious experience these are important.

The Baker, Langham, Carey, and Fison letters and reports in *Wesleyan Missionary Notices* (Australia) during the 1860s are extremely valuable historical material, both for the religious and secular historian and, as far as I know, have been practically untapped. My use of them in this monograph has been mainly to establish the narrow confines of the Christian era a decade after Kaba.

In order to evaluate the peculiar revival experiences of Viwa, Lakeba, Ono, and Kadavu, it becomes necessary to relate them to similar phenomena in the outside world. I have therefore made heavy use of two entirely different types of sources—Tyerman's *Life and Times of Wesley* in three volumes, and Knox's recent work, *Enthusiasm*. Both of these are rich in quotations and references to primary sources, and both writers were thorough in their examination of Wesley's own material. Other Wesley sources I have used sparingly. Their validity in this study is but for a single point—to establish whether or not there is a connection between the Wesleyan revival at home and those of Viwa and other places in Fiji.

In connection, with the nature of the faith of the native Christians under persecution, it is difficult to say that one source is more important than another. Possibly in my references I have drawn more from Thomas Williams' journal, a Mitchell Library manuscript, which we have in published form through the labour of Henderson. But I do refer to Margaret Cargill's *Memoirs* and to Fison's *Joeli Bulu*, and one might well have used many other sources. One does not have to go far to find evidence of the persecution of the early Christians. In connection with the actual experiences of the native agents and ordinary Christians, the testing of their faith in times of crisis, and for those most important (for this study) deathbed statements of faith, my source, wherever possible, has been a native document. These comprise two types: (1) stories and letters told and written by natives and translated into English by missionaries for publication (from the idiom they are manifestly translations, and usually it is so stated) as books, like *Old Sefanaia* and *Joeli Bulu* (Fison translations) or as short stories and letters in *Juvenile Missionary Offering* and other missionary publications, and (2) I have also a small assortment of original native manuscripts, and two of these are of considerable length. These are in Fijian, and I have had to translate whatever I have quoted. For a study of native faith and experience, these have, to me, become fundamental.

Such is the scope and nature of this monograph. I regret the impossibility of maintaining a single style of writing throughout, but that one part should be statistical and another psychological is the nature of the case.

The writing has involved me in a good deal of self-restraint, for it has not always been easy to go on without engaging in asides. Politics, for instance, persistently kept cropping up, for some of the missionaries and some of the Tongan teachers later did get tied up in local politics. But though they differed greatly among themselves in their political views (as in the church today), I feel their religious experiences were fundamentally characteristic. I hope that this little work will help the reader to clarify in his or her mind some of the issues that have been much misunderstood, especially regarding the nature of conversion among the early Fijians, and just what the effect of the conversion of a chief or a victory in war meant, and how far afield such influence would be felt, and whether or not there was a real spiritual factor in the conversion of Fiji.

No one will challenge the statement that the evangelistic attack on Fiji was an extremely dangerous venture from the start—it was dangerous for the missionary and dangerous for the Fijian who became involved before his chief, or the petty chief before his superior. Yet this happened—that is a fact which history cannot dodge. The venture called for brave spirits, men and women of faith from among the people. If we can discover the nature of that faith, we shall also discover the key to the conversion of Fiji.

These words of John Wesley to Alexander Mather in 1777 serve well to end this introduction: "Give me one hundred preachers who fear nothing but sin and desire nothing but God, and I care not a straw whether they be clergymen or laymen, such alone will shake the gates of hell and set up the Kingdom of God upon earth" (Carter 1951, 215).

REFERENCES

Carter, Henry. 1951. *Methodist heritage*, vol. 2. Nashville: Abingdon.

5
METHODOLOGY[10]

[for a research project in the Solomon Islands]

Immediately after the war the head of a Christian mission returned to what had been his station headquarters. The area was still under army occupation and, physically, all was desolation. Yet his report was one of thanksgiving. His people "had suffered hunger, nakedness, peril and persecution," but he was convinced of "the indestructibility of the Christian faith." He listed the congregations which had rebuilt the churches destroyed by enemy action and named many "strong Christian leaders," who had endured much and would certainly rebuild the church of the future (Goldie 1945–46). Nevertheless, within a few years, some three thousand persons from those very Christian communities he listed, under some of the leaders he had specifically mentioned, had rejected his church and followed an indigenous prophet with a Christopagan theology.

Solomon Islands Christianity (1967) presents us with a study in *growth* and *obstruction*. In both the first and second generations we face success and failure. When a historian and anthropologist is called in to investigate such a situation, the report which emerges is bound to be problem orientated. This does not mean, however, that he is unaware of the splendid pioneering work done by the various missions involved. It would be much easier for him to write a pleasant record of achievement. Such a record would be true, but it would not be the whole truth. The Department of Missionary Studies of the World Council of Churches determined on a research project for this region during 1964–65. This volume is the result.

This study is historical, but it is not a history. The record of each mission concerned has been written by its own competent historian. However, to understand the current problems faced by the churches, some historical perspectives are essential. Solomon Islands Christianity has grown and developed with clearly marked trends over the years. The study is historical also in that the techniques of historical method have been applied to the documents and other sources of information used. Most of this has been done from primary sources, secondary sources being evaluated in the light of their own specific purposes at the period in which they were written, rather than the period about which they were written.

---

10   Taken from *Solomon Islands Christianity* (London: Lutterworth Press, 1967), xiii–xiv. Used by permission.

This study is anthropological, but it is not an anthropology. It makes no attempt at presenting a total cultural analysis of a race of people or a village community, either diachronically or synchronically. Nevertheless, in methods of research—by participant observation in selected villages—in methods of handling informants and cross-checking their testimonies, this may be called anthropological research.

Essentially this is a religious study. It examines two of the young churches of the Solomon Islands, using historical and anthropological data to interpret the character of the local situations in which the churches have emerged or are at present emerging. It attempts to show something of the patterns by which people have come and are coming out of paganism into Christianity. It analyses the effects of social conditions and mission policies, in either stimulating or obstructing growth. It probes the problematics of both first- and second-generation Christianity. If the methodology is historical and anthropological, the purpose of the book is entirely religious. At heart many of the problems are ultimately theological.

One had to settle on some specific limits for the project. Regionally we are concerned with what is popularly known as the Solomon Islands, the group of islands stretching from Buin and Bougainville to San Cristoval and Ulawa.[11] Within these geographical limits, I have confined myself to the Melanesian people. I am well aware of the presence of Polynesians, Micronesians, and others in the region, and I recognise that in reality they are part of the situation—but so complicated a part that they warrant a special study of their own.[12]

At one or two specific points, studies have been conducted in depth, by my living with a village congregation for a period of time and sharing their religious and daily life. One research worker, even in a lifetime, could never learn everything of the Solomon Islands situation, and I hasten to admit awareness of the shortcomings of my research and knowledge. Many missionaries understand their localities better. My only advantage has been to see things over a fairly wide panorama, and to be able to look at them objectively, regardless of mission policy and administrative restrictions. My whole task was to discover what it means to be a Melanesian Christian in Melanesia today.

My task also involved me in a great deal of archival and library research in the scattered repositories of Oceanic documentary materials, and in interviews with many retired missionaries in Fiji, Australia, and New Zealand. I hope the total picture benefits from this expenditure of money, time, and effort.

The patterns reconstructed in this book are vignettes of the island life. Here the church grew. There it stopped growing. Here one finds dramatic action. There one meets

---

11   Politically, Buin and Bougainville belong to the Australian Trust Territory of Papua and New Guinea, but it is impossible to separate their missionary history or their cultural and economic connections from those of the Western Solomons.

12   The resettlement of non-Melanesians in Melanesian areas is receiving considerable attention from American anthropologists. A church survey by a Polynesian or Micronesian scholar should be valuable.

indifference. Here we meet a first-generation social group, in a face-to-face encounter with the powers of darkness. There the problematics of individuals drifting from marginality to nominality confront us. All these are real-life situations. As the subject is inexhaustible, I make no claim for completeness in the study. Missionaries in the area may feel there are important omissions. I can only claim their forbearance, for the number of localities I could visit in the time was certainly limited.

Before undertaking this study, I had myself served the church for twenty years in another part of Melanesia. This gave me some background for the analysis of Melanesian patterns in the Solomons, which were both similar and dissimilar to those which I had known.

REFERENCES

Goldie, John F. Chairman's report. Sydney: Methodist Overseas Missions, 1945–46.

6

THE HISTORICITY OF
ORAL TRADITION[13]

Certain methodological changes in both history and anthropology are now being initiated because of pressures brought upon them by ethnohistorical research and awareness. Possibly the most apparent area of this pressure is that of oral tradition. What is the evidential value of oral tradition? The argument over the status of ethnohistory has at least awakened both historians and anthropologists to their need for a determined effort at synthesis.

When A. L. Kroeber had worked through what the Mohave Indians believed to be their historical traditions, he described them as "*pseudohistory* and products of the imagination, of literary interest but not historical" (quoted in Sturtevant 1966, 27).

Robert Lowie protested against the treatment of oral traditions as history, although he accepted them as of "psychological significance" and admitted that their distribution, like that of artifacts and ritual forms, might have some historical connection, but this was as far as he would go—oral tradition is just not history (1960, 202–3). Certain elements might be regarded as the primitive counterpart of what we call history, but he would not validate oral tradition as such for the same reason that he would not validate Aboriginal pathology or biology (204). "We accept primitive observations," he said of astronomy, flora, and fauna, "in so far as they conform to what we independently ascertain by our own methods." Then he went on to make the astonishing statement (and this was in his retiring presidential address before the American Folklore Society):

> However we neither derive the least increment of knowledge from this primitive science, nor are we in the slightest measure strengthened in our convictions by such coincidence. Exactly the same principle applies in the domain of history.
> (Ibid., 205)

He wanted history to be a completely "objective" examination within his own ethnocentric criteria, and went so far as to say, "I deny utterly that primitive man is endowed with historical sense or perspective" (ibid., 206).[14]

---

13 Taken from *Aspects of Pacific Ethnohistory* (Pasadena: William Carey Library, 1973), 15–37. Used by permission.

14 One could dismiss this merely as evidence of how ethnocentric even the best anthropologists could be in 1916, when the statement was first made, but for the fact that DuBois in 1960, in a volume of selected writings of Lowie, choosing

Just as I would challenge Lowie, on a basis of my personal experience of what he (wrongly I think) calls primitive people, that we can derive no valuable knowledge from their botany, for example (true, it does not fit the Linnean system, but it has its own classifications and offers us much genuine information of value to medicine), so too the historical value of their oral tradition is immediately manifest once we cross the cultural barrier far enough to discover what it is about—its goals, its forms, its values, and its concept of time. It cannot be studied objectively by a foreigner. One has to enter the spirit and language. It is not a mere chronological record based on a foreign calendar. One has to distinguish between the *times of the gods*, the *times of the ancestors and heroes*, and *recent time*.[15] One has to tune himself with the media of communication—song, dirge, proverb, riddle, story—the symbolism of the form, the social situations, occasions, and institutions within which the communication operated of its own natural accord, its enculturative function, and many other things. It is the researcher's obligation to "get into the act" if he wants to understand it, and this will be more a subjective than an objective exercise. To appreciate the historical value of oral traditions requires an experience.

So while I would agree with Lowie that "we cannot substitute primitive tradition for scientific history," I would add the comment that we do not want to do so. But if we know the language and can get into the act enough to feel it, we will discover a rich field of historical and scientific data. Indeed there is no other way of reconstructing the cultural milieu, the worldview, the value system, which together form the context within which the history of these people has been enacted. The historical judgments of the cross-cultural historian have to be made within the values and thought forms of the people he studies—not his own.

Since Lowie's time the folklorists have gone their own way and collected tales, classifying the various kinds functionally—origin tales, explanatory tales, trickster tales, cultural themes, and so forth. Some interesting collections have been put together, which have considerable entertainment value and reveal commonalities of human nature in fables and other literary forms, but the emphasis has been more on the tale as a reflection of culture and as a type of literature than on history, and no adequate chronology has been recognised.

Before Lowie died in 1957 the methodology of *ethnohistory* had emerged. Strangely enough it has been developed mostly by students of the American Indians, of whom Lowie, an Indian specialist, said "Indian tradition is historically worthless (1960, 207)." I know of no revision of this opinion in his later life, and the journal *Ethnohistory* published no notice

---

thirty-three from three hundred options, selected this to include in the section entitled "Relation of Ethnology to Other Disciplines" and presented it on its own merits, without editorial comment, as if it were a recent article.

15   These are my own categories, and they came out of the data itself. The material I collected in Fiji over twenty years fell into one of these three types.

of his death. To attend the annual meeting of the American Association for Ethnohistory is to find oneself almost entirely confined to papers on Indian studies. Neither historians nor anthropologists at large express much interest. Furthermore their work tended to be obviously historical or anthropological. There was little synthesis.

Dorson complained of the gulf between folklore and history, which continues without fraternization in spite of efforts like the Oral History Project, because professional historians equate oral tradition with untruth and distortion, and because U.S. folklorists are not historically minded, using formal classifications rather than historical periods (1961, 12–13). In 1966 the first national colloquium on oral history tried to bring anthropologists and historians together and published a report. The reviewer in the *American Historical Review* doubted if oral history had yet crystallised sufficiently to be called a field. He found them concerned for their entity, and worried about the validity of their approaches, although the reviewer thought they do have a role to play and wished them well (Kahn 1968).[16]

In America, history, anthropology, and folklore go their own sweet ways, and the journal *Ethnohistory* seems to me to be the only serious effort to bring about a synthesis. The journal badly needs a special emphasis beyond the limitations of the American Indians.

Now let us take a look at the matter in Britain. One of the earliest men to take a serious look at oral traditions was E. B. Tylor. He distinguished between the mythical and historical elements, and claimed that things could be true either factually in the historical sense, or symbolically true in the ritual or religious sense. In either case he regarded them as of historical value. Let me give an example of each.

Seventy years ago, after his early works had become well known, he argued for a recognition of the remarkable memory element in many oral traditions:

> The South Sea Islanders, who till quite recently had no writing, were intelligent
> barbarians, much given to handing down recollections of bygone days, and in one
> or two cases, which it has been possible to test among them, it seems as though
> memory may really keep a historical record long and correctly. (1904, 292)

Among the supporting data, he told of a community of Ellice Islanders who claimed to have originated from Samoa, but offered no more evidence than a worm-eaten staff, pieced together and tied. It was used by the orator in their communal assembly and was so old that it was falling to pieces. The wood from which it was made did not grow on their island. It must have come from some other place: why not Samoa? The structure of the assembly was Samoan, and the role of the orator. But there was no other memory—just the notion that they had come from Samoa as the staff "proved." In time that staff was actually taken to Samoa, and two things immediately came to light. First it was indeed made of

---

16   This is viewed by an outsider. From inside I believe the Columbia University oral history program has operated for twenty-five years, and there are now 250 programs in the U.S. *Library of Congress Information Bulletin*, 30 March 1973, p. 110.

a Samoan wood and recognised by the people as such, and second there was in Samoa an old tradition of a large party of Samoans who went to sea a number of generations before and had never returned. Although not proved, the oral tradition is immediately credible (ibid., 293).

Another contribution of E. B. Tylor was in the reconstruction of "primitive" religion, which he regarded also as history. I recall a passage in which he described the flowing wine and burning meat sacrifice and the gods meeting in council. Yet of this obviously mythical episode he wrote:

> All this is not only history, but history of the finest kind. Looked at by the
> student of culture, even the wild mixture of the natural and supernatural,
> so bewildering to the modern mind is the record of an early stage of religious
> thought. (Ibid., 296)

There is truth and error in this statement. It is false because he was reconstructing the history of religion on an *a priori* frame of reference which was shortly to be discredited by anthropological research. He was right in assuming that the study of myths is basic evidence for religious reconstruction. He performed a great service for posterity by recording much data for the use of his successors, whatever they should think of his theoretical use of it.

Eighty years ago when George Laurence Gomme was president of the Folklore Society in England, he wrote a book for Lubbock's *Series in Modern Science*. He bemoaned the obsession of anthropologists with evolutionary landmarks at the expense of folklore. Even the historians, who occasionally drew on craniology, archaeology, and philology, rarely turned to folklore, which Gomme believed contained many ethnological facts which called for historical investigation, and that "a method for discovering them" had to be developed by scholars (1892, vi). Gomme found obstruction to the study of folklore because of the popular notion of its location in the nursery, and it being beneath the dignity of academic historians and philologists. He argued that the tale had value as a repository of information on beliefs, customs, and traditions, and he bemoaned the occupation of historians with only the political and commercial progress of nations (1–2).

Gomme himself had been much influenced by E. B. Tylor and was aware of the fact that folklore housed a body of significant data that needed some kind of classification. From this his own efforts as a folklorist turned to the matter of reconstructing religious belief and ethnic genealogies. Yet in spite of his enthusiasm and the inclusion of his work in Lubbock's series, Lubbock himself was cautious about the value and use of folklore. Grudgingly he admitted that it might "solve many difficult problems in ethnology" but that there needs to be very careful study "before this class of evidence can be used with safety (1892)."

The functionalists both helped and hindered the acceptance of oral tradition. Malinowski, with his synchronic rather than diachronic approach, discarded the historical potential of myths and concentrated on their relationships to social procedures and belief. The same applies to Radcliffe-Brown, who, in his study of the Andaman Islanders, saw myth as a "way of thinking and feeling about society and its relation to the world of nature." These men stressed the function of myth and/or oral tradition for maintaining social cohesion. Legends which relate the invention of weapons and customs may be related back to origin myths or hero stories—how the social order and practices came into being (Radcliffe-Brown 1994, 376–405), but they relate to current life and its artifacts and have no historical significance. Malinowski argued:

> They have no idea of a long vista of historical occurrences, narrowing down and dimming as they recede . . . Whenever they speak of some event, they distinguish whether it happened within their own memory or that of their fathers', or not. (1961, 300)

There are only two "time" categories—(1) that of their fathers or grandfathers (the number of generations the oldest inhabitant can remember or narrate), and (2) long ago, which is designated by an expletive, *lili'u* (301). This would agree with my own Fijian experience (supra. and footnote 2), except that I found the time depth of the recent period a little greater and recalled by physical events—epidemic, comet, eclipse, flood, etc. The same conception of time has since been reported from Africa (Jones 1965, 153, 160) and in Alaska (Hudson 1966, 56–58). Always there is a time gap between the remote past and the recent past. The great potential for ethnohistorians lies in the oral traditions of the recent past. It seems to me that we may have a preexistent state (timeless before the beginnings), the beginnings (hero stories), then a gap of which the islander does not seem to be aware until he is confronted with the problem by the investigator, and finally the recent (and perhaps subrecent) period for which he can produce epics, songs, dirges, proverbs, and narratives.

At this point in our discussion I have to differentiate between origin stories (which may have symbolic and exaggerated features), wonder tales, animal tales (maybe totemic or maybe literary imagination), and fairy tales (all of which may have great anthropological value), its function being religious, legal, educational, or for entertainment on the one hand, and material which purports to be historical on the other, even though it may be used to accompany a dance for entertainment: what the Fijians would call *ai talanoa* and *ai tukuni* on the one hand and *ai tukutuku* on the other.

Formulation of a Methodology

Having eliminated the religious and symbolic or mythical element of oral tradition, and having brought our focus upon that which actually purports to be historical, we shall now turn back to the question of reliability. "Written sources are better than oral ones." This is the maxim of a nonhistorian, declares Vansina.

> For the practitioner sources are sources. These can be good or bad, but there is nothing intrinsically less valuable in an oral source than in a written one. The

only advantage of a written source is that it is at the same time an archaeological document (Vansina 1960, 52).

Most encouraging results are coming out of new Africa, where many historians, including some highly competent Africans, are working on the oral traditions and exposing
much of truly historical value (Boston 1969; Shelton 1968; Alagoa 1966, 1968; Berger 1966;
Vansina 1960; Jones 1965; Ogot 1966; Gray 1965; et al.), and working out an appropriate
methodology for handling their material.

In 1966 Ogot took certain scholars to task for writing on African social institutions—
family, clan, religious cults, kingship, etc.—without paying adequate attention to their
historical traditions, both written and oral. He pointed out how the functions of these
institutions change through time, and that such changes are normally embodied in the
traditions and require historical investigation. He insisted that one has precisely the same
problems with both oral and written traditions—bias, reliability, conflicting accounts, and
so forth—so there are no reasons for accepting one and rejecting the other (1966, 140–45).[17]

Vansina, who researched the history of the chiefdoms of Kubu and found his sources
almost entirely oral traditions, formulated a set of theoretical rules for evaluating this
kind of source. He began by identifying oral tradition as different from reporting eyewit-
nesses (which would make the product *news* rather than records intended for *transmission*).
He felt the researcher had to acquire knowledge of (1) the language of the traditions, (2) the
society, and (3) the culture of the kingdom. Then he asked why this society had oral traditions at all, and why they were preserved in these particular forms and not in some other.
He sought to find the organic bonds which linked the forms of transmission to the rest of
culture. Eventually he classified the sources—formulae, poetry, genealogies, tales, com-
mentaries, and precedents in law. Some of these, but not all, had historical intention, but
they all had some historical value once the researcher understood their form and function. Vansina laid down an important foundation and discussed procedures and problems
of data collection. He found that village and clan records could be checked against each
other, and that sometimes traditions are preserved by specialised bodies, such as tribal
councils, and their recitation is checked (1960).

Berger (1966), working in Karagwe, used stories of the kings, genealogical lists, songs,
and recitations, and also found institutions for preserving traditions. She used regular
anthropological open-ended interviewing, working with the old men and with groups and
starting with the genealogy. Alagoa (1966; 1968) worked among the Ijo of the Niger Delta,
following Vansina's methods and working on proverbs which were built on historical persons and events. He stresses the importance of knowing the language and thinks that one
reason why oral traditions are neglected is the difficulty of the field work in data collect-

---

17   In passing he points out that the documentary sources for early British history—Gildas, Bede, Nennius, and the *Anglo
      Saxon Chronicle*—were all compiled from oral sources.

ing. Shelton (1968) studied a historical figure and wrote of the problems he encountered in identifying the traditions, verifying their historicity and the importance of identifying the purpose of the tradition before trying to interpret it—is it religious or historical, for instance? Boston (1969) programmed his research on the oral traditions of the Igala by dealing with three critical problems: (1) variants in the traditions, (2) chronology (because of gaps in the time span), and (3) separating political facts from their historical functions.

These are some of the ways in which African research is continuing with the use of oral tradition. It will be seen immediately that it implies a sympathetic attitude on the part of the researchers, a positive attempt to explore its hidden value, rather than that of "a detective trying to find fault with a text in order to condemn it" (Vansina 1960, 49).

One of the most fascinating pieces of ethnohistorical research to come my way was Raymond Firth's *History and Traditions of Tikopia* (1961), which will serve in this paper to bring us back to the Pacific. It throws light on the nature of change in traditional tales. Firth collected a body of traditional tales in Tikopia in 1928–29. About a generation later (1952) he returned and worked over the same material again, dwelling particularly on the revisions and modifications since his earlier visit. He found the tales represented continuity and discontinuity and revealed an important aspect of interpretation. One had to allow for variant traditions being the reflection of variables in the sociopolitical structure—the adaptation of tales to social and political events or changing situations. The tales can be regarded as true and interpreted symbolically, or they can be told for recreation, but they "belong to the group" and serve functionally as an "identity badge and a social rallying point" (Firth 1961, 171) The material is controlled by the approved leader of the group, and for him it held ritual power, which conditioned his health and prosperity. Not only do the tales reflect the unity of the social structure, but they also permit competitive elements and organisational pressures within the unity of that society. Firth stresses the fact that variations may not necessarily be "defects in the memory" or "embroidery of imagination" but rather "remoulding" due to the "social situation" of the narrator and his times." He goes on to argue that "realistic appraisal of Polynesian traditions in sociological terms" should strengthen the approach of scholars to this kind of oral tale for purposes of interpretation (ibid., 182).

REFERENCES

Alagoa, Ebiegberi Joe. 1966. Oral tradition among the Ijo of the Niger Delta. *Journal of African History* 7, no. 3: 405–17.

———. 1968. The use of oral literary data for history. *Journal of American Folklore* 81: 235–42.

Berger, Ruth C. 1966. Field work methods in the study of oral traditions in Karagwe. In *Prelude to East African history*, ed. Merrick Posnansky, 149–58. Ibadan, Nigeria: Oxford University Press.

Boston, J. S. 1969. Oral tradition and the history of the Igala. *Journal of African History* 10, no. 1: 29–43.

Dorson, Richard M. 1961. Ethnohistory and ethnic folklore. *Ethnohistory* 8, no. 1: 12–30.

Fenton, William N. 1961. Ethnohistory and its problems. *Ethnohistory* 9, no. 1: 1–23.

Firth, Raymond W. 1961. *History and traditions of Tikopia.* Wellington, New Zealand: Polynesian Society.

Gomme, Laurence George. 1892. *The handbook of folklore.* London: Kegan Paul, Trench, Trubner and Co.

Gray, Richard. 1965. Eclipse maps. *Journal of African History* 6, no. 3: 251–62.

Hudson, Charles. 1966. Folk history and ethnohistory. *Ethnohistory* 13, nos. 1–2: 52–70.

Jones, G. I. 1965. Time and oral tradition with special reference to Eastern Nigeria. *Journal of African History* 6, no. 2: 153–60.

Kahn, Herman. 1968. Review of *Oral history at Arrowhead: The proceedings of the First National Colloquium on Oral History. American Historical Review* 73, no. 5: 1471.

Kroeber, A. L. 1951. A Mohave historical epic. *Anthropological Records* 11, no. 2: 71–176.

Lowie, Robert H. 1960. Oral tradition and history. In *Selected papers in anthropology,* ed. Cora DuBois, 202–10. Berkeley: University of California Press.

Malinowski, Bronislaw. 1961. *Argonauts of the Western Pacific.* New York: Dutton. First published 1922.

Ogot, Alan B. 1966. Oral traditions and the historian. In *Prelude to East African history,* ed. Merrick Posnansky, 140–48. Ibadan, Nigeria: Oxford University Press.

Radcliffe-Brown, A. R. 1964. *The Andaman Islanders.* New York: Free Press of Glencoe. First published 1932.

Shelton, Austin J. 1968. *Onojo Ogboni. Journal of American Folklore* 5, no. 81: 243–57.

Sturtevant, William C. 1966. Anthropology, history and ethnohistory. *Ethnohistory* 13, no. 1: 1–51.

Tylor, Edward B. 1904. *Anthropology: An introduction to the study of man and civilization.* New York: J. A. Hill.

Vansina, Jan. 1960. Recording the oral history of the Bakuba. *Journal of African History* 1, nos. 1–2: 45–53, 257–70.

7

AN ANTHROPOLOGIST LOOKS AT THE JESUS DOCUMENTS[18]

In this little book we attempt to return to the world of the four Gospels and to look at them as independent documents or monographs. More particularly, we look in their subject matter at the person of Jesus and the band of disciples whom he prepared and sent forth on his mission to the world. The question that will most certainly arise is why this book is being written by a social anthropologist (or an ethnohistorian) rather than a biblical scholar or a theologian, seeing that it must ultimately be classified as a "theology of mission."

It is certainly not that I would usurp the research field of another discipline, but rather that I believe that all our disciplines are merely convenient abstractions for purposes of analyzing our data and setting up the criteria necessary for our evaluations. In point of fact, none of them are real, and once their practical value of providing a frame of reference for observing and testing facts has been achieved, they become more shackles than aids to our thinking. As historian Marc Bloch once said, "Man spends his time devising techniques of which he afterwards remains a more or less willing prisoner" (1964, 39). The tools of any discipline frequently go beyond their immediate purposes of analysis and classification and force an academic rigidity of the discipline on scholars, with two very unfortunate effects—they make the discipline meaningless to ordinary people and render the academicians closed against other methodologies. The value of interdisciplinary research is that we have a two-way process—a symbiosis of both giving and receiving.

I venture to write this gospel theology of mission as an anthropologist and an ethnohistorian, not in the sense of Saul being among the prophets, but in an attempt to reach out symbiotically to other disciplines. I believe my discipline has something to say to the subject, that we should be able to go even beyond symbiosis to some methodological syngenesis. There is a long history of anthropologists trying to speak to theologians—from the days of E. B. Tylor over a century ago (1871). This is a plea, not a criticism.

From both sides, the disciplines of history and anthropology, for example, have been moving together and speaking to each other. This has resulted in some exciting experi-

---

18   Taken from *The Jesus Documents* (Pasadena: William Carey Library, 2012). Used by permission. Manuscript written in 1972.

ences and some refreshing new kinds of writing. I begin this introductory preamble by giving a few illustrations of this interaction, and then I shall proceed to suggest a few ways in which it calls for a new approach to the biblical theology of mission.

The Interplay of Disciplines

Had anthropology not been discovered by the antiquarians and archaeologists, the historians must eventually have found it. When Wilde, in Ireland, and Keller, in Switzerland, were working on the remains of ancient lake-dwelling societies, a young historian in his twenties, Fustel de Coulanges, was struggling with the history of Greece and Rome. Shortly afterwards, in 1862, he delivered his inaugural lecture at Strasbourg. Among other things he described how the more he talked with his colleagues in history the more he became convinced that they were really talking of the French and British of their own day. Then he said:

> I then resolved to have no other teachers on Greece than Greeks, nor on Rome than Romans, and I boldly resolved to read the ancient authors . . . I encountered these writers in their magnificent diversity . . . historians took turns with orators, orators with poets, sometimes the tribune and sometimes the stage . . .
>
> Little by little I got better acquainted with the ancients; I saw their customs, their beliefs, their needs, their laws. Minor points seemingly insignificant and unnoticed, illuminated their institutions for me. It did not take me long to see that if these institutions are often misunderstood by us, this happens because we study them by themselves as abstractions without . . . giving thought to the state of mind and to the beliefs of the men for whom these institutions were made . . . I applied myself to the study of the beliefs of Greeks and Romans, and before long I thought I could see that between beliefs and institutions there is such a close bond that the one explains the other. (Stern 1963, 185)

The words of Fustel de Coulanges speak forcefully to me in a number of ways. In my travels across the missionary world in many countries, I have often been impressed with the fact that missionaries, and also the home constituency which sends them, are interpreting the gospel as if the biblical world were that of Lutheranism, or Anglicanism, or Presbyterianism, or Restorationism, or Universalism. I am not thinking here just of the foreignness of this—i.e., the problem of planting indigenous churches—but rather that most of us tend to see the scriptural world through our denominational spectacles. We force both the gospel characters and themes into our own garments and structures. Time after time this conviction has driven me back to the New Testament documents themselves in an attempt to discover what they were and to look at them whole rather than as a reservoir of proof texts for quoting.

I find four monographs, magnificent in their diversity, yet self-validating in their basic themes. I find people and social institutions which relate to each other. When I discover the cultural mazeways of the first century, I discover the early church, but above all I discover the nature of the Incarnation, the reality of the Word made flesh—and that in a precise social pattern, at a precise time in history, and at a precise place on the map. I see Jesus as so much a man of his culture and language that people speak of him as "the Galilean" or "the Nazarene."

The true humanity of Jesus and his voluntary acceptance of the bondage (cf. Phil 2:8) of Galilean culture is more than a cultural fact; it is a theological fact of greatest significance. The gospel narratives provide us with the validation of the Incarnation. It seems that such a subject calls for an integration of history and anthropology, and a perception of the nature of validation in cross-cultural documents.

Another historian, Lynn T. White Jr., in an exciting personal essay entitled "History and Horseshoe Nails" (1970) describes the effect of Kroeber's *Anthropology* (1948) on him. He suddenly discovered the "frightful limitations" of his historical training, which had been devoted to the critical analysis of texts. He was amazed at what history Kroeber could reconstruct without documentary texts, and began to apply anthropological methods to the history of the Middle Ages—after which he felt he was never the same man again. The result of this change of research methodology was his book *Medieval Technology and Social Change* (1962). His was an important discovery, not a rejection of the classical method of studying textual material, but an additional new dimension for professional historiography. It reminds his fellow historians of the ingredient of material culture in the study of social change.

In this present study we shall try to recognise the place of culture—a specific culture at a specific point of time (for cultures vary with time depth)—and to depict the disciple band following the Master in as accurate a cultural context as we can recapture. Both the material and social culture are important, but even so, White's essay does not take me far enough. At least, in this particular essay, I see nothing of the recapture of personalities. I see the horseshoe nails, but I do not see the blacksmith. To make the point clearer, let me call on another historian.

In his essay on "Afterthoughts," the English octogenarian, Vivian Galbraith, describes what he considers the problem period of medieval England. No historian has yet reconstructed a really adequate history of the period. We have no convincing portrait of the Black Prince, or Edward III, or John of Gaunt, or any other fourteenth-century worthy whose name is well known. And yet a great deal survives in the way of material artifacts—"full plate armour on monuments and on brasses" (1970, 17). More and more are anthropologists and ethnohistorians, and we may add also geographers, rediscovering ancient social patterns, but the great personalities often elude us. It is *only from documents* that we can recapture the words and thoughts and values of the key personalities, even though these may have been woven into laws and traditions, and be detected by their effects in behaviour patterns and evidence of social change. Men leave their mark on history, but they themselves often remain largely hidden in the shadow. Literary critics have made merry with personal problems. Was Socrates a real person? Did Bacon write Shakespeare? And so on, *ad infinitum*. Even when you have the documents, the personality may still be vague, but without documents the true personal portrait can never really be written at all. And unfortunately documents are the most perishable of artifacts.

An adequate theology of mission depends on our ability at recapturing a small community of people—the Master and the band of followers whom he trained in apostleship. The people, both the Master himself and the apostles, must reveal themselves before we can understand their message and mission.

Fortunately we have four early literary compositions that were assembled by quite different persons, with different styles, and with different immediate purposes. Our examination of these four presentations comprises the main body of this little book. We need to understand from the outset that these monographs are themselves compilations. The authors were creative persons who worked from earlier sources and from informants. They seem to have had access to some of the same sources, but each added some unique ingredients of his own, and *each wrote his own monograph.*

I have always felt that the biblical theory of the Synoptics (essential as it has been in the development of an understanding of how the Gospels were written) has so dominated the textual problems of *common* passages that we have lost sight of the fact that we are dealing with four quite *distinct* productions. But the significant common points in the Gospels are not merely formal and literary—they are (1) the person of Jesus, (2) the ecclesiological and missionary intention of Jesus, and (3) his message. Each Gospel writer has dealt with these in quite his own way. For this reason I shall devote a study to each monograph as an integrated entity, and only at the end attempt anything by way of a synthesis.

The ethnohistorian can become quite excited about the emergence of this collection of Gospel documents at such an early stage in the history of the young church. It was natural for her to begin with Hebrew models for communication, but more and more as the church became a community and then a world force did she feel the need for new kinds of expression, adequate for the world where the Christian mission was operating. The result was that in the Christian penetration of the Graeco-Roman world the church was herself stimulated to a new genre of literature in developing her efforts in mission and church nurture. Nothing but the ongoing work of the Spirit of God in the early church would have brought the writing of Matthew, Mark, Luke, and John together like this. They represent a deep-seated and dynamic quality the early church cultivated as it penetrated the world.

Let it be noted that there have been times like this in history when situations have called for new literary approaches and have produced the people for the occasion. A study of the literature of great movements through history would indicate this. Indeed, a few years ago, the American historian and essayist Richard Hofstadter suggested that, even now in our own day, a new historical genre is about to be produced by the interaction of history and the social sciences, that it will focus on *problems not hitherto raised* in most historical monographs and will develop *a new methodology*. He calls it "a sort of literary anthropology," the aim of which is "portraiture of the life of nations and individuals, classes and groups of men" and their basic human commitments (1963, 363). The emergence of the new missiology (and missiography) to deal with the postcolonial situations of our day is another example of this kind of interaction. To use the biological analogy—as we achieve an operating *symbiosis* we soon discover an exciting *syngenesis*.

What I am trying to say in this book is that something happened in the early church from two or three decades after the departure of our Lord, when in carrying out his commission the apostles and their successors left the enclaves of Palestine and reached out into the pagan world. The new situation, in which the teaching they had about mission was being translated into real life operations, demanded a new kind of literature, and four quite different men of God tackled the problems of their respective situations and have left their monographs to tell the story—the Jesus documents.

Not only have the historians been discovering anthropology, but anthropologists have moved into history, with the result that a methodology known as *ethnohistory* has emerged with its own technical journal that has run now for twenty years. Thus anthropologists themselves have been injecting their own methods into historiography like, for example, the application of archaeological "upstreaming" to the study of documents. They have differentiated between diachronic and synchronic reconstructions, and a good many fine case studies have been produced. This is merely mentioned to show that the historian/anthropologist relationships are moving from both directions with profound significance for missiography, and I believe that, if we could achieve the breakthrough of more acceptance by the critical theologians, the ethnotheologians could offer tremendous methodological resources for biblical interpretation.

The Holistic Approach

Another discipline from which anthropology has drawn a good deal is psychology, by which interaction we have a new area of research sometimes spoken of as *ethnopsychology*. Concepts of "basic and modal personality," studies of values and of abnormalities that are reversed in different cultures, dynamic cultural themes, and cultural configurationalism come from this interaction. One of these ethnopsychological ideas has a bearing on the methodology of this little book—this I should mention in passing.

Anthropology has borrowed a great deal from Gestalt psychology, which emphasises the organised character of human behaviour, the place of patterns or configurations, and the human drive for totality. When we apply this to communal societies, we come up with configurational anthropology. From the same source we have such words as "holistic" and "holism."[19] I must confess that my treatment of the four Gospel documents will reflect some influence of this philosophical position, in depicting both the documents themselves and also the Master and the disciple band they portray. The danger with critical analysis as a method of research is that it often obscures relationships and wholeness, and we end up, like *Time* magazine, with a compartmentalisation of society which is not real. The only way to avoid this is to study life or documents whole. This is not to say that the document may not have itself a network of component configurations. Indeed I shall endeavor to identify these and to show how the component ingredients relate to the total configuration of the whole document. However, I believe that we gain much which is otherwise lost if we read the New Testament books whole, each one at a single sitting.

If we recognise that each document came into being as a total thing at a particular time and place, quite independently of the other Gospel documents, we have to honor the integrity and uniqueness of each document. (This is not to argue that they did not use some of the same sources.) Each document is given a chapter to itself and any reference made therein to one of the others is purely incidental—perhaps a comparison or contrast in passing. The basic purpose of this book, then, is to discover the contours of the essential configurations that hold each document together as a unique thing in itself.

Because this work is in a sense experimental, I may not be able to capture very effectively in its pages the whole purpose I am trying to achieve, but I would ask the reader to strive with me. I am asking him to forget for the time being his own sermons on the Gospels, or the proof texts he has extracted from their contexts to argue his religious position, or the causes he has advocated. This, I believe, is the wrong way to go about achieving our present purpose. At this point we do not know exactly what we will find. We enter this Bible study with an open mind, and not looking for passages to support our already-accepted belief position. We read the documents whole to see what they seem to be saying to their own respective audiences.

I fully understand that it is somewhat presumptuous for an anthropologist to attempt this excursion into the domain of the biblical critics. But I have read a good deal of their writing, with very little satisfaction at this point, and this book is rather a "question to the critics" than a criticism of them. I also know that in recent times a number of the critics have themselves been looking at the notion of the Gospels "as self-contained wholes," with each by a single author (see Martin 1975, 119, 136–38), but this is very recent.

---

19   The reader is referred to Margaret Mead's biography of Ruth Benedict (1974) for an evaluation of her configurationalism, and to Barnett's appendix, "On Things" (1953, 423–47).

As the research methods I am using here are well established in anthropology, and especially in ethnohistory, it is natural that I should apply them to the book of my personal faith. We have seen how interdisciplinary study has resulted in benefit to each field, both in methodology and understanding, and I have long felt that biblical study (both theology and method) and social anthropology should be working together. This book is an attempt to move in that direction. It may be that the reader will find nothing really new in it. It may be that to the scholars some of my findings will be untenable. But, at least, I should like them to say: if an anthropologist looks at them this way, then maybe we should examine his speculations.

REFERENCES

Barnett, Homer G. 1953. *Innovation: The basis of cultural change.* New York: McGraw-Hill.

Galbraith, Vivian H. 1970. Afterthoughts. In *The historian's workshop,* ed. L. P. Curtis, 5–21. New York: Knopf.

Hofstadter, Richard. 1963. History and the social sciences. In *The varieties of history,* ed. Fritz Stern, 359–70. Cleveland: Meridian Books.

Kroeber, A. L. 1948. *Anthropology.* New York: Harcourt, Brace and Co.

Martin, Ralph P. 1975. *New Testament foundations.* Vol. 1, *The four Gospels.* Grand Rapids: Eerdmans.

Mead, Margaret. 1974. *Ruth Benedict.* New York: Columbia University Press.

Stern, Fritz, ed. 1963. *The varieties of history.* Cleveland: Meridian Books.

Tylor, E. B. 1871. *Primitive culture.* London: John Murray.

White, Lynn T., Jr. 1962. *Medieval technology and social change.* Oxford: Clarendon.

———. 1970. History and horseshoe nails. In *The historian's workshop,* ed. L. P. Curtis, 49–64. New York: Knopf.

8

THE STRUCTURE AND ANALYSIS OF AN EVENT:
An Exercise in Ethnohistorical Reconstruction[20]

> Bishop Patteson had been from the beach to a canoe-house, and was resting
> there when he was brutally clubbed with a mallet for beating native cloth, and
> shot with poisoned arrows by several assailants.

That is an event, a happening. No matter how many additional details are supplied, it will still be the record of an event which took place on 20 September 1871 on the island of Nukapu. Historically it is a record of a happening located at a point of time and at a point in space.

If that event is an isolate, it has no meaning. I can neither understand it nor evaluate it. The point of time requires time depth, and the point in space needs a wider field. Is there an appropriate model to guide us in our perception of such events? How may we cover their meaning and evaluate then? What does this mean for the ethnohistorical reconstruction of, say, our church planting case studies? How may we disentangle the various cultural and cross-cultural configurations that converge in the event?

Theoretical Preamble

The biblical view of history is not set on a structure of centuries and reigns or presidencies, as we arrange our almanacs. It is marked by *events*—the Fall, the Deluge, the Crossing of the Red Sea, the Giving of the Law on Mt. Sinai, the Captivity, the Return; and in the New Testament, the Nativity, the Crucifixion, the Resurrection, and Pentecost. These are events which speak historically and theologically to the people of God at *points of time* in their pilgrimage. They are focal points of experience and faith.

This approach to history by focusing on events is more reasonable than building up a record on a chronological grid of centuries and decades. It is an *interpretive* rather than a *measuring* tool. It may be argued that the ancient Egyptians, the Mesoamericans, and we Westerners have recorded history mathematically, but I imagine there still are more people in the world who find it more natural to measure time in events. They say "before

---

20   Paper presented in 1974 to the faculty and doctoral students, School of World Mission, Fuller Theological Seminary, Pasadena, California.

or after the measles epidemic," "before or after the war" or, for an individual, "before or after my marriage," as if these events were "watersheds" in their experience.

An event is an encounter or a crisis in a series of action, and the persons involved are never quite the same afterwards. It is significant because historical and social factors come to focus in the happening, competitive antecedent forces come to grip with each other in a crisis event, and values of the old period are tested, to be either valid or invalid for the new period being born. The notion of a crisis event thus becomes a useful concept for the study of culture change and other social processes. When competitive forces of a period of change come to grips in an event, the event differentiates and thus determines a new direction for the process of change. Such an event may shape new policies and stimulate innovations. It may become part of a people's literature, mythology, idiom, proverbial tradition, national ceremonial, or symbolism.

A significant event is always a theme for anthropological analysis, yet I do not know any textbook on anthropological theory which appropriates the concept of the event for the study of culture change.

The model for such an investigation would be:

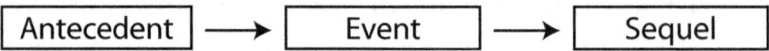

Perhaps the nearest to this was in Florence Kluckholn's essay on "Dominant and Variant Value Orientations," in which at one place she discusses the notion of *man in time* and speaks of the "three point range of Past, Present and Future" (1948, 347–48). But she is dealing with the point of time at which a people puts its emphasis, and the bearing of this orientation on culture change. Mine is a different problem.

A significant event which becomes a focal point in the literature and outlook of a people must have its antecedents and sequel—these together with the event itself are now *all in the past*, although they create an orientation and may condition current happenings and behavior. I submit that an ethnohistorical reconstruction which involves a significant event must deal also with antecedents and sequel. There are *three time dimensions within a time dimension.* The ethnohistorian has the advantage of looking back and seeing something whole as the participants in the drama could not see—he can look into their future because that future is now in the historic past.

One of the "distinctive qualities of culture" enumerated by Linton is the *cultural continuum*, which implies a *continuity* so that the present is always conditioned to some extent by the past. He makes the point that "throughout the length of the cultural continuum, therefore, traits are constantly being added and other traits lost," that "every culture is not only a continuum, but a continuum in a constant state of change." He goes on to attack the popular belief that "primitive" cultures are static, and argues that at whatever point of them you cut the continuum you will find "certain changes completed, others well under way, and still others just beginning" (1964, 294–303).

To take a cross section at a point of time is what we do when we focus on an event. This is a synchronic study. When Linton rightly says we see old processes running out and new ones beginning, we are immediately compelled to look back and to look forward, to look at the antecedents and the sequel, and this we can do in ethnohistory. Linton was writing of the culture pattern, but the same can be said of a society, a developing nation, or an institutional configuration like, say, the emerging indigenous church.

The cross section at a point of time may pinpoint the existence of various processes, but it will not show just how those factors or forces interact. If the ethnohistorical reconstruction is to be accurate, there must be some time depth in the sample. Linton perceived this problem before the development of the methodology of ethnohistory, but he left the study of "the processes of growth and change" to the historical method and assumed that the study of "processes of the interaction of cultural elements . . . does not require such historical studies," but rather "deeper levels of culture content" (ibid., 301) (i.e., the anthropological method). The ethnohistorical method is a serious attempt to work out a methodology for projecting the anthropological dimension into historical research. A very large number of present-day anthropologists are still where Linton was in 1936, compartmentalising history and anthropology to such an extent that research is distorted. Linton at least recognised the problem.

Time and time again in anthropological writing, an anthropologist will latch on to some historically reported event and give it some anthropological interpretation of his own. As long as anthropologists drew their allusions from history, they should also be competent historians. Likewise, if the historian intends to interpret cross-cultural events, he had better have some appreciation of anthropology.

When I was researching the planting of the church in Tahiti, I was continuously agitated by the careless use of cross-cultural historical events by anthropologists, historians, and missiologists, so much so that I included an appendix on the event of the conversion of Tahiti, in which I showed how an anthropologist, a missionary historian, and a missionary theorist had actually manipulated the event to serve their respective purposes. In point of fact, the event was rather a series of events, and they could not be isolated from a whole sequence of antecedents (Tippett 1972, 221–26, 269).

Now in this paper I shall take some well-known event out of the history of Christian mission in the Pacific to demonstrate an ethnohistorical analysis and discuss the method of analysis. One has the option of scores of significant events. One could take, in the case of Fiji, for example, the appearance of the first Fijian New Testament in 1847, or the conversion of the cannibal king, Cakobau in 1854, or the raising of the British flag in 1874, all of which were significant events because the processes of change at the time were thereby modified in some way—stimulated or redirected—and because they became historical focal points for subsequent generations.

We tend to think of the study of an event as synchronic as if it were merely a timeless cross section at a point of time, but even a synchronic study has its internal diachronic dimension. Each of these events I have suggested has its antecedents and its sequel from which it cannot be isolated. Despite their discreteness, the antecedent, event, and sequel are cohesively integrated.

In the historical literature of our Western culture (i.e., not a cross-cultural study), the historian who most nearly comes to using this approach is J. Wesley Bready, whose study of the Wesleyan revival the American public knows by an adapted version under the title *This Freedom Whence?* with the Statue of Liberty on the dust jacket. The larger original work had the title *England: Before and After Wesley*, which speaks for itself—here is a social history, an event with its antecedents and sequel cohesively integrated. In ethnohistory we try to do this cross-culturally.

So I cast about quite arbitrarily for a suitable event for our consideration, and I hit upon the death of Bishop Patteson of the Melanesian Mission. My procedure shall be as follows. First, I shall describe the event itself as objectively as possible, as one might read it in the newspaper. Then in asking how this event may be interpreted, I shall discuss the antecedents in more detail. Finally, I shall enumerate some of the significant factors of the sequel. Thus, although the event took place on a single day, its basic interpretive data extends both before and after. I could call this paper "The Southwest Pacific *Before* and *After* the Death of Bishop Patteson."

The theoretical point I am trying to demonstrate is that a significant event is only significant because it is the focal point of a dynamic situation; it has both anterior and posterior aspects, and if we are in the business of interpreting cross-cultural history, we need to see events in their cohesive totality.

The Event

Bishop Patteson's vessel, the *Southern Cross*, was cruising in the Swallow Group, thirty miles north of Santa Cruz. She was off the island of Nukapu on the morning of 20 September 1871. A year before, the bishop had been well received there. His party pushed off in a small boat from the *Southern Cross* about 11:00 a.m., with a small Christian party, and pulled, according to custom, towards the three canoes floating inside the reef. The tide was low and the boat could not cross the reef, so the bishop transferred to one of the canoes, leaving the others to follow when the tide was higher. The canoe took the bishop ashore, and his party saw him walk across the beach and disappear among the vegetation. All this was perfectly normal and according to custom. The other canoes remained with the boat, and the local natives engaged in conversation with the Christian party. The former then suddenly snatched up their bows and began shooting the Christian party, all of whom were hit before they regained the vessel, from which a boat was manned immediately to search for the bishop.

The party comprised seven men, three of whom had guns and instructions to use them if they were shot at. The tide had risen and they crossed the reef. Two canoes came out to meet them in midlagoon. One was an ordinary canoe. It cast off the other and returned to shore. The floating canoe contained the body of Bishop Patteson. His clothes had been removed and he was wrapped in native matting. A palm frond was fastened in the folds of the matting over his breast, the front being tied in five knots. The side of his skull was shattered, and his body showed multiple arrow wounds. His face was still smiling. The body had been subject to none of the indignities which were often inflicted on such occasions.

Once the boat crew had collected the body, the natives on shore yelled and launched their canoes, paddling fast towards them, and the boat crew pulled hard for the *Southern Cross*. No attempt was made at reprisals, and the bishop's body was buried at sea. The arrow had been poisoned, and two of the wounded Christians died, one of them in great agony from tetanus.

Mainly, I have followed here the story as narrated by Charles Sapibuana, who was one of the party of seven in the boat which rescued the body. This is not the only account of the event by an eyewitness. Joseph Wate's account is found in Fox's *Lord of the Southern Isles* (1958). He was on the *Southern Cross* but did not go ashore. Other details of what actually happened on shore have been described by a Nukapu man who ended up on a Fijian plantation. Further details of the wounded men may be found in Gutch (1971, 206–9).

In typical historical form, the historians have latched on to this event for intensive investigation because of the difficulty of precise reconstruction of details. The point of this paper is that the importance does not lie in those speculative details, but that the event of Patteson's death can only be understood by an analysis of antecedents, and can only be evaluated by an analysis of its sequel.

The Antecedents

When George Selwyn was appointed bishop of New Zealand, a curious error crept into the Letters Patent which fixed the boundaries of his territorial jurisdiction at the thirty-fourth parallel, registering it as "north" instead of "south," thus including all the Western Pacific as far north as Japan. Thus, humanly speaking, the Melanesian Mission came into being by mistake.

However, the mistake raised the highly significant question of the evangelisation of Western Melanesia. Selwyn made two long voyages through these islands, even as far east as Fiji, in 1848 and 1849, and in widely scattered Groups he found successful missions operating in Tonga, Fiji, Samoa, the New Hebrides, and the Loyalty Islands (Tucker 1879,

1:251–317). In spite of his Episcopalian biases, he was most impressed with the normal changes effected by the LMS [London Missionary Society] and WMS [Wesleyan Missionary Society] missions, and one of the things which affected him most was the effectiveness of the national evangelists:

> I am most drawn to them by their native teachers—men, who even in the infancy of their faith, have left home and friends to live among men of another speech . . . as Pioneers of the Gospel, to prepare the way by which the English missionary may enter (Tucker 1879, 1:346).

He found that some forty South Pacific martyrs had already given their lives in this pioneering thrust in the New Hebrides and New Caledonia Groups (King 1899, 154–55; Tucker 1879, 1:347).

Methodologically the Melanesian Mission was a departure from the regular missionary pattern. Selwyn's central idea was the operation of a college in New Zealand for training youths brought from the islands and subsequently returned as Christians to their own homelands. Despite opposition in both New Zealand and England, the college was set up in Auckland. In 1855 John Coleridge Patterson joined Selwyn and worked with the island people.

The Melanesian Mission was not one of the English missionary societies like the CMS [Church Missionary Society], the WMS, and the LMS. Selwyn designed it as an outlet for the New Zealand church, which had some considerable numerical strength from a Maori people movement and a considerable transfer growth by colonial migration. As Selwyn put it after taking over the Episcopal charge:

> However inadequate a Church may be to its own internal wants, it must on no account suspend its missionary duties; . . . this is in fact the circulation of its life-blood, which would lose its vital power if it never flowed forth to the extremities, but curled the heart. (Stock 1899, 1:448)

Patteson: Linguist and Communicator

As a boy at Eton, John Coleridge Patteson had been inspired by a sermon preached by Selwyn. The idea which gripped him was the notion of going out to the Pacific to found a church, and then to die there neglected and forgotten (Charles 1889, 290). In 1842 he was confirmed at Eton, ordained as a deacon in 1853, and as a priest the following year. In 1855 he joined Selwyn "with a view to work in Melanesia" (Page 1890, 156; Stock 1899, 2:89). On the voyage out he concentrated on two things: (1) learning the art of navigation, and (2) learning the Maori language (Tonga 1888, 1:116). He had acquired enough of this by the time he reached New Zealand to engage in conversation (Armstrong 1900, 24).

Patteson commenced working in New Zealand dealing with the island men. Eventually he became the first bishop of Melanesia, consecrated at St. Paul's, Auckland, in 1861.

By this time he already had a smattering of the languages. He had a natural determination to muster language, learning those from the islands from which the mission obtained their students (Yonge 1874, 1:307). He had a mastery of fluent conversation in over twenty languages, apparently achieved only by hard work, as Selwyn was wont to cite him as an example in industry (King 1899, 157). Selwyn was discussing the difficulty of language learning in a sermon on Isaiah 66:8–12 at the general convention, the great missionary meeting of the American church in 1871, and said of him:

> The difficulty is in setting about it. Do you suppose Bishop Patteson acquired a knowledge of twenty languages, so as to be able to converse in all, without some effort? You may talk about natural gifts and facilities for acquiring languages; but the real natural gift is to have in your heart a determination that you will give up everything that is necessary to be given up. (Tucker 1879, 2:322)

Having mastered so many of the languages of the islands, Patteson was able to communicate effectively. He was aware of the basic principles of cross-cultural communication long before the development of the technical linguistics as a science. In a letter to Max Müller, dated 27 May 1866, he said:

> I only illustrate my idea of a grammar as a means of teaching others the form of the mould in which the Melanesian's mind is cast. I think I ought to go further, and seek for certain categories under which thought may be classified. (Yonge 1874, 2:127)

He avoided translations but worked in native stories, ideas, aspects of the forest life, and so on (ibid., 2:122–29). He went further in the topic later in the same letter which was written at sea off Norfolk Island, now dated 6 June:

> Don't be in a hurry to translate and don't attempt to use words as (assumed) equivalents of abstract ideas. Don't devise modes of expression unknown to the language . . . Our Lord gives the model. A certain lawyer asked Him for a definition of his neighbor, but He gave no definition, only He spoke a simple and touching parable. So teach, not a technical work, but an actual thing.

I mention these fragments from his correspondence because they show a man who, given the basic vocabulary, certainly knew how to communicate. When a man of this kind is murdered by the people of the islands, we certainly have to clear the point of possible misunderstanding in communication. Patteson's communication and the manifest spirit of his behavior leave us with no possible misunderstanding. It was Max Müller, the philologist, who said, on hearing of his death,

> To have known such a man is one of life's greatest blessings. In his life of purity, unselfishness, devotion to man, faith in a higher world, those who have eyes to see may read the best, the most real *Imitatio Christi*. In his death, following so

closely on his prayer for forgiveness of his enemies—"for they know not what they do" we have witnessed once more a truly Christian death. (King 1899, 157)

Patteson knew all the islands; the people knew him. He was welcome everywhere, and somehow in our examination of the antecedents of the event of his murder we have to explain how such a thing could happen.

Patteson's Respect for Melanesia

The criticism that the missionaries were ethnocentric and disrespectful to native leaders as a generalisation is one of our modern myths. It is always revived in the press and anthropology classes whenever a missionary is murdered by native people, and always based on presuppositions of the missionary image.

When Selwyn had laid down the initial plans for the Melanesian Mission, two of his basic guidelines concerned this very point. First there was the declaration of what came to be called the *Melanesian ethos*: that any church planted had to be Melanesian in character, lifestyle, language, and material culture. Side by side with this was the ultimate goal of a Melanesian diocese, with its own Melanesian clergy and a Melanesian bishop. As a method of achieving this, the plan was to gather suitable youths from all the islands and train them at a central institution for return to their own islands as Christian Melanesians. I have explained this at greater length in *Solomon Islands Christianity* (1967, 33–37), but it is well documented in the writings of Selwyn and Patteson, and has been restated in all the historical writing since.

If the idea was first articulated by Selwyn, Patteson agreed with it from the beginning. The only major change he made in it was to remove the central location from New Zealand to Norfolk Island and thus move the operation nearer to the field situation. From the very beginning, the Melanesian Mission aimed at an indigenous form of Christianity, in spite of its English Episcopalian structure.

As Gutch has pointed out,

> Missionary effort to be successful and lasting, must be based on the people themselves and not depend on expatriate missionaries. He accepted, too, that there should be as little disturbance as possible to the people's traditional life. He abhorred any idea that conversion should entail the surrender of their Melanesian individuality in exchange for European ways alien to them and their surroundings. (1971, 10–11)

Stephen Neill's verdict on the same matter reads:

> He [Patteson] was far ahead of his time in his belief in the Melanesians, in his desire that as Christians they should continue to be Melanesians, untrammeled by western clothes and habits. (1970, 475)

That may be true for a man looking from Africa or India, but Patteson was by no means alone in the Pacific, not even in his own society. A contemporary of Lorimer Fison in Fiji, they were reading the same anthropological literature—Henry Maine and E. B. Tylor, and Fison had pointed out the significance of kinship patterns to Patteson (1871b, 1871c).

With respect to clothing and house building, his views were moderate. He was innovative but did not want English patterns. His own words were, "To adopt English notions and habits would defeat my object" (Charles 1889, 335).

He declined to give directions to a chief, or if a chief was present, because it would weaken controls and authority, and he would allow no one in his party to sit down higher than the local chief (Yonge 1874, 1:147). He warned his missionary assistants against presuming on the authority that might be given to them by the island people. Let me quote from his letter dated Tuesday of Holy Week, 1868, from Auckland, to his uncle in England:

> The heathen man will assume some arbitrary dictate of a missionary to be of
> equal authority and importance with a moral command of God, unless you take
> care. Of course the missionary ought not to attempt to impose any arbitrary
> rule at all; but many missionaries do. (Ibid., 2:113)

So I think we may assume that Patteson was alert to the human weaknesses of missionaries and was continually correcting them. He knew the custom and the courtesies of Melanesian social life and respected them.

Patteson had a great respect for persons. Savages he would not call them. "There are no savages," he said.

> The regular, wild, untamed fellow is not so pleasant at first—dirty, unclothed . . .
> his wigwam sort of place filthy, his food ditto; but then [he adds] he is probably
> intelligent, respectable and not insensible to the advantages of hearing about
> religion. (Charles 1889, 319)

Patteson as a Church Planter

How did Patteson view the pagan religion? Could there have been major objections from the animist islanders against his missioning, which might have exposed him to the kind of death he suffered?

There is no doubt about Patteson's personal faith and his determination to win men to Christ. There is no doubt about what he thought of heathenism. He saw himself in confrontation with the evil one in scriptural terms. There is a clear passage in one of his letters to his father (1 December 1860), in which he spoke of

> the awful power of heathenism! The antagonism, not of evil only, but of the
> Evil One, I mean the reality felt of all evil emanating from a Person, as St. Paul
> writes, and as our Lord spoke of him. (Yonge 1874, 1:313)

There are also passages in his letters about the experience of island Christians such as he required before baptism, which show that he was no baptismal regenerationist, but demanded faith in Christ. At Mota he tells of a man he baptised, a man dying of tetanus:

> I was satisfied with his expressions of faith in the Savior, of his hope of living
> with Him; he spoke so clearly of his belief in Jesus having been sent from the
> Great Creator and Father of all to lead us back to Him . . . he was so evidently
> convinced of the truth of our Lord's resurrection and the resurrection of us all
> at the last day—that I felt that I ought to baptize him. I had already spoken to
> him of baptism, and he seemed to understand that, first, he must believe that
> the water is a sign of an inward cleansing, and that it has no magical efficacy,
> but that all depended on his having faith in the promise and power of God; and
> second that Jesus had commanded those who wished to believe and love Him to
> be baptized. (Ibid., 2:159)

There never was any pressure for baptism or rapid intake into the church. Rather it went the other way. People had to witness a good profession to be baptised. If the bishop baptised three hundred to four hundred persons on a voyage (he recorded the details in his diary), we can depend upon it that there was no pressuring here and that a church was really growing.

Yet he recognised the problems of cross-cultural witness. Not only were the candidates for mission from England piteously few, but (as in his own case) they were not trained for cross-cultural evangelism and pastoring. Not all of them could present a gospel to the heathen. In a letter to his cousin and biographer, Miss Yonge (written at sea about August in 1865), he admitted:

> How greatly the Church needs schools for missionaries, to be prepared not only
> in Greek and Latin and manual work, but in the mode of regarding heathenism
> . . . It is not always easy to be patient and to remember the position which the
> heathen man occupies, and the point of view from which he must needs regard
> everything brought before him. (Yonge 1874, 2:100–101)

Patteson's respect for island custom included also a respectful approach, even to their pagan religion. It is difficult to see how he could have caused offence enough to bring the tragic death upon him. He saw their religion as a developed system with social and cultural ramifications through the whole of life. He saw—and in this he was far in advance of his day—that if the people were to become Christian, the structure had to become Christian. He is battling here with the problems articulated in our own day by Bavinck (1964, 169–90) and Luzbetak (1963, 341–54).

He shared his thoughts with his Uncle Edward, whom he addressed formally as "Dear Tutor" in a letter dated 4 June 1861, written at sea, within sight of Erromanga in the New Hebrides, just after his consecration as bishop, and only two weeks after the murder of the Gordons on that same island, which also claimed the missionary John Williams. This is what he wrote:

> Generally there is a settled system of some kind among them, and in the Banks Islands, an extraordinarily developed religion, which enters into every detail of social and domestic life, and is mixed up with the daily life of every person ... I think, therefore, that men are needed who have what I may call strong religious common sense to adapt Christianity to the wants of the various nations that live in Melanesia, without compromising any truth of doctrine or principle of conduct—men who can see, in the midst of the errors and superstitions of a people, whatever fragment of truth or symptom of a yearning after something better [that] may exist among them, and make that the *point d'appui*, upon which they may build up the structure of Christianity teaching. (Yonge 1874, 1:340)

That, by the way, is precisely the theme of my article on "Possessing the Philosophy of Animism for Christ" (1972, 125–43). Patteson's French phrase, *point d'appui*, meaning a "point of support" or base or fulcrum, is equivalent to what I have called "stepping-stones to the gospel." Apparently he used it frequently when writing to his close friends in England. There is another passage in a letter to his cousin in 1865, four years after the last excerpt I quoted:

> I think how the early Alexandrine teachers used the religious yearnings of the East to draw men to the recognition of their wants, supplied and satisfied only in Christianity. Often it is the *point d'appui* that the missionary must seek for. There is an element of faith in superstition; we must fasten on that, and not rudely destroy the superstition; lest with it we destroy the principle of faith in things and beings unseen. I often think, that to shake a man's faith in his old belief, however wrong it may be, before one can substitute something true and right, is, to say the least, a dangerous experiment. (Yonge 1874, 2:99–100)

This is an intensely penetrating passage which we could ponder at length had we the time. In passing, let me merely point out that both these passages are cast in the terminology of what the anthropologists call *wants* (Barnett) or *felt needs* (Linton) and *satisfaction* and *functional substitutes*. A whole, thoroughly up-to-date volume could be written on this single passage. A man who had developed this philosophy of cross-cultural encounter could certainly never be accused of iconoclasm.

Furthermore he was very perceptive in the area of *human universals* and *cultural relatives*. Because he believed that "to teach Christianity, a man must know the language well" he recognised all languages in his area. He spoke twenty of them fluently and understood more. Codrington was amazed at the "extraordinary quickness in which he passed from one language to another" and how jealously he guarded all those he considered to be true languages. Though he had mastered what was becoming the *lingua franca*, so much so that his translations of the Psalms, Codrington said, "are as lofty in their diction and as harmonious in their rhythm as anything I have read in any language" (Charles 1889, 361–62), yet nevertheless he always spoke the language of the people with whom he was dealing. What went for language, also went for custom in general. Christianity, however, was for all people. Thus he wrote to his uncle from Auckland in 1866:

> Christianity is the religion for humanity at large. It takes in all shades and diversities of character, race &c. The substratum of it is, so to say, inordinate and coextensive with the substratum of humanity—all men must receive that. Each set of men must also receive many things of secondary, yet very great importance for them, but in this class there will be differences according to the characteristic differences of men throughout the world. (Yonge 1874, 2:113)

It was this recognition of cultural diversity which made it possible for him to champion the policy which followed Selwyn's guideline of planting a Melanesian church in Melanesia. Although his universal [Christianity] had a very strong Anglican flavor about it, especially in its liturgy, nevertheless it remains to this day essentially a Melanesian manifestation—in language, art, religious paraphernalia, participation, and leadership. Even though the prayer book and collects reflect the English church, nevertheless the content is relevantly Melanesian. I find it extremely difficult to attribute the death of Bishop Patteson to anything religious.

He would not push the Christian religion or its system on people before they understood it. To Joan (stepsister) and Fan (sister) he wrote from Mota (23 September 1869):

> I dread the imposition from without of some formal compliances with the externals of religion, while I know that the meaning and spirit of them cannot as yet be understood. Can there be conceived anything more formal, more mischievous, than inculcating a Sabbatarian view of the Lord's Day upon a people who don't know anything about the Cross and the Resurrection. Time enough to talk about the observance when people have some knowledge of the vital living truth of a spiritual religion. (Yonge 1874, 2:247)

Later in the same letter he adds:

> A spiritual religion is imperiled the moment you insist upon an unspiritual people observing outward forms, which are to them the essence of the new teaching. Anything better than turning heathens into Pharisees!

The question now has to be asked: what kind of religious change did Patteson and his fellow evangelists bring about in the villages? Let us take a look at Mota.

Writing in his sea journal from Mota, 18 September 1860, Patteson summed up the degree of Christianity that he felt the people had acquired:

> The old customs and superstitions go on, but,

1. They know a better teaching has been presented to them.
2. They do not pursue their old habits with the same unthinking security.
3. There are signs of a certain uneasiness of mind, as if a struggle was beginning in them.
4. They have a vague consciousness . . . that power is passing from their witchcrafts, sorceries, &c, by which unquestionable they did, and still do, work strange effects on the credulous people, like Pharaoh's magicians of old. (Yonge 1874, 1:377)

Three years before Selwyn and Patteson had selected a young man, George Sarawia, from this area. He emerged as an acceptable leader and was ordained as a deacon in 1868 under the encouragement of Codrington, who also reported the following of Mota:

> The stir in the hearts and minds of those already christened might be called a revival, and the enquiring and earnest spirit of many more seem to be working toward conversions. During this time, there might be seen on the cliff, or under the trees in the afternoon, or on Sundays, little groups gathered round some of the elder Christians, enquiring and getting help. It was the work George evidently was able to do in this way that convinced everybody that the time had come for his ordination.

In one of his last letters, also from Mota (June 1871), Patteson wrote:

> There is more indication here than I ever saw before of a "movement," a distinct advance towards Christianity. The distinction between passively listening to our teaching, and accepting it as God's Word, and acting upon it, seems to be clearly felt. About two hours are spent daily by me with about 23 grownup men. They come, too, at all hours in small parties. (Charles 1889, 378)

These three references form a sequence of religious change developing in a single island. I believe they indicate that the mission operation was effective. The bishop records the numbers whom he baptised on his journeys. Clearly a church was growing.

The program was also producing an indigenous ministry of simple but competent leaders. To Miss Mackenzie, an English friend, Patteson wrote from Norfolk Island, 26 January 1871, where the men were training. This was shortly before his last voyage, and the bishop was discussing the requirements of a relevant ministry for Melanesian conditions. He wrote:

> We must consider the qualifications of one's native clergy in relation to the work that they have to do. They have not to teach theology to educated Christians, but to make known the elements of the Gospel truth to ignorant heathen people. If they can state clearly and forcibly the very primary, leading, fundamental truths of the Gospel, and live as simple-minded humble Christians, that is enough indeed. (Yonge 1874, 2:329)

It seems to me that, at least up to the time of Bishop Patteson's death, the religious progress was slow but steady, indigenous in character, and not provocative in any way that might have led to resentment against the bishop. The bishop was highly respected and widely known, and his visits were appreciated. We must look elsewhere for the interpretation of his death.

Patteson and the Slave Trade

One of the guidelines Patteson inherited from Selwyn was the commercial base whose trading principles were laid down and set forth in 1867. To some extent missionaries became dealers in yams and pigs, buying by weight, according to a pattern which was approved and accepted. However, the commerce was indirectly to bring about dialogue. The bishop's primary object was to obtain young men, who would go with him for a season and learn the new teaching (Belshaw 1954, 51). If the church was to be indigenous, this seemed essential. Over the years many young men went, first to New Zealand, and later to Norfolk Island. Their terms were short, and some of them went several times. Many of them became prominent churchmen in time, and the Melanesian ministry came from these young men. They returned to show the advantages of civilisation—tables and chairs, crockery and clothing, pots and pans—foreign goods to be sure, but all items the Melanesians were ready to borrow on their own account (109).

This system also got Patteson involved in the matrimonial market. The island custom was to buy young girls for later marriage to one's sons. Bishop Patteson took up the pattern, viewing the young men he had in training as his sons, and feeling that they would require Christian wives. So girls should also be trained and introduced to the concept of the Christian family. Thus on one trip he took to Norfolk Island sixty-two young men for training and fourteen girls (Armstrong 1900, 107–8). Some very fine Christian marriages and families came out of that experiment and served an educative function when the young couples returned to the islands, but the program exposed Patteson to some criticism, and the slave traders asked what the difference was between his buying wives and their enlisting labour. There was, of course, all the world of difference, for one was to plant an indigenous church with volunteers, the other was often kidnapping under fire against the will, and in such quantities that whole islands were depopulated. We now turn to examine this encounter between the missionaries and the slave traders.

Examination of Patteson's correspondence in chronological sequence will show from about 1867 an increasing amount of space given to references to the South Seas labour trade, especially that organised by planters in Fiji, who were enjoying a cotton boom due to the American Civil War cutting off supplies for the European market. The trade is variously spoken of as "blackbirding," the "kidnapping trade," and slavery. The nature and extent of this traffic I have investigated and written up elsewhere (Tippett 1956). What becomes clear in the Patteson papers is the increasing proportions of the kidnapping between 1867 and 1871, and the bishop's increasing discouragement because of it.

For a time he accepted the idea of a need for labour in the cane and cotton fields of Queensland and Fiji, and satisfied himself with attempting to obtain its regulation. Even as late as 1870 he pinned his hopes in this—licensed vessels only, only approved persons in charge, names of captains and vessels to be supplied to all missionaries, illegal vessels to be treated as pirates, the seas to be policed by men-o-war, and legal reforms to permit Sydney courts to deal with offences (Armstrong 1900, 112). But he obtained no hearing, and meantime the traffic increased and became more bloody. His letters home to England were full of it from 1868 until his death (Yonge 1874, 2:253, 278, 283–87, 296–97, 305–15, 340–41, 343–50, 359–69, 372, etc.). He had resolved to visit Fiji and Queensland after the completion of the voyage on which he was murdered (Armstrong 1900, 119; Yonge 1874, 2:372).

Among the last references in his unfinished letter, August and September 1871, he wrote,

> The deportation of natives is going on to a very great extent here, as in the New Hebrides and Banks Islands. Means of all kinds are employed—sinking canoes and capturing the natives, enticing men on board and getting them below and then securing the hatches and imprisoning them. Natives are retaliating. Lately two or three vessels have been taken and all hands killed, besides boats' crews shot at continually . . . Some islands are almost depopulated and I dread the return of these "labourers" when they are brought back. They bring guns and . . . run riot, steal men's wives, shoot, fight and use their newly acquired possessions to carry out more vigorously all heathen practices. (Charles 1889, 366–67)

The island of Mae was depopulated (Yonge 1874, 2:278); in the Banks Islands half the population over ten years of age had vanished (Armstrong 1900, 116). Patteson visited Santa Maria, Vanua Lava, and Saddle Island that year. He now had teachers ready for them, only alas, to find the people had been kidnapped. He was discouraged and "didn't know what was to be done" about Fiji and the trade (Yonge 1874, 2:340–41).

Several times his party was attacked, and much of his nursing ministry had been rendered to his Christian teachers who had been shot with poisoned arrows and died of tetanus. He had seen the process of preparing these with the fluid draining from putrefied human bodies (Holthouse 1969, 141). Everywhere there was talk of the "snatch-snatch" vessels and the "kill-kill" vessels.

The most despicable of all tricks was known as "the missionary act," and of this there is extensive documentation (Tippett 1956, 128–29). A slaver would paint up to look like the missionary ship and dramatise the missionary role until the people were on board and invited below deck to meet the bishop, and even for Holy Communion, to find the hatches closed on them until they reached Fiji. This was known as men-stealing and led to all kinds of retaliation. Sometimes an effigy of a missionary with a Bible was made and so placed on the deck of the ship as to be seen from the shore (Lambert 1907, 281). There is no doubt whatever that slavers used the good name of the bishop to expose people for kidnapping. It is also known that such activity was going on in the Santa Cruz Group precisely at the time when Patteson came along, and that he was indeed the victim of retaliation at Nukapu. The *Emma Bell* and the *Margaret Ghessell* were both in the area at the time. The historians disagree about which one was responsible.

The Sequel

The first repercussion of the murder came on the island of Nukapu itself, for not all the islanders had been involved in the event. The other islanders were angry when they discovered that the retaliation had been applied against the bishop, so much so that the avengers themselves fled from Nukapu or, more correctly, were banished. The leader of the murderers fled to Great Santa Cruz and landed at the northern end of the islands, but when the local chief heard that the victim had been Bishop Patteson, he would not shelter the exile and had him shot (Charles 1889, 396). Why the islanders would take this action against the murderer of the bishop is an interesting question. We know that Bishop Patteson had standing at Nukapu, that the people there were his friends, and together they passed through a ceremony in which they and the bishop exchanged names (Fox 1967, 24). This must have been very embarrassing when a party of their own people turned out to be his murderers, and probably this explains the anger and the banishment.

But the news of the bishop's murder sounded off reactions in the highest places. The British Queen dealt with the matter in her speech at the opening of Parliament in 1872, and "made it a text for some strong words about the Slave Trade generally" (Stock 1899, 3:76; Gutch 1971, 213). The murder drew public attention to what was really going on in the islands (Holthouse 1969, 86), and many questions were asked in public places. For some years the English press had subjected the missionaries of the world to scorn and criticism. Missionary outcries about the kidnapping had been treated as exaggerations. But already there had been a number of missionaries murdered, and now the Bishop Patteson, who had been a popular figure in England. He had distinguished himself at Eton and Oxford. England now began to listen to the missionary outcries.

A collection of documents on the slave trade in the New Hebrides was published by a Presbyterian missionary. The Pacific Islanders Protection Bill was passed, the text of which cited suggestions previously made by Patteson for the regulation of the labour traffic. Actually the bill was not effective—obviously nothing would work until there was an effective government in Fiji (Gutch 1971, 213).

In Australia, public meetings were held and motions of sympathy were passed for those carrying on in Melanesia. Lorimer Fison, a Wesleyan from Fiji, who knew the kidnapping trade from the Fiji end, seconded one of these motions with a long and perceptive speech, which the Australian press reported in full. (He already had standing as an anthropologist and had provided Lewis Henry Morgan with his Fijian and Tongan data for his famous work on kinship which appeared that year.) Fison pointed out that there were only a limited number of reasons why islanders kill white men. After enumerating them he dwelt on one particular reason: *revenge upon someone of the wrongdoer's tribe, the actual offender being out of reach.* He went on to analyze the murder anthropologically: the maneuvers of the canoes, the decoying of the victim, the five knots in the symbolic palm frond, the respect for the body of the chiefly victim, and the notion of revenge taken on another member of the same tribe. From this analysis Fison turned to discuss the offence which called for the revenge, and he did some plain speaking about the Queensland and Fiji labour trade and (Fison's oratory was very descriptive) the "sugar refined with brother's blood" (1871a). Shortly afterwards Fison rearranged this data in a long six-thousand-word letter with a grim description of kidnapping abuses. It was published in the *Sydney Morning Herald*, 18 November (1871b). On 4 December, he was in print again on the same subject, again mentioning Patteson and calling for government action (1871c).

Shortly after this, R. H. Codrington, another missionary anthropologist, addressed an Australian audience taking up the theme on a basis of the "feelings awakened by the death of Bishop Patteson." He had taken over Patteson's position in Melanesia (but was never made a bishop—his period is known as the interregum). Codrington described how four young men who witnessed the murder had been so impressed by the way the bishop met his death with a smile on his face, that they sought Christian instruction. Then he talked about the labour trade and about the guns that were brought back from Queensland. He had visited the plantations in Queensland and had met four men whose language he knew. Not one of them had been brought to Queensland legally (this was one of the things difficult to prove by those who fought the trade). Then he made a statement that "he would not accept the fact that the advancement of one race should mean the depopulation of another." At this point, the newspaper report indicates "Applause," so we may take it that Codrington was articulating a feeling of the meeting.

The battle against the South Sea kidnapping, having failed at the level of international law, was taken by Lorimer Fison into the Australian press—both the religious and the secular press. In the Sydney *Daily Telegraph*, *Sydney Morning Herald*, and the *Melbourne Age*, between 110,000 and 120,000 words of newsprint copy appeared from Fison's pen in a merciless attack on the South Sea labour traffic. He provided details—names of vessels, names of islands, dates of the raids, number killed and kidnapped. He had his facts, and he always held the "joker" in his hand to deal with anyone foolish enough to reply. It is one of the most dramatic stories of Australian history—through the press and the courts, and a classical episode in the House. Fison carried this on for three years—almost as if he was himself Patteson's avenger.

Eventually the showdown came in Britain, not in Australia. The case for the acceptance of the Cession of Fiji was being discussed in 1874. Alderman McArthur said in the House of Commons,

> This monstrous system of slavery cannot be extirpated until Fiji is put under the protectorate or sovereignty of Great Britain.

Mr. Eastwick M.P. asserted that

> an independent buccaneering movement has been established, which will attract all the desperate characters in Australia and the surrounding islands.

Sir Charles Wingfield pointed out that

> the Fiji Group is fast becoming the refuge of scoundrels and fugitives of all descriptions.

The Earl of Carnavon himself asked the House

> not to forget the labour trade that has grown up in the seas off the islands of Fiji. Those islands, though they do not cover the whole area of the kidnapping trade, rise, as it were, in the centre of it. No government can view with anything but deep interest everything that offers a means of putting down this iniquity.

With the fall of the Gladstone government and the change of policy under Disraeli, the Fijian chiefly offer of Cession was accepted, and under colonial government the labour trade—at least in its old unregulated form—came to an end.

We could say that the sequel ends there, but every now and again some historian revives the narrative of Bishop Patteson, but though they still discuss at length the precise details of the event of his murder, none has really grasped the significance of the sequel. Patteson had made his practical suggestions for regulating the trade and handling offences to Sir George Bowen, governor of Queensland (whom he had known at Oxford), but had achieved nothing (Gutch 1971, 196–97), and he had resolved to visit Fiji immediately after the end of the fatal voyage. He now knew that if there was to be any solution of the problem it had to be found in Fiji. It therefore seems appropriate that the sequel should be terminated in the debate in the English House of Commons about the future of Fiji.

The story would round off nicely there, but Patteson did not go to Melanesia to fight the slave trade, although it was this trade which certainly caused his death. He went there to plant a Melanesian church, and it is fitting that his memory is woven into its history and its symbolism. Immediately after his death, the penitent people of Nukapu wanted some visible evidence of the forgiveness he showed to them in his radiant death. (There is a record that he quoted the Lord's words from the Cross.) A memorial cross was placed at the site to be visible from the sea. Nukapu was never the same old pagan place after the planting of that symbolic cross.

In the cathedral at Honiara in the Solomons, I saw a memorial pulpit which bears the carved symbolism of his martyrdom. From that pulpit the gospel is preached to the descendents of the people for whom he died. A similar pulpit is found in Exeter Cathedral, depicting in carved wood the scene of his death and the five-knotted palm frond. Here he had been ordained as a deacon first, and then later as a priest, and thence he had gone forth to Melanesia. Thus also the descendants of those who sent him forth are not to forget the price he paid. For a bishop from Melanesia this kind of symbolism is appropriate. Neither his ministry nor his sacrifice is forgotten.

Conclusion

In this paper I have tried to demonstrate how a significant event is a focal point of one or more sets of action which project themselves in both anterior and posterior directions; in other words, we cannot have a significant event without antecedents and a sequel. We require knowledge of the antecedents to understand the event, and knowledge of the sequel to evaluate it.

In studying the antecedents of the murder of Bishop Patteson, we proceed to eliminate the configurational variables. Did the bishop lose his life because of any foolishness or foreignness on his own part (a frequent charge against missionaries who lose their lives in service)? We found him to be a competent linguist and communicator. Was he visualised by the Melanesian as an enemy? We identified his deep respect for all things Melanesian and his observation of the custom. Was there any objection of his methods of church planting? We found him respectful of their religion, using it as a stepping-stone to the gospel, certainly not iconoclastic, and not making changes without appropriate functional substitutes. There was nothing provocative about his methods.

We were left with one factor alone, and this was not his doing. The kidnapping trade was itself a whole configuration that grew out of economic development in Queensland and Fiji and employed bloodthirsty adventures in its operation. At first Patteson tried to bring it under control and regulation, but his correspondence shows his growing despair about it during 1870 and 1871. Although his death was due to this factor, it was indirectly so. The kidnapping trade was an uncontrolled instrument of culture clash, which made use of the bishop's own good standing with the island people to decoy their victims. The symbolism and procedure of the act of murder is morphologically Melanesian. The murderers acted according to pattern, as did also the islanders who expelled their murderous relations. The encounter was between the islanders and the kidnappers. The bishop was "sucked into the vortex at the meeting of the waters." This historical configuration is a cluster of cross-cultural interaction and values, which make it rather ethnohistorical than historical. Of all the writers who dealt with this event at the time, the man who understood it best was Lorimer Fison, and he was an anthropologist. He is the only writer who could look at the event from the various angles of the total complex. He understood the rationality of custom, the consequences of depopulation, and from his observation in Fiji he knew the nature of the economic pressure behind the Fiji kidnapping trade. He also knew the hopeless inability of the Fiji postcolonial government to deal with it. It was indeed a complex of cross-cultural configurations.

The event was certainly a crisis, an encounter of these factors. In the sequel, the various configurations sort themselves out and move each in its own direction. One works itself out in custom in the islands themselves. The problem of the kidnapping trade takes a new direction and is fought out in a three-year newspaper controversy, in which the rottenness of the whole business is thoroughly exposed—we might call it the humanitarian sequel. Then, on the political level among the nations, there is the battle in the House of Commons, with the fall of Gladstone, the establishment of colonial government in Fiji and an end of kidnapping—at least for British colonial recruiters. Then in the church which Patteson planned and planted in Melanesia, we have not only the symbolism of his memorials, but his biblical translations, his most relevant collects in the prayer book, and the unseen fruit of his ministry and that of his graduates. When I worked in Malaita, an Anglican area of the Solomons, most of the better things I saw there seemed in some way or other to go back to Bishop Patteson. Only from a distance may we truly perceive how those who sacrifice their lives contribute something abiding to posterity. If I may cite, in closing, from a famous pagan oration, that of Pericles over the Athenian dead after the Peloponnesian War:

> Their story is not graven only in stone over their native earth, but lives on far away, without visible symbol, woven into the stuff of other men's lives. (Zimmern's translation of Thucydides)

Thus an event has always a time depth greater than itself and a space bigger than the point at which it occurs. To understand it you must investigate the antecedents, and to evaluate it you must ponder the sequel.

REFERENCES

Armstrong, E. S. 1900. *The history of the Melanesian Mission.* London: Isbister.

Bavinck, J. H. 1964. *An introduction to the science of missions.* Philadelphia: Presbyterian and Reformed Publishing.

Belshaw, Cyril S. 1954. *Changing Melanesia: Social economics of culture contact.* Melbourne: Oxford University Press.

Charles, Elizabeth R. 1889. *Three martyrs of the nineteenth century.* London: Society For Promoting Christian Knowledge.

Codrington, R. H. 1872. Melanesian Mission. *Sydney Morning Herald.*

Dalley, W. B. 1872. The martyr of Santa Cruz. *Sydney Morning Herald.*

Fison, Lorimer. 1871a. Death of Bishop Patteson. Speech [seconding motion of sympathy, discussing the anthropology of the symbolism of his death, and attacking the labour trade.]

———. 1871b. Letter in *Sydney Morning Herald*, 18 November.

———. 1871c. Letter in *Sydney Morning Herald*, 4 December.

Fox, C. E. 1958. *Lord of the Southern Isles: Being a story of the Anglican Mission in Melanesia 1849–1949.* London: Mowbray.

———. 1967. *The story of the Solomons.* Taroaniara, Solomon Islands: Diocese of Melanesia Press.

Gutch, Sir John. 1971. *Martyr of the islands: The life and death of John Coleridge Patteson.* London: Hodder & Stoughton.

Holthouse, Hector. 1969. *Cannibal cargoes.* Adelaide, Australia: Rigby.

King, Joseph. 1899. *Christianity in Polynesia: A study and a defence.* Sydney: William Brooks.

Kluckhohn, Florence. 1969. Dominant and variant value orientations. In *Personality in nature, society and culture,* ed. C. Kluckhohn, H. Murray, and D. Schneider, 342–57. New York: Knopf.

Lambert, John C. 1907. *The romance of missionary heroism.* Philadelphia: Lippincott.

Linton, Ralph. 1964. *The study of man.* New York: Appleton-Century-Crofts. First published 1936.

Luzbetak, Louis J. 1963. *The church and cultures: An applied anthropology for the religious worker.* Techny, IL: Divine Word Publications.

Neill, Stephen, Gerald H. Anderson, and John Goodwin, eds. 1970. *Concise dictionary of the Christian world mission.* London: United Society for Christian Literature.

Page, Jesse. 1890. *Bishop Patteson: The martyr of Melanesia.* New York: Revell.

Stock, Eugene. 1899. *The history of the Church Missionary Society: Its environment, its men and its works.* 4 vols. London: Church Missionary Society.

Thucydides. 1939. *World order (Civitas Dei).* Vol. 2, trans. Alfred Zimmern, ed. Robert Curtis. New York: Oxford University Press.

Tippett, Alan R. 1956. The nineteenth-century labour trade in the southwest Pacific: A study of slavery and indenture as the origin of present-day racial problems. MA thesis, American University.

———. 1967. *Solomon Islands Christianity.* London: Lutterworth.

———. 1972. Possessing the philosophy of animism for Christ. In *Crucial issues in missions tomorrow,* ed. Donald McGavran, 125–43). Chicago: Moody.

Tonga. 1888. *Correspondence of Tonga government, premier's office.* 2 vols. Auckland: Australasian Wesleyan Methodist Church, 1888.

Tucker, H. W. 1879. *Memoir of the life and episcopate of George Augustus Selwyn.* 2 vols. New York: Pott, Young & Co. [Vol. 2 contains Selwyn's consecration sermon for Patteson, pp. 214–22.]

Yonge, Charlotte M. 1874. *Life of John Coleridge Patteson.* 2 vols. London: Macmillan.

PART TWO

Varieties, Location, and Use of Documents

9

PRIVATE LETTERS AND CROSS-CULTURAL VALUES[21]

In a significant paper presented about a decade ago, Jacob Gruber outlined the importance of personal documents in the reconstruction of the history of anthropology and discussed the intellectual breakthrough which resulted from personal encounters of scientific persons in specific situations. He argued that correspondence and private notebooks often indicate far more of the *moment of discovery* than do the works ultimately published, which are the tested and polished final statement. He recognised that,

> Much more important—and, of course, much more difficult to come by—are the informal and fugitive products—letters, journals, and impressions. From these we can glimpse a science in the making. (1966, 25)

Then he goes on to discuss manuscripts of men like E. B. Tylor and Lewis Henry Morgan in known archival repositories.

In reality this is only a beginning of the subject. Search for this type of material leads one into private repositories the wide world over, for government and missionary reports are also finished products and seldom reflect the *moment of discovery* or the series of experiences which led the district officer or missionary to write that report. One valuable type of repository for these more personal letters and journals is the magazine which features such correspondence. The missionary magazines of the last century published scores of letters written at *moments of discovery and confrontation*. These are by no means travellers' tales, and on the whole are remarkably frank. Frequently they are the only material for reconstructing the pre-Christian rites of passage, magical procedures, cannibalism, and other practices. In as much as I have been able to check a number against archival material, I have found virtually *no editing*, which cannot be said of the published books about missions of the same period. Quite apart from the history of missions, which is not our subject here, these letters are an indispensable data bank for any adequate diachronic or synchronic study of social organisation, political systems, language, myth, and religion

---

21 Originally presented at the annual meeting of the American Society for Ethnohistory, held at the University of Georgia, Athens (1971). Later published in *Aspects of Pacific Ethnohistory* (Pasadena: William Carey Library, 1973), 127–45. Used by permission.

through culture change. Here you see the culture pattern at the point of culture contact. Such documents become highly significant when they extend the time sequence diachronically into an earlier generation from that in which observations have been recorded.

Methodological Preamble

In my own studies, concentrating on Polynesia and Melanesia, I have identified a number of documentary corpora, each of which has its own peculiar value. One, in particular, I want to discuss here. The Fijian people became Christian over a period of about fifty years, beginning in 1835. One of the features of the missionary organisation was a printing program. There had been a press and printers there from 1838, and at an early stage the converts were already literate and were encouraged in self-expression. In the last decade of the century a small Fijian monthly newspaper began to circulate among the Fijians. *Ai Tukutuku Vakalotu* [hereafter abbreviated *T.V.*] had a remarkable number of indigenous Fijian contributors. About the same time the Fijian church commenced a missionary venture from British New Guinea (Papua). It already had one in German New Guinea (New Britain and New Ireland) and was shortly to operate in the Western Solomons. Fijian missionaries in all these fields contributed to the Fijian paper by sending in letters and reports in the Fijian language for their relatives and supporters at home to read. Let me make that clear: the letters were written by Fijians in their own language. These Fijians had a generation or so of Christianity behind them, but had not completely forgotten their pre-Christian vocabulary and practices. I doubt if a present-day Fijian could write some of the descriptions in these letters. In contrast to their religious and semantic change, these Fijian writers had a style of life, with subsistence and exchange economy, only slightly changed by culture contact. It was similar to that of the people they were describing in many ways. As their letters were written for Fijians at home, they made comparisons in house building, gardening, canoe construction and sailing, burial customs, and so on. Although in these comparisons one detects the Fijian value system as their criteria for comparison, it is only in religious values that this stands out in highly contrasting colors.

It has been popular to dismiss missionary documents on the score of their *bias.* Yet normally this is no more than the bias of any scientist who writes from the viewpoint and theory of his own discipline. Any critical reader must establish the subjective viewpoint from which his reading material has been written.[22] In any case, if you are studying a situation at, say, 1900 in Papua, and the missionary is there as an agent of change, *he is part of*

---

22   Bias and subjectivity should really be differentiated. Shafer's *A Guide to Historical Method* points out that the former is a judgment without really examining the data, the latter is an understanding in terms of personal values (1969, 149). If the missionary account is subjective, this is evidence in the dimension of cultural values and important. If the missionary is really biased (i.e., refuses to face the facts), what he writes is still of evidential value, since he was himself playing a participant role in the situation.

the situation, as Malinowski pointed out (1965a, xix), and a 1900 cultural reconstruction is incomplete without him.

However, much more difficult to evaluate than missionary bias, because they are latent rather than manifest, are (1) the purpose of the writing, and (2) the character of the audience. These two may be related and they may be complicated. For example, a missionary writes a letter to his board secretary, for personal reasons bearing on his service. The secretary publishes it in the missionary journal for promotional purposes. Both the motive of the letter and the character of the audience have been changed. Such documents have historical and anthropological value *if* the researcher can recognise these motivational rearrangements of the use of the documents. The essential information for really critical testing is whether or not the editor edited or clipped the letters.

In this case of the Fijian letter writers from Papua, the letters were written, not so much to the editor, as to the Fijian community at home. The editor was merely the "mechanism" by which their correspondence would be printed and circulated. These letters were personal documents which psychologically reinforced them in a foreign land by serving as their link with home, friends and relations. If these Fijians had any promotional motive, it was rather to keep up their numbers so that deaths and retirement would not deplete their ranks and their mission could be continued. The editor had the same motive. The anthropological descriptions in the letters can be taken at their face value, as what Fijians really observed.

This whole corpus of missionary letters, some of which are quite long, comprises about a hundred, if we include a few more formal reports that seem to belong with them. Those relating to Papua (Dobu and Kiriwina), to which I shall now turn, number forty-one. They are written in Fijian, and most of them are signed with localities identified.

A quantity of related documentation in English and Fijian also exists in the mission archives in Fiji and Sydney and in the files of *The Spectator*, a Melbourne religious newspaper. Names, dates, places, and the movement of Fijians can be checked from these where the letters do not indicate this. This means that the events, persons, and cultural institutions described can be located in time and place, making them possible focal points for *diachronic reconstruction* and specially valuable where cultural institutions have become obsolete.

The value of these letters is not confined to the *descriptive reconstruction* of conditions and institutions at the point of culture contact. We are also provided with valuable data of the *dynamics* of that culture contact. This is not another story of white missionaries, which we have in abundance, but the encounter of Melanesian with Melanesian, and within that encounter the differentiation between Christian Fijian and pagan Papuan values. In terms of the theory of cultural dynamics, as worked out for example by Barnett (1953), these letter writers would be the *advocates*, their purpose is religious innovation, and their letters are studies of how their advocacy met with *acceptance* and/or *rejection*. A whole study could be presented, using the data in the letters, to demonstrate Barnett's theory of innovation and his recombination thesis.

The Papuan letters come from the archipelago at the extreme southeast of Papua—including Kiriwina and Dobu, the happy hunting grounds of Malinowski and Fortune—islands of *kula ring* fame, and thus they push back anthropological description to a greater time depth than the major ethnological studies of these two men.

Content of the Corpus

Now let me turn to a few examples of the information in these letters and point up some of the cultural values reflected in them.

Cannibalism

Cannibalism is a recurrent theme. From J. T. Field's contemporary account to Fison (*Spectator*, 12 August 1898), we have a hard, gruesome, honest description of this ceremonial "inhumanity" as he had met it face to face. He knew he confronted it daily. Two of his missionary colleagues perished that way. He classified cannibalism, with *plunder* and *revenge*, as the three causes of war. The administration sought to correct this "offence" by punitive raids.

But these letters and reports show that *cannibalism was itself a result rather than a cause*. Papuan values went far beyond the feasting to the basic belief on which it rested to the acquisition of skulls and the build-up of *mana* repositories, because of the Papuan conceptualisation of *power encounter* and *survival*.

A Christian party was beheaded, disembowelled, baked, and eaten; the elder first, according to their pattern of protocol, in the presence of the others. The bodies were distributed over ten villages as gifts to be shared, but the skulls were preserved as highly desirable possessions. Whether of friend or enemy, the skull was valued, and its pedigree remembered. A man's power was measured by the skulls he owned. A punitive expedition, after killing thirteen and wounding many others, burning both their war canoes and light-draft fishing canoes, discovered and burned two large men's communal houses, each two hundred feet long and filled with skulls. This destruction of skulls was regarded as the height of their achievement. The two houses contained eleven hundred skulls (*T.V.* 45, June 1901; *T.V.* 47, July 1901).

Thus cannibalism is traced back to a *religious belief, the build-up of power for survival*, not merely a depraved taste. The flesh was given away, but not the skull. Indeed one letter tells how the Christian Fijians had to beware that human flesh was not sold to them as pork. It was the skull and not the flesh which had the "soul-stuff."

The Nature of God

Different also were the Christian Fijian and pagan Papuan ideas of God, his nature, and the life of man after death. One origin story is recorded. The people of Dobu are said to have sprung from a female, named Kekewakei, who appeared from out of the earth and gave birth to a child from whom the present race descended. One day the offspring went for water and returned to find the mother crazy. When the latter saw the child was afraid of her, she died and went to Buwebuweso, the abode of spirits (ghosts). This origin story links the ancestor with the spirit world for the dead (*T.V.* 2, March 1894).

It had similarities with the old tribal relations between the living and dead, which the Fijians had themselves rejected in becoming Christian. They understood this kind of encounter between ancestor worship and Christianity. It was a problem they understood better than the white missionary. They knew they were dealing with ancestral spirits rather than a high God, and they were concerned with supernatural power *per se*. It was a world of *mana*. The idea, if not the word, was there, as in old Fiji.

Josua Mateinaniu described a prolonged series of dancing, day and night, and day after day, to stimulate and entertain the ghosts of the dead, on the theological supposition that they were impoverished and hungry in the land of the dead. He described the presentations of food and entertainments and evaluated them in true Fijian style:

> There is nothing slapdash about the preparation of this feast. Each individual is
> responsible for the satisfaction of his own deceased relations, whether father,
> mother, uncle, nephew or niece, grand-parent, cross-cousin, elder brother, and
> so on. On the last night, before the conclusion of the ceremonies, after dancing
> all night until the crowing of the cock and the dawning of the day to the sound
> of the bamboo, the beating of the drum and the blowing of the conch-shell, they
> all run to the outskirts of the village, and send off the ghosts with the tradition-
> al farewell, "Go and sleep! Go and sleep!" (*T.V.* 19, March 1894)

Josua's concern, however, was not so much the futility of the ceremony and the waste of food and human strength (he could appreciate the communal values of the entertainment), but that the final stage clashed with Sunday and represented a "deliberate rejection of the better way" he believed he had to offer them. He had been only three years in this location and was just beginning to get results. His motive was to show the folk at home the need for the gospel, but in doing so he left a nice anthropological description of how they prepared their presentations and spread out a bed of leaves for the ancestral ghosts to lie on for the entertainment. He also left us an interesting picture of a conflict in Melanesian religious values.

The same conflict also showed up with respect to the moral nature of God. Setareki Tuicakau was much opposed by an elder named Mabundi, but apparently Mabundi realised that Setareki's God had too much *mana* for him, and that the best way of coming to terms was to buy the god from its owner. Fetishes, medicines, and magical formulae were marketable commodities for the manipulation of the owner. Setareki had been manifestly appraised as a fetishman. In his letter he tells the friends at home of the position he took. His God was not up for sale like a fetish or a charm. Neither was he the owner of the god with power to sell it. He was trying to communicate that God was universally accessible to all who believed, rich or poor, and had no material shrine or vessel (*T.V.* 54, April 1902).

A few months after this, Josua Mateinaniu wrote about a strong gale which brought down many houses and fruit and destroyed the gardens. This was attributed to the missionary, who, having seen the rapidly falling barometer had predicted the coming wind. As none in the village had heard of a barometer, he was designated a big wind-maker. The people of the district met at Boa, twenty-five miles from Dobu, and organised a huge presentation for him, that he not again bring such a wind upon them. Their request was that he "close his box of wind, that they may live." The barometer was regarded as his magical wind-making paraphernalia. There were repercussions. The Fijian evangelist at Duau could find no one to row him to Dobu lest the missionary release the winds again. The people, of course, were acting within their own conceptual framework. Did they not go to Bulitara, the pagan wind-maker, with a presentation when they required a calm for fishing? They were interpreting the foreigners by their own Papuan values. Their attitude to the wind-maker was ambivalent: fear of destruction, but readiness to draw on his resources (*T.V.* 59, September 1902; *T.V.* 62, January 1903).

Although this was a grave misunderstanding of Christian Fijian values and motives, nevertheless it shows that the people had recognised the Fijian presence and were feeling out towards the possibility of accepting it. Once they did this, some kind of status and role had to be ascribed to them.

Pailato Silimi reported that their own great God, known by different names in different localities, was far from a loving deity. He was rather responsible for bringing sickness on all kinds of people. This he did by *possessing* them. Correction of this possession-sickness required a priestly exorcist, who soon grew rich with presentations. This did not mystify the Fijians. There was an old pre-Christian character about it, and furthermore they had anticipated this kind of encounter (Silimi/Fison, 17 November 1891).

War

The war descriptions are quite numerous. One is led to believe that a serious war could commence with as small a thing as an argument over a pig. Someone is hurt and there is retaliation. Other villages are drawn in, fighting with spears, stones, and axes. In one such case of rapid diffusion, twenty-three villages were soon involved. On such occasions the Fijians frequently sought to become peacemakers. Josua Mateinaniu apparently won a reputation for this. He went out in the midst of nine hundred to one thousand angry Papuans and called them to see the foolishness of war and put in his "plug" for Christianity. Many a time he at least restored law and order, and even those who did not become Christian accepted his common sense and arbitration (*T.V.* 25, 1899; *T.V.* 33, 1900).

At other times war was premeditated and carefully planned. It began in the same manner as the wars of pre-Christian Fiji, the invaders surrounding a village by night and attacking at dawn from all sides to the sound of conch shells. The older Fijians had lived through this and knew how to deal with it. In any case the widespread destruction was always the same. Setareki Tui wrote from Kiriwina:

> This land is at war. I went to see the warriors from my village (Emarakana) and
> sat in their midst. They were mourning their dead. I was unable to conceal my
> own tears at the tragedy. Eleven villages have been burned this week—the food,
> animals and possessions all destroyed. (*T.V.*, February 1900)

He went on to describe how the pagan rainmaker and his younger brother had run to him on his return and wept. He described the stench of the plunder of war and the decimation of the coconuts (he uses a strong Fijian word for vicious and deliberate destruction). He certainly identified with the people with whom he lived. This time it cost him the house he had built himself and everything he owned. He went through five villages on the Sunday to preach, but the biggest group he could gather was eleven. All had fled. Even so, the preaching of a way of peace was not unacceptable (*T.V.*, February 1900).

Funerary Rites

The letters contain enough material on *the burial of the dead* to have devoted a whole paper to this. The accounts demonstrate the cultural diversity of the various islands. Juta Ranamalo reported from Dobu a burial in which the body was leaned against the grave with the head up, and covered by a pot shaped like a Fijian bowl. A few months later the skull having become detached from the body, would be taken away. Certain persons would sleep by the grave, and the mourners would stay nearby for a month or so, heads shaven and bodies blackened. A grave house was built over the grave, and shelters for the mourners, whose responsibility it had been to build the grave house. Mourning might go on for a year, the mourners continually talking of the generosity of the dead. On the day of the burial feast the relatives of the deceased would mourn at the grave for the last time, and when the widow ceased all would go to bathe (*T.V.*, June 1895).

A somewhat different account comes from Bwaidoga:

> A chief dies. His younger brother and his sons weep in the house. Other mourn-
> ers refuse to enter the house but sleep on the "village green" outside. In the
> morning a grave is dug and a "bed" of appropriate size is set up. The extended
> family makes a presentation of wealth—2 pigs teeth, 2 orange trees, bracelets ...
> The body is brought out of the house and everyone mourns. As the body is low-

ered into the grave they try to attract the attention of the dead by burying food, drinking nuts, and tobacco with him. Eventually they bring their weapons and fight with the spirits, until these are all dead. Then those who have so fought will receive some reward. (*T. V.* 56, June 1902)

Still another account comes from Poate Ratu. It begins as a typical Melanesian account would with kin orientation—and more precise responsibility.

When an elder, either male or female, dies, the mother's brother's son, *vasu*, or the mother's brother, *gadinana* (could also mean father's sister's husband), attends to the erection of a small grave house in the midst of the "burial place" with a "bed" for the dead, and a grave is dug beneath the small house. The body is lain on the bed until the burial. (*T.V.* 43, 1891)

The report goes on to describe how another body is lain with the dead as a cooked offering. The head man of the burial feast probes the cooked body with the rib of a palm frond or a fish bone so that some juice flows into the grave beneath the burial house. As the bodies decay, the head man of the funerary rites takes any piece of rotten flesh which is about to fall and wraps it up, placing it in the grave so it does not fall there of its own accord. Eventually the remaining bones are broken up and packaged in a mat and stored in the burial house until the end of the mourning feast. After the burial feast the skull is taken away. This is a very long account in archaic Fijian and describes the yams, puddings, fish, and pigs used at the end of the mourning feast, which might be delayed as long as two years. The food was supplied by the village of the deceased. The party with the feast moved to the house of the dead, where the last stage of the mourning was going on with vigor—wailing, screaming, kicking the wall, and making a song about the deeds of the dead. Mourners displayed the hair they had cut off (heads, moustaches, eyebrows), so the ghost of the dead would feel he was adequately remembered.

Now mourning was over. They bathed, oiled their bodies, and combed the new growths of hair. Taboo foods—pig, taro, puddings, and young coconuts—could be eaten again (*T.V.* 43, March 1891).

This is a piece of objective description, but in another letter from another area the same writer said,

In Fiji when our folk die we bury them with decorum, and bring as funeral presents, rolls of native cloth, mats, whale's teeth, sinnet, pigs and canoes. We strip ourselves to honor the dead. These people wail more than we do, but give little more than tears . . . They bury a few yams with the dead, that he may eat on the way [to the spirit land]. They bury him in a sitting posture in a hole lined with banana leaves like a Fijian banana-bread silo. They even cry over their war victims. They cry and sing a song called Women, beat their drums and wail until they decide where they will eat the bodies. (*Spectator*, February 1892)

One speculates that even the ghosts of those eaten by cannibal conquerors can trouble the living if not mourned by wailing. I think the Fijian account implies this, but it does not say so directly. If we add to all this a description of a burial ground by missionary Field in a letter to Lorimer Fison, we have a good body of data which predates Malinowski by twenty years and fits the diagram in Fortune's first chapter (1963, 1).

Sorcery

I have already mentioned the "Owner of the Winds" and the "Owner of the Rains," *Taukei ni Cagi* and *Tanhei ni Uca*. These and a few other magical roles were normally confined to males, but the references to sorcery usually concern females, and elderly ones at that. Apparently they were a jealous breed.

Poate Ratu reported from Dobu in 1894 that of two elderly sisters, the elder of the two had two children, both of whom died. The younger had five, all alive and married. The elder one was infuriated that her younger sister was well provided for by her offspring, while she had no one to support her. She declared she would apply sorcery against her sister, who immediately fell ill and died. Poate the Fijian buried her, for she had attended the Christian worship, but by night the angry sister exhumed the body, took it into the forest, cooked and ate it. When Poate heard of this he went to the grave and found it empty but for the mat. The civil authorities interfered and the sorceress was taken to Samarai and hanged (*T.V.* 4, September 1894).

Shortly afterwards Ananaiasa Benu (*T.V.* 7, June 1895) told of two sorceresses who tried to prevent his converts from joining the church by threatening that any who did would certainly die. Ananaiasa, the Fijian, countered by proclaiming that God had sent him to Papua to stop this kind of work of the devil, and God would certainly deal with any who tried to kill by sorcery. A week later the leader of the two lay down and died. The Fijians believed the power of sorcery could only be safely met in the name of the Christian God, whose power was described in the Bible. Here, philosophically, Papuan and Fijian shared a common value—*mana* working against one can only be overcome by a greater *mana*.

A 1904 report discusses the *Werebana*, old women sorceresses:

> When the moon is very red it is said that the sorceresses are eating it. The people say a sorceress has pierced it with a spear, so that it bleeds profusely and is therefore entirely red.

> These old women gather together in some quarter of the village for a lamentation, in which they mourn the moon's death, while it is being devoured. All these old women then discard their grass skirts; that is, their old, dirty skirts, and examine the inner cloth, [the Fijian term is *dau i taratara*, a method of detecting a guilty person by touch-divination]. When everything is discarded, the skirts are all burned, and then the sorceresses take a piece of mango wood and

beat it while the grass skirts are burning. They continue weeping while they
beat their drums, because of their love for the moon.

Then at the end of this quite objective reporting of popular opinion comes the encounter of values—"Alas, this is certainly foolish, when Christianity is there for the acceptance"
(*T.V.* 77, 1904).

This is a typical closing comment. In the same way, Opetaia Muani (*T.V.* 62, January
1903), after discussing a polygamous wind-maker and a rainmaker, simply adds in closing,
"This kind of darkness is wide-spread." Other letters are confined to their own positive
values. The inordinately large number of obituaries shows the price they paid for their
missionary program in Papua. These are absolutely typical Fijian Christians. One letter
from Josua Mateinaniu (*T. V.* 50, November 1901), about an infant almost drowned in the
sea, shows the Christian measure of health and hygiene. Several complained of the effect
of liquor in the islands. One blamed the white man's trade connections for hindering his
missionary work: this is not a Fijian reflection of missionary talk, it is the subsistence
economy speaking against "the enemy the Silini" (i.e., shilling).

Organisational Patterns

Here and there throughout the letters one comes on references to social organisation.

The Fijians were somewhat mystified by the ability of Papuan society to survive without a strong chieftaincy such as they knew in Fiji. Solomoni Tavatava told how the people
who had become Christian in a certain village, worked to build a church. There was no
head man in the village or in the Christian group, and they had no preacher or lay leader—
yet they put up a church building (*T.V.* 39, September 1900).

Poate Ratu also had commented on the absence of chieftaincy:

> These people have no real chiefs whose word all men follow, as we have in Fiji,
> and this is a bad thing. (Ratu/ Fison, February 1892)

And again he wrote:

> They have a word for "chief" which is *taubada*, but the trouble is they all call
> themselves chiefs, and every man is a chief in his own house. There are men
> who have a following, but there are no real chiefs.

In 1891 Bromilow, the missionary, mentioned in a letter to Fison that a certain polyga-
mist, Jikoro, had three wives but kept them in different villages. Poate Ratu, the Fijian, is
very much more to the point, and shows this is not merely to keep them apart:

> If a *taubada*, chief, here has 5 wives, each of those women belongs to a different
> town, and he has to go to visit her and his offspring are not his children, but
> are counted to her town. Your own offspring go to other tribes, but your sister's
> children come to yours. (*Spectator*, February 1892)

In a 1904 report, also from Kiriwina, surveying the decade, polygamy was discussed. It described how the woman's kin were responsible for building her house and yam houses, which were quite stable structures, and supplying her with yams. The particular reference is to the chief Enamakala who had twenty-two wives.

One Fijian, who no doubt came from one of the sailing islands of Fiji, has left us a description of Papuan sailing at Tubetube. We have also numerous other cultural institutions like peacemaking procedures and the transmission of obligations to relatives at the time of death. One could go on. There is more than this in the corpus of letters. Throughout these years, the Fijian business was to bring about religious change. Where they met obstruction, it was mainly resistance to their successes by those who were deprived of material advantage by the change—priests, magic men, exorcists, and elderly sorceresses. As Barnett points out (1953, 381) acceptors are more likely to be dissidents than the satisfied. Conceptualisation of Fijian Christians in some kind of priestly role opened the way for the acceptance of the new religion. Some demonstration of the power of the Christian God by his agents facilitated the decision making. Although the religious innovation was considerable, the indigenous culture was by no means destroyed. It remained an integrated thing.

The pattern of skull burial as an ocular demonstration of change of faith can be conceptualised in terms of Sherif's experiments as interpreted by Barnett as the reference point in a hitherto unstructured field (1953, 116–17). The burial was the decision-making symbol. In August and September 1891, Field saw them bury fifty-seven skulls in three group ceremonials, after the presentation of his message of peacemaking (journal, 6 November 1891).

Some Evaluations

We have been told by Kaberry (Firth 1964, 83) that

> for Malinowski an institution was multidimensional, having its personnel
> (social structure), its charter (or values), its norms, activities and material
> equipment. It was a construct, but it was a model closely linked to empirical
> reality, that is to social situations in which pairs or groups of individuals in
> defined relationships carried out activities in pursuit of certain ends.

I certainly agree with this theoretical statement. However, to read Malinowski and Fortune in the light of the corpus of Fijian documents is to feel a stress on magical practice at the expense of religious belief. Nadel detected the same imbalance without access to the Fijian corpus in "Malinowski on Magic and Religion" (Firth 1964, 205):

> Malinowski's account of magic is rigorously coherent and internally consistent;
> if you wish to quarrel with it you must quarrel with a systematic theory. Against
> this, the treatment of religion is loose and disjointed: there seem to be too many
> things incapable of conceptual integration.

Now I think it can be seriously postulated that both Fortune and Malinowski, whose data collecting was superb, actually failed to record what they saw—I mean the religious dimension—because they regarded it as acculturation due to mission influence. They were salvage anthropologists. Twenty years later Malinowski saw the missionary as part of a "new autonomous entity" (1965a: xix). Meantime, better time depth would have shown that *religion and magic do not change at the same pace, or with the same rhythm.*

Malinowski's own objection to the manner of gathering ethnological data from one dimensional accounts, that are incomplete because they ignore the social dimension (1948, 240), rebounds on him. This corpus of descriptive Fijian correspondence over a decade, written about the people of his own research area and their social *and religious* patterns by persons from a somewhat similar Melanesian and insular world could hardly be called one-dimensional. The letters form an archival collection, a multidimensional entity—what I have called a *corpus.* Indeed I think that by throwing this corpus up against the writing of Fortune and Malinowski we are able to add a *time dimension* which neither Malinowski nor Fortune had.

The big difference is the disappearance of cannibalism, which was mentioned in letter after letter in my data bank. Fortune's (1963) references to cannibalism are either historic cases (61, 90, 306) or described in the past tense (77, 80) or in oral tradition (302).

"Skull(s)" is not even in the index of any of the four Papua volumes of Malinowski I examined, and cannibalism is limited to references in the myths (Malinowski 1961, 321–22, 331) and by his only reference in *Coral Gardens* (1965b, 1:162), where he is discussing the possibility of endo-cannibalism in time of severe famine, he is indeed a feeble witness. In view of the huge collection of Malinowski's data, the absence of cannibalism and skulls shows the basic religious change which had taken place in the first decade of this century. No better example could be found to illustrate the shortcomings of purely synchronic research.

Josefa Malumu (to Fison, 13 November 1891), Panieta, described houses where the wall and end plates were entirely decorated with skulls—friends and cannibal victims. Pailato Sili (17 November 1891) at Ekaroi reported to Fison a collection of one hundred skulls from cannibal feasting.

When the Papuans were converted they buried the skulls. Poate, the most fluent of the Fijian speakers of Dobuan, penetrated into the mountains of Normanby. As a result of his efforts fifty skulls were buried in one village. Field thought cannibalism had vanished in Tubetube by 1898 (*Spectator,* 4 November 1898) despite the continuation of other non-Christian customs.

This must have meant a tremendous transformation in the whole religious value system. This kind of change had already begun to operate in the values of the *kula ring* before the arrival of Malinowski on the scene. Bromilow gave information on things like the secret gesture language, and claimed a change of character in the trade over the period I am discussing (Bromilow 1929, 127–301).

The spirit land Bwebweso, is frequently mentioned in Fortune, but he apparently did not explore mission archival resources. He drew on the physical facilities and linguistic work of the resident white missionaries and bracketed the mission and government as agents of change, blaming them for depopulation, but he refrains from mentioning the greatest destructive agency of all, the recruiting and labour trade which operated in the localities where he was working. The mission is not a single discrete entity, as he would have discovered if he had worked over the documents of the Fijian missionaries as against those of the white missionaries. Even the Pacific Island evangelists were not a discrete group, being Fijians, Tongans, and Samoans.

As Malinowski reported, the graves at Kiriwina had been moved outside the village shortly before by government intervention (1948, 257). One has the impression that the Kiriwinans regarded their old beliefs about ghosts less seriously. The people were not afraid of the dark or the spirits of the dead (152), and again the disrespectful removal of the grave goods before the ultimate interment (156, 258) suggests the whole event was a *mock substitute* for the more serious pre-Christian prototype described in my collection of letters, especially one account from Bwaidoga where the gifts included weapons of war to fight with the spirits (*T.V.* 56, June 1902).

Fortune distinguished between witches and sorcerers as female and male, making the point that the victims were *werebana*—mortal women (1963, 150–53), but he did not give us a great deal of information about their operations. He has a single reference to *jealousy* as a possible cause, and this is certainly supported in the letters, but the letters also indicate the *werebana* applied pressure by threat. Apparently a mere threat was enough to kill, and the government, knowing this, treated it as murder (Ratu, *T.V.* 4, September 1894). Bromilow recorded that the oldest chief of Dobu died through a woman's sorcery (journal, January 1892).

The terms *werebana* and *balau*, for the female and male practitioners, were also used for the spirits which possessed them (Field/Fison, 7 September 1891; Silimi/Fison, 17 November 1891), as with *kalou* in some localities of early Fiji. Fortune held that every disease was caused by an incantation of some kind (1963, 138), but the Fijian material indicates some diseases as caused by the spirit Werebana. In Kiriwina, Malinowski (1961, 76) found the *mulukwausi* and *bwaga'u* capable of causing sickness, and the *tauva'u* nonhuman but anthropomorphic malignant spirits who could cause death. What we have yet to establish, however, is whether the death by spirit possession was due to the spirit or initiated by a sorceress calling upon him for power.

Fortune's description of a Dobuan burial (1963, 193–200) is mainly comprised of kin responsibilities and feast exchanges, with a number of details which could have been innovations after 1900—i.e., *functional substitutes* for the pagan features which had disappeared with the acceptance of Christianity. I feel sure some features were *mocking substitutes*. The praises of the dead are retained, but in the feasting rather than the wailing (199). However, the grim associations of burial sacrifice, cannibalism, decomposition of the corpse before burial, and preservation of the skull as a *mana*-repository have no mention in Fortune, except for a few references which, because of the bare reference with no treatment at depth, I suspect come from an informant or oral tradition rather than observation.

Ruth Benedict pointed out the importance of early case study data for studying cultural process (1953, 18) and used Fortune on the Dobuans as her database. Yet the society she reconstructs was research at *a point of time only.* Malinowski, Fortune, and Benedict, who leans on them (120–59), all missed the point that the Fijian letters would have made clear; namely, that *the Papuans had just passed through a dramatic and rapid change of religious beliefs and values, but the magical patterns, which are usually corrected by slower educational processes had not yet been eliminated.* When the Fijian corpus is set over against Malinowski and Fortune, and the passage of time is taken into consideration, we are able to use the joint data diachronically. The analysis of Malinowski is synchronic. The description of the letters is synchronic. But bring the two together so that you introduce the diachronic dimension over the period of more than a single generation and some of the problems which Malinowski did not appreciate now become charged with new meaning. Malinowski is not the only anthropologist who has eliminated the religious dimension of an acculturated situation because of "mission influence," and the historical record of the process of cultural change is much the poorer because of these omissions. We have a great many gaps in our knowledge of sequences. The hope is that many of these can be investigated before it is too late. The living informants are dead. Only the study of personal documents can help us now, but the new availability of these throughout the Pacific makes possible a diachronic reconstruction at many of these broken sequences.

To return to Gruber's idea—these personal documents record much valuable information of *moments of discovery* and confrontation when major culture transitions began.

REFERENCES

Documentary Sources Used and Cited: 1894–1905

Collection of forty-one letters and reports from Kiriwina and Dobu Circuits; Trobriand, D'Entrecastreaux, and Louisiade Archipelagoes; from Fijian missionaries and written in the Fijian language and printed in that language in Fiji for their friends at home.

A few similar letters sent to Lorimer Fison in Melbourne.

Material from the journals of J. T. Field and W. E. Bromilow, also sent to Fison.

Contemporary Newspapers

Ai Tukutuku Vakalotu, Fiji, 1894–1905.

The Spectator, Melbourne, 1891–98.

Books and Articles Cited

Barnett, Homer G. 1953. *Innovation: The basis of cultural change.* New York: McGraw-Hill.

Benedict, Ruth. 1953. *Patterns of culture.* New York: Mentor Books. First published 1934.

Bromilow, W. E. 1929. *Twenty years among primitive Papuans.* London: Epworth.

Firth, Raymond, ed. 1964. *Man and culture: An evaluation of the work of Bronislaw Malinowski.* New York: Harper & Row.

Fortune, R. F. 1963. *Sorcerers of Dobu.* New York: Dutton. First published 1932.

Gruber, Jacob. 1966. In search of experience. In *Pioneers of American anthropology: The uses of biography*, ed. June Helm, 5–27. Seattle: University of Washington Press.

Kaberry, Phyllis. 1957. Malinowski's field-work methods. In *Man and culture: An evaluation of the work of Bronislaw Malinowski*, ed. Raymond Firth, 71–91. New York: Harper & Row.

Malinowski, Bronislaw. 1948. *Magic, science and religion.* New York: Doubleday. Essays first published 1916–26).

———. 1961. *Argonauts of the Western Pacific.* New York: Dutton. First published 1922.

———. 1965a. The anthropology of changing African cultures. In *Introduction to methods of study of culture contact in Africa*, ed. Bronislaw Malinowski, i–xxxviii. London: Oxford University Press. First published 1938.

———. 1965b. *Coral gardens and their magic.* 2 vols. Bloomington: Indiana University Press. First published 1935.

Nadel, S. F. Malinowski on magic and religion. In *Man and culture: An evaluation of the work of Bronislaw Malinowski*, ed. Raymond Firth, 189–208. New York: Harper & Row, 1957.

10
THE LOST LIBRARY[23]

Historical research done in connection with the centenary of Hunt's New Testament in Fijian has brought to light an interesting but regretted fact—viz., our knowledge of a lost library.

We are well aware, of course, that the American soldiers, who valued what we in Australia and New Zealand failed to value, bought up most material on the Pacific in our bookshops—a fact about which new missionaries are already sorely troubled, as these books, and especially those by early missionaries in English, were extremely valuable introductions to the history, customs, and languages of the Pacific. As I began, we are now sadly aware that this is already a lost library, but it is not of these that I want to write at length.

I refer to books written in the Fijian languages by our early missionaries and published by our mission press in Fiji during the first twenty years of its history. These were not about the experiences of the missionaries or native customs (which matters were reserved for the English language and published in Britain) but Scripture translations, sermons, catechisms, hymnbooks, and such. These were regarded as tools of work for the missionary and were, during the period of which I write, in dialect. What a valuable library this would be if only we could lay our hands upon it today.

The first book published in Fiji was the *First Wesleyan Catechism*, and this appeared in the dialect of Lakemba, in the Lauan Group in the year 1839 and was quickly followed by Mark's Gospel in the same tongue. These were the work of David Cargill. I know the British and Foreign Bible Society [hereafter B.F.B.S.] Library in Britain holds a copy of this Gospel, but I know of no other copy of either book.

Incidentally, when the natives saw the printing press at Lakemba, they at once declared it to be a god. They were soon disillusioned, however, and told that it was to be used in the service of the only true God—a statement which was most certainly proved to be true.

---

23 Taken from bound collection of articles entitled Historical Writing: Fiji, 1947–1967; Studies from the History of the Fijian Church, 1835–1967. Unpublished article.

Cargill worked on the language seriously and compiled a six-thousand-word vocabulary and grammar of this Lakemban dialect for the use of his fellow missionaries. This was copied many times. If only we could find a copy today, I feel its value would be immense, both as linguistic and anthropological data. Cargill, by the way, was particularly suited to this kind of work, having specialised in languages at Oxford and procured his MA thereby. Furthermore he had previously had experience in Tonga, both linguistic and racial. The whole movement of early missionary activity in the Pacific, in fact, which in men's knowledge of those days, could not possibly have been planned, shows yet such a perfect design that we are compelled to see in it the planning mind of divine wisdom—a subject which I hope someday to develop at length. Cargill also translated the four Gospels and part of Acts into the Lauan dialect and wrote a lengthy essay on the language and how it differed from others in Polynesia.

The press was now removed to Rewa, as a more central position in the group it was hoped to evangelise, and continued producing booklets and Scripture portions. For five years (1839–44) it remained there, until war broke out and for this reason was removed to Viwa, an island in the Bau area. The B.F.B.S. supplied a grant of fifty reams of paper (an act of generosity which was repeated after the appearance of Hunt's New Testament), and a serious project of Scripture translation was considered and commenced. The major problem was the matter of which dialect was most suitable. Each man began working in the dialect of his circuit, specific portions of Scripture being allotted to each one.

We now know that the following appeared and were circulated among the natives:

Genesis (twelve pages) and a Scripture lesson book.

In Bauan, work of Mr. Cross.

An alphabet and a book of twelve pages.

In Somosomon, probably by John Hunt.

Saint Matthew's Gospel (twelve pages).

In Rewan, probably work of Cross or Hunt (I favour Hunt, as it is known from his personal records that he began translating this Gospel five months after his arrival at Rewa).

Catechisms and other small works.

In each of these three dialects "and also in that of the windward islands."

A hymnbook of twelve pages.

In each Bauan and Lakemban dialects, work of Hunt and Lyth. (Thomas Williams says that it contained "fair imitations of some of the most familiar of Wesley's hymns." Anyone who knows how free are our hymn translations, will see in that quote the highest praise.)

A "Shorter Catechism," with Scripture replies to questions on doctrine and duties. Dialect? Work of Hunt. This was possibly the forerunner of a larger work
Hunt produced later in Bauan.

"Short Sermons," twenty-three in all, with a prefixed address to preachers and
native teachers, that contained among other things extracts from "Twelve
Rules of a Helper." Again the work of Hunt. In Bauan subsequently, and I presume also at this stage.

The last two mentioned, we are told by a contemporary missionary, "were much
esteemed by those for whom they were specially produced and by many of the converts
as well."

In addition to the above, there was a regular flow of class tickets, calendars, and such
items as the Morning Service from the *Book of Common Prayer* in the Lakemban dialect. At
the same time there must have been many manuscripts of which we have no record of
publication. Early in 1840, for example, Hunt had completed a rough draft of Matthew, and
had completed Genesis and part of Exodus. This would be in Somosomon, where he was at
the time. Lyth was working on a book of hymns in Somosomon. It is also on record that
Matthew and Mark had appeared in Lauan, Rewan, and Somosomon.

As far as I am aware, none of these books still exists today. This is nothing short of a
tragedy from whichever angle one looks at the subject—linguistic, anthropological, historical (especially from the point of view of Methodist biography), and as primary evidence in
missionary method. This last, at least, is worthy of a whole article.

Let us glance at the records of the district meetings and see what work was afoot:

District Meeting 1841: It was determined to coordinate the translation work in
some way, and to this end Hunt and Lyth were appointed a committee to examine all manuscripts. It was also agreed to work first of all on the New Testament
and to get this into as many dialects as possible before turning to the Old Testament (though some Old Testament work had already been done—e.g., Cross had
completed Genesis).

District Meeting 1842: Cross had translated Acts, Matthew, and Psalms into Bauan; Hunt and Lyth had completed John and a liturgy in the dialect of Somosomo;
Jaggar had done part of Acts and a liturgy in Rewan; and Calvert had produced
the Second Catechism in Lauan.

District Meeting 1843: It was not determined to allocate specific parts of the
New Testament to each man, for translation into the dialect used in the area
where he laboured. It was still desired to complete the New Testament in at least
the dialects of Lau, Rewa, Bau, and Somosomo.

The earliest reference to the use of a single dialect for the whole Fijian Group is
found in a letter of John Hunt, dated 15 May 1844.

District Meeting 1844: Reviewed again in 1844, the original scheme was discarded as providing no promise of a whole Bible in any one dialect. I wonder
what happened to those dialect translations, even if only in manuscript. I
wonder if any of the missionaries' descendants hold them today. The men on
the field at the time were Hunt, Calvert, Jaggar, Lyth, and Williams, and four of
these men were prolific writers. Jaggar was more than fully occupied with the
work of printing.

Another objection raised to their plan was that it would lead eventually to about fifteen different Bibles in the Fijian Group. (Actually there are more than twice as many
dialects, but I give the objection as raised at the meeting at the time.) This district meeting
of 1844, the five men mentioned above, and perhaps Watsford and Hazlewood, who were
appointed in 1844, made that day the decision which has meant more to Fiji than any other
of its history, with the possible exception of the Cession. They determined to adopt the
Bauan language as their medium. Because of the importance of the result, it is right that
we examine briefly the reasons given in that meeting for their decision. Firstly they fa-
voured it as the best from a linguistic point of view. Then, it was already the widest known
and, with the rising power of Bau, was anticipated would become more so. Those were the
two arguments which weighed most with Williams, who records the matter. True, some
objection came from Lakemba, and to satisfy them, hymns were still printed in their dialect for a time.

This decision had a great effect on the Fijian people as a whole. It was the first big
step in helping them to realise the unity of their race, it was the first important step in
their education after the adoption of the alphabet, it led to the standardisation of the language, it gave singleness of purpose to missionary activity and direction which could have
been achieved in possibly no other way. This—far, far more than the wars of Cakabau—was
the foundation step in the building of the Fijian nation. All that followed was built upon
it—Christianity, commerce, education, social order, and justice, to mention just a few of
them. Not only were they built upon it, but they were possible only because of it. It is not
often that five humble Methodist ministers who had thought to bury themselves in a place
away from their own race, can make a decision which turns the direction of a whole race
religiously, socially, and eventually politically. Again I ask: Could this decision have been
purely theirs? Or was there Another walking with them?

The honour which goes to David Hazlewood, writer of the *Feejeean and English Dictionary*
(published at Viwa in 1850), should undoubtedly have gone to Hunt, but for his transfer of
labour to Scripture translation. Hunt had prepared such a grammar and dictionary, which
he used himself during translation work, but of which he never found time for final preparation for publication, or perhaps he found himself continually adding to it and felt the
time was hardly ripe. Of the nature of this, we know very little, but seeing his translation

work was at least in three dialects and possibly in four, we may well imagine what a valuable document that dictionary would be. Once it was determined to use the Bauan dialect, he immediately set to work on the Scriptures at the expense of most other literary work. Most, but not all.

With the aid of an intelligent and trustworthy native, Hunt translated the Gospel of Saint Matthew (which he had already done in Rewan and Somosomon) and the Acts of the Apostles, and these were published at Viwa in 1846. A copy of this edition is in the hands of the B.F.B.S. Four thousand copies were printed: three thousand for immediate use and one thousand for binding eventually with a complete New Testament.

Up to this time others had been working on other parts of the New Testament. Williams, for example, records in his private journal references to his work on Luke and Corinthians, but in the district meeting of 1846, the other men declared that Hunt was the master in Bauan and gave him the task of completing the whole of the translation of the New Testament, which he had done by the early part of the following year. When it eventually appeared, he had done it all with the exception of John's Gospel, in which case he had revised the work of one of the other men. Jaggar was doing the actual printing, and Lyth was brought in for final corrections and proofreading. By July the printing was complete, and an advance copy (possibly unbound) reached Williams by 10 August, and another had been sent to Hazlewood, so I imagine that all the men had advance copies. Bound copies were not available for distribution until the following month. Hunt, who was chairman at the time, was away on a lengthy tour of the whole area, taking Walter Lawry, the general superintendent, with him. He was present at the district meeting, and it was here on 22 September 1847 that the supplies of bound New Testaments were issued out to the men. Hunt's trip with Lawry probably explains why a third man was called in to Viwa to handle the publication before the district meeting.

The various revisions and editions which followed may be seen in the B.F.B.S. Library in Britain, but the earliest which I have been able to find myself is Langham's and Heighway's revision of 1899. The 1847 district meeting also commissioned Hunt to carry on with the Old Testament. He revised the existing manuscript of Genesis, which subsequently disappeared, suspicion falling on the "intelligent and reliable native" mentioned above, so I imagine this work had to be done again. He then completed Exodus and had passed on to the Psalms, having completed forty-six, when his earthly labours came to a close. David Hazlewood took up the torch. Genesis, Exodus, and Psalms were published as a volume at Viwa in 1854, but the whole Bible did not appear until ten years later, and only then after Calvert had spent two years without pastoral charge and on a B.F.B.S. grant, revising the translation of David Hazlewood. Even then it was Lyth who finished off the revision of the Prophets.

It is a great pity that so many of these early efforts at Bible translation are no longer available to those of us who are now on the field. Revisions, of course, are necessary, especially in a country where the people are passing through rapid transition. I have no doubt that a young Fijian of today would read Mr. Hunt's New Testament with some difficulty. Fijians have often said to me that in the Old Testament we use at present (1902 revision) there are many words quite strange to them. On the whole the revisers have kept the language up to date and idiomatic, but I don't know that they have always retained the meaning of the original. Hunt and Hazlewood both were expert Greek and Hebrew scholars, and both worked from the originals, using the English text only as a guide or aid. I personally should like to own copies of these first editions for purely study purposes. Apart from satisfying my curiosity, I feel sure it would be an interesting and valuable study in semantic change, in a time of rapid transition when this island race is torn between a desire to be Western and a desire to preserve the best of its endemic culture.

The Viwa Press continued to produce a great number of books and pamphlets, very few of which remain to be read today. There were the usual items found in a Book of Offices, published separately, reading books, catechisms, Lyth's sixty-four-page *Teacher's Manual: A Confession of Faith*, 130 pages by Hunt, and 100 pages probably by Calvert, and Moore's *Teachings of the Bible*, a *Memoir of John Hunt* (a very desirable book), a reading book and catechism in the Rotuman language, and a seventy-two-page *Grammar and Collection of Fijian Idioms* (about which, alas, no one seems to know anything save its existence), and Hazlewood's *Feejeean and English Dictionary*, which was still the standard authority when I arrived in Fiji a little over six years ago, after over ninety years.

Some of these were revised and republished several times and could hardly be called rare, but the early editions are certainly all in the lost library, and it should be remembered that all the publications mentioned above go back to the first couple of decades of our mission history.

Hazlewood's *Feejeean and English Dictionary*, copies of which do exist but cannot be bought for all that, is an extremely valuable volume, both in its dictionary (281 pp.) and grammar (64 pp.). The only criticism I have ever heard of it is that it had become out-of-date, which, to my way of thinking, was its very virtue. The grammar is an interesting and informative approach to the subject. References to Cargill and Hunt seem to suggest that Hazlewood had the benefit of their researches. Not only was Hazlewood a great student of biblical languages, but he had, according to another missionary of that time, distinguished himself in the subject of the philosophy of languages. The appendix on the islands of Fiji holds its value not so much in its geographical value, but rather in its geography in the "historic sense," and its natural history section, which might perhaps have about seven hundred entries (of which Thomas Williams claims in his journal to have supplied seventy), is possibly better and has certainly less errors than the new government-commissioned dictionary which is more up to date and therefore useful in other ways.

On the subject of hymns, we seem to have lost track of much. Hunt and Lyth published the first hymnal, yet in our present book, Lyth has but one and Hunt is not represented. The hymnal in use at the turn of the century had 260 hymns, of which fifty-four were by W. A. Heighway, who is reduced in our present book to eighteen. If these men were capable of writing text books and translating and revising the Scriptures and doing the foundation work of our dictionaries, why are we passing over their hymns? Heighway, in fact, is greatly remembered by the Fijian people as our outstanding hymn writer. A good many of the hymns in our present book (1938) are the work of men of this century, and as a very rough estimate I should estimate that we have lost somewhere between 120 and 150 hymns of the church in the Fijian language, not to mention a great many in dialect.

In the main this study is meant to concern the early work of our missionaries, for space does not permit me to bring the subject right down to those books which are just recently out-of-print. The same tragedy applies to each period of our mission history. It is a great pity that no one knows anything about Dr. Fison's *History of the Jews*, and the *Concordance and Harmony of the Gospels*. Heighway's biographers give a list of books in Fijian about forty years ago. Of these only the Bible is available today. Eight I have seen, but the remainder (ten) are apparently lost.

During this last year the publications of our Mission Press at Suva, which appeared during the second and third decades of this century, have mostly become out of print. These include the work of Fison, Bennett, and others. I doubt if they will be republished. Fison's *Life of Paul* is replaced now by Bock's—a more detailed treatment, and illustrated. Fiji is demanding a completely new library now, but as it comes, I hope that the work of the past will not all be lost. For what has been done we give thanks; we regret what has been lost but know that what no longer can be put on our shelves has stimulated the fibres of a young nation.

> Now praise we great and famous men,
> The fathers named in story;
> And praise the Lord, who now as then
> Reveals in man His glory.

"Let us now praise famous men, and our fathers that begat us. The Lord hath wrought great glory by them through His great power from the beginning" (Ecclus 44:1–2).

11

A STATEMENT ON THE USE OF DOCUMENTS:
The Complexity of the Conversion of the Tahitians[24]

The purpose of this brief chapter is to show the real danger of the worldview of the particular ethnohistorian influencing his or her use and interpretation of the historical facts and documents. I cite here three different examples of reporting a single event, followed by an analysis.

Example 1: The Anthropologist

The first missionaries had very little success in the conversion of the people, though the material goods they brought were much appreciated. The missionaries were opposed, and many of them left the island in despair. When a fresh set of missionaries arrived some years later, Pomare was in a more chastened frame of mind. He had been defeated in battle and had taken refuge on the neighboring island of Mo'orea. The missionaries accompanied him there and began to make headway with him. Pomare had begun to distrust his gods because of his lack of success against his enemies. He began to flirt with the missionaries, in the hope that their god was more powerful than his own and would bring him the military success he wanted. At the same time he was chary of abandoning his own gods entirely. Thus, though the missionaries had hopes of converting Pomare, they could not get him to abandon his gods publicly. In view of the prospects, however, the missionaries ranged themselves on the side of Pomare and regarded his enemies as "heathen." In 1815, Pomare's enemies on the island of Tahiti invited him to attend a conference with them. Pomare, accompanied by his supporters and some of the missionaries, sailed over to Tahiti and, on a Sunday morning, he and his people attended a service conducted by the missionaries. During the service, the enemy was observed advancing with a large armed force, evidently to attack. The congregation became alarmed, and the missionaries were prepared to break off the service. Pomare, however, ordered the service to be continued to its proper ending and stated that the enemy could be attended to afterwards. The missionary writer, Rev. W. Ellis, had praised Pomare's piety and faith in the face of the enemy. The

24 Taken from *People Movements in Southern Polynesia* (Chicago: Moody Press, 1971), 221–26. Reprinted in Tippett's *Introduction to Missiology* (Pasadena: William Carey Library, 1987), 264–69. Used by permission.

truth is that any religious ritual that was broken off was regarded by the Polynesians as an ill omen for future success. The gods being invoked for assistance turned against their worshippers if the ritual was not properly completed. It was not Christian piety that induced Pomare and his followers to go on with the service but the fear of a broken ritual. At the end of the service both Pomare and his followers had plucked up courage in the hope that the Christian god would assist them in gaining the victory.

From the outset of the battle which ensued, fortune smiled on Pomare. The opposing leader, whose rank was immeasurably superior to that of Pomare, was killed with a musket-ball. On the death of their leader, the enemy retired and victory lay with Pomare and with the Christian god who had supported him. The power of Jehovah having been demonstrated, Christianity was accepted by the whole island of Tahiti, and Pomare became king of the group. Pomare handed over the material symbols of his native gods to the missionaries to be sent to England to show the people of that country what fools the Tahitians had been. A lucky shot had done more than seventeen years of preaching had been able to accomplish (Buck 1939, 65–67).

Example 2: The Missionary Historian

Pomare II walked in his [father's] footsteps ["fickle and brutal, offered thousands of human sacrifices to his gods"] until the missionary outlook became as dark as possible.

Prompted by the grave reports received from the field, a special meeting was called in London in July 1812 to pray for Pomare's conversion, and in that very month he gave up his idols and asked for baptism. This was the turning point of the work in Tahiti. Idolatry was completely overthrown, the king sent for a printing press to prepare Bibles and hymnbooks for his people, and at his own expense he built a huge church, where, in the presence of four thousand of his subjects, he was baptised. The light spread not only over all Tahiti, but also from island to island and other groups, through the efforts of the Tahitian Christians as well as from the missionaries, and Tahiti will ever be known as the seed-plot from which the gospel was scattered far and wide over Oceania (Glover and Kane 1960, 437–38).

Example 3: The Missionary Theoretician

After the missionaries had been labouring through a long night of fruitless toil lasting for years, the king made known his wish to be baptised. If after so many years of disappointed expectation the missionaries had been eagerly ready to grant the desire of the royal applicant, it would not have been surprising, but for four years he was kept back until more satisfactory proof was given of his knowledge of the gospel. The earliest missionaries were the children of the revival of the eighteenth century, and they took with them to their work standards which united puritan severity and evangelical spirituality, and they looked for and were not satisfied until they thought they had found evidence of a radical change of heart (King 1902, 378).

Analysis

At first it must be difficult for the reader to see that these three passages are each records of the conversion of Tahiti. Each at one point is sound and at other points quite wrong. Not one can be documented as it stands. All are faulty with respect to time depth, dynamic factors, and the total configuration. The historical reconstruction of both anthropologist and missionary historian is appalling. They create quite wrong impressions, and all suffer from oversimplification.

Each writer naturally has a different motive. There is no harm in this, nor in the selectivity this may involve, provided the integrity of the context is not distorted thereby. In this respect the anthropologist's manipulation of his source material is shocking.

The anthropologist is concerned with showing the acceptance of Christianity to have been a simple matter, almost an accident; the matter of "a lucky shot." He would presumably argue also that the great war of 1914–18 was entirely caused by the shooting of an Austrian archduke. To arrive at his conclusion he has to deliberately omit a great body of facts that hold together firmly within the very sources he uses.

The motive of the historian was to write a world survey. World surveys are, by nature, unreliable because they have to reduce complexities to simplicities and in doing so lose sight of patterns. By compressing a field of history worthy of a whole volume into a paragraph, both focus and time depth are wrong. They give the impression of something that just never happened. The one contribution is an allowance for the divine element. This is missing from the others.

The theoretician is concerned with an issue of missionary technique and cites the incident out of its context to illustrate his theoretical point. This is a common procedure, but it throws the responsibility on the writer, either to verify or document his source for the historical information on which the theory stands. Many of the myths of history are the supports of all kinds of theory. The third writer is quite correct in pointing out the slowness of LMS [London Missionary Society] baptisms, and the fact he stresses seriously undermines the other two impressions; not only is his own legalistic picture quite devoid of a dynamism that was certainly in the historic events, but he is careless about his figures. Whether Pomare II was kept waiting four or seven years does not injure his argument, as it happens, but this figure is the very support of his theory, and he happens to be wrong.

The anthropologist did contribute an interesting cultural point that was not in the historical sources. It came from his special knowledge in his Polynesian background, he being a Maori. But that same background has given Buck a mental set against the taking of Polynesian gods to England to show what fools the people were, and the iconoclasm of destroying ancient Polynesian sites, which we know from other writings also of this man. We see him in his own specific class—a salvage anthropologist[25]—with a certain cynicism which militates against his capacity for objective analysis when the question of missions is involved. Buck is denying missionary value judgments any validity (yet he is categorical in his own), drawing his own opinions of Pomare II, distorting the evidence of those who knew him face to face, and getting away with it because of his own Polynesian connections. He was, in the majority of his work, a good anthropologist, and because of this his opinions of Pomare II have been widely cited by other anthropologists as beyond dispute (for example, Howells 1948, 256–57). Yet his personal grievance against the Tahiti Christian teachers has been so vocal in other writings that we ought to be warned at this point. After all, if an anthropologist appeals to history, he or she is obligated to respect the canons and criteria of historical method. If out of the anthropologist's special knowledge, something interpretive can be added this is good, but facts cannot be selected, omitted, and distorted as set down in the documents. The anthropologist may disagree with them, but they must be stated and dealt with.

Glover and Kane give us the impression that the reason for the whole train of events lies in a certain prayer meeting held in London in 1812. It gives an impression of the complete overthrow of paganism because of Pomare II's conversion, and that the Bibles came from the press he sent for, and that he was baptised in a great, newly built church, and so on, one sweeping sequence of events in a limited space of time. All this was incorrect. The picture eliminates all the dynamics of the local events. Pomare II ate the turtle alone. He was kept seven years for baptism. No serious biblical translation work was done for another twenty years. As far as prayers were concerned, the evidence is that those of Tahiti were far more fervent than those in Britain. I have no doubt about the value of prayer, but to pin it to one particular meeting in Britain in 1812 is far too facile.

A brief analysis of the chronology of Pomare II's quest for baptism from sources that were public and not difficult for any of the writers to obtain will expose the weaknesses of each description.

> Pomare first asked for baptism after a conversation with Nott, who did not disclose it to the brethren at the time, lest they build hope on a vain boast. (Lovett 1899, 1:196–97)

> Either he must have feared disagreement on the matter among the missionaries or he himself was unsatisfied. Sometime later Pomare pressed his claim again, but during the interim he had been trying to win the support of some of his

---

25   A salvage anthropologist is one whose main concern is to salvage cultural items.

relations of status [Tamaloa, his father-in-law, and Tapoa, both high chiefs of nearby islands] but had failed.[26]

Seven missionaries had written to London about this. Pomare's words to the missionaries were, "You do not know the thought of my heart, nor I yours, but God does." This in itself is a simple statement of faith, which was worthy of support. He was told that two things were customary: first, instruction in the Christian way, and then a period during which his walking in the way would be observed and tested. That was all before July 1812. It shows Pomare II's leaning to Christianity and requests for acceptance long before the battle described in the first report, and before the London prayer meeting. At the beginning of 1815, three years after the prayer meeting, the situation was still the same. Some two hundred of Pomare II's people had been received before him by this time, as we have seen in the movement of the praying people. Pomare II was still being instructed and observed. At this time the missionaries wrote:

> The case of Pomare grieves and perplexes us. He wishes to be baptized ... but we are far, very far from being satisfied that he is a proper subject. He has extensive knowledge of the doctrines of the Gospel, but is a slave to drinking.[27]

After the battle of Bunaauia, when Tahiti had actually become nominally Christian, it was another four years before Pomare was eventually baptised—16 May 1819.[28] This makes the report of the 1812 prayer meeting look rather foolish. And Buck said Pomare II was chary about leaving his own gods, and drops the story of his eating the turtle from the source where he gleaned his other facts. Yet the documents are quite clear that he strove with the missionaries for baptism for at least seven, possibly eight years.

These passages have been arranged side by side to show the importance of critical testing and the folly of oversimplification like trying to reduce conversion to a single factor. We are dealing with highly complex configurations that build up over a period of time. While we are never certain of having observed all the factors, we can and must observe all the factors in the available sources. The three writers have given us cartoons, exaggerating one feature at the expense of the others to the distortion of the general effect. This is not good enough in anthropology, or history, or theory.

On the other hand, if only the published sources are examined carefully, it will be quite apparent that structurally there were several configurations of conversion movement operating in Tahiti and the neighboring islands. There were "praying people" building up into a small Christian fellowship. There was a large segment of Pomare II's family connec-

---

26   Letter of the seven missionaries dated 21 October 1812, cited in Lovett (1899, 1:198).
27   Letter of 14 January 1815, cited in several sources, including Lovett (ibid., 205).
28   Account of the event written three days later and cited in Lovett (ibid., 219–20). All these references are here shown to have appeared in the official published L.M.S. centenary volume, so that there could be no doubt about their availability to the three writers.

tions, both by blood and marriage, which he himself set out to win, and he was so engaged over a long period of time. Others were impressed by the idol burnings started by Patii. Only the rebel units came over after the battle, and only indirectly as a result of it—it was the postvictory policy of Pomare II ("Spare the rebels but destroy their religion"), not merely "a lucky shot." All this is found in the data in the printed works of the missionaries and the officially published history, although none have worked out the patterns. Church growth research assembles such data and seeks out the patterns, because knowledge of those patterns is of tremendous importance to all engaged in church planting today.

REFERENCES

Buck, Peter H. 1939. *Anthropology and religion*. New Haven: Yale University Press.

Glover, Robert H., and J. Herbert Kane. 1960. *The progress of world-wide missions*. New York: Harper.

Howells, W. W. 1948. *The heathens: Primitive man and his religions*. New York: Doubleday.

King, Joseph. 1902. Oceania. In *Christianity Anno Domini 1901*, vol. 1, ed. William D. Grant, 366–85. New York: Chauncey Holt.

Lovett, Richard. 1899. *The history of the London Missionary Society: 1795-1895*, vol. 1. London: Frowde.

12
NOVEL, FILM, REVIEWS, AND REACTION[29]

Hawaii, a mischievous novel in the hands of a still more mischievous film producer, is summed up by *Time* magazine in the following passage of gross misstatements which reflect a pernicious dogmatism far worse than that it seeks to expose. In my opinion it is provocative of hate to those who accept it and hurt to those who reject it.

> Hill & Co. selected two strong narrative threads [from Michener's novel] and with them delineated a simple, impressive picture of how God-fearing but life-hating missionaries destroyed the warm brown souls they came to save.
>
> The hero (Von Sydow) is a prune-faced New England parson insuperably identified with deity. Blankly unable to perceive that the islanders are more Christian than the Christians, this religious imperialist with ruthlessness throws down their god of love and raises up in its stead a god of wrath. With their religion in ruins, the Hawaiians lie open to the blessings of civilization: whisky, syphilis, and economic exploitation. By film's end the native nation in only 50 years has withered from 400,000 to less than 150,000 souls, and the parson is forced to assume the white man's burden of guilt and reparation.[30]

The only thing that saves a legitimate case for libel, in my humble opinion, is the fact that so many individuals have contributed to this pack of lies that it is hard to pin the blame on any one of them as an individual. There are at least seven or eight major untruths in that statement, quite apart from opinions that would be hard to prove (e.g., that the missionaries—a generalisation—were life-hating). The gods of the Hawaiians were not gods of love; the fall of the Hawaiian deities predated the arrival of the missionaries; the Hawaiians had been introduced to liquor thirty years before the missionaries came, and also to syphilis; the economic exploitation came into the Pacific through sandalwood and trading before the missionaries, as did also Western arms and ammunition and convicts (not mentioned); and the figure of 400,000 was Captain Cook's estimate, over thirty years before the arrival of the missionaries. The process of depopulation for all these reasons

---

29   Taken from "Evaluation of the Novel *Hawaii* and the Film Version" (unpublished manuscript, 1961).

30   *Time*, 21 October 1966.

was going on before the missionaries came, and the only efforts to counter these evils for many years (until a good government was established) was that of the mission. The Hawaiians were a dying race. The amazing thing is that the missionaries were able to save any at all. The would-be saviours had to fight the sandalwooders, the whalers, the convicts, and many of the sea captains. They have fought some battle for social justice at every period of the last century.

Yet the *Time* reviewer was not the only observer who accepted the film at its face value. Hollis Alpert, reviewer for the *Saturday Review*, though he found the movie burdensome because of Abner Hale, a "bigot" and a "bore," who "invaded the island without prior invitation" and when facing native customs was "not only against them" but "continually invites the wrath of his singularly narrow-minded God upon those who don't conform to … His precepts" so that "after a while you're all on the side of the natives." Let us suppose, then, that this is the picture the film gives to the average viewer. One is not too deeply concerned about this if one remembers the record of the writers of film scripts and the interpretive freedom of actors. If the American public knows William Bligh by the film version rather than the historical documents, they will do the same with the missionary. What alarms one, however, is that the presentation is so dramatically done that even the critical and professional reviewer is completely hoodwinked. Says Alpert:

> Evidently, Dalton Trumbo, the screenwriter … had the estimable aim of providing a truthful picture of the early conquest of Hawaii by the missionaries and traders.[31]

Let me go a step further. The religious missionary journal of the United Methodist Church published for their women (who raise a good deal of money for mission) an article showing changes in missionary policy and promotion. Bruce Hilton of the American Civil Rights Movement was the writer. Let me cite:

> The grim picture of James Michener's *Hawaii* is based on fact. The history of world missions is filled with preachers who thought the essentials of the gospel included covering up bosoms, teaching 19th century English hymns in place of "pagan" local music, and erecting Gothic stone churches in tropical forests.[32]

I do not dispute the point Hilton is making. I know that if we judge the missionaries by our twentieth-century anthropological criteria, they were ethnocentric. Nevertheless, it is untrue to say they regarded these as the essentials of the gospel. Furthermore one is surprised that fiction should be taken as fact and assumed without critical examination by the writer or editor of the paper.

---

31   Alpert, "S. R. Goes to the Movies," *Saturday Review*, 15 October 1966.
32   Hilton, "Should Missions Stop at U. S. Borders?" *Response*, January 1970.

Would you like to hear what one of the greatest living Hawaiians said about the film *Hawaii*? He described it as "a knife in the back of our Christian missions and must not be allowed to pass as truth." He was particularly annoyed at the fixing of blame on the missionaries for the matters mentioned above:

> *Hawaii* is a fraud when it comes to recording history correctly—particularly the impact of . . . missionaries on the lives of the islanders.[33]

This was his appraisal at the time the film came out. But what could a small national church do to fight a fourteen-million-dollar movie?[34] This year they celebrated the Sesquicentenary of the Arrival of the Missionaries, and among the features was a reenactment of the arrival with the brig *Thaddeus* sailing in and the missionaries coming ashore. There was more basic truth in this simple drama than in all the fourteen-million-dollar movie. Among the speakers for the occasion was Abraham Akaka. He took for his theme "Why I Am Glad They Came," and he said, starting from the point that the Hawaiians had rejected their gods and were without a religious system when the missionaries arrived,

> When a people loses the foundations by which they determine what is right and wrong, just and unjust, they are on their deathbed and ready to die. Unless there comes a new way they cannot live. The missionaries brought that new foundation.

A jet passed over, and Akaka stopped to let it pass. It gave me time to write it down. He repeated it as if to underline what he had said.

Albertine Loomis, a local historian, whose book *Grapes of Canaan* is the best available history of the foundations of the mission and sticks close to the documents, was also critical of the film for its historical distortions. She said and was reported by Reuters:

1. Christianity filled the void of a broken society in Hawaii, instead of the film version of joyless missionaries "invading a Hawaiian paradise where everybody is having fun, and where Kane the 'god of love' presides over a simple, joyful, pagan religion. Nothing could be farther from the facts."
2. The missionaries preached love, not the Old Testament wrath of the movie's Abner Hale.
3. The missionaries made the entire Hawaiian population literate in less than 25 years, instead of merely teaching the chiefs, as implied by the film.
4. "Missionaries and Hawaiians were co-workers in building the church" to such an extent that by 1843 the mission board "considered Hawaii no longer a foreign mission field but a Christian country."

---

33   Reported from Honolulu (RNS) in *Christian Life*, July 1967.
34   Bart, "$upercolossaliti$" *Saturday Review*, 24 December 1966.

Then the historian added—"No such incredible bigot, no such detestable fool" as the Hollywood version of the missionary could have effected such change. She agreed with Akaka that the film was a fraud.[35]

These are two of the typical reactions of people who know their Hawaiian history. I may add that the distortion of the film was deliberate. The company desired to use Akaka's church building, and he demanded to see the script. He pointed out the numerous items which needed correction, but was told the script could not be changed. Needless to say, they did not use Akaka's church. It would have been ironical for Bingham's own building to have been desecrated by Abner Hale.

The Hawaiian Mission Children's Society [H.M.C.S.], a body of missionary descendants, has a fine collection of books and manuscripts. No one can do adequate historical writing on Hawaii without the exploration of these documents, many of which are quite unique, like the manuscript journals and letters of missionaries. Here one will always find some critical scholar of Hawaiian history at work in the reading room. This society was so perturbed by the effects of the book *Hawaii* and the film version that a small booklet was published [1967] officially by the society—*Hawaii: Fact and Fiction* [hereafter *HFF*]. So many visitors to the Mission Houses Museum (the best and most historically informative tour in Hawaii) so frequently began by saying, "Of course I've read *Hawaii*," that the booklet became a necessary corrective, and its preamble says:

> Many have confused Mr. Michener's fictional account with the history recorded in these buildings. Now that the movie *Hawaii* has been released, even more of our visitors assume that the novel and the screen play have given them *the truth*. We can't agree, and offer here some of the reasons for our disagreement.

This review begins by pointing out that Michener claimed the book was a novel and that the characters were fictional, and maybe a number of small matters were deliberately fictionalised to establish this fact. The Hawaiian historians grant the novelist the right to such fictionalisations and "accept them as reminders that the book is *not* history."

The quarrel arises, however, from Michener's unqualified claim in the same introductory preamble that his book is "true to the spirit and history of Hawaii." To this the reviewers offer a categorical denial:

> So far as the missionary period is concerned, we who have studied both missionary and non-missionary accounts of that era say forthrightly that it is not [true to the spirit and history of Hawaii].

> The eighty-four men who served in Hawaii under the American Board of Commissioners [A.B.C.F.M.] between 1820 and 1863 possessed a wide range of personal traits and their share of human failings. But history shows none so

---

35   As reported in *Christian Life*, June 1967.

physically unattractive, so socially gauche, so cantankerously narrow and self-righteous, so crass and cruel as Abner Hale. He is not a real person or a composite of real persons; he is a caricature. The scenes in the novel that tend to soften and humanize him are so few and so fleeting that readers in general—and script writers in particular—ignore them. Consequently, the world now sees on the screen a missionary who is a hateful fanatic and an utter fool. (*HFF* 1967, 1)

I do not think there is any doubt that the general public saw Abner Hale as a real person. Those who knew the name Hiram Bingham saw him as Hale. It suited the antipuritan and permissive filmgoer to hiss at Hale as a real historical missionary. He was accepted as a type by many university students. In Hawaii most of my informants saw Hale as a lightly veiled attack on Bingham, and many academic (though not by any means missionary minded) persons resented the caricature as grossly unfair. The interesting thing about interviewing people who know their Hawaiian history is that they invariably pass the novel off as of no consequence and then gravitate to a discussion of Hale. No matter how antipuritan they may be, nevertheless they recognise Hale as an unhistoric monstrosity who has been popularly accepted as a missionary type. They feel guilty, it seems to me, because they know that all Hawaii has today in education and economic development is due to missionary foundations. Of course Michener does not ignore this in the novel. His historical tutor says you can recognise the characters down through the pageant by their names, but they are humanitarians or businessmen or visionaries[36]: Bromley and Whipple, or Hoxworth or Hale. This type of sociological classification is too textbookish. In reality, all these features are found, but it is not "true to the spirit and history of Hawaii" to present a single distortion so that the total context is obscured. One academic person said to me that "Michener had a conscience. He painted the mission black, and then, as if knowing what he had done, he added a touch of white."[37] When it came to the film, even the white was removed. Any book which directs the reader's attention and feelings on to a single eccentric character—real or fictional—can hardly be true to the spirit and history of Hawaii, which took so many people to build in so many ways. While the great length of the novel *Hawaii*, and the basic motive of showing the various ethnic units which make up modern Hawaii, indicate a very wide canvas, and many little units can be taken as fine descriptive vignettes, nevertheless public reactions were mainly to Part 3, "From the Farm of Bitterness," and created a missionary image that was entirely false.

---

36   Taylor, "Michener and Names," *Paradise of the Pacific*, October 1959.

37   A good example of these "afterthoughts of conscience" is found on pp. 767–68 of *Hawaii*, where a woman writer from New York, after four weeks in Hawaii, had written a scurrilous book about Hawaiian missionaries and their descendants and was basking in the glory of her literary success. She met Wild Whip Hoxworth, one of the renegade missionary descendants who never hesitated to tell his pious relations what he thought. He tells her the book is all "complete bullshit," and Michener gives him a speech of more than a dozen lines in which he informs her of what the missionaries have done for the economic development of Hawaii, and tells her to go home and write another book. But this "conscience passage" is lost in nearly 1,200 pages.

H.M.C.S. reviewers objected also to the manner in which the novel and film twisted cultural values:

> The conflict between the Hawaiian culture, gracious and in many ways admira-
> ble, and the customs and mores of foreigners has been so presented as to make
> the missionaries villains who destroyed a wonderful people. (*HFF* 1967, 10)

This is the modern form of the myth of the "noble savage." It recurs in the writings of fiction, especially Melville, who applied it most to Polynesia. At this point, however, the reviewers direct their thrust at the historical and social conditions of Hawaii just before the missionaries arrived. Apparently the film director was well aware of the historical inaccuracies (indeed Akaka pointed them out to him) and tried to pass them off as a point about which historians were in disagreement, but the reviewers would have none of this:

> Kane and Ku, Kanaloa and Lono had not protected the commoners from increas-
> ing misery nor restrained the lesser chiefs from greed. Although Kamehameha I
> begged his people to live by the established *tabus*, his death in May, 1819, opened
> the floodgates to drastic change. In November, 1819 (when the *Thaddeus* was still
> in the Atlantic) the Hawaiian *ali'i* destroyed their religious system and officially
> ended the pagan regime . . . We know of no recognized historian [in reply to the
> director's statement in the *Advertiser*, 20 October 1966] who doubts or denies that
> late in 1819 Kamehameha II, influenced by two strong-minded, chiefesses, pub-
> licly broke the *tabus*; that Hewahewa, the highest priest in the land, siezed a torch
> and began burning and despoiling *heiaus*; that a civil war followed, in which
> those who hoped to restore the old order fought against the king's forces and
> went down to quick defeat. When the missionaries arrived in April, 1820, Hawaii
> was a country without a religion. And because there was nothing yet to replace
> the old *tabus*, it was a country almost without law and order. (*HFF* 1967, 2)

The passage goes on to qualify this triumph as one which did take some time to be completely effective and to describe what might be called the "mopping up" operations of this religious war, and their subjection to rum and mammon rather than to Kane:

> To picture, then, a shattering conflict between an unwelcome alien doctrine and
> a treasured native tradition does not reflect the spirit of the 1820's in Hawaii,
> though admittedly it is an effective device for making an exciting story.

Neither novelist, film producer, or reviewers have considered, however, the anthropological fact that whether these movements take place before or after the arrival of the missionaries, they do not happen like this to a people unready for them. They reflect the strong influences of culture contact and a shift in cultural values which make a people ready for innovation or experiment (Kroeber 1948, 366–67). In this present case, this anthropological principle of culture change indicates that the missionaries were not the cultural disturbers, but found a disturbed people looking for a new way. At least in Hawaii it was this way.

What Really Happened in Hawaii 1819–21?

The H.M.C.S. historians insist, quite rightly, that "in a very important sense the old Hawaiian gods died in 1819 at the hands of their disillusioned worshippers." This is one of those basic historical facts which a historical novelist cannot bypass. By avoiding this, he changes the whole idea of the conversion of the people, he makes the missionary an agent of change to a degree quite untrue, and deprives the people of the initiative which was theirs and which created the historical frame of reference in which the people-missionary relations had to be worked out. For a historical novel, which purports to show how the various ethnic groups came to their present positions in the general Hawaiian complex, this is not playing the game by the rules, Mr. Michener! This permits him to create his own "spirit and history." To change the historic conversion pattern is a terrible distortion. One of the factors which mystifies Michener's critics is his (surely it must have been deliberate) avoidance of this evidence. It was either a deliberate rejection of a historical situation or shoddy research, for it is recorded in the reports, journals, and letters of the first mail back to America after the arrival of the missionaries in Hawaii. Neither do you have to go to the archives for these, for they were printed in 1821 and may be read in any missionary or seminary or university library that has a series of the *Missionary Herald* [hereafter *MH*]. That film director Hill should say "historians disagree" is sheer rubbish. Let me quote from the joint letter of five missionaries to Dr. Worcester, dated 23 July 1820:

> How were our hearts agitated with new, and various and unexpected emotions, to hear the interesting intelligence—"*Kamehameha is dead; the taboos are broken; the idols are burnt; the Moreeahs are destroyed; and the priesthood abolished.*" This victory was achieved by that arm alone, which sustains the universe . . . Long indeed did we expect to toil, with slow and painful progress, to undermine the deep laid foundations of the grossest idolatry, but He . . . commands us, as the feeble followers of the Captain of salvation to go up to "every man straight before him" and "in the name of our God, to set up our banner."[38] (*MH* 1821, 17:111–13)

In the same document, discussing the various locations which seem to be open for the gospel, the brethren said:

> The people are without any form of religion, waiting, as it were, for the law of Christ, though they know not his name, nor the way of salvation.

And again:

---

38   Letter signed by Bingham, Chamberlain, Whitney, Ruggles, and Loomis.

> From Atooi the call is loud and impressive, "come over and help us." . . . The chief
> is importunate in his intreaties, that some of us should settle, there;—prom-
> ises to give us houses and land, as much as we need; expresses a great desire to
> learn, and has begun the work in earnest.

This is a long and fascinating letter which shows the country religionless and exposed, some chiefs *desiring* their presence and instruction, others *permitting* them to establish themselves and interested in instruction. It was written less than four months after their arrival, and schools were in operation with good response from the chiefs and people. They were asking the board for a schoolmaster, "skilled in the Lancastrian method of in-struction," and "a tried physician," and "a pious, skillful and devoted ship-carpenter" to repair vessels. If Michener had worked this letter into his novel, it would have been a dif-ferent novel—its spirit and history would have been different. A qualified schoolmaster, physician, and carpenter: how much more down to earth do you expect a band of puritan missionaries to be?

Furthermore the letter indicates the process of depopulation going on when the mis-sionaries arrived:

> The heathen around us are washing away by disease, induced not by climate,
> but by their imprudence and vices.

Together with this letter goes another equally important manuscript item, *The Journal of the Missionaries.* The first part of this is known as *The Thaddeus Journal.* It was written on board during the journey of 164 days and was a corporate effort in many handwritings. It shows the missionary party as intensely pious, with a deep knowledge of Scripture. But it also shows them engaged in swimming, painting, and fishing.[39] The journal was continued after their arrival on 30 March 1820, and was copied out and sent to Dr. Worcester on 23 July. The portion from the arrival to 19 July was published in the *Missionary Herald*[40] and should be available at any library with this serial. Furthermore the missionaries them-selves kept journals and wrote letters. Many of these are available for inspection at the H.M.C.S. archives and library and in other libraries where copies of the A.B.C.F.M. records are held. Letters from Whitney, Ruggles, and the king and queen of Atui, and part of Thur-ston's journal were published in the same numbers of the *Missionary Herald*.[41] There can be no possible doubt about the "spirit and history of Hawaii" at the time.

Perhaps we may look at a letter written by one of the mates of the *Thaddeus*, a man who apparently had sympathy with the missionaries, though not one himself. He had been "previously acquainted with the Sandwich Islands."

---

39 A duplicated booklet of twenty-four pages, *The Voyage of the Thaddeus, 1819–1820* was distributed at the Sesquicenten-nial Arrival of the Missionaries. It is almost entirely excerpts from the *Journal.*

40 *Missionary Herald*, vol. 17 (1821), 113–21, 131–41, 169–75, running through three numbers of the paper.

41 Ibid., 123–24, 142–43, 175–78, in addition to editorial comment through the same numbers—4, 5, 6.

The great and important revolution, which has followed the death of Ka-mehameha, has opened the way for missionaries, and seems to insure them success. But they have a great work before them; having ignorance and the remains of superstitious prejudices to combat.

The great events of the revolution seem wrought by miracle. It was with aston-ishment that I heard, "Owhyhee's idols were no more." The great change was most apparent to me. Knowing, as I did, their former attachment and deep-rooted prejudices in favor of their *taboos*, and their superstitious reverence for their vain *akooahs*; that they were "no more" was what I could not realize, until I had trodden on the ruins of some of their late altars of abomination, and seen the ashes of their once sacred idols mingled with dust.

I now have the pleasure of seeing a part of the missionaries comfortably situ-ated at this place, having already commenced their work and appearing to enjoy many pleasures of domestic life, while all branches of the mission are enjoying the respect and confidence of the natives.

The king was the first to become a pupil; and the byword among all classes of the natives is "the A, B, C."

Sir, I doubt not that the blessing of God will crown all their labors with abun-dant success, both in civilizing and Christianizing this nation. (*MH* 1821, 17:122–23)

The mate must have been impressed to write this letter to the board secretary. As the writer knew the previous state and the attachment of the people to their idols and taboos, the letter is important evidence of the change which had already taken place before the missionaries arrived—its dramatic character, the missionary opportunity, the immediate commencement of education for all classes of natives (i.e., education was not confined to the chiefs, a point argued by Miss Loomis).

The king of Atui, who had acquired a knowledge of English through culture contact years before the missionaries arrived, now learned to write. He sent the following letter to Dr. Worcester by the same boat as the missionaries sent their *Journal*:

I wish to write a few lines to you to thank you for the good Book, you was so kind to send by my son. I think it is a good book;—one that God gave for us to read. I hope my people will soon read this, and all other good books. I believe that my idols are good for nothing; and that your God is the only true God, the one that made all things. My gods I have hove away; they are no good; they fool me; they do me no good. I give them coconuts, plantains, hogs and good many things, and they fool me at last. Now I throw them all away. I have none now. When you people learn me, I worship your God. I feel glad you good people come to help us. (Ibid., 124)

He has been almost four months under missionary teaching at this point of writing. The letter was his own composition and in English. He was helped with putting it into written form.

The writer of that letter was the father of George Tamoree, the Hawaiian whom the missionaries took back from America. The day before the king had written, George had also done so himself, assuring Dr. Worcester, whom he knew of course, of his father's goodwill to the mission, that he wanted the Christian teaching from men who would not behave like the "bad white men"—an interesting differentiation made by the Hawaiians from the beginning. His father asked for more missionaries—a minister (whom George actually nominated from those he knew in America), a farmer, some house and ship carpenters and cabinet makers (ibid., 142–43).[42] This letter shows that the missionary and Hawaiian requests to the board for personnel were in tune with each other and differs radically from the "spirit and history" of the fictional *Hawaii*. George's letter lines up with another written by Ruggles about a week later (123–24). George Tamoree also wrote of his own volition to the principal of the Foreign Mission School run by the A.B.C.F.M. in America, showing his friendship to the mission,[43] and his mother had written to the mothers of both Mrs. Ruggles (124) and Mrs. Whitney (143). At least for this locality of the Hawaiian Group, the critics have no right to suggest any uninvited imposition on the part of the missionaries.

So much for the letters which were made public and printed in the first emission of missionary documents. We might call these the April–June emission of 1821. The second came in November. Let me now turn to the journals. The June number of the *Missionary Herald* devoted four double-column pages to extracts from the private *Journal of Mrs. Thurston*, covering those eventful days from 31 March on to July in 1820 (ibid., 175–78).[44] She reports the fall of the old religion in the following terms:

> Brother Ruggles and Thomas [Hopoo] who accompanied it [the boat] brought new intelligence. They visited one of the Moreeahs; saw its walls and temples in ruins; saw the ashes of idols, and the bones of human victims, which had been offered in sacrifice to their gods. Since the king's death, which was on May 8, 1819, there has been war in Owhyhee. It was occasioned by abolishing the custom of men and women eating separately. *Krimakoo*, in favor of having the custom abolished, fought against a superior force and proved victorious. About one hundred fell in battle; many more were wounded. Even women presented themselves on both sides, and took an active part in the field of slaughter.

---

42   A "P.S." to this letter reveals the king's afterthought that he could also use a powder maker, showing he had not yet fully realized the nature of the new religion.

43   George Tamoree was the name used in America because he was the son of Tamoree. In Hawaii he had his own name—Humehume. Tamoree is really Kaumualii. See Loomis (1951, 326).

44   Private journal of Mrs. Thurston.

This interesting passage not only verifies the rejection of the old deities, taboos, and sacrifices before the missionary arrival, but indicates something of the nature of those taboos and sacrifices, and also the military struggle the fall of the gods had engendered. The battle had been fought, and the country was for the time at peace. The following day Mrs. Thurston described some women visitors whose faces bore the scars made by hot iron as the evidence of mourning at some time or other. Another excerpt describes the wretched living conditions of the villagers. Mrs. Thurston had no illusions about the "noble savage."

After describing the first Sabbath at Kirooah when Bingham preached on "The Isles Shall Await for His Law," the inquiries afterwards were made of the mission Hawaiians. The local people said it was good and expressed a desire to learn to read so that they might learn of the great God from the Bible. Hopoo found his father alive and desirous of receiving religious instruction. This is how Mrs. Thurston saw it.

The missionary journal described the rejection of the old gods in terms very similar to the letter to Worcester cited above but with a few more details and a discussion about the mind of Rehoreho and his openness to the gospel (ibid., 113–21, 131–41, 169–75). The journal specifies three characteristics: his desire for improvement in learning, his longstanding disbelief in idol worship, and his friendliness to whites, and thus they were led "to believe the time was ripe" for "the introduction of Christianity and the customs of civilized life"—a common differentiation in the missionary records all over the Pacific. (Though civilisation and Christianity were regarded as companions, they were never confused. The confusion of faith and form is a modern problem. All through the history of Pacific missions, in boards and among missionaries, the Christianity-civilisation debate has been a live one. Do you civilise in order to evangelise, or does civilisation come with evangelisation? The same issue arises in numerous forms with each generation, but it recurs.)

From this journal also we gain information of the small colonies of whites who lived there before the missionaries. These men had "favored the cause of the reformers, and seemed to rejoice in the destruction of the oppressive *taboo*." One of their number, John Young, had risen to a chiefly rank and served as an interpreter and advisor to the king and helped the missionaries present their credentials. On one occasion Bingham and Thurston called on him and found him reading his Bible. This was at Kirooah Bay. Later on in the journal (April), we meet with seven or eight European names, Spanish, British, American—five of them ship captains—with houses and storerooms at Hanaroorah (Honolulu) on Woahoo (Oahu). These people manifest some degree of prosperity, one of them having even a "framed house, two stories high," and some have cultivated extensive gardens of squashes and vineyards, fishponds, not to mention sheep and goats and a commodious eating house with an American table for boarders. All these are described in the journal of the first four months: things that were there when they arrived.

Furthermore they immediately find themselves bound up in the bundle of life. They have to deal with birth and death, to minister medical services to their neighbors. Their teaching program is in operation. Ships from the outside world come and go. They have already met the whalers. It all shows the culture contact as considerable and as predating the missionary arrival. One is astonished at the number of islanders who can communicate in English and at their use of European clothes. It all makes any talk about the missionaries coming in uninvited and changing a God of love into one of wrath, about life-hating missionaries, about their opening Hawaii to whisky, syphilis, and economic exploitation, and about their destroying the warm, brown souls they came to save, as dangerous and uncritical, as completely untrue to the "spirit and history of Hawaii" and as injurious to a mission board, which in spite of its shortcomings performed a great service when it was very badly needed. What can one say about the missionary image? If you read the missionary journals, you find something entirely different from the novel and film *Hawaii*. Human beings—yes, but men of profound courage and faith and far more humble than we are led to believe. The image that sinks into the mire as far as I am concerned is that of the film industry: $14 million for a brilliant but offensive misinterpretation of truth.

REFERENCES

Hawaiian Mission Children's Society. 1967. *Hawaii: Fact or fiction*. Honolulu: HMCS.

Krober, A. L. 1948. *Anthropology*. New York: Harcourt, Brace, & Company.

Loomis, Albertine. 1951. *Grapes of Canaan: Hawaii 1820*. Honolulu: Hawaiian Mission Children's Society.

Michener, James. 1959. *Hawaii*. New York: Random House.

Missionary Herald. 1821. Vol. 17.

13
MISSIONARY RESOURCES AND ISLAND LIFE HISTORIES[45]

One of the criticisms often made of the older types of Pacific missionary is that they wrote up their own exploits more than those of the Pacific islanders who worked with them—the "native agents" as they were called. The missionaries are often depicted as rather self-assertive, dogmatic, and biased. For this reason many anthropologists and some historians have rejected the missionary records as reliable source material.

This has been unfortunate and has invariably given an opposite bias to their own writing. Writing the essays in this book has convinced me of the great value of missionary documents on the Pacific. However, as with any research tool, one has to learn how to use them. One has to realise the variety of their types and functions, and evaluate them according to their basic purposes.

Missionary records need to be evaluated in the following manner:
1. Official reports intended for publication.
2. Official correspondence not for publication.
3. Private correspondence.
4. Private journals.
5. Printed books.

The moment the character and function are apparent, the researcher should know how to allow for any bias—recognising, of course, that all writing has some bias, including that of the administrative officer and the anthropologist.

Official reports and correspondence published in England or America (e.g., in *Wesleyan Magazine* or *Missionary Herald*) may be regarded as written with this possibility in mind, but where I have been able to compare the printed letter with the original, I have not found them edited for publication. The printed books vary in value. Those with imprints of the Mission Society have been prepared for the missionary-minded reader at home. Books from a secular publisher may be assumed to have a wider audience than the missionary constituency. The significance of the audience is important in evaluating a book. The book is more likely to have been edited than the letter or report. It may be promotional or

---

45   Taken from *Aspects of Pacific Ethnohistory* (Pasadena: William Carey Library, 1973), 193–202. Used by permission.

educational—i.e., for raising support or for interesting reading. Both are of value to the ethnohistorian, but one must first establish what the purpose is.

For the ethnohistorian the missionary journal is the most valuable of all these sources. The missionaries recorded their feelings and impressions and were frank in their descriptions, especially about things regarded as too delicate for putting in a book. They lived in the midst of the raw life of paganism, sometimes only ten to twenty feet from the cannibal ovens, and they were good observers. Sometimes their book editors removed items and substituted a phrase like "too disgusting to mention." In a later day these have been rejected by secular scholars as "exaggeration" or "missionary bias." Yet in the journals one frequently finds evidence of the reality of that "too disgusting" culture trait. Unfortunately this elimination was needed at the time as a corrective to the idea of the "noble savage."

Not all journals are of equal value. One has to measure one off against another. Fiji is rich in this kind of material—Williams, Hunt, Jaggar, Lyth; all of them available in one repository, and all very much in agreement. A little later on (in the 1860s), one finds a wider difference in the missionary personality types. From then on over the years, some men stand out as recorders of the changing way of life—Fison, Horsley, and others. From the same missionary continuum one can identify good observers and men with anthropological insights: Fison from the 1870s to the first decade of the new century, and then Deane later on. Fison was a contemporary of E. B. Tylor, Lewis Henry Morgan, R. H. Codrington, and Sir J. G. Frazer, and corresponded with them all. Fison and Deane left proper anthropological discussions.

Each repository has its own unique corpus of missionary documents and journals quite apart from the housing of mission archives.[46] In the Turnbull Library, Wellington, one can work on missionary journals and papers of Buller, Woon, Colenso, Kendall, Selwyn, Williams, Yate, Hall, and others, between 1800 and 1900, and also many reels of microfilm together with several files of mission society papers which have been alienated from their own archives.

---

46   These usually require the special permission of the mission concerned. The Methodist Overseas Missions [M.O.M.] Pacific documents, for example, are in the Mitchell Library, Sydney, and in the Fiji Government Archives in Suva, beside Roman Catholic Mission material. The M.O.M. collection includes much personal material assembled by missionaries—Royce, Jaggar, Hunt, Baker, Billings, Heighway, to mention only a few of them. The Mitchell Library itself has many others to go with these. I have mentioned only one Society. The early record of Pacific missions involves one in the study of the L.M.S. [London Missionary Society], the C.M.S. [Church Missionary Society], the Melanesian Mission, and several horizontal structures like the B.F.B.S. [British and Foreign Bible Society], and the Protestant Missions Medical Aid Society. The northern Pacific was the domain of the A.B.C.F.M., and some Presbyterian activity was located in the southwest. Catholic activity was widespread and involved four or five Societies—Marists, Picpus, Capuchins, Sacred Heart, and old Spanish missions and Jesuits if we cover the entire Pacific. A researcher will do well to cover the records on any one of these in his or her lifetime. Many of them have now microfilmed their materials and therefore are available in more than one repository, and some have photocopied duplicate sets: thus, for example, the A.B.C.F.M. records are both in America (Harvard University, Cambridge, Massachsetts) and in Honolulu.

The A.B.C.F.M. [American Board of Commissioners for Foreign Missions] records and correspondence of Hawaii and Micronesia, and files of individual missionaries may be used at the H.M.C.S. [Hawaiian Mission Children's Society] repository in Honolulu, amplified by the superb island collection of books, theses, documents, and microfilms at the Gregg Sinclair Memorial Library at the University of Hawaii, and the Library of the Bishop Museum. These places between them offer many missionary journals—Chamberlain, Mrs. Ruggles, and others—mission station reports, and many rare pamphlets.

In Sydney, Wellington, or Honolulu one can work on missionary material to his or her heart's content—more than any one can use in a lifetime.

Indigenous Sources

The Fiji missionaries did not bypass the "native agents" in their writings. They knew well that the small staff of British missionaries could not do the job that was opening up before them, and they recognised their dependence on the native agency. They did not bemoan this necessity but rejoiced in it. They recognised the superiority of the nationals for breaking new ground with the gospel and used them at every level of Christian education. The missionaries recognised their ability to endure the climate better than a white man, better ability to mix with the people, and better communication through superior knowledge of the language (Calvert 1860, 430). A few select men were given posts of oversight at an early date. Twenty years later, Calvert wrote of the 1848 decision to admit four islanders as assistant missionaries with all the rights of the ministerial office:

> We were somewhat timorous of taking this step; but it answered well, and many
> have been chosen for the work since that time. There are now 44 of these de-
> voted and useful men, already thus ordained, or on trial. (Calvert, 1870, 562–63)

Calvert updated this in 1884 when the missionaries, eleven in all, were outnumbered by fifty-one Fijian ministers, thirty-two catechists, and 1,729 local preachers (laymen) (1884, xiv).

If these Fijian agents received little publicity in England, it was because the folk there wanted to know about "our missionaries" (i.e., the men "we send forth and support"). But in the private records of the missionaries, their Fijian colleagues figure prominently, and the missionaries themselves frequently inspired the island leaders to write down their stories. In this way Fison acquired the autobiographical account of James Havea and Joeli Bulu. The latter being of book length, he translated it for publication. Fison's translation retains the character and rhythm of the original—I have read them both (1871). R. H. Codrington did the same with the autobiography of Clement Marau, the Melanesian deacon. Fison's little book on Sefanaia Bilivucu is probably also a translated autobiography—it has the music of Fijian narrative about it.

The life story of Osea Ligeremaluoga has been translated by Ella Collins and published under the title *The Erstwhile Savage.* It is a New Ireland story told in a delightfully conversational style, even to his impressions of the preaching of a Fijian missionary (1932, 78–80), and his experience in connection with preaching his own first sermon (80–81).

During my Solomon Islands research in 1964 I came across a small book, *From Heathen Boy to Christian Priest*, about Taloifuila, which although written by a missionary, A. I. Hopkins, was a biography which seemed to have been built up on reminiscences. There are, of course, many biographies written by missionaries, like R. C. Nicholson's *Son of a Savage*, based on the life of Daniel Bula; and biographical articles—for instance, "Harry Raeno," "Solomon Damusoe," and "Timothy Loe," etc., among the *Metcalfe Papers*, which have now been microfilmed by Pacific Manscripts Bureau.

The biographies written by missionaries may offer an appreciation or evaluation from the angle of a Westerner, but when the rhythm and idiom of the prose strongly suggests translation, it may be assumed that much autobiographical material has been included. This usually stands out very clearly to one who knows the vernacular language. Sometimes a missionary narrated his own experiences, identifying them throughout with an island fellow worker. Paton's *Lomai of Lenakel* is a good example of this type. Such works do point up the personal cross-cultural relationships between Christian workers, at least from the missionary side, and within such limits are valid evidence.

Also not to be overlooked are the memoirs published immediately after the death of some prominent islander, a life story reconstruction by a writer who knew the deceased personally, and in a book which was circulated among others who knew him. The most famous of these was Dwight's *Memoir of Obookiah*. It has been recently republished as a paperback after a century and a half.

Another source of indigenous autobiographical material is the large excerpts from their accounts translated by some missionary for inclusion in his own book. A good example of this is the "Narrative of Peter Vi," fairly literally translated in West's book on Tonga (1865, 360–68). I found this important data for my study of the people movements in Southern Polynesia (1971, 79–82).

R. H. Codrington and Lorimer Fison were not the only anthropologically orientated missionaries to set out to preserve the biography of outstanding islanders. Another was George Brown, author of *Melanesians and Polynesians* (1910). In 1898 he wrote an article "Life History of a Savage," which reconstructed the story of a New Britain individual from his birth to his death, not the narrative of a particular identified person, although he had assembled it from observing people he actually knew.

The methodology for handling biographical and autobiographical data of this kind has been discussed by Kluckhohn (1945). He points out the need for exploring the potential of these documents and how research based on them may be developed, controlled, and tested (79). He also believed that, because these documents are so widely scattered, their "collective bulk is probably not appreciated, even within the profession" (80). Annotation should be done by a person familiar with the material, the culture (146), and the language used in the documents.

There is no shortcut to this kind of research, at least to those who pioneer the field. Even if someone has paved the way by translating a manuscript, one still should know the language and be able to feel the rhythms and emotions of the translation. One only has to listen to an evening entertainment of both Polynesian and Melanesian artists to realise that all Polynesians are not rhythmically identical, even though they borrow from each other.

Kluckhohn is certainly correct about the scatter of these mission documents. The observation raises another question—what can be done about the restoration of the integrity or wholeness of archival collections (*respect des fonds*, as the archivists call it)? Supposedly it is desirable (Muller et al. 1940, 34, 38), but is it ever possible? One thing which impressed me on my travels around the manuscript repositories of the Pacific was the presence of *archival strays*. I came across a collection of letters in one place which had strayed from the Methodist Overseas Mission Archives in Sydney. They were all letters to the general secretary. One might presume he had left them behind in New Zealand en route to the islands or on his way home. Four, at least, of the letters were important to me. One was the only letter I know in the handwriting of Crawford, a young missionary who died really before getting into "harness." It is the only historical portrait I know of his personality. Another was a letter of Calvert's on a political issue of some significance, on which we badly need confirmation. Another was a letter of Edward Martin, a fugitive seaman converted under the influence of Hazlewood in Fiji, and who trained as a printer there and stayed for many years of noble service. I know all the handwritings except Crawford's, and so the genuineness is in no doubt. We can only hope that the new accessibility of documents will expose other items like this, because some of these archival strays speak to major anthropological and historical problems that are still unsettled.

Richards, at Lahaina in 1824, produced a *Memoir of Keopuolani, Late Queen of the Sandwich Islands*, within four years of the commencement of the mission. The first two chapters thrust back into the premission period, and the material must have been gathered from Keopuolani herself or other Hawaiians who knew her well. In any case it is a good picture of Hawaii at the mission contact period.

I have often thought that every Pacific mission field should produce a good volume of essays devoted to its most fascinating indigenous characters. This would require much research but it could be done. If Joeli Bulu, Ratu Cakobau, Sefanaia Bilivucu, Henry Obookiah, Daniel Bula, Clement Marau, David Vule, and Jack Taloifuila can provide enough material for a whole volume each, the men who planted the church in Fiji—say, like Ilaija Varani,

Paula Vea, Ra Esekaia, Solomoni Raduva, Josua Mateinaniu, and the missionary Wilisoni Lagi—could at least provide material for an essay on each.

Oscar Maurer's useful little booklet *Three Early Christian Leaders of Hawaii* (1945) is an interesting example of what I mean—but it is only a small sample. The three men Maurer selected were Bartimea Lalana Puaaiki, the blind preacher of Maui; David Malo, Hawaiian preacher of social righteousness; and James Kelela, first ordained Hawaiian minister and a missionary to the Marquesas. The most important of these studies is the third because Maurer is able to quote Kelala verbatim at some length, which gives the man's personality a chance to break through nicely. The extent to which this may be done would surprise many researchers. Twenty years ago [1954] in writing a long monograph, *The Christian (Fiji 1835-67)*, I found that a great many letters of indigenous Christians and their reports had been preserved for the use of anyone with the patience to search them out. At the time, the Fijian church was moving towards independence, and the process of discovering its own selfhood was not confined to the present and future. The people were aware that their own forebears had contributed much to the spread and building of the church. I made it a rule of my life to have a fund of anecdotes about the great Fijians of the past to use on all kinds of occasion, and I never once failed to get a hearing. Furthermore, I must confess, that I became more and more impressed with the character and calibre of these pioneer Fijian Christians. Some day they must claim a major volume. No history of the islands is adequate which passes them by.

As for those which were written at the time the subjects were remembered by the readers, many of these might well be reprinted now that we seem to have entered the age of facsimiles—with an introductory essay perhaps. The republication of the memoir of Obookiah to commemorate the sesquicentennary of his death was a good idea, and likewise the introduction by Albertine Loomis and the fifteen historic illustrations. This work is largely comprised of Obookiah's correspondence, and this throws much light on the character of his conversion and the burden on his heart. It shows up the historic role he played in inspiring the church in America to undertake the mission to Hawaii. "Slender and simple as it was," says Miss Loomis, "this book shaped the future of Hawaii" (1968, xi).

This article makes no attempt at a comprehensive survey of missionary material. For example, I have not discussed material in private hands to any great extent, letter books, newspaper cuttings books, obituaries, book reviews and vernacular publications for purposes of Christian growth of converts, translations of Scripture and hymns, all of which exist in abundance. There are enough editions of the Fijian Scriptures and hymnbooks to study semantic change in them over 150 years. I have merely intended to make two points, namely that (1) the primary sources are there for any who undertake to prepare themselves to use them, and (2) there is far more historical and anthropological raw material of very high value in the missionary sources than has generally been realised.

REFERENCES

Brown, George. 1898. Life history of a Savage. *Proceedings of the Australian Association for the Advancement of Science* 7: 778–90.

———. 1910. *Melanesians and Polynesians: Their life histories described and compared.* London: Macmillan.

Bulu, Joeli. 1871. *Joeli Bulu: The autobiography of a native minister in the South Seas.* Trans. Lorimer Fison. London: Wesleyan Mission House.

———. n.d. *Ai Tuhituku ni Noqu Bula.* Unpublished manuscript.

Calvert, James. 1860. *Fiji and the Fijians.* Vol. 2, *Mission history.* London: Alexander Heylin.

———. 1870. *Fiji and the Fijians.* Vol. 2, *Mission history,* 4th ed. London: Charles H. Kelly.

———. 1884. *Fiji and the Fijians.* One-volume edition. London: Charles H. Kelly.

Dwight, Edwin W. 1830. *Memoir of Obookiah: A native of Owhyhee.* Philadelphia: American Sunday School Union, 1830.

———. 1968. *Memoirs of Henry Obookiah: A native of Owhyhee.* Ed. Albertine Loomis. Honolulu: Woman's Board of Missions for the Pacific Islands, Hawaii Conference, United Church of Christ.

Fison, Lorimer. n.d. *Old Sefanaia, the Fijian herald, by a friend of his.* London: Charles H. Kelly.

Havea, Jemesa. n.d. *Ai Tukutuku ni Noqu Bula.* Unpublished manuscript.

Hopkins, A. I. 1949. *From heathen boy to Christian priest.* London: Society for Promoting Christian Knowledge.

Kluckhohn, Clyde. 1945. The personal document in anthropological science. In *The use of personal documents in history, anthropology and sociology,* ed. Louis Gottschalk, Clyde Kluckhohn, and Robert Angell, 78–173. Bulletin 53. New York: Social Science Research Council.

Ligeremaluoga, Osea. 1932. *The erstwhile savage: An account of the life of Ligeremaluoga.* Trans. Ella Collins. Melbourne: Cheshire.

Loomis, Albertine. 1968. Introduction. In *Memoirs of Henry Obookiah: A native of Owhyhee,* ed. E. Dwight. Honolulu: Woman's Board of Missions for the Pacific Islands, Hawaii Conference, United Church of Christ.

Marau, Clement. 1894. *The story of a Melanesian deacon.* Trans. R. H. Codrington. London: Society for Promoting Christian Knowledge.

Maurer, Oscar E. 1945. *Three early Christian leaders of Hawaii.* Honolulu: Board of the Hawaiian Evangelical Association.

Metcalfe, John F. n.d.(a) The Gumi family. Unpublished manuscript.

———. n.d.(b) Harry Raeno. Unpublished manuscript.

———. n.d.(c) Solomon Damusoe. Unpublished manuscript.

———. n.d.(d) The three brothers. Unpublished manuscript.

———. n.d.(e) Timothy Loe. Unpublished manuscript.

Muller, S., J. H. Feith, and R. Fruin. 1940. *Manual for the arrangement and description of archives.* Trans. A. H. Leavitt. New York: Wilson.

Nicholson, R. C. 1924. *Son of a savage: The story of Daniel Bula.* London: Epworth.

Paton, H. L. 1903. *Lomai of Lenakel: A hero of the New Hebrides.* New York: Revell.

Richards, W. 1825. *Memoir of Keopuolani, late queen of the Sandwich Islands.* Boston: Crocker & Brewster.

Rycroft, Harold R. 1926. *From savagery to Christ: The story of David Vule.* London: Epworth.

Tippett, Alan R. 1954. *The Christian (Fiji 1835–67).* Auckland: Institute Publishing.

———. 1971. *People movements in Southern Polynesia.* Chicago: Moody.

Vi, Peter. 1865. Peter Vi's narrative. In *Ten years in the south-central Pacific Islands (Friendly Islands).* London: Nisbet.

Waterhouse, Joseph. 1866. *The king and people of Fiji.* London: Wesleyan Conference Office.

14

THE RELEVANCE OF ARCHIVAL DEVELOPMENTS IN THE SOUTHWEST PACIFIC[47]

A Fiji government department recently set its imprint on a quasi-official history without any qualifying comment and placed it on the official list of publications (Eason 1951). The book concerned Rotuma,[48] in which two semipublic bodies were much interested. The book was also highly biased and inaccurate. The colonial secretary found it necessary to write to one of these bodies,[49] pointing out that the book was not official and had to stand on its own merits. The other body[50] published a series of highly critical articles in its monthly journal, and substantiated its claims. Subsequently a high government official expressed his opinion to me that the book should never have been printed. Had the bodies concerned been other than Christian missionary organisations, it is probable the government would have found itself in serious legal trouble, for there is libel in the book.

The episode brings to light a number of relevant facts. Had there been properly established archives in the colony at the time, the whole thing need never have happened. The government was in difficulties because other institutions had their records available and could produce evidence quickly, challenge the so-called historian, and substantiate their claims. From a government point of view (or from the viewpoint of any other agency, for that matter), one of the stated purposes of archives and records is protection of the government or agency. The history in question is a typical work of the writer who gleans most of his facts from secondary sources, selecting what suits him, rather than evaluating them carefully, making judgments in the light of present-day affairs instead of seeing things in the historic sense, confusing characters who happen to have the same surnames, quoting passages completely out of their context, paying no serious attention to sequence, failing to observe facts that should be related, reading his own mind into sources instead of quoting correctly—or to put it in a single phrase, making every error of historical method.

---

47 Taken from the bound collection of articles entitled *The Distribution and Use of Documents in Oceania*, 1972. Unpublished article, written in 1955.

48 Rotuma, three hundred miles north of Fiji, distinct in race, custom, and language, is, however, under the administration of the British crown colony of Fiji.

49 The Methodist Church in Fiji.

50 The Roman Catholic Mission in Fiji.

Yet the government not only accepted his work but published it, placed a government imprint on it, had the administrator of the area write an introduction, and placed it on their official list. How was this possible? It was possible because the colony needed a history of Rotuma, and needed it badly. There was no other person in the field but the person who wrote that book, no one who knew the subject well enough to evaluate it before its publication, and no archival records catalogued so points could be verified. The poverty of its bibliography indicates the superficiality of its research, and I myself can testify to the fact that semipublic archival matter was available for him to use, and offered, but declined, or at least not used, which indicates that he was writing his own point of view, not a history at all. So the government's only history on Rotuma in the official list is a personal viewpoint of a present-day observer. This covers a period of local tension, religious and political, and of grim culture conflict.

Its importance is more than local, as it was one of the islands, for instance, which came under British legislation aimed at dealing with British subjects in islands belonging to no great power, and the most important of these acts to Rotuma is not even mentioned.[51] The failure to state this legislation invalidates his judgments on the events. Unfortunately the book may be taken as reliable overseas, if for no other reason than because of the government imprint. This has significance to all students of British foreign policy in the Pacific. Quite apart from the damage this may do away from the colony, sooner or later historians are bound to discredit it, and that will bring discredit to the Fiji government. Fortunately there were historically minded people in Fiji who knew enough to realise what had happened, and an expression of disapproval was made at the time.

The illustration, however, is not meant to throw light on this particular book, but rather on the predicament with which a government found itself faced, through leaving its own responsibility to historically minded private persons. Ever since the French Revolution, the two concepts of the government's responsibility to (1) preserve public documents, and (2) make them accessible, have been well known, and most British countries have at some time or other since then inserted these two elements into their legislation. Preservation and accessibility would have saved the government from much embarrassment. Well-organised archives are certainly a protective institution.

The illustration quoted does not by any means stand alone. Many colonial officials, preparing reports for printing, though providing valuable current data, bring their whole work into discredit, and leave the critical reader wanting to debate historical points instead of dwelling on the findings of the paper, which are actually the purpose of its compilation. Furthermore, in the countries of the southwest Pacific, like Fiji, Tonga, Samoa, New Caledonia, and the New Hebrides, where there is a fairly rapid change under culture contact, it

---

51   *Pacific Islands Protection Bill*, 1875.

is essential for administrators, educators, missionaries, and other leaders (who belong to the new culture) to get their historical backgrounds correct. This is not a mere interest in history for history's sake, but in the environment itself, wherein they work, where the real problems of the present arise from the historical issues of the recent or subrecent past.

Thus, for instance, it is not good for the press to report one day the text of a speech delivered by the director of medical services on the history of Saint John's Ambulance activity in the colony, and to find the same paper correcting his erroneous statements a day or so later.[52]

The Stephens Report on Education was eagerly awaited. Educational policy was to be reorganised in the light of it. Alas, it contained over 160 inaccuracies, many of them of basic historical and cultural background (Colony of Fiji 1944). Annual reports of the director of education (of all people) have revealed the same shortcomings (*Fiji Times and Herald*), and the Colonial Office has a somewhat superficial and biased historical survey, which is reprinted with each annual report of the colony of Fiji, despite the criticisms of it that have been made locally.

From time to time statements are made in the legislative council by unofficial or Indian members, which reveal the existence of important source material on official matters, which is apparently not readily available in official circles. A statement of this sort I remember being made recently by an Indian member regarding the breakdown in repatriation of Indian indenture labour. The statement had to pass, as records could not be produced readily (if at all) to deal with it. Although this was a statement of history many years ago, it had a current value on a "live" issue. There is a story in circulation, in what I take to be reliable circles, of the destruction of a great quantity of official records relative to this subject, when the chest which housed them was required for other purposes.[53]

These items, mainly of local interest, serve to show something of much wider import— viz., that archives and historical records can have a current social and political significance long after they were compiled, perhaps in any community, but certainly in an insular one. It also demonstrates the importance of accessibility and efficient catalogue procedure, and the perils and insecurity faced by a government which doesn't attend to the matter. This real situation is seen, furthermore, to be accentuated in a community where culture change is rapid or productive of tension, especially where native land tenure, foreign race infiltrations, population changes, and Western commercial expansion are all met with together, as in Fiji, for instance. It is as essential for administrators, missionaries, and public leaders to have an appreciation of local history and the cultural elements of local society as it is for them to be competent workmen in their respective fields. I fail to see how this is possible without extension of archive and library facilities. That is my judgment after

52   *Fiji Times* and *Herald*.

53   Described by a Western Pacific High Commission (W.P.H.C.) archivist at a meeting of "The Fiji Society."

fifteen years in the last-mentioned colony. Something is being done now, and a competent archivist has been appointed for duties that will be specified later in this paper. The financial assistance, however, though it has made possible a good practical beginning, is quite inadequate for anything like what should be done.

The basic finding of this section of the study is that the subject of developing archives and historical library facility in the southwest Pacific is relevant. The local situation itself demands it. Let us now investigate whether or not there is sufficient historical interest in the southwest Pacific to make it relevant to the wider world.

[A lengthy section on the wider international relevance of Pacific documents has been deleted.—Ed.]

What Pacific Material Exists and Where Is It?

In the National Archives in Washington, one may see certain planters' journals set out for display. They throw light on the planters' way of life, and in particular their relations with the nearby Native Americans. These journals may be taken as characteristic of the English-speaking people who settled the out-of-the-way parts of the world. The same type of thing exists in abundance with relation to the Pacific. Many perhaps are still buried among "Grandfather's papers" in the attic, but many have found their way into public libraries, museums, missionary society offices, and private collections. They are important documents, because they were compiled by individuals who lived in the experiences they describe, at the time, and in the places mentioned. Many of them predate the days of constitutional government; some of them witnessed the first immature attempts at constitutional government under native potentates. They are basic historical data. But alas they are widely dispersed throughout the world.

A master of arts candidate in New Zealand discovered in the Turnbull Library, Wellington, a valuable collection of documents assembled by J. B. Thurston to Captain C. W. Hope. Hope had experience in Fiji as a British naval officer on official business, and Thurston was an official in King Cakobau's government, and subsequently, after Cession, became governor. He had also served earlier as British consul. This correspondence throws light on his private opinions of official matters. It is only one of many valuable manuscripts in the Turnbull Library (Crane n.d.). The MA thesis has since been used in an official history of Fiji (Derrick 1946a). This library has also produced the finest Pacific bibliography yet to appear (Taylor 1951). Another similarly valuable manuscript collection of the same period is "The Swanston Papers" in the Fiji Museum. Here again is a private record of the leading politician of the (anti-Cakobau) Ma'afu party (Derrick 1946b). They make a valuable contrast for the student of an important period.

Similar documentary sources of equal importance in the earlier period are found in the Mitchell Library, Sydney—journals and records of Thomas Williams, David Hazlewood, and Dr. Richard Bursdal Lyth, who did pioneering work in education, translation, and medicine in the 1840s and 1850s. No authoritative history on Fiji, mission or secular, covering that significant period, 1835–55, can ignore these works. Someday a medical history of the Pacific will have to be written. The writer will have to spend many hours in the Mitchell Library. The same applies to any history of the orthography of the Fijian language, though this will also require access to the Hunt Journals in London. The Mitchell Library is a recognised depository for Pacific documents, with strict custody rules.

The missionary societies which pioneered the Pacific have all their record depositories, preserving a wealth of informative material, by no means all religious. Here again we must confine this survey to one particular society, taking it as our type. We select the Wesleyan Missionary Society because it is relevant to Fiji more than any other society. At the same time, however, it must be remembered that all missionaries over the period kept records, they all wrote long reports to their parent societies, and that despite their theological differences of opinion they were alike in many ways. So this is typical only.

The Methodists have several depositories housing a great quantity of extremely valuable material on every aspect of life and culture, and to a large extent the concept of provenance has been retained. Material sent from Fiji, Australia, Tonga, and New Zealand up to 1855 is in the London archives of the missionary society, together with other material deposited there by descendants and relations of returned missionaries. Some of the rare original records have been copied, and bound typescripts are available for working copies, reference being possible to the original if required on an important point. This applies to the Hunt Journals—indispensable for custom, folklore, and language study of the pioneering period.

A separate Wesleyan Conference was created for Australia, New Zealand, Fiji, and Tonga in 1855, and the archives from that date are housed in Sydney. For practically a century they accumulated in the Sydney office, bundled or boxed as they had been used. The space they occupied was required, and an agreement was made with the Mitchell Library, which attended to the work of appraising, cataloguing, and preserving on behalf of the Methodist Overseas Missions, by which name the society now is known. The library is merely custodian, and access is possible by authority given by the society, which still retains ownership. As source material on the four countries mentioned and Samoa, which in politics, as events have turned out, represent five different types of government, these archives are important. Owing to the conception of concomitancy, which was accepted at an early date in the Pacific, a searcher would thus turn to the Wesleyan archives for Fiji, but to the Presbyterians for New Caledonia and to the London Missionary Society for Tahiti, for the fields of Protestant overlap were very few. The provenance has been retained.

Over the whole period the complementary part of records and correspondence has been retained in Fiji and the other places concerned. That in Fiji comprises official records, accounts, annual reports, minute books, letter books, rolls and registers, agendas, rough notebooks, records of special investigations, and inward letters in bundles according to subject, in which form they were arranged at the time they were received. A good deal of provenance is retained because they have been preserved hitherto in bound volumes or bundles. There are significant gaps here and there—probably due to fire and hurricane, but no doubt if the whole could be properly housed and catalogued, copies of missing material if sufficiently important could be obtained from the complementary archives. It is intended to provide proper facilities for these records in the new administrative offices shortly to be built in Suva.

These records throw light on all periods of the colony's history and contain much that has been missed by the historians. Too much has been written about the South Pacific by travelling journalists, and their work has been quoted as history. We are now faced with rewriting much of that history in the light of the evidence of documents of the period. The writer, for example, produced a monograph a year or so ago, which was based mainly on his own manuscript library and these particular archives (Tippett 1954). An English historical publication [*Journal of the Wesleyan Historical Society*] reviewing the monograph said that much which had been written of Fijian history now required to be rewritten in the light of the evidence documented in the monograph. Actually the monograph had only investigated several aspects of a single issue. Other similar issues are awaiting attention.

The official archives of the Western Pacific High Commission (WPHC) have now been established at Suva, Fiji, although Fiji does not fall under the jurisdiction of that body. This establishment houses some unique material of great importance to the study of international affairs in the Pacific. To take a single example—I myself have worked there on a certain bound volume, which contains the outward correspondence of the British consul in Fiji during the 1860s. I was seeking information regarding the attitude of the consul towards the matter of the murder of the Rev. Thomas Baker by the mountain cannibals. I not only found my answer, but also elements of background which had not been found in the scores of documents from other sources which I had examined beforehand. It was found to tie up with social and political issues of major importance, the matter of native lands and foreign settlement, and consular interference in local politics. In other words, a story, hitherto taken to be of more domestic importance, has to be reevaluated. It is no longer an isolated episode, but important evidence in the study of local tensions at the time.[54] That is but an example of one piece of evidence, in one very large volume in a most interesting collection of documents.

We have here also material of a highly official nature relative to developments in islands some distance from Fiji—Tonga, the British Solomons, the Gilbert and Ellice Islands.

---

54   Baker's own journals are in the Methodist Overseas Mission Archives in the Mitchell Library, Sydney.

It covers official inquiries into disturbances, instructions from the Foreign Office,[55] references to agreements and treaties, and a great number of reports, correspondence, and routine administration documents. Anyone contemplating research on the islands that fell under the WPHC, will see at once that they should visit Suva.

Since the provision of a building and the appointment of an archivist, a great deal of appraisal, cataloguing, and physical work has been done, and much valuable material is now accessible. The work was hindered by the bad state of the material, heavy damage by cockroaches and silverfish, water damage through hurricanes, and the fading of ink through tropical fungi, and the disintegration of paper through the same cause. Certain inks used about a century ago have apparently contained chemicals which have eaten through the paper, so that it tends to disintegrate along the strokes of the letters. Inward correspondence of the colonial period was folded horizontally, usually in four. Experience shows these to have split along the folds. Insects also have chosen to eat along the folds, and often important phrases are thereby lost. At present, material is being flattened out for preservation in flat folders.

The British consular outward correspondence referred to above is in excellent condition and almost unaffected by any of the tropical forms of depreciation described. The quality of the paper is good, the ink has retained its color, and the binding of this huge volume is sound.

Furthermore it reveals interesting information on the British consular office procedure for preserving records and the classification of the same. It conforms to the old type of registry system, in that outward and inward correspondence are segregated. This volume in question—outward mail—has been written by hand, each communication being carefully copied from the original prior to its dispatch from the office. Being a bound volume, the letters are in chronological sequence, but the registry system used is constant throughout.

A brief description—little more than a title—appears at the head of each letter and indicates that the letter is from the British consul or acting consul at Fiji, to the Foreign Secretary, or the Commodore of the British Pacific Squadron in Australian waters, or the American consul in Fiji, or whoever else it might happen to be. So the letters are neither classified according to subject dealt with nor recipient. This has some importance to the student of history, as letters written at the same time to entirely different persons often are seen to have bearing on each other.

An identification number appears in the top left-hand margin of each letter. These symbols conform to type in this respect—that the first two digits represent the third and fourth digits of the year, and after a crosshatch, appears the number of the letter for that

---

55   In the consular period Fiji came under the Foreign Office not the Secretary of State for Colonies.

particular year. Thus a letter bearing the symbol 67/102 would be the 102nd letter written in 1867 from the consular office. In many cases a code letter is also used. I believe this to be a reference to a complementary file of inward correspondence relevant to the letter in question. The letter *S*, for instance (I write from memory on this point), refers to the South Pacific Squadron file.

As to the archival material of the British crown colony of Fiji, its availability for research will depend entirely on the finance and the staff provided by the government. The work of appraisal alone that has to be done is a tremendous one, particularly so as there is no basic history of the period since Cession, no extensive bibliographies or other aids. It is appraisal under difficulties over a period when the colony has had three official languages—English, Fijian, and Hindi.

Mention of languages other than English brings us to what is probably one of the world's most unique archives. I refer to the official findings and holdings of the Fijian Native Lands Commission. This was a huge project that was conducted in a most thorough fashion over the period of many years. Its ultimate aim was to establish the land holdings of the tribes and clans, throughout the whole of the 280 islands of the Fiji Group, by the investigation of their tribal oral histories, migrations, wars, and settlement. It was commenced under the guidance of a highly competent European and fluent speaker of Fijian, but in later years it has been under Fijian leadership.[56] The inquiries have been conducted throughout in the vernacular, and in consequence this archival source is entirely in the Fijian language. It has been a monumental task, and a huge quantity of records have been assembled to describe the possession of the lands by the people. These records, as the investigated and accepted oral traditions of hundreds of tribes, have legal status. Their social importance is no more than their scientific value to the anthropologist, however—provided he will learn the language. Here is a mine of information on folklore, culture, old religion, and migrations. Access, however, is difficult. Enquiries conducted by the Commission were in harmony with the methods for investigating tribal histories as laid down by Capell and Lester for research workers (1941).

Suva's nicely planned museum stands in the Botanical Gardens. It has among its treasures a small collection of historic documents. Some of these have bearing on the activities of Cakobau, the paramount chief of Fiji, at the time of Cession. There is a good assortment of reference magazines, bound, files and photographs, and a few odd items like the sea journal of David Cargill, who came to Fiji in 1835 from Tonga. The Bishop Museum and Library in Honolulu has some similarly valuable material.

Several government departments have highly interesting archival materials (quite apart from their normal records), most notably the Lands Department and Department of

---

56   Ratu Sir Lala Sukana, an Oxford graduate.

Agriculture. The former has many original documents of historic significance. For example, I have seen there a parchment throwing light on the policy of Ma'afu, and his dealings with Cakobau and revealing something of the background of the establishment of small Tongan settlements or colonies in many parts of the Fiji Group; quite important data for a historian. The Department of Agriculture had assembled valuable research records from Fiji and other tropical places. Interest has long been shown in nearby island groups, especially those with destructive insects, and information over a wide field has thus been collected. The post office records are considerable, and have been used on several occasions recently by philatelic historians for articles in overseas publications. The Medical Department has a most interesting history. Some of its special projects interest medical people far afield—work on tuberculosis and leprosy are two cases, for instance. The inter-island project of a central medical school for the South and Western Pacific was aided in its commencement by Carnegie Foundation funds, and students from American islands are in residence there.

The fact that valuable records have been indiscriminately burnt to provide space, shows that the time has come for central archives in Fiji on a big scale, and for the establishment of legal procedure for the reception, appraisal, cataloguing, and preservation of official documents of permanent value and the disposal of material of no permanent value.

To pass now from official and semipublic archives to those of commerce and private persons, I confine myself to two examples.

Sir Alport Barker, the proprietor of the Suva newspaper *Fiji Times and Herald* has among his exceptional collection of Pacific books and documents, a complete file of series of newspapers published by his predecessors and himself. They are his official record and, therefore, may be classed as true archives. He has at times made them available for research by *bona fide* students. They were a major source for Mr. Crain's thesis mentioned above. Although they naturally represent a viewpoint, they are pertinent for all research on public issues, labour problems, racial conflict, popular ideas, and public criticism of policy of a government that always has an official majority.[57]

My second example is the Dr. Lorimer Fison Archives, which are also in Fiji. These cover the period of two decades from 1864, as far as Fiji is concerned. Prior to that they have important bearing on the Australian gold rush, and subsequently to political troubles in Tonga. Fison also did much anthropological research on tribes of Australian Aborigines which are now extinct. He corresponded with eminent anthropologists in all parts of the world, and the archives contain this material—Tylor, Frazer, Codrington, and many

---

57 Although the Fijian, European, and Indian citizens have their representatives in the Legislative Council in Fiji, there is always an official majority. They may thus register protest to a measure, but they cannot defeat the measure. At best they can ask it be sent to a select committee. This makes the view of the Fijian newspaper very much the more important to the historian.

others being among them. One lot of correspondence, unfortunately, has been alienated. That was sold I think to Yale—the correspondence of Lewis Henry Morgan [this correspondence is now at the University of Rochester]. The Fison Archives include not only inwards correspondence but letter books of outward mail, journals, private correspondence with government officers and political figures (with private opinions on public issues), cuttings books, manuscript copies of Fison's scientific papers, sketch maps of islands and other localities visited eighty years ago, showing villages no longer in existence, notebooks, printed papers with his marginal notes, material prepared for publication before his death, extensive research on kinship, island mythology, comparative language study, research on obscure cults, and on land tenure customs and terminology. He had provided his Fijian friends with small notebooks in which they wrote accounts of their experiences, and also described customs, myths, vows, and many other matters. He served as newspaper correspondent to the *Sydney Morning Herald* and kept a file copy of his articles. They provide a sequence of valuable nonofficial commentary on public affairs in Fiji at the time. He participated in the great controversy on the South Sea slavery issue, and kept press cuttings, both for and against. He figured in two historic law cases, with merit in each, and has preserved the data of the cases.

Useful Adjuncts

In addition to these records, there are half a dozen good private libraries of Pacific literature in Fiji. Most of these are owned by active members of the Fiji Society, which indicates that they have been assembled for the sake of their subject matter rather than as mere collections. Their owners are students, and many of the articles published by the Fiji Society[58] are the result of their labour.

These libraries contain a basis of printed books, primary sources in that they were written in the first place by men who worked in the Pacific and collected original data for them; they tell their own experiences and observations. There are some hundreds of them, produced by missionaries, naval captains, and scientific persons.

Then in addition to these, there exists a great number of secondary sources of more recent composition, themselves based on library research. These vary from very poor to very good, but some of them provide excellent bibliographies and are useful aids for the archivist.

Some of these libraries also have collections of vernacular literature, written perhaps for entertainment, religious, or educational purposes; they provide valuable linguistic material for the student. Most important of all to the historian are the files of *Na Mata* and *Ai Tukutuku Vakalotu*, the government and missionary monthlies which have been appearing for about sixty years. They give the historian who can read Fijian the official and mission

---

58   Published as Proceedings of the Fiji Society.

viewpoint on public issues over that long period. The former has also published much data from the Native Lands Commission reports, and the latter is essential for a picture of the Fijian missionary enterprise in New Britain, New Ireland, Papua, and the British Solomons. Scores of valuable letters written home to Fiji by the Fijian missionaries are published in full. It is the only known source of material of purely native origin that has not gone through the translator's hands, on those tremendously interesting native missionary activities. A collection of early copies of *Ai Tukutuku Vakalotu* is indeed a treasure. An almost complete set of that period exists in Fiji.

Finally these private libraries, each in its own peculiar field, have some good manuscript material, important and unique. Some of the collectors have gone to some trouble also to copy records beyond their reach and prepare a typescript for information and working purposes. As manuscripts they have no legal status, but as working tools they are most useful.

Because of the activity of this small group of scientifically and historically minded people, much valuable material has been rescued, and much brought into the limelight. There is a deeper interest in these things today than there was before. The fact that so much has been assembled in a decade or so, that was not known to have existed before, is itself evidence of appreciation of historic records. This increasing appreciation must eventually lead to some more adequate provision for preservation of the things appreciated. We hope it will not be too long delayed.

[Conclusion and Recommendations not included.]

REFERENCES

Capell, A., and R. H. Lester. 1941. *Local divisions and movements in Fiji.* Sydney: Australasian Medical Pub. Co.

Colony of Fiji. 1951. *Colony of Fiji.* Suva: H. M. Stationery Office.

———. 1944. *The Stephens report on education in Fiji.* Suva: H. M. Stationery Office.

Crane, E. A. n.d. *King Cakobau's government.* Unpublished manuscript.

Derrick, R. A. 1946a. *History of Fiji.* Vol. 1. Suva: Fiji Government Printer.

———. 1946b. The Swanston papers. *Procedings of the Fiji Society* (July).

Eason, W. J. 1951. *A short history of Rotuma.* Suva: Fiji Government Printer.

Fiji Times and Herald. 1951. History and progress of education in Fiji, 20 February.

Taylor, C. R. H. 1951. *A Pacific bibliography.* Wellington, New Zealand: Polynesian Society.

Tippett, Alan R. 1954. *The Christian (Fiji 1835–67).* Auckland: Institute Publishing.

Wesleyan Historical Society. *Journal of the Wesleyan Historical Society,* London.

PART THREE

Synchronic and Diachronic Studies

15

A SYNCHRONIC ETHNOHISTORICAL RECONSTRUCTION[59]

One of the profitable dimensions of ethnohistory as a research methodology is the reconstruction of the synchronic ethnographic description at some precise point of time in the past (Sturtevant 1966, 6–8). This is being explored more and more since the breakdown of colonialism and the new availability of historical documents from the old colonial archives. The exploration in these new facilities by scholars in the disciplines of history and anthropology has revealed many hitherto untapped resources with tremendous potential. From among these resources many personal documents—diaries, journals, and correspondence—have been brought to light. The majority of these new resources are official, but one is continually surprised at the discovery of important personal records created by planters, missionaries, traders, and slavers from Oceania—all of which give a different viewpoint from the official records.

A diary of this kind covering, say, a decade of history in a remote island in the period of Pacific kidnapping, permits a synchronic reconstruction. So much of the popular Pacific "history" has been *created* by historians and historical novelists, rather than *re-created* by historians capturing the relationships which give a diary its cohesive entity. This distinction was articulated by the historian Gottschalk (1945, 9), who insisted that the historian's imagination be directed to re-creation rather than creation.[60] We create, for example, when we go to our sources to select evidence to establish our hypotheses about historical events. We re-create history when we take our primary sources whole and struggle to discover their own implications.

I believe we have still much to learn about discovering the wholeness of a journal or diary as a primary source. One journal may be worth more than a hundred apt quotations. I am reminded of Lord Acton's letter to the contributors to the *Cambridge Modern History*

---

59 Taken from *Aspects of Pacific Ethnohistory* (Pasadena: William Carey Library, 1973), 105–25. Used by permission.

60 Historical novelists have been particularly irresponsible at this point. James Michener's treatment of Hawaiian history is a good (or bad) example of *creation* where one might have expected to have found *re-creation*. Although he admits the book is a novel and the characters are fictitious, nevertheless he claims his writing to be "true to the spirit and history of Hawaii." Herman Melville, in an earlier period, manipulated what he saw. His claim of four months residence in Typee, by the logs of ships is found to be four weeks, which makes a great deal of difference for the validity of his anthropology.

in which he spoke of the historian Froude consulting 100,000 papers in manuscript for his major work, and to which Acton added, "That is still the price to be paid for mastery" (Stern 1963, 248). I would certainly agree that the price of relentless industry has to be paid, and I feel bad about one of my students imagining he has completed his thesis when there are still unexplored resources in our own library. However, I would rather have my manuscript confined to the analysis of a single journal and capture its cohesive implications and wholeness than be distinguished for its voluminous footnotes. I very much doubt that 100,000 papers can ever be adequately studied by a single person, if one has to project himself historically into another period of time, or ethnographically into another culture.

Before taking an actual journal for examination and discussion, I need to make three comments about this kind of primary source material.

First, in the disciplines of both anthropology and missiology we are much concerned today with social or cultural change—terms which cover, among other things, the process of conversion from animism to Christianity. Allied to this religious experience is the whole area of cultural dynamics, including the how and why of the acceptance and rejection of new ideas or innovations. In the history of the last century or two in the Pacific, there are many gaps in our information just at this very point. The phenomenological regularities in culture change (including religious change) have not always been noted. Kluckhohn ascribed this shortcoming to paying "too little attention to the concrete individuals in whom the changes actually begin" (1945, 136). One main thesis of this paper is that the use of a missionary journal or an administrator's personal diary, when studied as a whole, often makes it possible to rectify this shortcoming. In the Pacific area the sandalwooders, missionaries, whalers, planters, traders, and escaped convicts were all agents of change— conscious or unconscious—and many of them kept journals of their experiences. Such a primary source from any one of them is valuable, because we meet the author as a reacting personality in his real-life context.

Second, much so-called history is far too simplistic with events frequently attributed, for example, to a single cause. Writers on Pacific missions in particular have time and time again interpreted conversion (especially group conversion) to a single cause. I devote an appendix to this in *People Movements in Southern Polynesia* in dealing with the case of the conversion of Tahiti (1971, 221–26). Behind a conversion movement one usually discovers (1) a whole complex of specific events, (2) a significant number of key persons, and (3) a set of distinct and precise relationships between them. As Barzun says of the ways of culture history, there is

> no short cut to arrive at an understanding of relationships . . . cultural life is in-
> tricate and emotionally complex. One must be steeped in the trivia of a period,
> one must be a virtual intimate with its principal figures. (1963, 394–95)

A personal document may thus not only fill in a gap in the record of historical information, but also reveal something of the situational complexity and the personal interactions of the characters. Such discoveries are truly exciting.

Third, we have a concept from the historian Renier (1965, 97–105), who takes the Latin word *vestigium*, meaning "the *trace* left by the sole of the foot and also the sole of the foot itself." He speaks of documents, diaries, memoirs, and letters as *traces*, because either by direct statement or by implication they are traces of the original writer's desire to record events he had experienced for future reference. The fact that the word can be used for either the footprint or the foot is employed to imply a fairly close relationship between the footprint and the foot which made it. Renier discusses historical method as *discovering traces*, and then moving from the traces to the events which caused their imprint, from the primary sources to the *events* which stimulated the long since deceased writer to record them in his lifetime.

After that rather long introductory preamble, I now purpose taking such a personal document as I have been discussing theoretically, and examining its contents in some detail by means of a suggested research model. I shall try to reconstruct a synchronic description at a precise point of time, bringing out the social factors and personal relationships in a decade of culture change in a remote Pacific island, and proceeding from the traces to the events.

The Methodological Tool

From some scores of possible personal documents, I have selected the *Journal of the Rev. John Geddie*, which comprises five exercise book volumes, located at the Latrobe Library in Melbourne. The journal covers the period from 29 July 1848 to 11 December 1857—a few months short of a decade. Geddie was a minister of the Presbyterian Church of Nova Scotia and planted the first Christian church in the island of Aneiteum in the New Hebrides.

The journal reveals a drama of cultural change being played out in a dynamic struggle between three different types of people with very different value systems—the native animists of the island, the missionaries, and a number of white adventurers. In each group I could go on further and break down the categories into personality types or individuals, for the data is open to a more sophisticated analysis than the length of this paper permits. We have to be satisfied with the three basic groups, which are very clear-cut. I am saying here that in this ethnographic synchronic reconstruction we find three clear-cut cultural complexes *in a state of tension and interaction within a cohesive whole*. In behavior, social values, morals, and religion the three complexes are quite distinct from each other and clash at every point. Yet the very clash gives a dynamic wholeness to the greater configuration which the journal depicts.

Against this threefold encounter, which was the New Hebridean world of 1848–57, the Christian gospel was offered, and a church was planted. It was a decade of culture change. Here is a study in microcosm of what was going on in many parts of the Pacific. The key factors of the 1840s and 1850s converge and focus on Aneiteum, and here is a record of it left by the man who planted the church in that island. But it is an equilibrium of tension and not merely a biography that lies hidden in these five exercise books.

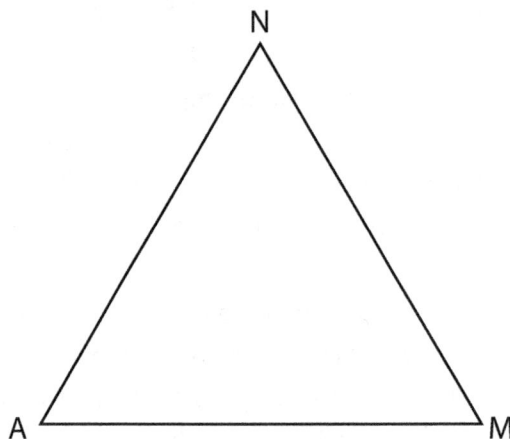

To coordinate and present my material I shall use a research model as a methodological tool. I call it the *triangle of personal relationships*. In the triangle NAM, N represents the native animists, A the foreign adventurers, and M the missionaries. The sides of the triangle represent the personal relationships between the two parties represented by the alphabetical symbols—NA, AM, or MN as the case may be. The perimeter of the triangle represents the total configuration.[61] By using such a model I hope to establish Barzun's claim that "in history no single element is a prime mover, no single kind of clue an explanation of everything else" (1963, 392). To this I want to add my own claim that conversion does not result simply from the relationship MN, or that between the advocate and the acceptor (using those terms anthropologically [Barnett 1953]), but always takes place in the ramifications of a configuration involving many persons and forces.

The triangle is a useful tool. It does help one to ask the right questions about the different relationships. But it is theoretical. When you actually struggle with the data and identify MN or MA, you will never find them in isolation. You are continually brought back, not to the side of the triangle, but to the perimeter. Always to describe MN I had to introduce both MA and NA. We are reminded that analysis is always abstraction and, hav-

---

61   The triangle is the simplest possible model for this kind of reconstruction. In reality one might require a multisided figure. The point is, however, that a simple MN relationship is never an adequate explanation for conversion. Furthermore, there is always at least one kind of A—maybe many. The motives of the sandalwooders, whalers, escaped convicts, and blackbirders were never quite the same, but they can be grouped because they all came into conflict with the missionaries and actively obstructed church planting. Their social values were also similar.

ing served its purpose, in reality you are still left with the synthesis with which you began; and there is something in the synthesis which is more than the sum of its parts.

Many missiologists say that, because the Scriptures show that M should establish an advocate relationship with N (Matt 28:20), there is nothing more to say on the matter. But it is better argued on a basis of John 17, where the emphasis is on the world to which the apostles are sent, that the Christian mission takes place in a context not a vacuum, and that there cannot be an MN relationship without there also being an MA and an NA relationship. For purposes of study we break down our model into its parts, but in reality it always remains a whole thing.

The Journal as a Cultural Complex

John Geddie arrived at Aneiteum in the famous LMS [London Missionary Society] vessel *John Williams*, taking with him teachers from Samoa. Later he mentioned Rarotongans also. This lifted Geddie out of his Nova Scotia Presbyterian background and associated him with the LMS work of the southeastern and south-central Pacific, which had over fifty years of Pacific mission experience before 1848, where the journal starts. These Samoan and Rarotongan helpers were Polynesians. The people of Aneiteum were Melanesians. Thus the assistants whom the missionaries (and missionary historians) usually regarded as "Pacific islanders" rather than precisely as Polynesians were not differentiated from the Melanesians. Indeed the documents about the Melanesian blackbirding trade speak of these islanders as Polynesians. This imprecision of terminology led to much cultural confusion. Westerners did not realise that Polynesian missionaries to Melanesia were just as much *foreign* missionaries as they were themselves.[62]

The Samoans had been placed in Aneiteum before the arrival of Geddie and were able to interpret for him while he was learning the language. Geddie accepted this as adequate for the start, but I should add that the early Polynesians themselves had trouble articulating some of the Melanesian sounds and were not always good communicators once they went outside Polynesia.

Neither were they always particular about Melanesian custom. One of the first problems Geddie experienced in the NM relationship was due to the frequent offence taken by the local animists because of Samoan behavior with respect to their customs. For example, a taboo had been placed on a crop of nuts so that they would be preserved for an approaching feast. This is a normal practice all over Melanesia, and one is surprised that the Samoans ignored it. It put the missionaries in a bad position with the people. Geddie had to come to terms on behalf of the mission, apologize for his ignorance, and promise to observe these taboos (*itaup*) thereafter. This was not the only case. The teachers had taken

---

62   For example, for some time the Indian indentured labourers were treated as Pacific islanders in Fiji. The first Fijian pastor appointed to minister to them was selected because he had done overseas service in New Britain.

coral from the reef to make lime for housebuilding (an art they had learned from other missionaries further east, and at which they were very skilled). Thus we see them as agents of change in the area of material culture as much as the white missionaries and traders. Apparently they collected the lime without ascertaining first that the reef was taboo. Eventually the Christians had to agree that after completing this project they would burn no more lime. A third incident concerned their "closing of the path to the sea," a religious obstruction, as indeed they all were. The fact that a number of such incidents appear in the early part of the first volume, and the accompanying fact that Geddie devoted so much space to recording them, shows up this relationship as a major problem of their initial contact which very much threatened the rapport of M with N.

For this relationship to be meaningful to the modern researcher, he has to draw from other material in the journal that concerns the New Hebridean spirits (*natmasses*). Geddie saw from the start that he "wrestled not against flesh and blood." The shortage of nuts would not merely upset the social organisation for the feast—the spirits would be angry. The burning of the lime would also make the spirits angry. These spirits were supposed to live in a small hill near the mission. They required a "path to the sea," but the mission party had closed it off, and the spirits were angry again. When the spirits became angry, they were disposed to demonstrate it by causing sickness. Even if they did not interfere with the foreigners, sickness and death would fall on the local people. The missionaries had thus found themselves involved in an encounter of religious worldviews, before they understood what they were up against, and as a result the whole of the relationship MN was threatened.

Geddie was apparently a diplomat. He went to the chief and people to arbitrate on behalf of his teachers. He found the New Hebrideans reasonable. When they saw he wanted a good relationship between them and was ready to listen to them, the chief was satisfied and made a ceremonial presentation of taro to terminate the disagreement. Let me quote what Geddie wrote in his diary. (Remember, this was 1848 and Geddie had received no training in anthropology. He was learning it the hard way.)

> Missionaries among a heathen people ought, as far as possible, to guard against everything that would outrage their feelings. Our zeal in the cause of God must be tempered with prudence, or we are in danger of defeating our object in living among them.

Feast days were sacred. When a village was preparing for a feast, no stranger could enter, without enquiring first and then doing so by a circuitous route. Failure to do this would again anger the spirits. Although Geddie had paid for the trees that surrounded his house, even so he aroused anger when he cleared a space. No doubt there was an animist ritual act for preventing offence to the spirit of the tree, but Geddie did not know of it and thus angered the spirits in general.

The spirits sometimes *possessed* people. The land and sea spirits fought each other in a great battle. The sea spirits were angry with the land spirits for allowing the worship of the Christian God on their land, and determined to destroy the people. This led to a communal demonstration of spirit possession, which supposedly strengthened the people to fight against the sea spirits. Geddie reported it as a noisy business which left the possessed persons quite exhausted. The ceremonial offerings which had to be presented at the gathering were considerable.

The incident of the burning of the coral lime was explained in terms of the smell of burning, which both interfered with fishing and angered the sea spirits whose domain had been invaded. Although the missionaries had obtained approval to complete the building project if they did not offend again, they had only won this approval on the basis of a religious argument which the New Hebrideans could not answer: God made the sea, the coral, and the fish, and as Creator he had control over them all. At this point one might speculate that the chief, desiring no conflict with an unknown God, was glad enough to compromise. This kind of NM relationship runs through the first six months of the journal.[63]

Ramifying through all this are many kinds of radiations from A—the white adventurers. When Geddie arrived he found "no manifestations of kindly feelings" from the native people, but a "distinctive coldness," which he subsequently interpreted as due to their dealings with the white men, who wanted no missionaries in their islands. So the missionaries' first obstruction was the white man image which had preceded him. Some islanders were ready to fight all white intruders, because as Geddie said:

> Their [native] lands had in some instances been seized, their wives and daughters stolen and their plantations robbed by men of Christian lands.

However, as one reads through the journal, one has a feeling that the island people soon began to distinguish between sandalwood trader and missionary. Geddie felt the relationship changing steadily. He thought it might be partly due to the presence of home life with missionary wives and children. The Protestant home life stood out with its own set of values, as different from that at the traders' posts where they "saw firearms and other weapons of destruction in abundance."[64]

The improvement of NM relations was hindered also by a visiting Tanna chief, who argued that all kinds of sickness came upon them in Tanna with the presence of missionaries, and that when the missionaries left the sickness departed with them. The Tanna chief therefore advised the Aneiteum people to leave Christianity well alone. The year 1849

---

63   The journal is a valuable repository of descriptive material on pre-Christian Aneiteum animism, which was never the same after the first six months of Geddie's ministry.

64   This was Geddie's opinion. Perhaps the Christian natives had told him this, but he does not say so. One would get a different point of view from, say, the journal of a sandalwooder. In the same library as that in which I found my source for this article, I spent some time on the photocopy of the diary of a supercargo of a labour vessel, which traded in the same part of the Pacific.

began with the arrival of the cutter *Harriet* with the survivors of the *Revenge*. The latter had been driven ashore at Erromanga, where the islanders had plundered the vessel. The crew had escaped in the boat, but Geddie reported them as "very wicked and hardened characters."

About a year after Geddie's arrival in Aneiteum, the AM relationships deteriorated considerably. The journal entry for 20 October 1849 reads:

> We begin to suffer much persecution from our own countrymen on this island. They begin to see that if we succeed, their wicked influence over the natives will be lost. Some of our enemies have urged the chiefs to drive us off the island and burn our houses. I know parties who have threatened more than this if we do not leave.

He goes on to describe "our efforts to arrest licentiousness."

> The conduct of the traders here is too abominable to be described. The poor women are chased by them and seized for their violent purposes. Females are bought from their husbands and parents to become the concubines of the white men, and the brutes sometimes purchase women from the chiefs, who sell them without the knowledge or consent of their husbands. The house of one of my neighbours was entered by some white men and one of his wives forcibly carried off, and her husband threatened with instant death if he dared to resist. My house has often been an asylum for the poor women from their wicked pursuers. The opposition which we suffer is no new thing in the history of missions. Oh, what an impression it must make on the minds of the poor natives, when they see men from Christian lands far excelling themselves in wickedness! I have never seen manifestations of depravity as among the foreigners here. Little do we know the wickedness that is bound up in the hearts of our own countrymen. It is only when they are placed beyond the restraints of civilization that we see many of them in their true colours.

It has been common for many scholars to reject this kind of evidence as "typical missionary bias." On the contrary, in that it does not emerge for twelve months, this suggests it was the result of growing disillusionment. In any case its value lies in what it shows from the angle AMN, standing at the missionary position M, and looking at the relationships MA and MN. Without this data our information of interpersonal relationships in the context would be deficient.

Exactly two months later the schooner *Rover's Bride* arrived from Erromanga to report that a boat's crew of five had been massacred by islanders, and Geddie commented in his journal:

> To those who are acquainted with the doings of the sandel [sic] wood men on
> these islands it is no matter of surprise that such occurrences take place, the
> wonder is that they were not more frequent.

In this particular case the Erromanga chief had been badly beaten on board the vessel, and an innocent native, who happened to be on board when the five were killed in retaliation, was murdered there and then and thrown into the sea. On the first day of February the following year, Geddie was himself attacked by a seaman from a sandalwooder, a Spaniard and "a son of the Cross," and the mission house was damaged. Again Geddie recorded that the sandalwooders dislike the missionaries for their "exposure of the horrors of the sandalwood trade."

By 1851 we enter into a period of struggle between the missionaries and a certain Captain Paddon and Underwood his boatbuilder. They blamed Geddie and his wife for protecting native women from the white men. We have here a highly important series of journal entries, and a most needed corrective picture to the character of Captain Paddon. Paddon met up with Bishop Selwyn and convinced him that his dealings with the islanders were perfectly fair, and his understanding with them so good that he had maintained the sandalwood trade for years to the satisfaction of all. Selwyn even called Paddon his "tutor" (Fox 1958, 5). In *Solomon Islands Christianity* (1967, 355) I expressed doubt about this boast. Belshaw (1954, 17) also discusses Paddon's trade and movements. The record of "Paddon at home" in Geddie's journal is hard evidence which corrects a number of errors in the supposed record of this man. In March 1851 he initiated a raiding party against the Christian natives. "The sandelwood [sic] establishment," Geddie says, tried to work through the Anglican bishop to have Geddie removed, and listed a number of frivolous charges made against the missionary. The bishop had two interviews with Geddie and was not deceived. To Geddie he said, "Go on as you have been doing, and by the blessing of God you will prosper." Geddie records that the sandalwooders were just as abusive about the bishop himself when it suited them to be so. Of Captain Paddon, Geddie wrote on 24 October of that year:

> Captain Paddon . . . has long been an avowed and bitter enemy and [Mr. Underwood] is no less hostile. I heard a few days ago that Underwood offered a black man 10 gallons of rum to rid the island of me, and when he heard that a heathen had speared a cow belonging to me he said, "I wish to . . . that it had been himself."

On 28 November the mission house was set on fire, but no lives were lost. On the basis of evidence in the journal, we may assume that five natives had undertaken to burn the house and church at the instigation of Captain Paddon. The incident had an interesting effect on the island people. The incendiary involvement of Paddon and Underwood and their general hostility to the missionaries divided the heathen and Christian natives, and revealed that the strength of the Christian community was growing rapidly. This indicates another "thread of the story," which one finds running through the pattern of events, and to which I shall return shortly. The involved heathen confessed their complicity in the incident with the sandalwooders.

Thee year 1852 began with the report of the sandalwooder *Deborah*. On a nearby island the captain had argued bitterly with a young chief. The latter was murdered and thrown overboard; but his brother, who had also been there, escaped. On shore some white men were seized for retaliation, and were saved only by the intervention of some Christian teachers, who negotiated a settlement. Even so, not to be outdone of their "pound of flesh," the islanders swore revenge on the first white man's vessel to come along.[65] It happened to be the *Rover's Bride* (Paddon's), but the teachers sent a warning ahead. Meantime Geddie wrote in his journal:

> If all the massacres which have of late years taken place in these islands were
> inquired into it would be found that in most cases white men were to blame for
> them. The sandel [*sic*] wood trade is a bloody business, and those who engage
> in it soon become more hardened than the natives themselves. The sooner the
> wood is exhausted the better for the cause of humanity and Christian missions.

Eventually Paddon saw the "writing on the wall" and departed. Even so, the fourth volume began with the arrival of the *Black Dog*, seeking a place to establish another sandal-wood station. Geddie also records his version of the murders of the missionaries Williams and Harris at Erromanga, sometime before. These had been victims of the kidnapping or blackbirding trade. This is an important statement on one of the major issues of Pacific history.

Efforts to control these incidents from Australia and New Zealand by the Royal Squadron had not been successful.[66] In 1854 Geddie copied out in his journal Fitz Roy's "Proclamation" on the purchase of native women, to cover Fiji and other islands in terms of *slavery*, and to this he added the following note:

> The above proclamation was much needed. It has been the custom of the
> sandelwood [*sic*] traders to purchase females from their friends for licentious
> purposes. Almost every white man among them has his woman. These they con-
> sider their special property and sell them to one another. I am well acquainted
> with a native woman on this island, who was sold at auction and purchased by
> a Tahitian with whom she still lives. All the sandelwood [*sic*] vessels that I know
> are floating brothels. (Entry, 4 July 1854)

---

65   "Revenge on the first white man's ship that happened to come" had awful consequences, evidenced by the record of
     a long list of murders of innocent men, many of them missionaries. The record of Erromanga was the worst of them
     all.

66   The officers of the British Squadron could never win a verdict against the blackbirders they caught, because the
     colonial courts would not accept native evidence against the word of a white man (Palmer 1871).

In the last volume of the journal we meet up with another historical figure, Captain Towns, who figured in the early development of Australia and introduced island labour onto the stations. However his sandalwood establishment in the New Hebrides suffered loss by fire, two houses being destroyed with £1,000 damage in January 1856.

Sandalwooders were not the only adventurers in the Pacific during the last century. Later in the same year Geddie made the following entry of the whaler *June*:

> 6 October. The whaler, *June*, of Sydney, Capt. Waibrow, sailed today. We rejoice at her departure. The conduct of her crew on this island has been infamous. The men were permitted to come on shore for licentious purposes. One sabbath day they went 4 or 5 miles distant from the mission station and offered payment all the way for women, but were defeated in their object. They returned d[is]appointed and enraged. The[y] said much to the natives against the missionaries. They also stole bananas and sugar-cane.

Woven in between entries of this kind are references to a growing Christian community. The MN relationship reflected in a mood toward acceptance of the gospel on the part of the islanders is seen to have a clear effect on the NA relationship as evidenced by their refusal to sell women, annoyance at thefts of their food, involvement in brawls and murders, and so forth.

An entry for 28 April 1857 tells of the *Lady Leigh*, a whaler from Hobart Town, from which, after a brawl, eight deserters were reported. These deserters were all dangerous escaped convicts from Tasmania. Although both Geddie and the chiefs objected to the captain about leaving these men on the island, they did so to no avail. This is the only reference to convicts in this journal, but this type of thing happened all over the Pacific, and escaped convicts figure in many of the missionary journals. They were most obstructive to the missionary cause even when they posed as friends for their own profit, especially if they were there first and knew more of the language than the missionaries. One can imagine what eight convicts could do in such a situation. Of the whalers Geddie said:

> The Hobart Town whalers have an established character on these islands on account of the injuries which they inflict on the natives. The fewer that come this way, the better.

Now let me backtrack and take another look at the MN relationship. In the first year the missionaries had come into encounter with the Aneiteum spirits (*natmasses*), the indigenous taboos, and spirit possession. The customary way of dealing with neighbors or strangers who created problems within the terms of their worldview or value system was to fight and kill. The missionaries tried to demonstrate "a better way," which required no weapons of war or magic. Today it would be called "the way of dialogue." In 1849 a hurricane did much damage. Thinking within their own worldview, the islanders reasoned that this misfortune had been the result of enemy manipulation, and by popular vote the enemies who had supposedly caused it were to be exterminated. The resultant war was effectively terminated by the missionaries through arbitration and reason. This gave them an opportunity to press the interests of a new religion which tabooed war and had a new set of values. Peace was made in the ceremonial manner.

However, traditional values were set against this kind of success on the whole, and Christian missionaries and teachers were frequently blamed for natural calamities. When persons and goods were shipwrecked, the islanders regarded the spoil as their peculiar property by act of the spirits, and believed they could use them as they wished. A chief's child died, and because of this two women were strangled and the Christian teacher's house was burned. Geddie and his party almost lost their lives at Ipece due to an accident in which an unfaithful woman of that place went to live with a chief in the locality where the missionaries happened to live. The chief had rejected the husband's messengers, and boasted that he would "make fish" of any further messengers of reconciliation ("make fish" = kill and eat). Geddie knowing nothing of this chanced to visit the locality of the offenders. He and his party were immediately regarded as "fish," and indeed were fortunate to escape with their lives. This is a good example of how a chief may regard a missionary who elects to live in the region of his rival.

The missionaries had set their faces against a number of practices they regarded as inhuman—cannibalism, live burial, and strangulation. In 1850 numerous cases of cannibalism were cited in the journal. Two years later the matter was no longer taken for granted, but had become a public issue—"cannibalism versus burial," and the growth of Christian values over against the animist may be seen in the following reference of January 1852:

> The parties who sought the body to bury it, would themselves have lately taken
> a part in this tragedy. What a change does the Gospel make! Christianity abol-
> ishes all former anomosities [*sic*] and old enemies become on[e] in Christ.

Strangling was a recognised form of human sacrifice. We have seen that when a chief's child died two women were strangled as a sacrifice. Sometimes the reference in the journal merely reads, "Another strangling case," as if it were quite commonplace. On 28 December 1849 a young man and a girl were strangled to honour a woman who had committed suicide. Two weeks later a woman set out to strangle herself but was saved by some natives who, though not Christian, had been listening to Geddie on the subject. Such cases were reported until well on into 1851 (15 August). However, before the end of the journal one reads for the date 17 March 1857:

> The chiefs and people believe that strangulation is finished on Aneiteum.

The journal as a total thing reveals a process of change.

In March 1853 Geddie took a census of Aneiteum, and he discovered more boys than girls, and proportionately many more adults than children. This disproportion led him to a "flashback" on the subject of infanticide. He recorded that parents exposed their children in the bush or on the shore at low tide, so "the high tide takes them," and that this was especially done with females. Two years later (11 August 1855) he entered information in his journal about a woman who had died in childbirth. Once the child would have been wrapped in a mat and buried with the mother, but "this time Christianity saved the child." Thus again the recording of simple daily facts in the journal reflect a major shift in social values over the decade.

The same may be said in the area of religion. I have already mentioned the place of spirits, of feast days, of taboos and spirit possession in the first six months of Geddie's term on Aneiteum. The tendency was for the islanders to interpret all calamities as due to the anger of the spirits. When a Christian died, that always told against Christianity. By 4 February 1852—still less than four years after his arrival—Geddie was able to write:

> Heathenism is declining fast. The old objects of worship are being forsaken by the natives. Two celebrated disease-makers have recently joined us. They declare that they will no more serve the Devil and ruin their souls. As an evidence of their sincerity they sent me their charms for making sickness. These were done up in two native bags. I opened them in the presence of a number of natives who were amused at their contents. They contained some earth of a dark colour, leaves of a sacred plant chewed up, portions of human hair, fragments of women's dresses, sugar-cane chewings, &c, &c. When a disease-maker wishes to cause sickness he endeavours to procure a portion of a person's hair or some fragment of his food. He then chews up a quantity of sacred leaf and puts the whole into his charming pot, which he sets on the fire. He then prays to his *natmasses* to inflict disease on the person whom he wishes to charm. The process is called *naragess*, and those who practise it are much feared by the people . . . This class, however, is hated as well as feared.

In spite of the decline of the old religion, these sorcerers remained actively opposed to Christianity and used their arts to obstruct the conversion of individuals.

Turning now to the actual response of the people of Aneiteum to the gospel, we find that by the end of the first year about ten islanders were attending the Christian fellowship group. A year later this had grown to forty-five. Missionaries from further east had reported to Geddie that the general pattern was that the people waited for their chief to become Christian before they actually took the step themselves. Geddie, on the other hand, found the women and young people more responsive. After the beginning of the third year about eighty persons were attending. Although the chief felt he gained prestige by having a resident missionary, and valued his medicine, nevertheless many of the other chiefs were obstructive.

In August 1851 Kapaio, brother of the chief, came to Geddie asking for Christian instruction. He confessed that he had regarded the missionaries as liars when they first came with the new teaching, but having observed that their living supported their teaching, he was now prepared to accept their word as true. That was on 20 August. Five days later several chiefs and priests renounced the old religion. It was this movement to Christianity on the part of the leaders which stimulated Capt. Paddon to stir up the heathen islanders to burn the mission house, and thus accentuate the division of the islanders on a basis of their attitude toward Christianity.

At this time, "the chief himself had a large piece of sacred ground cut down and cleared for a plantation," which Geddie claimed would have been the "precursor of death twelve months ago." So had times changed!

Walking with the chief, Nohoat, one day Geddie came upon a woman preparing food from a certain bark, an agreeable food, but one forbidden to chiefs and sacred men, and used only by commoners. Geddie asked if he could try a piece. The woman obliged and Geddie ate. The chief looked at him strangely, and then asked for a piece himself and ate of his own accord. Thus was a sacred food taboo broken.

Less than a month later (20 December) Geddie described the process of religious secularisation going on at the hands of the people themselves:

> In the district where I reside there has been a great destruction of sacred
> groves. The Christian natives are now cultivating these spots . . . The sacred
> stones likewise, which were worshipped as gods, are despised by the natives.

The conversion of the two celebrated disease makers followed only a few weeks after this, and again Geddie reported that in one village where the people had lost their faith in the old religion, but had no substitute for it, they were afraid to destroy the village *natmass*, a "piece of durable wood which branched out" like "the horns of a deer" (showing the term was used for both the spirit and the fetish).[67] They authorized a Christian native to destroy it. He broke the heavy sacred object, burned part of it in their presence, and carried the remainder home for some less dignified purpose than it had hitherto enjoyed. Shortly after this event Geddie recorded the formation of a church (congregation) and reported another thirteen baptisms. Even the heathen had accepted the notion of Christian prayer, and some of them had asked native Christians to pray for them. A visiting Tanna party expressed surprise at being able to walk about Aneiteum without spears and clubs,

---

67   This is an important anthropological observation; viz., that the same term is used for both the spirit and the "shrine" it inhabits. Many anthropological writers on Melanesia have entirely missed this fact and thereby misinterpreted their data. Note also that Geddie's term for sorcerer is "disease-maker."

and the chief of the party broke down and wept at the idea of a community existing without fighting.

27 October 1852: The oldest man in the island, an inland native, came ten miles to confirm the news of the gospel which had reached his village. He accepted Christian instruction, sent his stone god to Geddie, and thereafter enjoyed a new lease of life—both physical and spiritual. Two weeks later some distant islanders brought in their sacred paraphernalia, including the skull of a high chief. The pre-Christian practice was to bury the dead chief in a shallow grave, leaving the head exposed, and to present sacrifices there until the head separated from the body. Then it was placed on a pole as an object of worship. Now they brought the skull for burial, that the old form of worship might be ceremonially terminated.

By 1854 the Christian community had been organised with congregations, ordinances, school program, and regular itinerations. Work was going forward on a New Testament translation. In 1855 a printing press arrived with supplies. The Christian effort was beginning to reach out to other islands—Erromanga, Tanna, and Futuna. Geddie began to discuss the notion of native laws and government with the chiefs. He thought codified legislation should grow with the people and have its own indigenous authority—two good anthropological principles. Many of the chiefs, especially Nohoat, were themselves good advocates of the gospel and witnessed to other chiefs. On the second day of 1857 the Gospel of Matthew came off the press, and here, most appropriately, the journal of John Geddie ends.

Conclusions

I have by no means exhausted the subject matter or the valuable historical evidence on some critical points and anthropological issues, which still remain open. The journal narrates many episodes which concern Erskine of the *Havannah*, Bishop Selwyn of the Melanesian Mission, Walter Lawry the Wesleyan area secretary and other missionaries—among them Harris, Williams, and Inglis, who figured in the labour trade controversy; also historically significant seamen like Paddon and Henry, and colonial figures like Towns; and a great wealth of material on the sandalwood trade. Quite apart from the value of this journal for its own sake, these references confirm or challenge statements based on other documents, and therefore are an essential part of *a Pacific world of interrelating documents*.

For my own immediate purpose in this presentation, I have used a grossly oversimplified model, namely that of a *triangle of personal relationships*, the triangle being the simplest possible geometric figure by which I could demonstrate my claim that a conversion pattern requires more than just an advocate and an acceptor in a face-to-face dialogue. It has to be a complex or a configuration of some kind—a *multirelational engagement*. There is always a context with social factors and usually with other persons. In reality the figure often has more points than a triangle. Thus, for example, the white adventurers, A, might have been treated as whalers, sandalwooders, sailors, or convicts; the islanders or native people, N, might have represented those in the territory where the missionary lived, or those in the territory of the enemy; and the missionary, M, might have been Geddie, the Presbyterian, or the visiting Anglican bishop. Even more complicating would have been M, the renegade missionary mentioned in the journal, who because of the discouragement and early persecution lost his faith and turned to exploit the South Pacific for his own personal profit. He shifted from the point, M, to point A and did much mischief to the missionary program. In 1851, when Paddon and Underwood were stirring up opposition against the missionaries, a missionary named Archibald "joined the sandalwooders and disgraced the mission." On the other side of the account, however, Geddie had also spoken of a man, Henry, as a helpful sandalwooder,[68] "the only one." Was this perhaps the trader by that name, son of a Tahiti missionary? These sidelights show how grossly oversimplified my model is. Nevertheless it points up my general thesis that we are dealing with complex configurations when we consider conversion. The forces impinging on the decision-making process are truly multitudinous.

Finally, I believe these five exercise books, which I have treated as one whole primary source (they represent a unified account of one man's experience over a limited period of time in a single locality), demonstrate the value of the personal document for filling the gaps in our historical knowledge by means of the *synchronic ethnohistorical reconstruction*. It is synchronic as it cuts across time for a single decade in the days of the Pacific sandalwood trade, and depicts a set of personal relationships in the lifetime of one missionary, from the original point of missionary contact to the production of a printed Gospel for the Christian island community. It is more than a biography. It is a dynamic panorama of interacting people and events. Furthermore, in the archival repositories of the South Pacific, scores of similar journals remain untapped. If this essay helps any Pacific scholars to undertake further research of this kind, I shall feel more than rewarded.

REFERENCES

Acton, Lord. 1963. Letter to contributors to the *Cambridge Modern History*. In *The varieties of history*, ed. Fritz Stern, 247–55. Cleveland: World Publishing, 1963.

Barnett, Homer G. 1953. *Innovation: The basis of cultural change*. New York, McGraw-Hill.

Barzun, Jacques. 1963. Cultural history as a synthesis. In *The varieties of history*, ed. Fritz Stern, 387–402. Cleveland: World Publishing.

Belshaw, Cyril S. 1954. *Changing Melanesia: Social economics of culture contact*. Melbourne: Oxford University Press.

Fox, C. E. 1958. *Lord of the Southern Isles*. London: Mowbray.

---

68   Samuel Henry had a good name among the missionaries from Tahiti to Fiji, and figures in missionary records as early as the 1830s (Williams and Calvert 1884, 231).

Geddie, John. n.d. *Journal of Rev. John Geddie, first Presbyterian missionary in the New Hebrides.* 5 vols. Latrobe Library, Melbourne. Unpublished manuscript, ref. MS8774.

Gottschalk, Louis. 1945. The historian and the historical document. In *The use of personal documents in history, anthropology and sociology,* ed. Louis Gottschalk et al., 3–75. New York: Social Science Research Council.

Kluckhohn, Clyde J. 1945. The personal document in anthropological science. In *The use of personal documents in history, anthropology and sociology,* ed. Louis Gottschalk, Clyde Kluckhohn, and Robert Angell, 78–173. Bulletin 53. New York: Social Science Research Council.

Palmer, George. 1871. *Kidnapping in the South Seas.* Edinburgh: Edmonson & Douglas.

Renier, G. J. 1965. *History: Its purpose and method.* New York: Harper & Row.

Stern, Fritz, ed. 1963. *The varieties of history.* Cleveland: World Publishing.

Sturtevant, William C. 1966. Anthropology, history and ethnohistory. *Ethnohistory* 13, no. 1: 1–51.

Tippett, Alan R. 1967. *Solomon Islands Christianity.* London: Lutterworth.

———. 1971. *People movements in Southern Polynesia.* Chicago, Moody.

Williams, Thomas, and James Calvert. 1884. *Fiji and the Fijians.* 2 vols. London: Charles H. Kelly. First published 1860.

16
ETHNOLINGUISTICS AND BIBLE TRANSLATION:
A Diachronic Case Study—Fiji[69]

Historical Preamble

In 1835 the Fijian culture lay in its highly institutionalised forms of cannibalism and war, supported by an elaborate magico-religion which was devastatingly equipped for self-extermination. The population had been reduced drastically in the century before the arrival of the first Western Christian missionaries, with some twenty-five years of prior culture contact with the West.

A small colony of escaped convicts and runaway mariners and sandalwooders established themselves and participated in cannibal war to such an extent that they completely secularised the institutions of cannibalism between 1809 and 1835. The evidence for this is ethnohistorical and ethnolinguistic, and bears in a way on the work of the first Bible translators in Fiji.

Down to the documented arrival of the first white men, cannibalism was a highly religious institution with a strong eschatology. Christianity overcame cannibalism, virtually unaided, and when the Fiji Islands were ceded to Great Britain in 1874, only a couple of mountain tribes in the centers of the largest two islands of the Group still practiced this way of life. The story of that transformation is preserved and verified in the semantic change as seen in the vernacular documents of the century—the Christian hymns, devotional aids, and the translation and revisions of the Bible.

Cannibalism in precontact Fiji was interwoven with the war patterns distributed over this Group of some three hundred odd islands. At the end of the eighteenth century when the first missionaries entered the South Pacific and settled in Tahiti, Fiji comprised some eight political "kingdoms," who by cannibal war were in the process of reducing themselves to seven. The early missionaries reported seven cannibal wars being waged at one time just before midcentury. Sometimes they were completely cut off from their missionary fellows behind the lines of two warring enemy kingdoms. The missionaries Hunt and Jaggar describe the same events in their journals from opposite viewpoints. They reflect

69   Taken from *Notes on Anthropology and Intercultural Community Work*, nos. 6–7 (1986): 67–78. Used by permission.

differences in the way the two kingdoms made war, and how their institutions operated (Tippett 1954).

There was probably no greater missionary achievement than the overpowering of the institutions of cannibalism and widow strangling without destroying the culture itself, unless perhaps it was the reduction of the Fijian speech to a written form as a *lingua franca* for the whole Group. This was all the more remarkable because seven or eight political kingdoms were at war, every one of them holding a cluster of tributary states with dialect differences. And, moreover, with that *lingua franca* they provided thereby the capacity for unification as a single crown colony before Britain ever came into the picture.[70]

When the islands were ceded to Britain after some forty years of missionary activity, there remained only a couple of interior tribes to be brought under control.

After three years at Lakeba, with the arrival of new missionaries, the policy of distributing workers over the Group began. This exposed each man to some regional dialect.[71] They had farmed out the biblical books to each man for attempts at translation, but the policy was soon abandoned because of the multiplicity of dialects and the variability of their translation skills. At a district meeting a decision was made to concentrate on the Bauan language as a *lingua franca*. John Hunt was to concentrate on a translation of the New Testament. It was a momentous decision.[72]

Bau, as the strongest of the kingdoms, had the most widespread distribution of subject states. It was a sea power whose canoes could come and go collecting tribute. A study of the diversification of Bauan nautical vocabulary supported the thesis that this language had the best capacity for diffusion, and the decision to put the New Testament into that language was certainly a significant one.

The conversion movement to Christianity began in the communities of Tongan carpenters who were located at the chiefly centers mainly for canoe building, trade exchange, and contact with Tonga. Christianity made such a profound difference to the morals of these communities that it attracted observation by the Fijians, and the movement spread, mainly through group decision making, through the windward islands under Lakeban authority. The missionaries and their first island evangelists came into Fiji from Tonga through these socioeconomic political Tongan/Lakeban links. The first lexical work was done on Lakeban, so that there were many borrowed Tongan words in Fiji, even before any

---

70 The colonial administration adopted Bauan as the *lingua franca* and used missionaries Fison and Langham to serve as go-betweens with the chiefs in the codification of their laws.

71 These were Lakeban, Rewan, Somosomoan, Bauan by 1842. Work started on Lakeban in 1835, with Cross and Cargill involved. Cross moved to Rewa in 1838 to be joined by Hunt. Cross, Hunt, and Lyth worked on Somosomo. The press moved to Rewa and subsequently to Viwa, where Hunt worked on the Bauan New Testament.

72 The decision to make Bauan the *lingua franca* was made at their district meeting in 1843. Matthew and Acts were translated and printed, then other books followed, with enough copies of each printed for them to be bound together as a full New Testament (in 1847).

translation attempts. Christianity itself was the *Lotu* (a word that marked the spread of the religion through Polynesia). There were already Tongan practices, cultural institutions, and magical performances in Lakeba, and a cultural process had begun of rival Tongan/Fijian interpretations of "the way things ought to be done" and their supporting myths. It was through this door the gospel came into Fiji, and with it came the notion of putting a spoken language into a written form that was precise and not hieroglyphic, needing interpretation.

Adapting Cannibalistic and Magical Terms for Translation

The culture of Fiji showed a strong semantic diversification in the direction of cannibal war and destructive magic. For example, the vocabulary of population extermination in Bauan as it looked at its nearest enemies, the Rewa and Verata, has many terms meaning "exterminate" or "depopulate," with a variety of different modes for achieving it: *kawabo-ko, kawayali, vakalala-taka, qeavu, ravuravu, samuta, bokoca laivi, vanua lala, veirakarusai,* and no doubt there are many others. These terms were all in daily use in the first missionary decade and can be seen in the contact documents.

In addition to Bauan descriptions of exterminating their enemies, one can find terminology of the magic man and sorcerer. For example, note the words which indicate victims ensnared in devices of plotting and black magic: *bacana, corita, verata, tudaitaka, temaka, lawakitaka,* and so on.

The institutions of war and sorcery were basically religious. That is, they both employed some ritual form of offering or incantation to secure the success of their war, cannibal, or sorcery intentions. Thus we have, for example, *veikaci, kaciyalo, veinocati, vei-vakadraunidautaki,* and so on. In all of these a religious practitioner calls upon a spirit or deity of some kind to empower the performance.

On the other hand, one never meets with a destructive mechanism without some form of approved countersorcery or corrective measure. True, they are in a state of imbalance. The cultural pattern displays a destructive purpose, but the escape is also always there. It is the presence of that option for correction that opens the door for any message or way of salvation. There is only one general term for extricating a victim from sorcery (that is *sereka,* "to free or loose"), although there are ways or modes of freeing the person (like *gunuva,* "I drink on his behalf," or *bikai,* to "press down" the power of a hostile whale's tooth, *tabua,* with another tooth). So the cannibal understood very well the nature and function of a salvific mechanism.

Given this mental set, an evangelist or translator could use one of the regular methods of word expansion to create an adequate salvation terminology. A meaningful source existed in the linguistic structure before Christianity came to Fiji.

In *Solomon Islands Christianity* (1967) I give a long account of how salvation in terms of Christ as Peacemaker was the means of a tribal conversion after a prolonged crisis situation of feuding. As long as a complex or corpus of words can be built up around a root, the language has the capacity for natural expansion. Sometimes the process is achieved by a lengthy circumlocution.

Cannibal Fiji never actually conceptualised the idea of "peace." It was rather "the times when gardens were not plundered and there was plenty" (*sautu*). The first Christian effort at "Peacemaker" was a long circumlocution *O Koya sa Vakayacora na Veisaututaki*, "He who brings about the State of Plenty" because there was no war. That term was actually being used in contact times. The point is not the long circumlocution, but the fact that it was quite meaningful to the Fijians, and utilised their own mode of word creation, although the positive moral notion of peace as a quality only came with Christian usage. For the time being it meant a period of rest and plenty between the more normal periods of war and destruction.

Let me give one more example. The idea of "reconciliation" was quite foreign to the Fijian. A "war of the chiefs" was a war of extermination for one side, and of exterminating for the other. I have seen in Fiji scores of overgrown village foundation sites which tell this tragic story of population decrease.[73] The acquisition of the land for the mission at Davuilevu was possible because the whole tribe was wiped out with no offspring. What were the alternatives? Either there was enslavement or normally there were cannibal ovens for the men, the captive boys being used as spearing targets by the boys of the victors, and the women as prostitutes in the unmarried men's houses. In each case after serving their purposes, they were consigned to the ovens.[74] There was no place for reconciliation here, because each of these tragic fates met a particular felt need that demanded satisfaction for social reasons. Being therefore conceptualised as desirable, and undergirded by cannibal theology, it was no easy matter "to break down the middle wall of partition between Jew and Gentile," as every translator and preacher soon discovered. Four attempts in the contact period revealed major circumlocutions: *vakayalovinakatakatale*, *vakavinakatitakatale*, *vakamaliwavinakataka*, *veivaka-meautaki*. As time went on preference was given to the simple reciprocal form *veivinakati*, which means "mutually liking each other." The suffix tale in the first two examples means "again," which implies the idea of restoring a good attitude which may have been present.

---

73   More information on a "War of the Chiefs" is in Hunt's journal which he wrote during his observation of the events. See my use of the data in Tippett 1973.

74   See my field correspondence and notes on Davuilevu at St. Mark's Library. Information on spearing of boys comes from Jesse Carey in his studies on Bau.

Another new theological word which came into use was the causative form *vakavoui*, "the being made new." This was a secular use taken over for theological purposes. A cannibal would speak of an act of renewal of, say, a sinnet design on the wall of a house, a rethatching of a piece of leaking roof, patching a leaking canoe, or putting a handle on a battle-axe or adze. This entirely secular act of renewal, a passive verbal noun, had the potential for expressing the idea of spiritual renewal as "regeneration." Although the meaning of the word was clear, it was not understood until the experience of spiritual conversion, or spiritual paradigm shift. Then it suddenly became a meaningful revelation. For translator and preacher a word selected in translation required two elements: (1) a technical structural capacity to give true meaning, and (2) a paradigm shift to reveal that meaning in its spiritual dimension.

The men who made their mark both in translation and in preaching or theology with the Fijian emerging church (Hunt, Lyth, Hazlewood, and later Fison) were all men who were ready to see conversion in terms of "power encounter" moving from one religion to another, as a shift from one religious paradigm (however depraved) to a better one. The less effective translators and evangelists (if I may venture my opinion) saw heathenism as dark, as a nonfaith position. They saw conversion as moving from nonfaith to faith. This accounts to some extent for their Western, paternalistic, ethnocentric presentation. Occasionally in the deputation documents one sees statements of "a people having no religion," and in conversion moving "from nothing to faith." A century of anthropological research is against them.

From my early days one of my heroes in church history was Ulfilas, who ran into the problem we all face in cross-cultural mission of putting a pure gospel into the vulgar language of the Goths—or the cannibal language of Fiji (Tippett 1975, 14, 32). For, as Malinowski pointed out (1949), every word the missionary translator had to use derived its meaning for his audience from the heathen context where he got it.

The presupposition that even a cannibal society had a religious base for the translator or preacher to build upon for a meaningful Christian faith implies certain elements:

(1) *The Fijians were a religious people.* Their social structure, and even their inhumane practices within cannibalism and widow strangling, patricide, and infanticide were based on their notions of meeting communal felt needs in this life and progress towards, and entry into, a world beyond. It is therefore quite wrong to consider the animist as simply materialistic, however earthy his sexual drives and acquisitive values were. However weird to us his view of gods and spirits, he recognised their reality, and developed an elaborate system for approaching them and coming to terms with them and securing their support. He had no trouble differentiating material and spiritual. Without such a base, any kind of gospel at all would have been meaningless. In language as well, his adjectival descriptors indicate material and spiritual distinctions.

The translator and preacher, therefore, had to find a way of getting, not from the material to the spiritual, from nonfaith to faith, but from a false religion to a true one, from a false god to the true One.

(2) *The animist cannibal had developed a series of institutionalised modes of approach to the spirit beings.* What did it mean to the evangelist and biblical translator to discover there were both terms and the actual institutions through which mankind had access to his gods and their resources? He paid homage. He prayed. His prayers included confession, intercession, thanksgiving, both individual and corporate. The missionary task was surely one of selecting and sanctifying. Aspects beyond redemption, if any, required functional substitutes that met felt needs. If there were ritual blessings associated with crop planting, with firstfruits and ingathering, there had to be Christian functional substitutes, or the converts would have been torn apart in fear for the cultural void left without them. The translation problem therefore, was: Do we retain the pagan vocabulary or find a new term? Do we append a Christian adjective to the term? Whatever is done, there must be no void, if there is to be an indigenous Christianity.

(3) Arising from that second aspect of the religious base, the religious cannibal realised that *somewhere beyond himself, that divine being or spirit force of which he was aware, and conceived in some anthropomorphic ways, had tremendous resources of power.* The cannibal, in the manufacture and use of weapons of war, and cultivation of a garden plot, differentiated quite clearly between his own scientific knowledge and his dependence on resources beyond himself. There are passages in the Hebrew worldview of the Old Testament which also make these precise differentiations.

(4) The aspect of *the cannibal capacity for understanding a gospel message* appears to have been more apparent to the missionaries of the 1840s than to those half a century later. At the end of the Victorian Age imperialism convinced the white man of his intellectual superiority over the "child races," such that he saw the savage as in the childhood of human evolution, a kind of "survival" of an era long past. To the late Victorian the cannibal was a child. However, the great missionaries like Hunt and Fison treated the people as adults with a mental capacity for mature decision.[75] Fison struggled with the recognition of the Fijians as adults with a mind world of their own. He spoke of worldview under that term "mind world" a century ago and would have no truck with any notion of child minds. He researched the Naga cult of the interior and described its ritual as a mature, if weird, procedure within a rational system of thought (Fison 1884). He respected their capacity for reason, for evaluation of a situation, for mature judgment within the contours of their own system of thought. He studied their marriage structures, pioneered the classification of kinship structures, and so on. People who could think out such a system, and moreover,

---

75   Fison said this many times in his public lectures as an anthropologist in the 1880s and 1890s. See documents at St. Mark's National Theological Centre Library.

make it the rule of their lives, had a capacity for a deep level of scriptural understanding, including the salvation motif.

No white man in the whole history of Fiji mastered the conceptual depths of Fijian thought like Hunt and Fison. They both found the Fijian people to be good informants, not children, but people who could understand cause and effect, and had descriptive skills to no end, could identify misunderstandings, and had a wide range of knowledge of dialect differences. The same two men had no trouble communicating theology in depth to the Fijian evangelists. The Fijians saw them as good listeners and opened their hearts to them.[76]

The animist not only ascribed a meaning to everything, but he rationalized on the problem of meaning itself. He was a good listener, a good informant, and a good communicator of new ideas. He had capacity for appreciating the gospel, and skill in communicating it.

(5) Although the diversification of mechanisms for destruction were more developed than those for preventive or protective measures, those which existed were highly innovative. *They brought together the felt needs of the victim with institutionalised mechanisms for escape and survival, with a theological undergirding.* Basic to any idea of salvation was the underlying awareness of right and wrong, good and bad. What was good or bad, of course, was determined by the worldview, which was cannibal. But both cannibal and Christian had ideas on the right way and the wrong way, and that there was a penalty of some kind due for those in error.

Error was seen as just clumsiness and something unwittingly done, or as premeditated, deliberate, so there was a gradation of penalty, and a whole cluster of idiom, especially related to the former. Somehow these wrongs had to be righted. They caused a loss of social equilibrium and crisis situations. Somehow things had to be brought back to normality.

In *Solomon Islands Christianity* (1967) I ventured a simple typology for island people to suggest a South Pacific view of "sin." I depicted sin as *antisocial* (offending against the social group or a member of the group), or as *theological* (against a deity for breaking taboos or behavior controls which had divine authority in myth, proverb, legend, etc.), or as *extra-communal* (against spirit forces of bush or sea, normally committed accidentally, and often the cause of sickness). The typology fits the Fijian situation as far as it goes. Any of these may cause a "crisis situation" which calls for a "salvation corrective."

An example of an escape or salvation mechanism was a large rock outside a mountain village, which was a location of escape of a "manslayer" in flight from the "avenger of blood." This "rock of refuge" has a strangely Old Testament ring about it corresponding to the record of the Hebrew cities of refuge. It was precisely the same social setup: the recognition of error, the awareness of the penalty of death in reprisal, and the obligation of the avenger of blood to see to justice, the means of escape, and the ultimate restoration of

---

76   Both kept good notebooks and journals. Both were involved in teaching the Bible to Fijians, and both have left good
      basic material in Fijian, which is available for study and evaluation.

normality. We have here the basic mental set for a theology of salvation, as well as lexical evidence with it.

All this, then, required the translator and the expositor to perceive these religious basics in the people, in spite of their inhumane practices of cannibalism and widow strangling.

Why then translate the gospel into a language of cannibals at all? For these five reasons indeed: (1) they were a religious people and therefore open for redemption; (2) they had developed a series of institutionalised approaches to spirit beings and thereby expressed their felt need; (3) they had realised that there was a reservoir of spiritual resources of great power, and therefore they desired to tap it; (4) they had a capacity for mature reflection and were adult, not child mentalities, and could consider the gospel for acceptance; and finally (5) although their destructive institutions outnumbered the salvific ones, there were mechanisms for escape and survival which were built on a recognition of error and the felt need for its correction. Hunt, Lyth, Cross, Hazlewood, and Fison all agreed on this as over against the rival theory of mission at the time that a people had to be civilised first in order to evangelise (Tippett 1971). The policy brought good results.

The Sacrificial System and the Recovery of Normality

I will now comment on the notion of sin and its demand for correction. Probably all humankind, including cannibals or Christians, feels uncomfortable in any kind of crisis situation. The crisis situation drives people to explore corrective mechanisms, to make innovations, to confess their shortcomings or their failures, and to make sacrifices to restore harmony.

Wallace (1956) showed how prophetic movements and various kinds of nativism or revitalization movements emerge in crisis situations and bring people into a new kind of steady state. The crisis situation might be due to any one of a number of possible causes: a manifestation of disloyalty within the lineage, the death of the chiefly leader by sorcery, or a mysterious epidemic. People then have to find means of restoring normality. In the case of disloyalty, the offender is forced to flee to safety. He is ostracized, put down, dismissed (*sa vakasoburi*, or *vakasivoi*). The latter term is used in Christian situations for "disciplined" or "dismissed from office." In the case of murder by sorcery, necromancy (*ilovi* or *yarasasa*) was used to call the spirit of the dead to possess some person, normally the priest, and disclose the cause of death, whose sorcery was responsible, and approve the execution of justice. In an epidemic, a priest or diviner is required to call the tribal spirit, to ascertain what (or who) caused the epidemic, and how to correct the matter. This will determine the kind of sacrifices to be made.

With conversion to Christianity there is very little change in the phenomenology or psychology. The forms of sacrifice pass away, the appeals to the tribal deities cease, and there may be some moral elements which are removed. But it is a corrective phenomenology. There is a confession and an approach in prayerful petition, but now to Christ the

Lord. It is still an act of faith, be it a better faith. The subject still acts to correct his feeling of error. The crisis is dealt with and normality is restored again. This is the same both on the individual and communal levels. Normality means the mind is steady again, but the experience is new.

In most strongly sacrificial societies the Christianisation needs an Old Testament context, leading into the New Testament. This is why the letter to the Hebrews is so essential for early translation. Many converts are just exactly where those Hebrew converts were when that letter was written. The journals of men like Hunt and others speak frequently of "two conversions," one from pagan faith and deities to the Lord of Power, and then later to the Cross and a discovery of grace. This journey from Mount Carmel to Calvary has a special lexicon to deal with both experiences.

All corrective rituals which aim at setting the mind at rest, such as removing guilt, relieving the anger, preventing danger, ensuring the right standing with some god or spirit, or groping for a solution to some unexplained mystery, demonstrate that mankind solves his crises by means of religious practices. Such salvific institutions include sacrifices, atonements, formal confessions, worship, and chanting. The ethnotheological psychology related to these cultural practices did not change with conversion to Christianity, although the nature of the faith and its ethical outworkings certainly did. There were still prayers, devotional acts, sacraments, and rituals of restoration. This shows the importance of rituals as functional substitutes, and this was certainly reflected in the semantics of the Fijians' developing faith.

Let us now consider a case of necromancy and its practical function in Fiji. A young man in the full prime of life, a leader of his people, and one on whom everybody depends, suddenly dies quite unexpectedly. The whole community is in a state of shock. In two cases the people resorted to necromancy, one by *ilovi* and the other by *yarasasa*; the former using a mirror and lantern to call back the spirit of the dead, the latter having him ride on a coconut branch dragged to a house where the inquirers sat in the darkness. The spirit of the dead possessed one of the party in the darkness (in older times it would have been the priest of the tribe, but the custom is now irregular and it would be the person who initiated the ritual) and spoke through him indicating how he died. Of course he was killed by sorcery, and the instigator of that act was so-and-so. Unless the spirit of the dead indicated otherwise, there would be a customary form of retribution. Note that the cause of the crisis is clear, the course of action is clear, and it is dealt with to the satisfaction of all concerned.

Necromancy was not done in the name of another god set up in opposition to the Lord. It was a mechanism from olden times to resolve a crisis. Although the Scriptures tell us that it is a wrong method (1 Sam 28), Saul turned to necromancy when confronted by a crisis. Where people are living in an Old Testament context with a New Testament gospel, we have a similar situation.

There are many evangelicals today who use the Christian promise box. This is divination. Its purpose is not to worship another deity or spirit, but to learn what to do about a crisis situation.

All I can suggest is that when a forest people are suddenly projected into Christianity they need a good translation of the whole Bible, accompanied by good teaching on how to use it and how to pray, because the study of the Word and the prayer patterns will have to be the functional substitutes of divination. If we delay those religious aids we cannot expect the converts to live with a void in their lives. Forms of divination (and necromancy is only one of them) will not only survive, but develop new dimensions to fit the cultural changes going on.

The Christian Impact on the Fijian Language

Although the original selection of words tends to remain, semantic change is an ongoing process. It requires some time depth before the subject can be studied, and this makes the Fijian Bible a good subject for research. It has passed through several revisions, and every revision shows up some significant shifts in meaning. One way of illustrating this is in the translation of the Lord's Prayer.

Cannibal Fijian had no word for "forgive." The nearest equivalent was the idea of a victorious chief to deal with his conquered enemy who was appealing for mercy. That would mean a sacrifice, a pot of his earth, his war club, and his daughter's hand in marriage. Each of these were the symbols of his subordination, designed to save him from the cannibal oven. His request was, "Do not be angry with me for my rebellious indiscretions." He might survive with his life if the victorious chief so decided. That was the nearest equivalent to the idea of forgiving. Perhaps it was a poor substitute, but it represented any unusual event when a conquered chief was pardoned, and was the cannibals' concept of "forgiveness." The term and prayer were inbuilt for three or four generations. Following cannibal times a Fijian community emerged with Christian values and forgot all about their ancestry. Theological development rendered the translation inadequate, but the form continued. A century passed before the Fijians were convinced the term ought to be changed. Eventually when the educational system included blackboards and chalk, the idea of "rubbing out to begin again" was substituted as a more positive figure for "forgive." However, the matter was argued in church committees for years, and eventually the passage was related to the sin of the pray-er, which needed rubbing out. (The concept of sin had also developed over the years.)

The new wording was printed in the hymnbooks just before World War II, but the church was still divided about the change. Some congregations used the old form, and others used the new. Many older Christians never did make the change, because they said, "How can we change the word of the Lord?" This shows how easy it is for word form to become sacralized at a cost of the meaning.

Let me now tabulate the findings of many years of research in studying the Fijian Scriptures diachronically from the contact period to my own time:

1. The church took over the linguistic forms of the cannibal people. The gospel, with its theology and ethic, was presented in Fijian thought forms, and this led to great lexical and expressive development.

2. Foreign borrowings were deliberately restricted to:

   a names of people and places,

   b new terms for new cultural innovations,

   c elements from the wider world which were bound to be soon introduced into Fiji, and

   d unique terminology required for church life and practice.

All such foreign borrowings were made to conform to Fijian form, rhythm, and sound.

3. Many old Fijian terms from pagan ritual, sacrifice, and so on, were retained but acquired new Christian dimensions. New ideas were developed by familiar patterns of word expansion, especially by causatives and reciprocals, and by compounding nouns with adjectives.

4. As Christian experience developed, so did the theological meaning of terminology.

5. Some significant choices were made, such as the preference for apostolic over priestly terms for the ministerial office and roles. The Fijian church captured the true apostolic equivalent of the early church by these choices.

6. The extensive Fijian word combinations widened the scope of the language for expressing an indigenous theology and ethic. Concepts like "incarnation" and "transfiguration" were quite meaningful.

7. The church developed her own original and unique terminology in (a) organisational practice and pattern, (b) widening religious experience, and (c) a growing demand for ethical expression.

8. By reducing the spoken language to written form, making it the *lingua franca*, translating the Scriptures, composing hymns, preparing the catechism and other devotional aids, and eventually a church paper, the church standardised the language, expanded its vocabulary in step with the expanding experience of her members. They also produced many new terms with finer distinctions of moral discrimination than do our own English words.

In conclusion I must make one more theological and historical point. When the gospel came to Fiji, it did so "in the fullness of time." Cannibalism had been secularised. The effect of the introduction of Western arms and ammunition had greatly increased the number of bodies for the oven. Taboos were being broken everywhere. Women and children were becoming addicted to the taste for human flesh. Practices developed which actually helped children acquire the taste for it, although there was a fairly wide reaction against this because of its secularisation. Many people were ready to listen to the new message brought by the missionaries, whom they saw as a different kind of white man.

The missionaries challenged the undergirding of Fijian theology of the nature of the afterlife and spoke of a heavenly land. This cultural readiness for change, the innovation of the written Word, a heaven-centered hymnology, the Christian use of indigenous liturgical forms, and a better eschatology, left the Fijians questioning their old beliefs, so that many were ready to desert their old gods. The combination of translators with skill, and preachers with conviction, certainly came at the right time. Hunt, who translated the New Testament, also trained an army of Fijian converts in how to use it, giving them the bones of their sermons and expecting them to flesh them out on a basis of their own personal experience. It had people-movement responses.

I remember once hearing a Fijian close a meeting in prayer. He asked God to use us as the *waqawaqa* of His Spirit. It was a daring idea. It was a pagan word. It was used on an ancient diviner calling on a god or spirit to possess him. I would not have dared to say that, but upon reflection, what is wrong with calling on the Spirit of God to possess us, especially for the revelation of His will? Furthermore, it was the thought form of his context of situation that prompted his prayer. And the congregation said, "Amen."

Appendix

The Fijian Concept of Man as an Active Being and the Linguistic Capacity for Ethical Expansion

In considering man as an active being or person, the Fijian of the contact period used three terms. The *yago-na* ("body") manifested its activity in the *yalo-na* ("spirit" or "nature"), the *loma-na* ("mind" or "thinking"), and the *tovo* ("behavior" or "doing"). This set of terms was open for development with the acceptance of the Christian faith.

The language had a capacity for expansion by the compounding of the noun with an adjective, like *ca* or *vinaka* for "bad" and "good"; resulting in *valoca* and *yalovinaka*, *lomaca* and *lomavinaka*, *tovoca* and *tovovinaka*, indicating that the attitude, the thinking, or the behavior was good or bad as the cannibal context required.

By the time the Christian Bible translators had worked on this procedure, they had developed a wide ethical and spiritual lexicon, such as:

yaloca:	"evil-spirited," "angry"
yalovinaca:	"good-hearted," "generous"
yalokocokoco (intensive):	"covetous"
yalodina:	"true-spirited," "genuine"
yalododonu:	"right-spirited," "righteous"
yalosavasava:	"clean-spirited," "clean," "holy"
yalobatabata:	"cool-spirited" (i.e., without enthusiasm)
yalokatakata:	"hot-spirited," "enthusiastic" (in some cases, "hotheaded")
yalololoma:	"merciful"
yalobalavu:	"long-spirited" (i.e., "slow," "takes a long time")

(Other combinations: *vakayalo* "spiritual," *yalovata* "of one spirit," *veiyaloni* "of one spirit.")

Likewise with *loma*, there is: *lomadina* "true-minded," *loma-savasava* "pure-minded," etc. Or it might be *lomadei* "steadfast-minded," *lomalialia* "foolish-minded," or *lomasoli* "a mind to give." Likewise, to *tovoca* and *tovovinaka* were added *tovodina, tovododonu, tovosavasava*, and so on.

REFERENCES

Fison, Lorimer. 1885. The Nanga of Sacred Stone Encolsures of Wainimala, Fiji. *Journal of the Anthropological Society of Great Britain and Ireland* 14: 14–31.

Malinowski, Bronislaw. 1949. The problem of meaning in primitive languages. In *The meaning of meaning*, ed. C. K. Ogden and I. A. Richards, 296–336. London: Routledge and Kegan Paul.

Tippett, Alan R. 1954. The nature and social function of Fijian war. *Transactions of the Fijian Society* 5, no. 4: 137–55.

———. 1967. *Solomon Islands Christianity: A study in growth and obstruction.* London: Lutterworth.

———. 1971. *People movements in Southern Polynesia.* Chicago: Moody.

———. 1973. *Aspects of pacific ethnohistory.* South Pasadena: William Carey Library.

———. 1975. Christopaganism or indigenous Christianity? In *Christopaganism or indigenous Christianity?* ed. T. Yamamori and C. Taber. South Pasadena: William Carey Library.

Wallace, A. F. C. 1956. Revitalization movements. *American Anthropologist* 58: 241–81.

17

THE ABNORMALITY OR NORMALITY OF A FIJIAN CANNIBAL CHIEF[77]

Database

This paper is informed from descriptions of cannibalism in autobiographical manuscripts of island observers like Joeli Bulu and Jemesa Havea; from missionary letters and journals (most notably those of John Hunt, David Cargill, Thomas Williams, Richard Lyth, and later Lorimer Fison and Joseph Waterhouse (all of whom lived in cannibal times); and from records left by shipwrecked mariners like William Lockerby and Samuel Patterson. Not all these are directly cited in this paper, but collectively they form a corpus of documents from which the general picture of cannibal patterns can be reconstructed.

Myths and epic poems about Cakobau were extensively collected by Jesse Carey, and several missionaries recorded odd items. This corpus of material was produced between 1835 and the late 1860s and is scattered over various libraries and archival repositories in the Pacific: New Zealand, Australia, and Fiji.

Introduction

Fijian cannibalism may be considered from either one of two angles: (1) objectively and descriptively, or (2) functionally and interpretively. The first is simple because of an abundant database, and because the missionaries, sea captains, shipwrecked sailors, and sandalwood traders who supply the database were more or less in agreement. Apart from regional variations there can be no doubt about the general features of cannibal behavior, its widespread distribution and intensity, and its institutionalisation.

On the other hand, its meaning, function, and origin can be debated. Elsewhere (1973), I describe at length the nature of Fijian cannibalism, and in this present paper I shall merely mention the essentials required for the discussion before us. I also demonstrate in another paper (1972), using the ethnohistorical method known as "upstreaming," the history of Fijian cannibalism, working back in diachronic reverse beyond the periodic strata of colonialism, missionary contact, first Western culture contact, into the period of myths. That paper revealed that cannibalism was originally ceremonial and sacrificial, highly

---

77   Presented at the Annual Meeting of the American Society for Ethnohistory, Albuquerque, New Mexico, 1976.

institutionalised and controlled by taboos; that the introduction of Western arms and ammunition at the beginning of the last century led to secularisation of Fijian religion and a breakdown of taboos due to the accelerated warfare and increase of bodies (*bokolo*) for consumption. More important for this present paper is the missionary period from the arrival of the first missionaries (1835) to the Cession of Fiji to Britain (1874). This was the period of encounter between Christianity and cannibalism, without any pressure from colonial law or soldiers. The battle between Christianity and cannibalism in Fiji was not fought out in the colonial situation but in a complex of warring native kingdoms. From the perspective of our investigation, therefore, most of the colonial variables are eliminated from our data, and we should have a good "laboratory" for research, as we examine the phasing out of cannibalism and the phasing in of Christianity.

Theoretical Considerations

The purpose of this essay is to focus this study of Fijian cannibalism in a single personality, for whom enough documentation exists for a reliable construction. The best subject for our purpose is probably Ratu Cakobau of Bau, although Ra Esekaia of Bua, Ratu George of Dama, and Ratu Ilaija Varani of Viwa might all have served our purpose. These men were all chiefs in their respective regions, and all had convincing conversions, followed by dramatic changes in their behavior patterns.

It would be easy to speak of the change from "club rule and cannibalism" to that of "law and order," but this would be an unfair presupposition. It would be to assume that club rule and cannibalism was the opposite of law and order, whereas in reality it is merely another kind of law and order. The thesis of this essay is that the change brought about by conversion to Christianity was a change of *character orientation* or *mental set*, not a change of physical or intellectual capacities. The personality type can still be observed in terms of the same basic abilities and qualities. These men were still the leaders of their people. They still played the same social and political roles. They still had to deal with the same kind of problems and issues from the same personal capacities and skills. Becoming Christian did not destroy a man's capacity for leadership, although it did change his mental set. For both the individual and the society this meant a directional reorientation, what is currently known as a paradigm shift (Kuhn 1970; Barbour 1974).[78]

When the cannibal becomes what the theologian calls "a new man in Christ," physiologically and intellectually he is still the same man. The newness is manifest in behavior, values, ethics, and mental set, which proceed from his religious experience. If this be true the cannibal cannot be treated as an abnormal personality or one who is "mentally sick."

---

78 See Kuhn's chapter on "The Priority of Paradigms" and Barbour's discussion of it. Group conversion, like a scientific revolution, is a community paradigm shift.

His condition is determined by cultural factors like his worldview and religion. There is nothing physiological or psychopathological here.

The ethnocentric Western individualist has difficulty in understanding the individual in communal society. Nothing shows this up clearer than the common Western notion that a cannibal is mentally ill, because we look at him as a physical isolate instead of seeing him in his communal context. Ruth Benedict argued that people like the Fijians provide an excellent laboratory for psychological study, because their historical isolation has provided the opportunity for the development of local forms of social interplay. She questions the absoluteness of our normal/abnormal categories by asking if they are not rather functional mechanisms of culture. In pressing her argument she insists that whatever kind of "abnormality" we choose to illustrate the case, whether an extreme instability or some sadistic character trait, there are societies where "these abnormalities function at ease and with honor, and apparently without danger and difficulty to the society" (Benedict 1956, 183–84).

One feels disposed to bring Benedict's argument to bear on Fijian cannibalism in the pre-Christian society when she says, "The most spectacular illustrations of the extent to which normality may be culturally defined are those cultures where an abnormality of our culture is the corner-stone of their social structure" (ibid., 188).

Benedict's argument that normality is culturally defined raises the question of what happens to a behavior trait complex and the individual who operates within it, when that society and the individual pass through a great value change or basic paradigm shift, such as conversion to Christianity.

This present paper purports to answer that question and to throw light on the *relativity of normality,* for not only does normality vary from culture to culture but also from era to era within one culture. Benedict goes on to point out that it is possible for a society to achieve critical self-analysis and create its own new normalities (ibid., 198). This is what happens in people-movement conversions,[79] though Benedict does not discuss this.

The anthropologist Gillen struggled with definitions of the normal and the abnormal. He was disposed to regard normal persons as "culturally adjusted" and abnormal as "culturally mal-adjusted," but as this made normality and abnormality relative, he raised the question of whether all supposed abnormalities should not be differentiated as *cultural* or *absolute* (Gillen 1948, 589). Is the cannibal abnormal absolutely, or culturally (meaning abnormal only to someone in another culture)? Is he, like an imbecile, abnormal in any society? Or is he normal in his own society, whatever he may be to us. And if we proceed from diagnosis to prognosis, is the correction to be achieved by medical attention or directed cultural change?

---

79   See "The Structure and Validity of People Movements" in Tippett (1971, 197–220), and its database (1971, 9–136).

It occurs to me than an ethnopsychological (rather than theological) study of the conversion of the Fijian people from cannibalism to Christianity, whether we consider its stimuli as from outside by evangelism, or from inside by self-analysis, we have a case of society creating for itself a new normalcy. This is not a case of a passage from abnormality to normality, but of the processes of culture change from one era to another in a perfectly normal human community.

One does not get far along the track of pondering the data before he comes up against the problem of the *individual* and his *community*. We are not dealing with an isolated individual convert over *against* his social group, which would make his conversion idiosyncratic or abnormal. Unfortunately many Christian missions have tried to grow this way. But this was not so in Fiji, where waves of conversion swept through localities and lineages by group decision or consensus. People were converted together within their groups, and new group normalities emerged at the same time, in the totality of the multi-individual conversion movements. (For the psychology of this creation of new group norms, see Tippett 1971, 210.)

Fijian Cannibalism and Religion

John Hunt, who lived among the cannibals of Fiji (1838–48) before the conversion of Cakobau, and for half of that decade had a cannibal oven a few feet from his door, was firmly convinced that cannibalism sprang from Fijian religion:

> The religion of the Fijian *requires* cannibalism. When the priest promises the applicants that they shall be successful in war, by slaying some of the enemy, the bodies are given by the gods not to be killed only, but to be eaten also. Human flesh is not cooked in the ovens or vessels used ordinarily. Cannibalism has its poisoned source in their religion. (quoted in Nettleton 1906, 32)

Even when personal motives like revenge and love of notoriety were quite manifestly the immediate reason for cannibal acts, nevertheless these were executed *within the institutionalised pattern*, and *performed as religious acts* and *with the authority of religion*. Not only were sacred cooking utensils used, but also different modes of cooking (Seemann 1862; MacDonald 1857). But frequently the killings were for *purely religious* purposes without any personal motivation. In his journal, Thomas Williams (25 October 1849) spoke of his experience of cannibals in Bua "hunting for men for a heathen sacrifice," and added, "There was no revenge in this case, they were not enemies, merely the need for sacrifice."

As far back as we can go into the myths of the precontact period, *the gods were cannibals*, who made war on and ate the enemy. They expected an offering of bodies in sacrifice from those they assisted. The standard pattern of the epic myth finishes with the hero, having derived *mana* from the ancestor, heaping up his victims as a sacrificial offering before the ancestral dwelling place:

A thousand legs are laid together
And all the feet are tied together
This food for the oven.

The cannibal gods of the people, *kalou kanari*, many mentioned by name (e.g., Degei, Tuisicidra [Deane 1921, 226]) are set off in contradistinction to Jehovah in the period of encounter with Christianity (see journals of Lyth and T. Williams)—and this is *a Fijian differentiation*, not a missionary one. It was the indigenous obstruction offered against one's becoming Christian, as Cakobau himself said, when unable to answer an evangelist's argument of the advantages of becoming Christian: "Wonderful is the new religion, no doubt? But will it prevail? Will it prevent our having men to eat? Not it!"

David Cargill also, the first Western missionary in Fiji, though revolted by the very idea of cannibalism and the cruelty and revenge that went with it, recognised that "they are a decidedly religious people," but this "religion is the poisoned *source* from which these demoralizing qualities have been derived." The "poisoned source" is a phrase also used by Hunt. This may suggest the missionaries had discussed among themselves the relation of religion to cannibalism.

In any case, acceptance of a new religion like Christianity had to deal with cannibalism. There could be no such thing as a political conversion without encounter at the religious level. This I have documented elsewhere at great length (1967b, 1971).

Ratu Seru Cakobau: The Cannibal Chief of Bau

Pre-Christian Fijian epics describe the young Seru in a bloody episode that took place at the island of Moala somewhere about 1822, in which the young child hero clubbed his older and bigger eight-year-old victim and pounded him until he died. They were violent days, and the children were merely reenacting for themselves the approved behavior and values of adult life. The epic poems were still chanted, and several missionaries had the words of them before Seru's conversion thirty years later. Waterhouse subsequently used them later in his work *The King and People of Fiji*, which he wrote after sixteen years of residence in the locality: "The boy chief puts aside his heavy weapon to gaze on his first sacrifice to the customs of his people. Thence he departs to wash his hands, and partake of food, feeling himself every inch a man" (1866, 7).

Seru entered into Fijian political history dramatically in 1837 and, between that date and his conversion in 1854, he was to devour a thousand human bodies, many of them killed by his own hand and scored on the handles of his war clubs.[80] A political revolution in 1832 had sent his father, Tanoa, into exile. After five years the young Seru planned and carried out a counterrevolution, which reinstated Tanoa and literally exterminated the

---

80 The writer has a pencil rubbing of the score marks on the haft of one of Cakobau's throwing clubs (*ai ula*).

rebels, sacrificing them to the ancestral gods and giving their flesh to the Lasakauans.[81] One rebel, who was brought before Seru, had to witness the chief devour his tongue raw, and suffer other mutilation of his body while he begged in agony for a speedy death. This mockery was itself no mere innovation of the bloodthirsty cannibal, but an *institutionalised pattern* of revenge (*seledrutia*). After a period of torment, the miserable victim was killed and eaten (ibid., 62–63).

Seru derived a new cluster of titles from this accomplishment, after the Fijian practice of giving a "name with a meaning," *yaca vakaibalebale*. His enemies henceforth called him Cakobau, meaning "Bau is at War," as the kingdom indeed was thereafter continuously until his conversion, and for a year afterwards. The chiefly party on Bau called the young man Cikinovu ("Centipede"), because he had demonstrated his capacity to deliver a sudden, sharp, and unexpected bite. He also earned the name Bi from some of the Bauan chiefs. A *bi* is a turtle fence, where captured turtles are kept for feasting when required. The name is also used symbolically for human bodies kept for sacrificing and cooking. *Lewe ni bi* (literally, "turtles within the fence") was a popular idiom for captives held prisoner for eating when required.

All these terms appear in the chants and dance songs that celebrate the event, and to Seru himself they gave great personal satisfaction. With Tanoa restored and Cakobau now established as War Lord (*Vu ni Valu*), Bau was indeed to continue as the major center of cannibalism in Fiji, outdoing both Rewa and Somosomo, rival kingdoms of gory fame.

> Seru won renown and glory
> Also won suggestive titles.
>
> "Turtle-pond," "Na Bi," they named him
> For his deeds had filled the ovens
> With the flesh of human turtles. (Carey's translation 1891, 259)

The Lasakauans (who resided on Bau) and Viwans (on another island two miles north of Bau) were responsible for keeping Bau supplied with bodies for the cannibal functions. There were some thirty heathen temples at Bau and, during the Bau/Rewa War for two years, "the Bau ovens were never cold" (Waterhouse 1866, 111–12).[82] Concentrations of religious temples and concentrations of cannibalism came together in Fiji. William Cross, who lived just opposite Bau on Viwa, wrote in his journal:

> The dead bodies of human beings are in continual request at Bau. The building
> of temples, chief houses, taking down the masts of new canoes, visits of Somo-

---

81   The Lasakauans were the fighting seamen of Bau, a social unit with a residential locality of their own and the last unit of Bau island to become Christian.

82   I believe this was a saying in Fiji at the time. It recurs in a number of records. The missionaries certainly used it, but I believe it came from the Fijians themselves and should be placed in the same category as the name Cakobau.

somo people with their canoes and property, are all occasions of numerous
murders. (9 June 1839)

Raivalita (who apparently, under Christian influence, had some conscience about how
far custom should be stretched) tried to restrain Cakobau's particularly vicious instructions about how certain victims were to be killed by offering Cakobau his new canoe, as
a substitutionary atonement gift on their behalf. Cakobau snapped, "Keep your canoe. I
want to eat men." So the men had to dig their own ovens, cut their firewood, make the ba-
nana-leaf cups into which their blood would be drained and drunk in their presence, while
they were still alive. And they had to see their own limbs cut off one by one and offered
back to them in bitter mockery to eat. Then fish hooks were to be placed in their tongues,
which were to be drawn out and cut off, roasted and eaten before their eyes. Then, if they
had still not expired, their bowels were to be removed (Waterhouse 1866, 82–85). This treatment was prescribed for the escapees of the Namena massacre. It needs to be remembered
that politically Namena had long been a "thorn in the flesh" to Bau. Cakobau's motivation
was not sadism. He lived in a cannibal society in which clubbing was "an easy way out." To
maintain his authority as a cannibal chief, he had to perpetuate his image as a ruthless
autocrat who was dangerous to oppose.

A Fijian society rejoiced in the strength of its war lord—his fame, his status, his reputation—his ferocity guaranteed the security and perpetuity of the society, and the people
took comfort in this.

Seru was a firm believer that survival was possible in Fiji only by success in war and
ruthless discipline. When John Waterhouse[83] talked to him about this brutality in war,
Cakobau replied: "We will fight till we die: we will teach our children to fight, and our children's children shall fight" (1944 [14 June 1841]).

This was shortly after the plot against Namena, when over one hundred persons were
killed in an hour, and the bodies were taken to Bau for cannibal purposes.

Bauan Society Becomes "Ripe" for Change

Although Bau lived in splendid isolation, lording it over the other states of Fiji, and Cakobau claimed to be King of Fiji (*Tui Viti*), nevertheless both the powerful state and the War
Lord were not unaware of the religious changes going on in the Group under missionary
influence.[84]

An interesting feature of the journal of John Waterhouse's tour of the Fijian mission
areas in 1841 is the contrast between all the accounts of war and cannibalism through-

---

83   John Waterhouse, father of Joseph, was general secretary over all Wesleyan missions in the Pacific. He lived in Aus-
     tralia and visited all the island missions.

84   Communities under Bauan authority were becoming Christian in small groups all through the 1840s (1841, 134; 1842,
     356; 1843, 420; and so on). Lau had all turned to Christianity by 1849. Cakobau's conversion was not until 1854.

out Greater Fiji with his report of conditions in Lau (the windward islands), Lakemba in particular, where no cannibalism had been reported for two years. The missionaries had been working there for the comparatively short time of six years. This widespread change affected the whole society, not just a few odd individuals.

A decade later the "Introduction" to a book written by the wife of a *beche-de-mer* trader, described the life of Fiji, and spoke of the Fijians as the Ishmaelites of the South Pacific, whose natural ferocity and cannibalism had discouraged many attempts to civilise them. It went on to point out that under the influence of Christian missionaries they were *found to be interesting people*:

> Beneath their wild and uncouth exterior have been found marks of intellec-
> tual power and sagacity. Minds have been discovered there, which, under the
> discipline of refined culture, might have ranked high upon the scale of mental
> attainment . . . Many of these islanders have abandoned their cannibalism, and
> introduced into their habits of living, the manners and forms of humanized life.
> (Wallis 1851, vii–viii)

If we allow for the literary style of 120 years ago, the writer was saying that there was nothing psychopathological or abnormal about cannibalism. It was *culturally conditioned normalcy*. The society had *the capacity for critical self-analysis and the creation of new normalities*. The above quotation referred to life in the Christian communities in Lau and Viwa. Bau had not yet changed. Cakobau was still a cannibal. Her book has no index, but I noted over twenty descriptions of cannibalism in Mrs. Wallis' experiences. Her stay in Fijian waters was long enough to observe clearly the difference between cannibal and Christian values and behavior.

In 1853 Joseph Waterhouse was permitted to live on Bau, and he began to reason with Cakobau against his war and cannibalism. There is some evidence that this was possible because the rank and file of the people of both the Bau coastline and the Rewa delta were tired of continual war. Waterhouse was articulating the younger Fijian folk, and his writing seems to imply that the continued demand for cannibalism was confined to the older folk, who clung to the traditional religion based on it (1866, 242). Certainly during 1853 and early 1854 Bau as a society was moving collectively towards conversion to Christianity.

The notion of resistance to innovation by a society not yet socially ready for it was developed in anthropology by Kroeber (1948, 366–67); and the presence of an "adoption period" between awareness and decision making, by Rogers (1962, 105–20), and with special reference to group conversion in non-Western society, by Tippett (1967b).

In the case of Bau and its War Lord, a complex of sociopolitical factors was closing in on Cakobau, and some drastic socioreligious change was necessary to avoid a crisis.

Epenisa Cakobau, the Christian

In 1854 Cakobau became a Christian. His motivation was very complex, and does not concern us in this paper. It should be noted, however, that having made what seems to me to have been a sincere decision in private with his wife, Litia Samanunu (already a Christian), and the missionary, he called together his extended family (*vu vale*) and discussed the situation at length and then the public announcement he was about to make. The next day he called together the leaders of his kingdom (*matanitu*) and went through the same procedure. As a result of this corporate sharing, on the following Sunday, when Cakobau entered church and "bowed the knee to the Lord" (*cuva vei Jiova*), a great number of his family and friends accompanied him, and a group conversion movement began. But it was multi-individual and not mass movement. They did not follow the chief like "sheep." Each week another group of persons followed. After twelve weeks from Cakobau's conversion, about eight hundred Bauans had become Christian, and his kinsmen on the island were 50/50 Christian/pagan (Bau Circuit 1854).

I have commented on the great difference between Christian Lakeba and cannibal Bau through the 1840s. In 1854 there were Lauan youths fifteen years of age who had not heard a cannibal drum in their own island, but they knew they lived under the fearful shadow of Bau. The Bauans left them alone only because they found enough Rewan bodies nearer at hand. When the Fijian leaders in Lakeba heard that Cakobau converted, one of them said:

> There is an oven in which all the Fijians are being cooked to be afterwards
> eaten. That oven is Bau, and that oven is now closed. A remnant of our race will
> yet live, to cultivate the soil, and to occupy the country God has given us. (Waterhouse 1866, 263)

Cakobau now placed himself under Christian instruction for three years, accepted Christian marriage, and was baptised in 1857. He now received a "name with a meaning," Epenisa, from the Bible, saying, "Hitherto hath the Lord helped us." This was a cultural element shared by the Hebrews and the Fijians.

The transformation recorded of Cakobau's behavior after his conversion is remarkable and well documented. The conversion was the signal for his enemies to gather and to plot his downfall. He knew full well that hundreds of Fijian cannibals would have delighted in taking revenge on him in the institutionalised cannibal Fijian way. They would have shown no mercy, and he knew it. He knew also that many in the coastal villages who were loyal to him when he was the cannibal War Lord would desert him when he turned to worship the Lord who was not a cannibal god. His loyalist forces—mixed Christian and pagan—met the rebels at the Battle of Kaba about a year after his conversion. As it happened, the forces of Cakobau were victorious, and Cakobau had to face a more subtle test than a cannibal oven. He had to decide how a Christian victor handles the hundreds of captives taken by his forces, many of whom were themselves still cannibals.

Waterhouse was on Bau at the time and saw from the hilltop the victorious Christians on one side and the Lasakauan cannibal loyalists on the other. The former were actually ministering to the wounds of their captives, the latter coolly killing them. But Cakobau took charge of the situation and, contrary to his previous behavior pattern, would tolerate no butchery. A spy, who would certainly have been eaten, and indeed expected this, was recommended to become a Christian, and escorted back to his town unharmed (Bau Circuit 1855). Two hundred captives who had vowed (*bubului*) to eat the Christian chiefly convert were brought before Cakobau after Kaba (where his authority was reestablished and the rebels were put to flight) and were frankly forgiven and returned home. This even included Koroi Ravulo, on whose head Cakobau had put a price years before his conversion (Waterhouse 1866, 293). The pagans were amazed at this new value of forgiveness manifested in place of revenge. More than any other single factor this led the villages along the Bau Coast to follow Cakobau's example and become Christian in the two or three years which followed. This movement has all been statistically graphed on a flow chart (Tippett 1967a, 86–89).

The old killing stone against which Cakobau had previously had his captives torpedoed, head first, before putting them into the oven, was not used again for this purpose after his conversion. Five years later, Thomas Baker (shortly afterwards to be killed and eaten in the highlands) saw it there overgrown by vegetation (Baker 1859–61). Subsequently Cakobau had it made into a baptismal font and placed in the new Christian church on Bau. The church itself was made from the stone foundations of seventeen Bauan pre-Christian temples which fell out of use during the 1850s and 1860s. The new Christians, led by Cakobau, destroyed the old evidences of their cannibal religion and built their salvaged materials into functional substitutes so their children would not forget that they have been saved from a cannibal religion.

The importance of this to the theme of this paper is that it shows Cakobau still as the leader of his people. His mental set had certainly changed, but his capacity for leadership remained the same.

Deane, a missionary of a later day (but not so late that he was prevented from collecting and recording the cannibal drumbeats), reflecting on the past and present, wrote:

> We who have lived in Fiji have reason to believe, from the evidence which is to
> be seen in Fijian society today, that, if circumstances be changed, the appetite
> caused by them dies away also. (1921, 239)

Perhaps I may cite also a district commissioner of the old colonialist type, who was no particular admirer of Wesleyanism and loved having a slap at it, but nevertheless gave his judgment of Cakobau thus:

He was thorough in all things. As a cannibal he was terrible and bloodthirsty; when he embraced Christianity he did it with his whole heart; and finally as a subject of the Queen he gave her his full obedience. He was a typical old-fashioned South Sea chieftain, cunning in council, brave and resourceful in war, yet simple and patriarchal in life and habits. As an example to his people he cultivated his food plantations with his own hands, and as becomes a chief he excelled in all things that he undertook. (Brewster 1937, 281–82)[85]

Conclusion

When I look at the man Cakobau, whether in the period of his cannibal or Christian days, I find him a normal human being within his own religio-cultural frame of reference; a man with full self-control for behaving or operating as a social being—for survival, for adaptation, for development. He operated within his worldview and value system, and when his religious belief changed he manifested a tremendous capacity for rapid adjustment in the crisis.

A born leader of his people (they accepted his leadership and felt secure under it), he demonstrated a capacity for self-awareness, for social awareness, for planned action, for speculation, for integration of values, for responsibility, and for intellectual adjustment. He saw those who depended on him as "his people" and showed a paternal concern for their security and survival.

He understood much about the nature of social change in the Fijian way of life, and when he saw that change was inevitable, he took control of it and channeled it. Were this a book instead of a paper, I would illustrate each of those points comparatively from both his cannibal and Christian years. These capacities are human universals, and signs of normalcy. Benedict's point is well made, when we Westerners look at Cakobau, the cannibal, in his own society:

> Those organizations of personality that seem to us most incontrovertibly abnormal have been used in different civilizations in the very foundations of their institutional life . . . Normality, in short . . . is culturally defined. (Benedict 1956, 194–95)

Thomas Williams (who lived in Fiji from 1838 to 1853) pointed out with respect to cannibalism that it was "one of their institutions, it is interwoven in the elements of society; it forms one of their pursuits, and is regarded by the mass as refinement" (1844, 175). Truly does Melville Herskovits, the anthropologist, say, "The very definition of what is normal and abnormal is relative to the cultural frame of reference" (1951, 66).

When the Fijian chiefs, unable to deal with their internal strife and other factors which do not concern us here, sought to cede their islands to British rule in the 1850s, Britain re-

---

85   In Fiji at the time he was Adolf Joske. Like many British Germans he changed his name during the Great War (1914–18).

jected the request on the report of a military man, Col. J. W. Smythe, because it would take a force of "not less than a wing of a regiment," a warship and light draught tender (both steamers) and considerable cost to accomplish what the missionaries were doing slowly through the process of conversion. (Text of the report is in Smythe 1864, 208–9).

The missionaries, of course, were advocates of the new religion and value system, but the real innovators were the people themselves (Barnett 1953)—the multi-individual society. If we compare the beginning and the end of this period of encounter between cannibalism and Christianity, and consider the paradigm shift, we discover the *relativity of normality*. People-movement churches tend to be more indigenous than those built by converting odd individuals out of their social structures, because the individual and the society are in step with each other through the process of religious change. We have a personal paradigm shift, but the natural capacities remain the same. In the specific case we have discussed of the chief, Ratu Cakobau, as cannibal or Christian, he proved to be a normal person and a competent one in either worldview.

REFERENCES

Baker, Thomas. 1859–61. *Journal.*

Barbour, Ian. 1974. *Myths, models and paradigms: A comparative study of science and religion.* New York: Harper & Row.

Barnett, Homer G. 1953. *Innovation: The basis of cultural change.* New York: McGraw-Hill.

Bau Circuit. 1854–55. *Annual reports.* Wesleyan Missionary Conference.

Benedict, Ruth. 1956. Anthropology and the abnormal. In *Personal character and cultural milieu,* ed. Douglas Haring. Syracuse: Syracuse University Press.

Brewster, A. B. 1937. *King of the Cannibal Isles.* London: Robert Hall.

Carey, Jesse. 1891. *The kings of the reefs.* Melbourne: Spectator Publishing.

Cargill, David. 1841. *Memoirs of Margaret Cargill.* London: John Mason.

Cross, William. 1838–42. *Journal.*

Deane, Wallace. 1921. *Fijian society; or The sociology and psychology of the Fijians.* London: Macmillan.

Gillen, John. 1948. *The ways of men: An introduction to anthropology.* New York: Appleton-Century.

Herskovits, Melville J. 1951. *Man and his works.* New York: Knopf.

Hunt, John. 1838–48. *Journal.* 2 vols.

———. 1846. *Memoir of Rev. William Cross.* London: John Mason.

Kroeber, A. L. 1948. *Anthropology.* New York: Harcourt, Brace and Co.

Kuhn, Thomas S. 1970. *The structure of scientific revolutions.* Chicago: University of Chicago Press.

Lyth, Richard B. 1836–50. *Journal.* 5 vols.

MacDonald, John D. 1857. Proceedings of the expedition for the exploration of the Rewa River and its tributaries, in Na Viti Levu, Fiji Islands. *Journal Royal Geographic Society* 28: 232–68.

Nettleton, Joseph. 1906. *John Hunt: Pioneer missionary and saint*. London: Charles H. Kelley.

Rogers, Everett M. 1962. *Diffusion of innovations*. New York: Free Press.

Seemann, Berthold. 1862. *Viti: An account of a government mission to the Vitian or Fijian Islands 1860-61*. Cambridge: Macmillan.

Smythe, S. M. 1864. *Ten months in the Fiji Islands*. Oxford: John Henry and James Parker.

Tippett, Alan R. 1967a. The dynamics of church planting in Fiji. Unpublished manuscript.

———. 1967b. Religious group conversion in non-Western society. Unpublished manuscript.

———. 1971. *People movements in Southern Polynesia*. Chicago: Moody.

———. 1972. The cultural dynamics of Fijian cannibalism. Unpublished manuscript.

———. 1973. The idiom of honorable and dishonorable killing in Fiji in the contact period. Unpublished manuscript.

Wallis, Mary D. 1851. *Life in Fiji; or Five years among the cannibals*. Boston: William Heath.

Waterhouse, John. 1944. Journal (1841). *Wesleyan Magazine* 67.

Waterhouse, Joseph. 1866. *The king and people of Fiji*. London: Wesleyan Conference Office.

Williams, Thomas. 1838–53. *Journal*.

———. 1884. *Fiji and the Fijians*; and *Missionary labors among the cannibals*. Ed. James Calvert. One-volume edition. London: Charles H. Kelley. First published 1860.

18
THE EARLY GROWTH OF THE CHURCH IN FIJI[86]

The passage of the gospel from Troas to Philippi in New Testament times was a transmission from Asia into Europe. McGavran calls such transmissions "bridges of God." In the same way the church passed from Polynesia to Melanesia, via Tonga and Fiji.

The Tongan Bridge

The Fijian Group was still relatively unexplored. To navigators its prospects were terrifying. When the missionaries wanted a vessel to take them from Tonga to Fiji, the captain demanded an exorbitant price and would take them no further than the Polynesian fringe. But this was enough, for God had prepared a bridge, and the "fullness of time" had come. The Tongan language was understood in the Lauan islands of Fiji and in many of the chiefly centers, as many chiefs had acquired attractive Tongan wives. Tongan influence had been felt in eastern Fiji for a century or so. Tongan colonies were dotted about the Group, in particular at the chiefly centers. Many Tongan wanderers had settled down and married Fijian women. Tongan influence had already imposed itself on Fijian material culture—design, carving, house building—and mythology. Tongan craftsmen and entertainers had prestige in Fiji.

The same may be said in a less appreciative way of the roving bands of Tongan filibusters who went from island to island attaching themselves to any chief who would pay them well enough to fight his local wars. This gave the young Tongan adventurers status at home after they had "won their spurs" on some plundering expedition.

On a more pleasant note, we observe also that there were many trade contacts between pre-Christian Tonga and Fiji. The Tongans went to Macuata for sandalwood to scent their oils, to Yasawas and Kadavu for sail mats for their canoes. The red feathers of the Kadavu parrots were used for the royal regalia of Tonga and to trim the fine mats of their chiefs. The green feathers of the same bird the Tongans traded with Samoa. Fiji also offered food, water, and oil receptacles and other forms of pottery—jars, dishes, and lamps—and an

---

86   Taken from bound collection of articles entitled *Historical Writing: Fiji, 1947–1967; Studies from the History of the Fijian Church, 1835–1967.* Unpublished article.

abundance of wood carving, weapons of war, and food dishes, also timber for great canoes. Tonga traded whales' teeth and bark cloth. Tongan carpenters usurped the canoe-building profession of Fiji and became resident. Tonga had more contacts with white traders and whalers and served as interpreters. Some centuries earlier pigs, fowls, and muscovy ducks found their way from Tonga to Fiji and more recently axes, hatchets, chisels, fishhooks, plane irons, knives, calico, and prints. Tongan mercenaries supplied their own powder and shot. Acculturation began in Fiji because of the Tongan, not the white man.

This was the state of affairs when the Great Awakening came to Tonga. This significant people movement not only brought the Tongan people to Christ but expressed itself in an expanding missionary drive. After 1834, converts began thinking of and praying for Fiji, and by the end of 1835 the first missionaries were already established in the new land. All procedure and communication was performed within the correct chiefly pattern. The Tongan king had often sent presentations and messages to the Fijian chief at Lakeba, but never one quite like this, with two white missionary families, a Fijian petty chief converted in Tonga, and a party of Tongan evangelists. These latter were selected men with some chiefly status so that the missionaries could be introduced with dignity. The first gospel communications were in the Tongan language. The first converts in Fiji were Tongans, and the profound difference the conversion made to their behaviour convinced many Fijians to take a serious look at this new doctrine.

The Fijian who had come from Tonga became the spearhead of the missionary attack on his pagan homeland. At each point before a new advance he was sent ahead to "spy out the land." As a matter of strategic policy he went to the chiefly centers; this being the correct Fijian procedure. But the Tongan settlements were all at chiefly villages. In these places the Tongans listened eagerly to the Fijian's testimony of the great happenings in Tonga. News that Tonga had turned to Christ gave the Fijian evangelist an attentive audience, and within a short period of time families and groups accepted the new faith. Thus the first converts were Tongans, and they came as groups. It was an outreach of the Tongan movement itself.

The First Melanesian Christians

With the Fijians it was a different matter. They listened at first to the Word with interest, but it was more important to them that the new missionary residents brought stores of axes and fishhooks. For some time there was no sign of acceptance of the gospel.

Before long the truth dawned on the Fijians that these boisterous Tongan migrants had undergone a remarkable change of life; whatever this gospel was, it had certainly worked a mighty transformation in them.

The earliest Fijian converts were mostly individuals who joined the Tongan Christians first as mere occasional hearers then later with commitment due to the preaching of the

Word. The preaching in Tongan won the Tongans for Christ but very few Fijians. When the Word was preached in Fijian, the truth dawned on the indigenous people that this gospel was being offered to them, that it was not merely a movement among the Tongans. Though this had been stated from the outset, when the gospel was heard in their own tongue they became impressed with the seriousness of the invitation.

At the end of the first year of the Christian mission to Fiji, the Christian congregation at Lakeba comprised 131 members (all adults who had been baptised) and sixty-four under instruction as members on trial. Only four of these were Fijians. It is interesting to note that the full training system was in operation during the first year of the mission and the first Fijian individual converts had come in.

The church in Tonga rose to the occasion magnificently and for years sent many of her best evangelists to Fiji, but the tendency was for the Tongans converted in Fiji to consider whether or not their reformed ways permitted them to stay there indefinitely. Within the first decade many hundreds of Tongans had been converted and had returned to Tonga.

They had been good pioneers. They had provided a Christian nucleus that permitted the early individual Fijian converts to have a fellowship from the beginning and build up some Christian maturity that stood by them well under the persecution they were to experience before any people movements began in Fiji.

The early Fijian church grew from the beginning on the biblical principle—"Let the redeemed of the Lord say so." There was praise and testimony when the converts, regardless of status, would tell "what the Lord had done unto them." They strengthened each other in the faith in the fellowship group, and as individuals each man was himself an evangelist. They built houses for worship. They participated in stewardship from the start. They faced persecution with courage, and thousands of them died for their faith. The first individual converts very quickly brought their nuclear families and sometimes a larger family unit.

More missionaries arrived in 1838, and immediately a forward thrust was made into the heart of Fiji. Each locality saw the church planted in this way—a movement among the Tongans, then a few Fijian individuals, small families, and then larger groups—in time whole villages and lineages. The early stages were always days of persecution. In the eastern islands the realm of the King was won for Christ by midcentury. It took fourteen years. This was the area of strongest Tongan influence and served as a stepping-stone into Melanesia. A strong Christian center had been established at Viwa in the heart of Fiji in the first decade. From this strategic station thrusts went out in all directions. Here the New Testament was translated and printed by 1847—a memorable achievement. From this center early institutionalism and regular itineration were kept in relationship to each other. Here Fiji's own indigenous evangelists were trained in the use of that book. These men, more than any missionary, won Fiji for Christ.

At the end of 1838 Fiji was separated from Tonga as a missionary district, and the missionaries had their own powers and autonomy. During the 1840s the missionary thrusts extended through Ovalau, Taveuni, the Bau coast, at several points on Vanua Levu, and to Kadavu.

The great event of the 1850s was the conversion of the celebrated cannibal chief, Ratu Cakobau, and shortly after this the Battle of Kaba when his authority was challenged. These were years of great people movements, many of them with no relation to Bau, Cakobau's kingdom. Paganism died hard, and in some places whole Christian villages were wiped out in raids by night. Yet the church grew mightily by aggressive evangelism. The young church produced a regular "army of prophets." After thirty years of mission the coastal people of the greater islands and the island communities had been won from paganism and were enjoying regular and disciplined Christian worship. The hill tribes, culturally and linguistically different, secure in their mountain strongholds, still remained solidly pagan and cannibal, but everywhere they were encircled by Christians.

Features of the Early Christian Church in Fiji

(1) Anyone who believes in a God who is active in history will have ample evidence for his belief in this story of the beginning of the church in Fiji. Because of the Tongan bridge the eastern islands lay open to the gospel. The conversion of the chief Mateinaniu in Tonga, his role of "spying out the land" before each forward thrust of mission, and his good standing with both Tongan and Fijian and many other significant events, which the secular historian might regard as coincidence and fortunate, when contemplated cumulatively are impressive. The Hebrew prophet would have said again, "I have gone before you and made the crooked places straight." The church came into Fiji in God's time and in His way.

(2) One is impressed in working through the archival descriptions of the spiritual movements which were a feature of this mission's activity from the beginning. The Spirit of God certainly worked on groups of people as it did in New Testament times. Many remarkable group experiences of Pentecostal power have been described and the records preserved.

(3) God used the ordinary people who were ready to bear witness to the wonder of their salvation experience and new life in Christ.

(4) The translation achievement was remarkable in itself, but the Bible in the hands of the Fijian was a most powerful factor in Fijian life. God used the written Word to convince men of the truth of the gospel. It changed lives of converts who were willing to act upon it. It gave Fiji a linguistic and social unity it never had before.

(5) The church in all its parts operated from the start. The fellowship was fully participant. If the way they trod in the pagan world was a way of the Cross, it was also the way of victory.

(6) Evangelism was the converts' primary responsibility. It was an indigenous church with outreach from the beginning.

19
PIONEERING EDUCATION IN FIJI (1835–42)[87]

Serious misunderstanding has arisen through the publication of uninformed statements like these:

> The early missionaries had no knowledge of educational method.

> In the early schools children and adults, men and women were all taught together.

> Nothing was done for girls in their special crafts until recent times.

Many such statements have appeared in official publications of both the Methodist Church and the Education Department of Fiji. It is therefore the purpose of this paper to investigate the nature of the schools and teaching in the first seven years of mission history in this country.

First Missionaries

The Wesleyan Mission to Fiji was an offshoot of the Tonga Mission, the outcome of the people movement into Christianity during 1833–34. There had been considerable intercourse between the two groups prior to this, trade and labour connections and also large migrations. The Tongan language was well known in the eastern islands of Fiji, and it was therefore natural that the new mission should commence in Lakeba. The project had been contemplated for some time, but the people movement created a missionary passion, and the two men selected to lead the new mission were both experienced in the Tongan work and fluent speakers of the Tongan language. David Cargill, a master of arts in languages, was specially selected for pioneering Fiji because of his linguistic ability; and William Cross, his companion, although not so academic, had experience in instructing young people before becoming a missionary, and had been a missionary in Tonga for eight years (Hunt 1846, 13).[88] When, three years later, the team was strengthened by the addition of three men from Britain, two of them had been theologically trained and the other was

---

87   Taken from bound collection of articles entitled *Historical Writing: Fiji, 1947-1967; Studies from the History of the Fijian Church, 1835-1967*. Unpublished article.

88   Cross attended his first service in Tonga 11 Nov 1827, when the Tonga Mission seemed to be an utter failure.

a Kingswood-school man (Cargill 1841, 203).[89] The next to follow was a qualified medical man (Henderson 1931),[90] and two of the team were competent printers (ibid., 204),[91] one was highly proficient in both Greek and Hebrew (and therefore a natural choice for Scripture translation),[92] and within the decade the greatest linguist of them all had arrived,[93] and also a trained teacher from one of the best schools in the Colonies.[94] All these were ministerial missionaries, and among those who had no particular academic training, one turned out to be a first-class infant teacher,[95] and another a practical man who made his own educational aids, including a globe.[96] The claim that the early missionaries had no knowledge of educational method is highly suspect the moment one looks at the list of names and compares the general standard of the ministry in Britain at the time with that of the rank and file of teachers.

First Schools

Cross and Cargill arrived in Fiji on 12 October 1835. On the last day of that month Cargill reports in his *Journal* that a simple school system had been started. The male school commenced at sunrise each morning from Monday to Friday and lasted for an hour and a half. It was conducted by the missionaries in the open air, and reading and writing were taught. In the afternoon a female school was held under similar conditions, some fifty attending and receiving instruction from the wives of the missionaries (Cargill 1841, 107). This is an important record. It reveals a definite pattern in schoolwork from the very beginning, and the schools were graded, men and women being segregated according to Fijian custom and their work differentiated. The primary purpose was to teach reading so the people could read and learn scripture portions, hymns, and catechism.

It should be remembered that most of those who attended were Tongans, and both the men and women among the missionaries were fluent Tongan speakers. Mrs. Cargill, for instance, had a good knowledge of Tongan and needed no interpreter. She lived a regular life with rounds of visiting, caring for the sick, teaching sewing, and running female groups for discussing sermons and so on (ibid., 107). Cross had lost his wife in Tonga, and his second wife had had less opportunity to learn Tongan. I have traced no specific references to her teaching beyond sewing. Mrs. Cargill set to work immediately to become a competent

---

89　John Hunt did full three years in Hoxton, James Calvert part time, Thomas Jaggar was the Kingswood-school man. They arrived December 1838.

90　Dr. Lyth, who had spent sixteen months in Tonga before coming to Fiji, and spoke fluent Tongan (Henderson 1931, 11 July 1841 and elsewhere).

91　Calvert and Jaggar.

92　John Hunt, who translated all the New Testament, save for John's Gospel, which was the work of Watsford.

93　David Hazlewood, who compiled the grammar and dictionary, which was used as the standard for almost a century.

94　John Watsford, had been a teacher at King's School, Parramatta, his own school. His juvenile school at Viwa was famous later.

95　John Malvern, who set so many health and hygiene lessons to rhyme to fit simple tunes, both English and local.

96　Thomas Williams. See Henderson 1931, 4 January 1849, for reference to the globe.

Fijian speaker, and her husband prepared his grammar and vocabulary on her account (Cargill 1841, 110),[97] although it was copied by all the missionaries for some years.

Twelve months after the commencement of the first schools at Lakeba, there were some 252 under instruction (Cargill 1841, 131), and by January 1837 there were more than thirty Fijians attending school (if I read the text correctly) at Nukunuku (148). The 1837 report, written just two years after the start of the mission showed about four hundred at school (153).[98] Shortly afterwards there is a report of a school at Waitabu (151), and another at Waciwaci, this one for Fijians (158). This should serve to show that the missionaries were concerned seriously with schools from the outset.

Indigenous Agents

It follows, however, that their main activities must have been confined to the centre where they dwelt, and that Tongan and Fijian agents were used as monitors and teachers for the schools established in other villages like Waitabu, Nukunuku, and Waciwaci. As yet there were few agents sufficiently advanced. Josua Mateinaniu, Fijian teacher, who had come with Cross and Cargill from Tonga, was now in charge at Oneata (Hunt 1846, 82),[99] but the team of six selected men from Tonga, which made such an evangelical impact on Fiji in the 1840s, did not arrive until June 1838, and had to begin by attending the Fijian school and learning to speak better Fijian (Cargill 1846, 184–86). The management of the female school under Mrs. Cargill was good, and despite her domestic duties she was seldom absent from her post. The discipline was good, and reading and Scripture study was taught in addition to sewing and other female occupations.

Even in the outer schools, scholars were soon able to read without having to spell out the words, and could write a plain legible hand (Cargill 1841, 155). Josua Mateinaniu had been taken to Waterhouse's institution and had acquired a wider range of knowledge including something of geography. He was a fluent speaker and wrote a good hand (Hunt 1846, 139). The missionaries themselves taught reading, writing, singing (or used their wives in this respect), translating texts, composing hymns, and printing. They also gave a little instruction in carpentering and gardening (ibid., 116) and house building.[100] They formed the habit of making regular inspections of the indigenous teachers' work, and cat-

---

97   Henderson (1931) suggests the title ought to have been Grammar and Dictionary of the Lau Dialect of the Fijian Language. Actually the title was Hints to a Friend on the Rudiments of the Feejeean Language.

98   The actual number was 399.

99   Appointed in February 1836. Although the Tahitians had been provided with paper, pens, ink, and slates (Henderson 1931, 43–44), they had made no attempt at learning Fijian or Tongan or teaching the people to read (Hunt 1841, 83). Josua was to organise schools as at Lakeba for men in the morning and women in the afternoon, five days a week (ibid., 82).

100 Thomas Williams gives an account of building and furnishing his home in Henderson 1931, 15 October 1841.

echising the scholars, usually dealing with the male school in the mornings and the female in the afternoons (Cargill 1841, 191).[101] This became the regular pattern.[102]

A great impetus was given to the work with the arrival of a large canoe from Tonga under the chief, Job Saokai. He brought six selected Tongan teachers,[103] who were given a special course in Lakeba and appointed to villages (ibid., 184). By the end of the year Messrs. Hunt, Calvert, and Jaggar had arrived, and there were already over six hundred at school in Fiji (ibid., 201). Cross had moved into Rewa and was teaching reading and Scripture to a school of thirty-five by September (Hunt 1846, 99).[104] By the end of that year Namosimalua of Viwa had asked Cross for a teacher and built the teacher a chapel (Williams 1884, 244). In 1839 the work was extended to Vatoa, and Ono was virtually Christian (ibid., 269).[105] By June 1840 the work centred at Viwa controlled five teachers and 120 scholars, and thirty to forty were attending school at Somosomo (Bau Circuit 1840).[106]

The mission had been in Fiji for only five years, yet these figures show great expansion. Each new preaching place or village opened to evangelism demanded a teacher and a school. Thus we observe, from the outset, what has been unto this day a big problem of education in Fiji—the staffing of more schools than the mission could really carry, and the demand for teachers in excess of the supply available. This fact determined the major change which came with the chairmanship of John Hunt and the adoption of the Viwa Plan, as an attempt to deal with teacher training in an elementary way (Hunt 1843). It is significant that an attack was made on this problem at such an early stage in the history of the mission.

Translation Program

Another element that should be pinpointed perhaps is that reading cannot be taught until the language is reduced to writing. The basic work was done by Cargill, but the orthography for the simplification of *th* to *c*, *ng* to *g*, *ngg* to *q*, and so on was the suggestion of William Cross and has proved to be a device of great significance which makes the language perfectly phonetic. With the assistance of the Fijian, Josua Mateinaniu, the Fijian alphabet was prepared in Tonga and some printed material taken to Fiji by the pioneering party.

101　Mr. and Mrs. Cargill cruised Lau in a canoe visiting schools and examining scholars and the work of the teachers in October 1838. Where necessary they appointed assistants, which I imagine to mean "monitors" (e.g., at Namuka on 17 October 1838).

102　Thomas Williams records similar visitation in June 1842, examining the male school in the morning and female in the afternoon (Henderson 1931, 20–22 June 1842).

103　Joeli Bulu, Jone Havea, Julius Naulivou, Silas Faone, Nesele Langi, and Jeremiah Latu. They arrived on 26 June 1838 and after their course were appointed respectively to Narocake, (Lakeba) Ono, Nukunuku (Lakeba), Rewa, Rewa, and Moce.

104　He began his open-air school in January.

105　Vatoa, population 66, was all Christian and demanding a teacher. Ono had 4 teachers. Its schools had 168 males and 160 females.

106　Actually Viwa; term Bau used till 1843.

Modifications were made soon after arrival and have stood the test of time. The early part of Saint Matthew's Gospel was prepared in Fijian and printed in Tonga, twenty-four pages in twelve months (Williams 1884, 229–32). Cargill's grammar and vocabulary was written out by hand for his wife and was copied by all the missionaries, up to the time of the appearance of Hazlewood's grammar and dictionary (1872). Cargill had also been at work translating the first Wesleyan Catechism. He and Mrs. Cargill copied out a number by hand and sent them to Ono for the use of the teacher there (Cargill 1841, 182–83). The Somosomo Hymns, a collection prepared by Hunt and Lyth, were also handwritten and copied by each person who wanted to use them.[107] William Cross, who did no literal translations, but wrote paraphrases of Scripture narratives, did so by hand and made scores of copies for teachers and readers.

Printing

We do not wonder that the missionaries appealed to England for a printing press (Williams 1884, 232). It arrived with the three men who came in December 1838 (ibid., 249). In February it commenced operations and the 1st Wesleyan Catechism was the first work printed, and Mrs. Cargill was selected to put the first copy through the press (Cargill 1841, 205). From that time onwards the press was kept busy, first at Lakeba, then at Rewa and finally at Viwa. It produced a continuous supply of alphabets, readers, Scripture portions, New Testaments, hymnbooks, and other school materials, in four dialects.[108]

The emphasis in the pioneering period was thrown on reading, writing, handcrafts, hygiene, singing, and especially Scripture knowledge. Handcraft classes were segregated—sewing, cooking, and mothercraft for females—carpentry, gardening methods, etc., for males. On the whole, schooling interested only those who were concerned with Christianity as a religion. The missionaries sought to persuade heathen folk to learn to read also, but few responded. The heathen priests pressed that schooling was religion.[109]

These are the essential characteristics of mission education under Cargill and Cross, 1835–42.[110] No thought had been yet given to the selection of a *lingua franca*, or a central model institution. These came under Hunt's chairmanship and prepared the way for the Glasgow System in the 1850s.

---

107 Report of Translating and Printing Department of Fiji District 1842 says, "Messrs. Hunt & Lyth have prepared a number of hymns in the Somosomo dialect." 1843 report says that a hymnbook on the plan of the Somosomo MSS is to be prepared in Lakeban, Bauan, and Rewan. For full detail of the project, see Index Volume, pp. 204ff in *Lyth Records* in Mitchell Library, Sydney.

108 2nd Conference Catechism was printed in Bauan in 1841, and twelve pages of Luke's Gospel in Somosomoan; the Hunt and Lyth hymns came out in Bauan first, then Lakeban. By 1842 the four dialects were in use (Williams 1884, 359).

109 Stated definitely to be so by Hunt (1846, 116, 158). A case is cited of Tuidreketi withdrawing his daughter from school through the priest pressing this argument. But there were good exceptions—witness Varani of Viwa. Hunt/London Committee, *Wesleyan Magazine* (1846), 926.

110 1835–38 under Tonga. 1838–40, Cargill chairman. 1840–42, Cross chairman.

REFERENCES

Bau Circuit. 1840. *Annual report.* Wesleyan Missionary Conference.

Cargill, David. 1841. *Memoirs of Margaret Cargill.* London: John Mason.

Hazlewood, David. 1872. *Fijian-English and English-Fijian dictionary*; and *Grammar of the Fijian language.* First published 1850.

Henderson, G. C. 1931. *The Journal of Thomas Williams.* 2 vols. Sydney: Angus and Robertson.

Hunt, John. 1843. *Viwa report.* Wesleyan Missionary Conference.

———. 1846. *Memoir of William Cross.* London: John Mason.

Williams, Thomas. 1884. *Fiji and the Fijians.* Vol. 1, *The islands and their inhabitants.* London: Kelly.

20
THE PLACE OF WOMEN IN EDUCATION AND EVANGELISM IN FIJI (1835–1900)[111]

It is commonly thought in Fiji (and often stated in public) that women's education was hardly touched before this century. On several occasions in the last couple of years official statements have been printed, which so read as to belittle missionary activity of the past by praising what is being done by other bodies at the present time in terms strongly suggestive that nothing has been done before. This applies to technical, agricultural, health, and girls' education. It has been both misleading and unfair, as those of you who have been trained as nurses and teachers probably know.

Perhaps to some extent we are to blame in this matter ourselves as some of our own missionary publications, anxious to glorify the achievements and view them as a gradual progressive development, have deflated the work of the pioneers. Better research would have prevented them doing this. For example, the missionary journalists who wrote the following did not dig very deeply:

> There was practically no differentiation between the type of instruction given to girls and boys. The schools, primitive as they were, tended to develop along academic rather than practical lines. The curriculum, if so high sounding a term can be applied to such fragmentary instruction, was modelled on English ideas rather than on native needs, as much of the education, viewed as a means of eliciting the best response from the scholars, was useless . . . very little was attempted for the girls.

And the last clause was qualified by stating it was "restricted, spasmodic and unsystematized" (Burton and Deane 1936, 96). This is an unfair statement which is certainly not supported by the journals and reports in the Archives of the Methodist Church in Fiji.[112]

---

111 Address given to the Women's Group of the Jubilee Methodist Church in February 1951. Taken from bound collection of articles entitled *Historical Writing: Fiji, 1947–1967; Studies from the History of the Fijian Church, 1835–1967*. Unpublished article.

112 Archival sources show this statement to be wrong in the following points: (1) There was clear differentiation between the various forms of education. (2) If schools were primitive, this was only because they were dealing with primitive people after their own culture pattern as much as possible. The educational method was advanced and essentially practical. (3) The curriculum was perhaps a bit limited, but it was not fragmentary. (4) It elicited a good deal of

Such statements have supplied ammunition for our critics, and this afternoon I hope to show something of what has been done for women and girls from the early days down to the turn of the century. The church was well aware of this form of educational need from the start.

Beginnings

The early ministerial missionaries were men of varied qualifications, having among their numbers several competent linguists, craftsmen, trained teachers, and a doctor. Their wives also were competent, and two at least were teachers before marriage.

They reduced the Fijian language to writing, translated reading material, printed textbooks, manufactured educational apparatuses,[113] organised schools and dispensaries. Their wives also learned the language and gave lessons to the women and girls in the vernacular.[114] The women's classes were systematic and efficient. Let us begin with this—these classes were in capable hands, and they were regular, not spasmodic. There were usually two families on a station, and one of the women could always be free for a class, and although there was coeducation for children up to the age of twelve years, there was segregation for specialised girls' and boys' work, and an industrial class for girls over twelve and for women. Mrs. Hunt, Mrs. Cargill, Mrs. Collis, Mrs. Hazlewood, Mrs. Binner, and others formed a capable team. They lived lives of regular habits in prayer and Bible study, were industrious in sewing and other handcrafts, and read serious literature together with their husbands on free evenings.

The first school for women and girls was established by Mrs. Cross and Mrs. Cargill at Lakeba in 1835—a highly efficient institution according to the standards of the day. The course offered by these and those who followed included practical crafts and handwork, general hygiene and special reference to feminine hygiene, reading, singing, and Bible study. They also ran special classes for Bible instruction and handcrafts for women who were too old or whose eyesight was too defective to learn to read letters. These classes were well attended and even by many who had not yet become Christian. Year after year the continuous operation of these schools is reported in the records.

One of the interesting results of the methods and work of these women may be seen in the way in which it fitted the Fijian culture pattern. The Fijian women committed to memory long passages of biblical narrative and psalms and used them for chanting after

---

response. (5) Girls' education was well organised, systematic, able, and continuous. (Witness the Collis reports of Lakeba schools in the 1850s.)

113   Some of this apparatus required patience and technical knowledge for its manufacture (e.g., Thomas Williams manufactured a globe).

114   Mrs. Hunt's vernacular was highly proficient, and after the death of her husband she proofed the Fijian Scriptures for the British and Foreign Bible Society in London.

the manner of their ballads and myths. The missionaries encouraged the practice and were astonished at the phenomenal memory of the Fijian people.

Some of these women assisted with the infant classes, which were greatly developed by Messrs. Watsford and Malvern; the former of whom was a trained schoolteacher before he entered the ministry. When the ministers went on their field evangelistic trips, the infant classes were carried on by the women.

The "primitive" period came to an end in 1852 when the Glasgow System educationalists arrived in the country. They were known as "training masters" rather than "teachers" and aimed at training the children in the "whole life." The preparatory work had been well done. Collis at Lakeba, and Binner at Levuka, took over the existing institutions, made a few modifications, and before long were making inspections of the surrounding village schools. The system had to be adapted to the Fijian scene, but Collis especially was a man inspired with the virtues of the plan.[115]

It has often been stated that the early schools functioned on an "all in together" principle. This was the exception rather than the rule. Even in a village school this was avoided by the use of monitors. The regularity of the lives of the missionaries is astonishing to us; rather than mix classes they overloaded their own timetable.[116]

Great advance was made at Lakeba when Mrs. Collis, herself a trained teacher, began to apply the Glasgow System to the women's work. Thus not only was the Fijian teacher better trained to go out to a village, but so also was his wife. Mrs. Collis was able to send out women with a fair knowledge of reading, Bible knowledge, sewing, and hygiene, and in this she had the help of Mrs. Lyth and Mrs. Polglaise.

Both the girls' and boys' education was essentially practical. They built their own houses and equipped them. Yet this was all thoroughly Wesleyan.[117]

The arrival of the Glasgow educationalists enabled the staff to distribute itself more effectively, and a complete Glasgow unit was soon at work in Lakeba, and the ministers diverted their attention to the senior and theological sections.

---

115   The British government was so pleased with this system of education that it made a grant of £7,500 to the new normal training centre opened in that year (1851), and Methodism herself sank £30,000 into the scheme—a lot of money for those days.

116   For example, David Hazlewood, alone on his station, with his wife sick unto death, ran his infant classes on Monday, Wednesday, and Friday mornings and his adult classes on those evenings, and had general instruction in religion on Tuesdays, and special classes for preachers and teachers on Thursdays in reading, arithmetic, geography, theology, Bible study, preaching methods, and prayer. On Monday and Thursday nights he held a singing class. There is planned activity on a graded basis four years before the arrival of the Glasgow educationalists. In his spare time he wrote his 345-page *Feejeean and English Dictionary* and translated the whole Old Testament into Fijian. So he lived and died within a decade of service in Fiji.

117   This was set out in *The Wesleyan Methodist Training System for the Young.* A Methodist educational training centre in 1850 required four institutions to be a complete unit—(1) an infant school, sometimes called an Initiatory School; (2) The Juvenile School (coeducational because family education is coeducational); (3) The Industrial School (for girls); and (4) The Senior School, for higher education of the type desired.

The Industrial Schools for girls and women became key institutions in the preparation of teachers' wives, a noble body of women who did much towards the uplift and evangelism of Fiji. Unfortunately the demands for teachers in remote parts prevented them having a long stay in the institution, but this was a contemporary problem and should not be made a criticism against the institutions or the educational pattern.

Collis felt that conditions in Fiji required industrial training for girls from the age of nine years upwards, but he had these segregated from the older women. They concentrated on cleanliness, order, and industry.

Within twenty years of the arrival of Cross and Cargill in Fiji in 1835, there were five central industrial schools for girls in Fiji, run by the women who came to this country with their husbands, and whose names are equally deserving of remembrance though often forgotten. In the same way we often forget the fine band of Fijian women, especially the wives of the teachers, who endured as much as their husbands for the evangelisation of their country, and hundreds of whom died martyrs for the cause.

They went out into pagan villages, and they went out to establish their own Christian homes in a heathen setting, they preached by faith and clean living, by orderliness and industry, what Christianity had done for them. By their example they won many followers. This did not make Christians, but it did cause enquiries and opened opportunities. Education comprises much more than teaching reading, writing, and arithmetic. There has to be an attitude of the people towards education in the first place. These tiny Christian cells throughout the country were slowly but definitely preparing Fiji for a new day.

But education in Fiji is not a matter of simple and straightforward evolution. There have been advances and recessions. An examination of the documents relative to the later decades of the century is most disturbing. Things were clearly not nearly as advanced as they should have been. Perhaps the situation can be explained under four points thus:

(1) Educationally and spiritually Lau advanced out of all proportion with the rest of Fiji between 1850–55, and was virtually all Christian. Collis' system was firmly established, and regular tours of inspection were made throughout the islands; many of his students became almost his disciples. Of course, he built on a good foundation, but both Collis and his wife built well.

Viti Levu represented an entirely different proposition. The conversion was not completed until British times. In Collis' day Lau was at peace, but Viti Levu was torn by war for another twenty years, and in Vanua Levu the Christian party was passing through the worst period of persecution in the Christian history of Fiji. Even so the great movement into Christianity had begun, and from all parts requests were coming for teachers. Alas there were none to send. The needs of Viti Levu and Vanua Levu took every teacher who could be trained in Lau and Viwa; many were obtained from Tonga (not always satisfactory). With the conversion of Cakobau the movement into Christianity increased in

Lomaiviti, and Kaba added more impetus to the movement. Whole villages discarded their old gods and demanded teachers.

Tonga had little more help to offer. Lau and Viwa had to carry the load. Teacher after teacher, trained by Collis, was uprooted from his Lauan island and sent to deal with pagan enquirers further afield. The raw material these teachers had to work with was less than productive, but they did well and many died at their posts. These tens of thousands of new enquirers might well have disorganised the whole system of education. The wonder is that it was held together as well as it was.

The supply of teachers was exhausted; students were withdrawn from the institutions. Any who would go, were sent—preachers, readers, anybody.[118] They did a splendid job, but it played havoc with Collis' organisation.

On the other hand there was a levelling of measure, which was not altogether unfortunate. The level in Lau dropped, but it was distributed not lost, and the best teachers were at work in backward places. Furthermore it was an important step in the unification of Fiji, which at the time was a tragic need.

(2) The second cause of the "slump" in Lau was that Collis was removed to Bau. This was a strategic move of tremendous importance in Central Fiji. It was a move into the centre of Fijian life which indirectly determined much of the pattern of Fijian church life. Collis himself was astonished at the differences between the materials he had to work on in the two places. He worked hard but never repeated the achievements of his Lauan station. Binner also had a tough time at Levuka. The gospel had done fifteen years work in Lakeba before the arrival of Collis, but he came into Bau with the mass movement from paganism into Christianity; it meant greater numbers, poorer discipline, greater ignorance, and less appreciation of what education was.

It goes to show that the methods of Cross and Hunt were more suited to the real primitive people, and the way for modern education has to be prepared.

The peculiar nature of the mass movement into Christianity in the mid-1850s led inevitably to the concentration of the white staff and institutions in middle Fiji—Viwa, Bau, Rewa, and Levuka. Yet the strain was still falling on Lau, whose quarterly meeting now resolved to forbid further exodus of their teachers.

(3) During the 1860s there was a respite and a period of consolidation of gains and steady expansion. A good central institution was now established for training teachers and their wives—the best part of one hundred were in training. The educational standards were only fair, but Scripture knowledge was good.

---

118   Thus, for example, after three unsuccessful attempts to establish the gospel in Kadavu, Paula Vea (the fourth) commenced to obtain results and wanted more teachers. Moore, at Rewa, chartered a boat and combed Lau seeking teachers. Eventually at Matuku, he collected nineteen men, all with evangelistic fire but no training. These he placed with their wives round Kadavu. They did a fine job as evangelists, but their teaching had many shortcomings.

One reads the documents and is left with great admiration for the young church, which could come through this crisis and retain as much as she did. It says much for the solidarity of the pioneering work. From now the lowered educational level began to rise slowly, but the movement was heavier now as the load was so much greater.

(4) No sooner had the young church recovered from the shock of the mass movement crisis than she was faced with a problem of an entirely different kind. The measles epidemic carried off forty thousand Fijians, including literally hundreds of teachers and their wives. Langham lost forty teachers at Bau, Webb at Rewa lost ninety. Fison at Lakeba recorded the list was too great to write their names. Every circuit in Fiji fared in the same way. Of the Fijian ministers, catechists, and teachers who died, only a rough estimate could be made, but we do know that within a matter of a few weeks the church found herself with over five hundred empty teachers' appointments.

The central institution of Navuloa was barely meeting the demands of normal conditions. Its capacity was but for one hundred students. To have increased this by 20 percent would still have required twenty-five years to have made up the shortage of teachers. How would the critics of mission standards of education have met that problem? A decade after the epidemic, the circuit of Cakaudrove alone still had fifty villages without teachers, which meant no schooling at all for all their children between the ages of five and fifteen. Empty circuits again cried out to Lau and Viwa, who generously suffered further impoverishment for the sake of Fiji as a whole.

The church had no alternative but to reduce the term of training, and this meant lowering the general standards, and that the situation was as repaired as it was by the end of the century speaks worlds for the Fijian teachers themselves and their wives. True, the European missionaries had given them the machinery, but they kept it going—and it involved more than just teaching. It meant food supplies, medical services, law, and order.

The last three decades of the last century were dangerous years—the Colo Wars against Cession and Christianity, the measles with its forty thousand dead, the increase of Western industry, the substitution of indenture for a form of slavery, the economic depression and moral landslide of the 1880s, the realisation that the Fijian race was steadily increasing its mortality rate, and other features.

The Fijian church faced up to those facts. She staged big celebrations for her jubilee in 1885; she launched an attack on the moral evils of her day and raised the moral standards she demanded of her members; she trained her teachers and their wives in simple first aid and child welfare; and launched out on a campaign of church building in the villages; opened up new mission fields in New Britain, New Ireland, and Papua, and a few years later in the Solomons; and offered some hundreds of her sons and daughters to that form of service.

Men said the Fijian church was dying. She was not dying. These were her birth pangs. Help came with the new century. Methodism had achieved union in Australia. New educational projects were launched, adjusting policy to meet the changing Fijian needs—postprimary, technical, and agricultural institutions were established and equipped, and new types of girls' schools commenced. So came the twentieth century with its great improvements, but let us not forget the Fijian church fighting with its back to the wall for those last three decades of the nineteenth. It can be set beside the period of persecution in Vanua Levu as a modern epic of gospel triumph in the Pacific.

Towards the end of the century certain movements came into prominence, two in particular, concerning women's work.

One of these was the Hygienic Mission for Women. The government was now alarmed at the decrease of Fijian population and sought mission aid in the form of a supply of women from abroad for hygienic work in the villages among the Fijian women. The required qualifications were set out, and it was hoped that in this way and with mission aid in time to establish a team of Fijian health sisters.

The mission pressed for something more definite, and the chairman (Lindsay) in an interview with the governor and colonial secretary gained these points:

1. Where our trained teachers were appointed, their wives were to be also appointed as hygienic sisters with authority.
2. This authority, as the governor's wish, was to be stated in the publication *Ai Tukutuku Vakalotu*, and a periodic sermon was to be preached on health.
3. The government was to supply qualified inspectors to give public addresses in the villages from time to time.
4. The mission was to appeal to Sydney for European sisters for village health work.

All these were carried out as planned.

The machinery was already established for the carrying out of the Fijian side of the project. Health education at Navuloa under Heighway was really good, and Mrs. Heighway had a class for teachers' wives in mothercraft, a task for which she was particularly well equipped. For years she had been engaged in village hygiene work in Kadavu, and inspected hundreds of homes each year, having government authority to deal with anything insanitary, especially relating to kitchens and outhouses. She had the right to enter any village school and speak on health matters and the prevention of disease. By this method between 1898 and 1901, or over those four years the Kadavu mortality rate was arrested, and Heighway himself saw to it that the government was acquainted with the figures.

Meantime the government had pressed again for mission sisters. Eventually European sisters were brought for child welfare work, and the missions (not only the Methodist Mission) carried on this work for years until the government was ready to take over the child welfare work itself and develop the work with new devices like mobile clinics with a greater expenditure than the missions had available. Even so it should be remembered that the church pioneered this work and carried it for years and used Fijian women in the task. On the whole they did a good job.

Likewise the government moved in 1898 in some definite way to deal with the fall in vital statistics, but the individual missionaries had been pressing for some such action for years.[119]

The second movement that came towards the end of the century was the establishment of a girls' school at Matavelo, on the vision and practical work of William Slade. The school opened in 1899 under the head mistresship of Miss Morehead and began with ninety-five scholars. By 1900 it was working well, and the first annual exams were held in June. Several other sisters were also at work, and they extended some of their efforts along the Ba Valley in the form of hygienic and welfare work.

This brings us to the new century, which is another story. This is but the introduction—a story of ups and downs but never of neglect, and honour is due as much to the Fijian teachers' wives as to the planners like Mrs. Collis and Mrs. Heighway.

REFERENCES

Burton, John W., and Wallace Deane. 1936. *A hundred years in Fiji.* London: Epworth.

---

119   Take, for example, the connexional year ended June 1884: 4½ years before any official move was made. The Viwa superintendent pointed out that in his area there were 1,081 deaths against 718 births during the year, a decrease of 362; the Bau superintendent reported 401 deaths against 197 births, a decrease of 182; the Rewa superintendent had 1,150 deaths, which he said was "an astounding decrease." This accounts for the ready action of the mission the moment the government felt disposed to face the facts.

21

CONTEMPORARY DEPARTURES FROM TRADITIONAL CHRISTIANITY IN CROSS-CULTURAL SITUATIONS:
A Melanesian Ethnohistorical Case Study[120]

No topic has generated more enthusiasm for research in Melanesia than the study of its nativism, by which I mean the large homogeneous ethnic units, sometimes whole lineages, breaking away from the traditional Christianity which emerged in the era of colonial missions.[121] It has been argued that these movements are the result of stress situations which arise when two very different cultures clash or come into acculturative contact. The clash is said to derive from: (1) the inherent cultural differences, (2) the conflicting values and attitudes of the two societies, (3) the precise nature of the dominance/submission situation, and (4) the effect of forces which emerged with World War II in the Pacific, with the G.I. in particular as the catalyst.[122]

The movement may be resistive or reformative, perpetuative or accommodating, aggressive or passive.[123] It may seek to reintegrate the whole subject society, or merely some subordinate homogeneous unit within it; either by the rejection of alien elements in it, or the modification of new elements (i.e., by accepting the forms but ascribing their own meanings to them), or a syncretism of basic ingredients from the two cultures. The literature on the subject is tremendous,[124] and the typologies are numerous.[125] In the literature the movements may be viewed negatively as ("nativistic movements" or "cargo cults") or positively (as "people movements" or "revitalization" [these two are distinguished by the

---

120 Taken from *Introduction to Missiology* (Pasadena: William Carey Library, 1987), 270–84. Used by permission.

121 The phenomenon is not peculiar to Christianity, to the postcolonial age, or to Oceania. History is replete with accounts of such movements in Africa, Asia, and America, but in Africa and Oceania especially they have increased by hundreds since World War II.

122 Nativistic movements frequently follow in the aftermath of wars. One of the best studies of this theme is Wallace's investigation of the relation between war and religious group movement in the history of the Delaware Indians (1956, 1–21).

123 The passive type, such as the Gandhi resistance in India, does not appear frequently in Melanesia. There have been a few minor strikes among students on mission compounds (see Crocombe 1954, 6–21), but Melanesian movements are notably aggressive, the aggression rising or falling according to the way in which the administration or mission handles the disturbance.

124 See the bibliographies in Worsley's *The Trumpet Shall Sound* (1957, 277–83), Lawrence's *Road Belong Cargo* (1964, 276–80), Kamma's *Koreri* (1972, 300–19), and Leeson (1952).

125 Typologies for nativism were developed by Linton (1943, 230–40), Kobben (1960, 117-64), Clemhout (1964, 14-15), Worsley (1957), Turner (1974), and many others.

possibility of a foreigner or outgroup person being the catalyst in the people movements, whereas revitalization may be stimulated only by an ingroup person]). Figure 16 illustrates some of the various approaches in the literature.

FIGURE 16
Approaches to the Analysis of Nativism

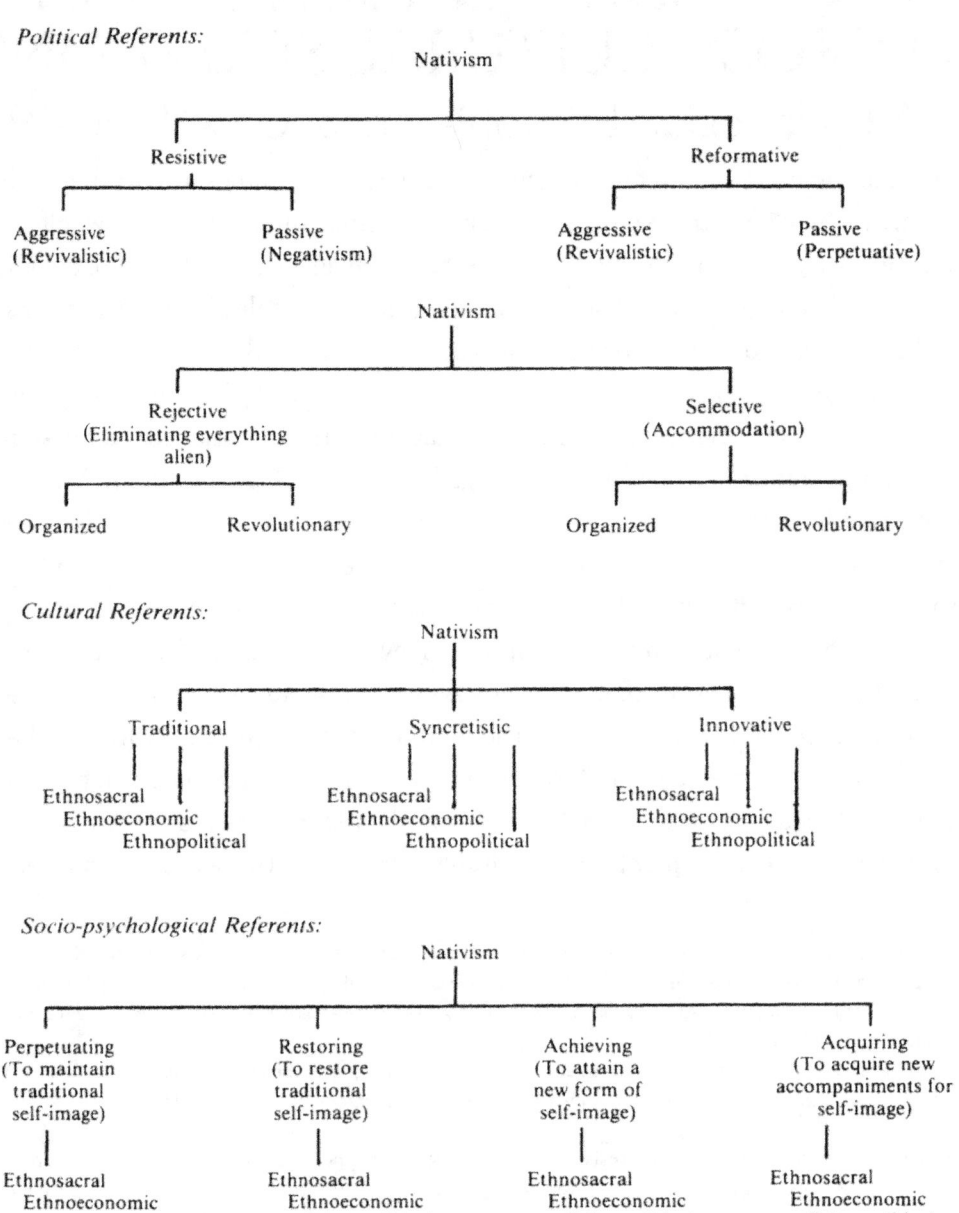

This chapter is focused on Melanesia as far as the database is concerned (although there is even more data for Africa, which would also introduce us to concepts like "Negritude").[126] The findings, I believe, apply also to Africa.[127]

In Melanesian research most of the investigation has been focused on the components of the nativistic movement or cargo cult, pinpointing such features as messianism or millenarianism in the eschatology, its antigovernment or antimission motivation, its aspect of counterconversion, and endless speculations as to the real causes of the defection from traditional Christianity. We have also been weighed down with generalised speculations about a "theory of nativism." This is a somewhat negative approach which has suited the mood of the cultural relativists, who since the 1930s set themselves up as "judges over Israel." I think a more positive approach to our subject is possible when we ask, not what was lost (or thought to be lost) but what really emerged in Melanesia after World War II. This is not to reject the existing research, or the numerous typologies, which all provide different frames of reference for investigation, and certainly aid our ethnological description. But a positive approach will certainly save us from the error of interpreting these movements as necessarily disintegrative or chaotic.[128]

We need to see that, although the traditional missionary Christian worldview of the colonial age has been rejected (either in part or whole), the new emergent state is not one of chaos. It is an integrated and homogeneous structure, functioning as an autonomous, ongoing concern. The notion that change has to be disintegrative is entirely wrong.

In 1964 I was sent by the World Council of Churches to the Solomon Islands to investigate why some twenty or more villages had broken away from traditional Christianity. It was a breakaway from a church whose members had received fifty years of Christian instruction.[129] My Western and some Anglo Solomon Islander informants mostly saw the whole thing as chaotic and disintegrative.[130] But however tacit a Christian missionary may consider the heresy which emerged in the breakaway of these tribal groups, one cannot honestly say they were in a state of chaos. They were dynamic, vibrant with life, self-expressive, with a cohesive structure and a programmed daily life and religious routine.

---

126 The concept of "Negritude" was used to describe the resurgence of Bantu paganism, and the exaltation of the African past (Steenberghen 1959, 287–88).

127 The Christian church in Africa was made widely aware of this phenomenon by a growing body of literature on such movements which appeared about 1948. The most notable work was Sundkler's *Bantu Prophets in South Africa*, published in 1948 and updated in 1961. But there are many others—Welbourn (1961), Barrett (1968), and Baeta (1962)—and by Comparative Religionists like Lanternari (1963) and many others.

128 Early writers on "culture contact" used the term "culture clash," which was subsequently discarded because it gave the impression of a powerful culture destroying a passive or static one. Later anthropologists pointed out that the less powerful one was not disintegrating, but that sooner or later, after the initial culture shock it would reformulate its structures and continue as an ongoing organism. Culture contact is a two-way process of interaction.

129 For the report of the research, see *Solomon Islands Christianity* (1967) and in particular pp. 212–14, 217–66.

130 Somewhere in the same source is a report of an interview on this subject with an Anglo Solomoner. An Anglo Solomon Islander is an acculturated or Westernised native. In this case, despite his acculturation he still subconsciously cherished his tradition.

When I sit down with the data of religious innovation in Melanesian Christianity since the war, I find the case studies fall into three basic categories. I am not analysing on a basis of my own conceptualisations of forms, function, or attitude, but rather I find the data falls into three "heaps," with different views of selfhood. We discover (1) the cultic group, nativistic movement, or "cargo cult" which emerges with an aggressive, syncretistic theology and is in direct opposition to regulations and beliefs, and sometimes its morals; (2) the indigenous church, which has emerged from a Christian mission structure by a process of evolution, and retains a character of faith and practice (and sometimes a structure) indigenised, but very little different from the mission prototype; and (3) the independent church, which breaks away on a revolutionary principle, has often assumed folk elements in the process, and demonstrates its autonomy by featuring strongly those elements which were either paternalistically controlled or neglected altogether—say, a healing ministry.

The African data which has come my way will fit the same three categories. How does it come about that the same set of causative factors suggested above can lead to three quite different but equally autonomous solutions? Furthermore, how is it that in no case do we find the breakdown of traditional Christianity leads to anything resembling a state of chaos? For better or for worse we are dealing with dynamic, functioning, autonomous living organisms.

Most of the missionary churches of Melanesia and Polynesia were planted as the result of people movements, which I have described elsewhere at length,[131] and mostly these were power encounter situations in which the old animistic divinities or their shrines were formally (i.e., ceremonially) rejected by the groups concerned by means of an ocular demonstration in which the responsible official (headman of the village, chief of the lineage, priest of the temple, or head of the household) destroyed or abused the *mana* repository or symbolic locus of power (skull houses, ceremonial skulls, fetishes, idols, monoliths, sacred groves, or taboo totem animals). The mode of destruction was by burning, burial, drowning, or devouring according to the local conception of *mana* disposal.

These people movements usually led to the planting of Christianity as a functional substitute for the original animistic religious structure; and although they took from one to ten years to run through the sometimes scattered tribal unit, from subunit to subunit, they resulted in reasonably total substitutions.

These Christian churches have continued in some parts of Melanesia since about 1840. Most parts (except for the New Guinea Highlands) had a time depth of more than half a century of Christian history by the beginning of World War II in the Pacific, which means they had survived the first generation of Christian converts from animism.[132] Quite apart

---

131   *People Movements in Southern Polynesia* (1971) is entirely devoted to this subject. See also *Solomon Islands Christianity* (1967, 42–43, 60).

132   Christianity entered Fiji in 1835. For a record of its diffusion in statistically large movements, see my monograph *The Christian: Fiji 1835–67* (1954).

from the psychological effect the war had on them, Melanesian Christians of the postwar period were mostly persons who had been born to Christian parents in traditional missionary island Christianity. They had never themselves rejected animism, burned their fetishes, buried their *mana* skulls, destroyed their idols, or cut down their sacred groves. That is, they had never experienced a power encounter deliverance from the old life, and frequently (but not always) they had been quite cut off from the animistic worldview and mental set by mission education.

Historically the period following World War II was not only one of rapid social change due to acculturation, but the changes in technology and electronics going on in the West itself were also being felt in the islands. These changes were social and political as well as religious, and I think we are wrong if we assume we can really study the religious change in isolation; politics, medicine, economics, electronics are all part of the picture, and the religious life suffered no more than any other of these configurations, or "integral institutions" as Malinowski calls them.[133] I make the point, not because I want to discuss it here but because it is often overlooked, and this chapter is really not a complete study without this dimension.

The experience of the war introduced the Pacific islanders to resources far greater than anything they had ever dreamed of—the number of warships, the power of their armament, the quantities of canned food in the cargo ships, the aircraft in the sky—the islanders were completely bewildered by such resources of power and quantity. Added to this was the vocal anticolonialism of the average G.I., who saw a good deal of the people in his off-duty time.[134] We do not wonder that many of the innovative reactions to traditional Christianity and colonial government grasped on "cargo" and "airplanes" and "ships" as their symbolic reference points,[135] as they also did of the American military system itself,[136] and the notion of administrative authority.[137]

Recognising that this capacity for group movement with some symbolic reference point was inherent in the Melanesian situation anyway, whenever some prophetic or

---

133 This concept developed in a most important essay on "The Functional Theory of Culture" found in *The Dynamics of Culture Change* (1961, 41–51). He also describes these institutions as "systems" and as "instrumental imperatives" (ibid., 46).

134 In my own field research on the Eto Movement, I repeatedly had expressions of this opinion from my Solomon Islander informants.

135 Many movements had secret clearings in the forest with a model of an airplane, for example, setup as a symbol. One example of this was the John Frum movement. The symbol is illustrated in Attenborough's *Quest in Paradise*, facing p.154.

136 The Marching Rule Movement in Malaita was structured on the model of the U.S. Army. For a description see *Solomon Islands Christianity* (1967, 204–9).

137 The classical example of the symbolization of administration was a wartime movement in Ysabel (Solomon Islands) which spread through Gela, Savo, and San Cristoval, which related to native representation on the Advisory Council. The Melanesians raised a flag together with a wooden chair and a wooden rule. They also agitated for higher wages. As an outcome of this movement, plans were initiated for native courts (see Belshaw 1950).

charismatic leader emerged to grasp control of it, it is not difficult to see how the war first, followed by technological and electronic change, led parts of Melanesia into periods of innovative religious movements.[138] Melanesia began (if she had not already thought of it before) to see herself as deprived of her "place in the sun." Sometimes she felt she had lost something from her past by culture contact. Her old religion was gone. Had the white colonial administrators and missionaries robbed her of her birthright: her cultural heritage, authority, wealth, and religious power? Were these to be regained by totally rejecting the government and the missions? Sometimes she felt she had something valuable in traditional Christianity which she should not cast lightly away. How could she master it, deal with it, and use it in her own way, as something indigenous rather than foreign, autonomous rather than paternalistic? Soon after the war many missionaries were found working towards this end, especially from about 1945 to 1946, and indigenous churches began to emerge.[139] Where this did not happen, many ethnic groups broke away and established independent churches or, better called perhaps, "folk churches," which though they claimed to be Christian, were inclined to be syncretistic or bibliomythical.

Using then an ethnohistorical referent, I find that these three types of innovative movement have characterised the postcolonial period: the nativistic cult, the indigenous church, and the independent folk church. The character of Melanesia as a missionary field has thus been completely transformed since the war. The old paternalistic type of traditional Christianity has been greatly reduced. I do not intend reconstructing in this chapter the nature of the old missionary traditional Christianity, except indirectly by way of comment in the following descriptions. It was too uneven to describe here. Let it suffice to say that it ranged on the scale from pathetically paternalistic to remarkably indigenous, and I do not need to do more than point out that traditional Christianity at the former pole tended to suffer after the war from nativistic cults, while those at the latter pole passed from mission to church with little serious culture shock. Let me now turn briefly to the three types one by one.

The Nativistic Cult

This type of movement, commonly called a "cargo cult" (although in reality not all such forms of nativism feature cargo), utilises the term "cargo" to focus on a concept of wealth. It came out of the war, when white man's wealth came to be envisioned in cases of canned meat, such as were seen in the army supplies. A whole mythology developed about it and described how the white man had stolen the islanders' heritage and wealth back in prime-

---

138 This was certainly so in the Paliau Movement in the Admiralty Islands, researched by Margaret Mead (1961) and Schwartz (1962). (For Mead's reference to electronics see 1961,141 and 1970, xvii–xviii, 58.)

139 This was discussed in a lecture I delivered in Melbourne, Australia, in 1947. It was subsequently printed under the title "Fiji's Tomorrow" (1947).

val times.[140] These myths may be collected in hundreds, and they have been interwoven in the origin tales. This, in itself, is a return to pre-Christian values and aesthetic forms and is a rebellion against Christianity and a claim that something was lost at culture contact. The army stores of food and arms revolutionised the islanders' conception of the meaning of plenty as unlimited, and it was natural for them to latch on to this symbol. This mental set is found in the church especially along the north coast of New Guinea, where the missionaries of today call it the "cargo mentality."

Wealth in canned goods became an element of a new eschatology. It promised a new day which was about to dawn for the islanders when they would regain all they had lost—lands, authority, wealth—and which were rightly theirs from the beginning of time. This conception of Melanesian paradise was soon formulated into an apocalyptic belief structure, for which the model was sometimes the New Jerusalem in the New Testament, and new villages might even be given biblical names. When this Golden Age is articulated, we speak of the movement as millenarian.[141]

The millenarian element is often accompanied by the emergence of a prophetic or charismatic figure around whom the group rallies (though all prophetic movements are not millenarian). The interesting factor, in my experience at least, is that this leader usually turns out to be one who has previously been trained in some white man institution in a role of subordinate leadership: a teacher, a policeman, an orderly in the army, or a catechist. The man has had authority under authority, and has Melanesianised the white authority pattern in his nativistic cult.[142]

Most nativistic cults are highly structured after the nature of a church organisation, an educational complex, an administrative system, or a military organisation. They may include such features as drill parades, marching formation round a flagpole, with commissioned and noncommissioned officers and men, or an administrator in control behind a desk. The white man's authority, like his wealth, must be returned to the Melanesian in the Golden Age.

The key personality of the movement has a prophetic character. He is not always a natural orator, but gains power by his authoritative utterances in the specific situation of crisis—he is a man for the hour. The movement depends on him. It may be economic, political, or religious, depending on the nature of the situational crisis, and by the same criteria the role of the charismatic figure will be seen. It does not follow that a nativistic cult has

---

140 A useful aid in identifying the self-image of the movement is to ascertain whether it builds its ritual around a collection of hymns or myths. One might at least start from this position. This would place Etoism as an independent church, in spite of its heavy syncretism with pre-Christian elements.

141 Millenial visions and apocalyptic aspects of these movements featured in Linton's original essay (1943) but he did not include them in the classification descriptors in his typology.

142 Of the leaders of the Solomon Islands movements of which I gathered data, Silas Eto was a mission catechist, Paukubatu a teacher, Taosin trained as a teacher also but failed to graduate, Pekokoqore was a discharged policeman, and Timothy George had witnessed the Sydney dock strike in 1913 (Tippett 1967, 201).

to be religious. If the crisis is purely political, as in the case of Marching Rule, there may be no religious aspect. A number of Christian pastors actually held office in this particular movement, for example.[143]

However, it may well be that the movement is entirely religious, or religious and economic, as with the John Frum movement.[144] A religious (sacrosyncretic) cult will develop a religious doctrine of some kind, and perhaps a verbal creed and a liturgy. A collection of hymns emerges, usually quite heretical from the biblical standpoint. The institution of hymn singing will be regarded as an essential functional substitute for its Christian counterpart, and (in the absence of a printing press) there may be a handwritten hymnbook, which each member copies by hand as part of the reception into membership ritual.[145] Likewise we may expect an organised prayer system, and perhaps a few written prayers for worship.[146] The doctrine of the movement will be found in the hymns and liturgies, and may even be the composition of the charismatic leader himself. I found this myself in a Solomon Islands case. The theology reflects a syncretism of biblical ideas and elements from the ancient myths—either truly remembered or imagined.

Quite frequently this role of the prophet is extended as more and more extravagant claims are made of him. He becomes the promised one of imagined ancient myths. This type of situation acquires the descriptor "messianic."[147] Once the figure becomes messianic the movement usually becomes millenarian, and in extreme cases (one known to me personally) the messiah goes beyond this to deification. We now have on our hands a fully developed sacrosyncretic nativistic cult (in terms of cultural referents), and a sacrorestorative cult (in terms of sociopsychological referents) if the movement purports to restore the faith of the ancient heritage, as the act of deification may well do. In still another classificatory frame of reference we may say we have a revolutionary selective accommodation; in other words, a breakaway from traditional Christianity which selects its desirable elements for modification in terms of the pre-Christian past and validation by means of myth.

We must remember that no two movements are exactly alike, and any classificatory system is not only merely approximate, but is indeed in the mind of the observer as his or

---

143   Fifteen percent of the leadership of Marching Rule was said to have been borrowed from the Christian churches (Allen 1950, 41). See also Fox's autobiographical account (1962, 127–35, especially p. 134).

144   This movement sought to rid the land of the taint of European money, of European trade, of immigrant natives, and to return to the old customs prescribed by the theocratic Presbyterian Church, as Belshaw puts it (1950). It was both anti-Western economic and anti-Church. See also the writings of Guiart (1956, ix; 5, etc.; 1959).

145   The Eto document did this. When I was living in Wanawana, I procured such a collection of hymns. It became a major source for *Solomon Islands Christianity* (1967, 253–64).

146   The pietism of the Eto Movement prayer pattern was highly institutionalised. Members recorded the score of their prayers by inserting the midrib of a palm frond in the hair. These tallies marked the building up of merit (see Tippett 1967, 233).

147   There is always a key personality in any group movement, either to or from Christianity. Even in communal groups where new group norms are sought, the momentum begins with an individual (see Tippett 1971, 199–214).

her own abstraction. As long as we have the large number of variables—cultural values, historical antecedents, complexities of the crisis situation, and different responses to the movement beginnings by the local authorities—we will never find two exactly alike. Neither will two be the same to two different observers. So within these limitations, and using my own ethnohistorical referent, let me identify the normal characteristics of a cultic nativistic breakaway from traditional Christianity as having the following features:

1. a new, accommodating mythology,
2. a symbolic locus of power transfer,
3. a new eschatology,
4. a syncretistic belief system,
5. a speculative reconstruction of pre-Christian values, and
6. a mythologization of the worship structure.

All these are dynamic and evolving factors. The extent of their development will depend on the impact they make on the community and the reaction of the civil authorities and church, or any other against whom they may be directed. In the above features I have omitted the immoral dimension because it is not a constant, but when it appears it is usually the major factor, as in the case of the Hahalis Welfare Society, in which the Baby Garden was to provide the society ultimately with the birth of the messiah.

The Indigenous Church

We should not imagine that the entire world of Melanesian traditional Christianity has dissolved into revolutionary nativistic cults. Statistically they represent only a small percentage of the island world population. Possibly the biggest of them would be covering twenty or so villages. Over against this we have numerous churches of 200,000 practising members. The process whereby these strong indigenous churches have emerged is clearly evolutionary rather than revolutionary or rebellious.[148] These churches conduct their own business, social, and religious affairs on the village, national, and international level; and where they still have white workers (fraternal workers rather than missionaries), they are under the authority and discipline of the island churches. These island churches manage their own property, administer their own finances, pastor their own churches, train their own leaders (except perhaps at the highest level for which they may be sent overseas), and integrate their own evangelistic efforts, publication programs, social service projects, and in every way represent the voice of the church in the community. Furthermore they belong to the new world of our day and interact with the representatives of other churches in international conferences.

---

148   For my own historical account of the evolutionary emergence of an indigenous church, see "A Church Is Built," which was the feature article of the inauguration program of the autonomous Methodist Conference in Fiji (1964).

Yet although they have retained many of the traditional church structures, they differ from their prototypes in many ways. They maintain a basic continuity especially in their theological foundations. They study the Bible in groups all over the country and regard it as their norm for faith and practice. They retain many features of the old preaching pattern, although this had already assumed some indigenous features in former times. Their hymnologies are well developed and theologically biblical, and many of the hymns are their own composition, for island hymn writers are very creative when given the opportunity. They will have no dealings with any attempt to speculate on, or seek to recover anything of the pre-Christian mythology, and are quick to detect and oppose syncretism with old myths. They are vocal in opposition to anything approaching a nativistic movement, and if one arises in a small group or village they immediately discipline the offender as "backsliders" who have "fallen from grace."

On the other hand, they differ from the prewar missionary church structures at a number of significant points. The white foreign missionary has no longer any authority over them. Where they have fraternal workers, they have been invited to be there by the island church bodies and have been stationed by them through the regular elective and appointive mechanisms, which deal also with indigenous appointments.

I remember myself once being assigned a clerical task by my Fijian colleagues somewhere about thirty years ago. Two of us had to eliminate the adjectives "European" and "Native" from the Fijian lawbook, which was in their language. A Fijian-controlled synod had appointed and instructed us in our assignment, and told us to bring a revised script for discussion and ratification at the following synod. If I remember correctly the Fijian to Australian ratio of that legislative body was about fifteen to one. When I first went down to Fiji before the war, the most critical issues were determined by a European synod, which was the highest court of appeal in the island church. It was comprised entirely of missionaries. About the end of the war I was involved in the procedures which disposed of their synod. It could only be done by the Europeans of the synod organising their own demise. The matter was discussed over a series of conferences by the composition of the text of a new constitution, which was then submitted to the Fijians, who discussed it for some days on their own. And suddenly the European synod had gone, and with it a century of white missionary authority. Fijians and missionaries alike were now "pastors," "catechists," "teachers," and so on without adjectival descriptors. About a dozen white workers found themselves in the midst of 160 Fijians. They had no longer the power of autonomy. They were a minority voice. Thereafter the Fijians determined our appointments.

At the World Methodist Conference in 1956 I presented a paper on these developments, and I identified three highly developed configurations in the island world:

1. an increasing responsibility in leadership roles on the level of local church activities,
2. constitutional developments constructively moving in the direction of indigenous government and autonomy, and
3. the emergence of new and indigenous forms of evangelism.[149]

As far as Fiji was concerned, this stage lasted for seventeen years. Over this time as the European missionaries retired one by one, they were frequently replaced by indigenous nominees. Theological training was strengthened, select people were groomed for responsible positions, and a bilateral curriculum was developed for ten transitional years to provide indigenous ministers for the very different rural and urban (and academic) ministries.[150] Some cooperative beginnings were launched to bring Fijian, Tongan, and Samoan programs into step as a move towards the standardisation of entrance requirements for a hoped-for central theological seminary in the South Pacific where a divinity degree might be obtained. Eventually after the T.E.F. (Theological Education Fund) Consultation on Theological Education in the South Pacific this dream materialised.[151] The Pacific churches now have both university and seminary resources in Fiji.

Today the Fijian church, over 200,000 strong, is completely indigenous, and by its own choice has affiliated with the Australasian General Conference as a full status and equal body with Australian and Island Conference on an international level. I have used the Fijian Methodists because I knew them best and have served under them, but this is only one of many examples I might have cited for an indigenous church.

The indigenous church is the diametric opposite of the nativistic cult, both at the theological level and at the level of harmonious working with the mother church. In both these respects one rebels and the other develops, one is revolutionary the other evolutionary. Both have in a way withdrawn from the parent body. Both have undergone dramatic change in the process, but one is reactionary, the other cooperative.

Before passing on to the third type, I should point out that the attitude of the white missionaries undoubtedly was one of the crucial factors in each case. In the former they were authoritarian, unbending, and paternalistic. In the latter they recognised that the traditional missionary churches had to change with the changing times; that the church was a dynamic organism and could not be treated as a static organisation. They accepted the no-

---

149 This was published in the *Transactions and Proceedings of the World Methodist Conference* held at Lake Junaluska, North Carolina, in 1956, under the title "Methodism in the Southwest Pacific."

150 A full account of the emergence of theological education in Fiji was multigraphed and distributed to delegates at the Theological Education Fund Consultation on Theological Education in the Pacific in 1961. See also the report (Dearing 1961, 65–68) for a synopsis of the same.

151 The Pacific Theological College at Suva Point, Fiji.

tion of change as appropriate. The task was not always easy. It was like navigating a banana raft on a flooded river and trying to keep in the current without upsetting the craft. The missionaries recognised this and let the current carry the raft, working themselves with their poling, not to increase momentum but to keep them facing in the right direction.

Independent Churches

The question now arises: what happens when the people do not desire to return to pre-Christian mythology, and when the Christian faith meets their needs but the missionaries continue to be paternalistic and resistant to change?

The natural thing is for them to break away from the missionary church and to form an independent church of their own. To this extent they are revolutionary, and they may be quite antiwhite; but they keep nearer to Christian Scripture, are strongly evangelistic, and their new theological emphases are Bible based. Often these are indigenous elaborations of some biblical ingredient which had been neglected in the missionaries' training program, maybe, say, the doctrine of the Spirit or the rites of healing, and there are some elaborate developments of baptism. Africa can supply us with hundreds of documented examples of this, but we do meet them also in Oceania. Another strong element is catharsis.[152]

They are often prophetic or charismatic, strongly liturgical, and present us with an abundance of functional substitutes for the Christian vestments, rituals, and sacred paraphernalia. They have less syncretism than the nativistic movements, but some are borderline cases. Their main difference is that the independent movements are clearly Christian. They have not rejected the Christian religion of the white man and his sacred book. Rather they want to claim it for themselves, and they want to be able to achieve status beyond what they can in the white church, and to express themselves indigenously in participant roles. They do not strive to recapture the ancient animism from which their fathers departed.

The probability with this revolutionary departure from traditional Christianity is that it leads to a rapid institutionalisation of the breakaway movement that ultimately becomes quite rigid. The forms become set. They do not have the internal flexibility of the indigenous churches mentioned above, or their intellectual exchange from outside contacts, or the quality of their theological training. Most cases that I know or have read about have manifested these shortcomings, and I think it probably natural because whereas in the indigenous church, missionary controls have been phased out slowly over a period of time in a smooth evolutionary manner, in the other, the revolutionary cutoff has demanded a

---

152   The catharsis relates to the struggle with sin and may be violent. It may recur, and reduce in intensity each time. It is seen as a power encounter with Satan. It may well be stimulated by some kind of rhythmic beating, tapping, or clapping. It may have strong similarities to voodoo and may lead to possession.

whole complex of institutions "overnight" and the new officials have not been properly trained for it.[153]

Usually such an independent church will be forced to work out its constitution to get public recognition, and if it has day schools they will be at a much lower educational level.[154]

Sometimes we meet with borderline cases between the nativistic cult and the independent church. The borderline marks not so much the degree of syncretism, as to whether or not it is consciously and deliberately intended to go back to native values which predate the white man's presence, or whether it is a failure of a theologically unsophisticated prophet to discriminate between what is Christian and what is not. It may well be that the prophet believes he is biblical and claims the right to his own interpretation.[155] Such men have often argued that as each denomination interprets Scripture in its own way, why should not a Melanesian also do so.[156]

However, the common point between the nativistic cult and the independent church is the revolutionary character of the breakaway, as opposed to the evolutionary character of the passage from mission to church in the case of the indigenous church.

The common point between the indigenous and independent churches is the manifest intention to retain their Christianity, as against the intentional rejection of Christianity by the nativistic cult.

The tragedy of the independent church is that in all probability it need not have happened that way had the mission policy been different. The same may be argued of the nativistic cult. The number of Western features retained by all three types of movement demonstrates the Melanesian readiness for cultural borrowing from the West. Unless there are factors I have not identified, we are left with the following residue:

1. A process of change under the rapid acculturation and end of insularity was inevitable.
2. Ultimate resistance against Western paternalism and overloading authority had to come sooner or later.
3. The Melanesians inevitably had to develop a new self-image adequate for the new day.
4. World War II provided the crisis situation for the emergence of Melanesian prophets and saviors.

---

153 A schismatic indigenous church which breaks away from the main body (which retains the institutions and more sophisticated pastors) may be confronted with this same problem as it was the last century in Tonga.

154 In 1967 I pointed this out in the case of Etoism (1967, 225). I understand that since then they have been forced to secure a constitution to gain their recognition, and even be permitted to run schools.

155 For example, Silas Eto argued that the Bible was a reference book which he would cite when needed. It was not for the people to read.

156 For example, the Hauhau Movement, which followed the Maori Wars, was established on this attitude to Scripture.

These were common factors for all three new and nontraditional forms of religiosity we have discussed. The Melanesians found three different ways of reacting to these factors, and to some extent at least it may be argued that the manifest operations of the white traders, settlers, and especially the public servants, administrators, and missionaries influenced the precise form of the Melanesian reaction.

REFERENCES

Allen, C. H. 1950. The marching rule in the British Solomon Islands Protectorate: An analytical study. Canberra: Australia National University. Microfilm.

Attenborough, David. 1960. *Quest in paradise.* London: Lutterworth.

Baeta, C. G. 1962. *Prophetism in Ghana.* London: S.C.M.

Barrett, David B. 1968. *Schism and renewal in Africa.* Nairobi: Oxford University Press.

Belshaw, Cyril S. 1950. The significance of modern cults in Melanesian development. *The Australian Outlook* 4: 116–25.

Clemhout, Simone. 1964. Typology of nativistic movements. *Man* 64: 14–15.

Crocombe, Ron. 1954. The theological student's walkout, Raxoconga 1954. *Journal of the Polynesian Society* 79: 6–21.

Dearing, F. M. 1961. *Theological education in the Pacific.* London: T.E.F. Committee of the International Missionary Council.

Fox, Charles E. 1962. *Kakamora.* London: Hodder & Stoughton.

Guiart, Jean. 1956. *Un siècle et demi de contacts culturels à Tanna, Nouvelles-Hébrides.* Paris: Musée de l'Homme..

———. 1959. *Destin d'une église et d'un peuple.* Paris: Mouvement du Christianisme Social.

Kamma, F. Ch. 1972. *Koreri.* The Hague: Martinus Nyhoff.

Kobben, A. J. F. 1960. Prophet movements as an expression of social protest. *International Archives of Ethnography* 49: 117–64.

Lanternari, Vittorio. 1963. *The religions of the oppressed.* New York: Knopf.

Lawrence, Peter. 1964. *Road belong cargo.* Manchester: University Press.

Leeson, I. 1952. Bibliography of cargo cults and other nativistic movements in the South Pacific. Sydney: South Pacific Technical Paper 37.

Linton, Ralph. 1943. Nativistic movements. *American Anthropologist* 45: 230–40.

Malinowski, Bronislaw. 1961. *The dynamics of culture change.* New Haven: Yale University Press.

Mead, Margaret. 1961. *New lives for old.* New York: Mentor Books.

———. 1970. *Culture and commitment: A study of the generation gap.* Garden City: Doubleday.

Schwartz, Theodore. 1962. *The Paliau Movement in the Admiralty Islands, 1946-1954.* Anthropology Papers 49. New York: American Museum of Natural History.

Steenberghen, Pera Rombaut. 1959. Neo-paganism in Africa. *Frontier* 2: 287–88.

Sundkler, Bengt. 1961. *Bantu prophets in South Africa*. New York: Oxford University Press.

Tippett, Alan R. 1947. Fiji's tomorrow. *The Link*.

———. 1954. *The Christian: Fiji 1835–1867*. Auckland: Institute Printing and Publishing.

———. 1956. Methodism in the southwest Pacific. Proceedings of the World Methodist Conference. Lake Junaluska, North Carolina.

———. 1961. Consultation on theological education in the Pacific. Unpublished manuscript.

———. 1964. A church is built. Fiji: Methodist Conference.

———. 1967. *Solomon Islands Christianity*. London: Lutterworth.

———. 1971. *People movements in Southern Polynesia*. Chicago: Moody.

Turner, Harold W. 1974. New religious movements. *World survey charts*. International Association for Mission Studies.

Wallace, A. F. C. 1956. New religions among the Delaware Indians, 1600–1900. *Southwestern Journal of Anthropology* 12: 1–21.

Welbourn, F. B. 1961. *East African rebels*. London: S.C.M.

Worsley, Peter. 1957. *The trumpet shall sound*. London: Macgibbon & Kee.

PART FOUR

Nondocumentary Sources

22

FIJI:
Whale's Tooth Ends an Era[157]

There were reverberations in diplomatic and political circles, but the Christian world was particularly shocked by the tragic news. Thomas Baker and a band of Fiji Island Christians bent on evangelising the interior had been cruelly massacred and eaten by cannibals.

Baker's colleagues had chosen him for the difficult mission to the interior because of his outstanding evangelistic ability and fervor. The small islands of the Fiji Group had been won for Christ, but in the two large islands Christianity was confined to the coastal belts. The home church had used the wonderful story of the conversion of coastal Fiji for missionary promotion and had fallen into the danger of presenting an incomplete picture. Supporters said, "Fiji has been won," and relaxed effort. Field missionaries called for help to follow up the strategic advantages they held.

"Converted?" wrote Jesse Carey. "When? Where? About one third perhaps." In another letter he added, "The alarming fact before us is that nearly every island tribe settled say within eight or ten miles of the coast is still heathen and cannibal."

The missionaries reconsidered their strategy and deployed their most effective penetrating evangelist, Thomas Baker.

Baker's new station was at Davuilevu, originally the land of the Big Shell people who were wiped out in the eighteenth century by a plague brought by a foreign ship. Fresh from successful evangelism in Vanua Levu and Yasawa, he wrote from his new hilltop station,

My work is specially the heathen in the interior . . . I am living about 12 miles up the Rewa River. We occupy a border position, all below being Christian, while those above us are heathen, except two small towns that have been *Lotu*, Christian, for some years. From our door we can see the first heathen town and hear them sing their heathen songs.

Baker's Last Trip

Reference to Christian towns in a pagan region illustrates how Fiji was won by conversion of social units.

---

157   Taken from *World Vision Magazine* 11, no. 8 (1967): 6–8. Used by permission.

During 1866 and 1867 Baker made journeys inland, up the Rewa River and its tributaries. He saw Soloira, Siria, Navunidakua, and Dawarau come to Christ. Extended families, lineages, and villages were "fields ripe unto harvest." He attended family and village discussions presenting the gospel. He knew Fijian custom and procedure and was careful not to offend. Then, with a party of Fijian Christians, he crossed into the next geographic and ethnic area where the field was green and far from harvest.

Conversion by Social Units

Baker and Setareki Seileki, a Fijian minister, shared the sermons and devotionals and engaged in dialog with groups that inquired about the gospel. Baker's letters speak in expectant terms: "People are turning from heathenism . . . I do not fear the (mountaineers) we hope to do them good . . . If Navosa should *Lotu*, turn Christian . . ." His last letter to his wife told his motives for the dangerous journey—he wanted to do them good, he saw no obstacles, and he felt this was the day of opportunity.

But Navosa was virtually another land. Its waters ran southwest rather than southeast. Cultural factors which had opened the Rewa headwater areas to the Spirit of God did not yet apply in Navosa.

At Dawarau, the last frontier village beyond which the gospel had never been preached, a sympathetic but pagan chief consulted his oracle and warned the party to go no further. The people here had discarded heathenism only one month before and were adherents under instruction but not members of the church.

Baker and his party pressed on, but soon ran into opposition. At Ngeladelavatu the hospitality was grudging and formal. There was open hostility to the gospel. Preaching was forbidden, and only because a few individuals were curious were they even permitted their own devotions. Seileki led Saturday night and Baker Sunday morning. The few pagans who witnessed this were concerned with Christianity as a possible supply of axes, arms, and ammunition. Ironically, that very morning—21 July 1867—Baker was cut down with a Western axe, and some of his party were shot with foreign guns. Taken by surprise as they left the place where they had slept, all but two were murdered.

Death drums communicated the news across the plateau. The bodies were carried to Yarawa, accompanied by the strains of the cannibal death chant and a rising chorus of yells followed by the lewdest of pagan dances.

The people of Yarawa refused to associate themselves with the crime. An old woman, Masima, made an honorable offering of a flask of oil and a mat as a sign of respect to the murder victims. (In pagan Fiji society a dead body was always either honored or dishonored.) Though she was not yet a Christian, she made known by her act that she wanted to keep the way open to her.

The murderers carried the bodies on to Nadrau and again were rejected.

Bodies Disposed of—Apparent Defeat

Retracing their steps, they came to Cubue. Here they cooked the bodies, dissected them with bamboo knives, and disposed of the parts in as many villages as they could thereby implicate.

Christians were puzzled by the apparent defeat. It looked as if the mission had been a complete failure. One hundred years later, is it possible to view the event from a better perspective?

The scrupulous Wesleyan records of 1868 show a small drop of adherents that year—from 107,771 to 105,782. But this was the only figure which dropped, and it may be accounted for by the general war situation in Fiji, the direct loss of 250 Christian lives because of this murder and the pagan massacre of two whole Christian towns in Vanua Levu. Furthermore, any unstable or "fringe" Christians registered at the adherent level.

What happened in the core of the church? Nearly twenty thousand persons were introduced to education that year in the newly converted communities. Over a thousand new converts came into membership preparation classes, and a thousand more into full membership. The number of class leaders increased by seventy, and one hundred members assumed the responsibility of lay preaching. A qualitative growth was taking place within the church in spite of the massacres and cannibal ovens.

Two Critical Years

The years 1868 and 1869 were critical in political and military affairs. The fact that Baker was British adversely affected the situation. The British consul continually pushed the Fijian Christian king to punish the mountaineers. This gave the pagan interior cohesion against Christianity. In spite of this, the 1869 records show 25,995 pagans turning to Christ in one year. This remarkable movement revealed depth within the church. Many were brought into catechumen classes, and fully committed communicant members increased by 8,614. Class leaders increased from 1986 to 3,048 and lay preachers from 614 to 1,499, showing qualitative and organic growth and responsible participation. On the level of stewardship, in mid-1868, 529 congregations built chapels for worship that year, and 289 new congregations began to meet. Clearly the massacre of the pioneer missionary party did not obstruct the growth of the church, either quantitatively from paganism or qualitatively within.

With no other men available, the discouraged missionaries had to close the Davuilevu station temporarily. The mountain area was worked from Rewa. When reopened, Davuilevu was established as an educational center.

Even before the interior was fully won for Christ, the Fijian church began to develop overseas missionary perspective. Seven years after the Navosa tragedy, a large party of

Fijians volunteered to take the gospel to New Britain and New Ireland, despite pressure against it from the British resident commissioner.

Before the first decade was half gone a Fijian minister, Sailasa Naucukidi, took a party of young converts into the interior, and the Baker drama was repeated. Only one of the party escaped to tell the tale.

The two incidents were remarkably similar. The effects were the same—the church grew mightily.

"The ashes of the martyrs drive away demons," Chrysostom wrote in the fourth century.

Shortly after the murder of Baker and his party, the murderers' town was reduced to ruins. A missionary who visited the place in 1885 saw its foundations already buried under secondary vegetation. Near the site of the murder he baptised five men, two of whom had taken part in the crime. In Cubue, where the bodies were cooked and eaten, the cannibal ovens were never used again.

Tooth of Death

Subsequently the real instigator of the crime was discovered to be the pagan Naitasiri chief who lived almost in sight of Baker's station. He had sent a *tooth of death* into the mountains seeking Baker's death. This whale's tooth had been rejected by chief after chief until it reached Ngeladelavatu.

The unhappy instigator found neither personal satisfaction nor peace nor prosperity for his people. "Evil times fell on the land," confessed the chief's son, now the chief himself, when he visited the annual synod the church held at Rewa thirty-five years later. He came with another whale's tooth, a huge white *tooth of atonement*. With full ceremony he presented it to the church and confessed publicly his father's involvement. He admitted that everything had gone wrong with the fortunes of his lineage and community, and he wanted to set the matter as right as he could set it.

A strong indigenous church in Fiji is commemorating 1967 as the one-hundredth anniversary of the martyrdom of Thomas Baker and his associates. The once-pagan society has become Christian. Virtually all of the islands' 190,000 Fijians regard themselves as Christians today.

Baker Memorial Hall stands on the hilltop, a solid building locally designed and built entirely by Fijian voluntary labour without cost to the mission or the church. Men called to be ministers and catechists performed this labour of love that the gospel for which Baker and his party died might be better studied and understood and more effectively communicated. From that building emerged a mighty army of the Cross.

23

FIJIAN MATERIAL CULTURE:
Conclusions[158]

Throughout this study we have tried to re-create the contexts in which our selected arti-facts belonged and operated, and to examine the people who made and used them, and the institutions which gave them value. This has confirmed our basic contention that every artifact has a context, and that understanding of the context is required to give meaning to the artifact. We have seen the artifact as a point of reference through time for the study of cultural change. We began by schematising this context as a triangle, ABC, and showing the artifact in relationship with the person(s), AB, and with institutions, AC. We also saw it in a variety of perspectives or angles, BAC, and so on. We found that different persons in different roles within a context had different attitudes toward the artifact, the artifact serving a different function for each—B1A1C1, and B2A2C2, and so on. We have sought to reconstruct contexts in their totality (that is, in these three dimensions) by taking first the item of material culture, examining the terms used to describe it by the people who made or used it, and using this as a methodological starting point. By means of local informants, archival records, writings of other investigators, and my own participant observations, a number of contexts were re-created. These were studied through time. Such questions as what changes took place, when, and why, were explored. Now we must ask what the four studies have contributed in particular findings, and then what are the general findings of the whole investigation.

Case Study of Clubs

Fijian craftsmanship suffered from Tongan competition. This rivalry is reflected in craft myths and "copyright" engravings on clubs of Tongan origin. By supporting Tongan crafts, Fijian chiefs reduced the prestige of indigenous club makers.

The war context in which the clubs were used experienced a major breakdown with changes in the belief and value systems brought about by Christianity. The new religion opposed cannibalism, war, human sacrifice, the shedding of blood, the sanctification of clubs, and the eschatological beliefs associated with funerary rites and ritual death danc-

---

158 Taken from *Fijian Material Culture* (Honolulu: Bishop Museum Press, 1968), 173–80. Used by permission.

es. This deprived society of the function of club-person relationships, AB. In terms of the old religion this was secularisation.

The Christian value system was reinforced in the early years of colonial administration by the establishment of its authority. The civil government introduced constitutional law after Cession. In the Colo Wars the last opposition was reduced, arms and ammunition were confiscated, and peace was established. The role of the club "intimidators" was thereby dispensed with, and the need for club-authority patterns passed away. Relationship AC disappeared.

As a result of the new religious and civil values, not only did the clubs and guns become useless, but war fortresses fell into disrepair, unprotected coastal settlements became more permanent, and people turned to new agricultural pursuits. The ceremonies of the war context, such as the *bolebole* and *taqa*, vanished, and a whole segment of war vocabulary with them, because the need for them had gone.

We saw how war orientation provided ways and means for a man to win prestige and a title. Henceforth this was transferred to new peacetime occupations in the church, the administration, and in economic life. This is reflected in a new ceremonial terminology, "*vakavanua, vakalotu, ka vaka-matanitu*"— "pertaining to the land (birth), the church and the administration." The successful businessman, although accepted socially, is not yet ceremonially recognised.

The need gone, the club disappeared. The only clubs which remain in use today are dance clubs and the colonial mace. The mutual reinforcement of the authoritarian club of the chief, the spirit club of the priest, and the war club of the warrior seeking honor and glory, had vanished by the 1880s; not, however, leaving voids, for each was replaced by a new pattern. Old needs were met in new ways. No more significant evidence could be required of the functional outlook of the Fijian people. When the function was met by other means, and the need disappeared, so did the club.

The change did not come suddenly. The acceptance of Christianity took fifty years. Preadaptation was an important factor. A century of Tongan preadaptation prepared the way for Christianity from Tonga. Christianity undermined the war orientation and its associated beliefs and values. It prepared the way for the administrative takeover. The new government added what the new religion did not have, physical power and authority. They reinforced each other. In this way war clubs became mere museum pieces, because the context, the ABC which made them valid indexes to society, had disintegrated.

Case Study of Canoes and Boats

The canoe study showed a series of dramatic cultural changes. Many features have passed away, but others have survived. Innovation and stability are seen side by side.

The symbiosis within the community has been reduced and stripped of its religious overtones. Sacred canoes are no longer built, and the craft have disappeared, resulting in the loss of the associated institutionalised communal activities. These interrelationships and interresponsibilities held the old society together and provided naval security as well as communal pride in fine craftsmanship and achievement. The subcontracts of canoe building have also vanished; for example, sail making, for which the Yasawas and Kadavu were famed, has given way to the making of mats for cash.

The secularisation of canoe building was inevitable after the changes in the belief and value system came about. War, cannibalism, and human sacrifice had been basic in the canoe context, in the building and launching as well as the naval warfare itself.

The termination of war opened the way for individualism. This is reflected in the patterns of canoe building and canoe ownership. One reason for the survival of canoe building in its secularised form is this scope for individualism with respect to both building and ownership. This was not possible with large sacred canoes that required so many years of building and demanded such costly presentations. Individual building and ownership have been accompanied by a reduction in the size of canoes. Even so, deep-sea types, *camakau* and *tabilai*, are still extant. Society has adjusted itself to this individualism. The individual carpenter, who has replaced the guild, and the individual owner—irrespective of status—who has assumed the role of the group, are accepted as useful persons to have in one's village.

Yet these canoes continue only in Lau and Kadavu, localities where there is need for them. Even so it is interesting to note with Gladwin (1958), commenting on canoes in Micronesia, that they do continue to exist even where Western substitutes are available. The mere provision of a substitute does not necessarily satisfy a need. Control of time and movement and general accessibility of transport to fit one's schedule is all part of the need.

The development of the banana trade for overseas markets has assured the permanence of the river raft (*bilibili*). Coastal communications, markets, and fishing guarantee the survival of the flat-bottomed boat (*boto*). Island trade in copra, bananas, and trochus shell will always require the cutter or some equivalent, which, because of its availability for hire, has substituted for the sacred canoe in transporting ceremonial exchanges. Pseudo-Western types such as the *boto* meet the changing needs and reflect the shifting focus from sacred to utilitarian economic needs. This adaptability of boats has permitted their survival through a period of change. This tendency was apparent before the arrival of the white man, when coastal carpenters transformed the mountain *takia* into the coastal *waqa vakatau*.

Even before the arrival of the Westerner, craftsmanship was beginning to decline. The monopoly of the craft guild had been challenged both by unskilled Fijians and by Tongans. Confronted with a loss of prestige, the craft guild strengthened its claims by appeal to mythological traditions. The divine right of craft monopoly was threatened by individual opportunists and foreigners. The attitude of the chiefs toward the foreigners did not help the local craftsmen, who more and more turned to other professions or to general carpentry. Craft guilds began to disintegrate. By the turn of the century canoe-building units could no longer be found. Only a few individuals remained, operating alone or with low status, attached as servants to the household of some important chief. Today some individual carpenters and village cooperatives build *boto* for cash, but canoe building is confined to Kadavu and Lau. In spite of the fact that the craft remains heavily institutionalised in these two provinces, it is thoroughly secularised and individualised.

Case Study of Turtle Nets

The turtle-fishing fraternity was widespread throughout Fiji, and these groups were interrelated (*vuvata*). Their craft was a monopoly, and their proficiency in it guaranteed them good property exchanges for their catch. The reference point for the sacred ceremonial and approved behavior was the sacred fishing net, their own monopolistic craftwork.

A Togafiti myth indicates pre-Christian rivalry. The myth reveals an encroaching alternative technique for net manufacture, for catching turtles, and for a ceremonial mode of disposal of the catch, that won the acceptance of certain groups in the Rewa delta and threatened the monopoly.

Acceptance of Christianity lessened the faith in the fishing divinities and the fear of turtle-fishing taboos, and this also militated against the monopoly. However, an economic issue had been injected into the situation prior to these Christian values, for the *beche-de-mer* traders exchanged muskets, ammunition, and hardware for turtle shell in large quantities in the decade before the arrival of the first missionaries. For this there is good documentation.

Fishing for the sacred turtle was a religious matter. Only specified persons could catch or eat them, and only at specific times. The sacred nets were made in the only approved ceremonial manner by the fishermen themselves and no one else. Divination was practiced at every stage. The sacred turtle club was featured in the key ceremonies. A rite was performed on the canoe when a turtle was caught. The whole complex was encircled with taboos of food and procedure which preserved the fear of the deity. These taboos also preserved the turtle from extinction. Acceptance of a new system of beliefs and values changed all this. Later on, the missionaries approved turtle fishing for their converts on the score that God's creatures were for all men, but they did confine the pursuit to specific occasions, such as church-building programs when large numbers of men had to be fed. Furthermore they had chiefly precedent in doing this. Even so it did represent a challenge to the monopoly and, from the point of view of the old religion, was a step toward secularisation.

Viewing these changes diachronically, the great changes came after Cession, when the monopoly was lost altogether. The reasons were these: (1) non-turtle-fishing groups of Fijians usurped the rights of the turtle fishers; (2) many individuals did likewise; (3) non-fishers were able to make nets by using imported twine as a substitute for the sacred secret process; (4) other methods of fishing were introduced both by groups and individuals: noose catching, spearing, and so on; (5) any person who wished to fish for turtle or eat the creature could do so without fear of taboo or law; (6) many raids were made on the breeding places; and (7) turtle fences were established in hundreds of villages.

Every one of these factors broke some taboo. This was not the effect of Christianity, although Christianity helped to open the way for the change. The colonial administration actively supported individualism and enterprise.

Economic reward was considerable. Turtles were systematically caught and the shell sold. This went on for a century. Today there are not enough turtles in Fijian waters to support a turtle-fishing program. As long as the taboos prevented excessive fishing and the fishermen alone made the nets, the supply was enough for the institutional complex to be maintained, and to serve the social and religious purposes for which it existed. Once the monopoly was lost, the secularised individualism that took its place was self-destructive; it destroyed itself by exhausting its own source of supply.

Two attempts have been made to rehabilitate turtle fishing. There was the reestablishment of the institution known as *Na Veibuli ni Tunidau ni Bau*, and a belated effort on the part of the administration to preserve the turtle by controlling the fishing season.

The first attempt sought to restore an institutional context on a basis of the personal relationships within it, B1-B2, *tunidau* and chief, with the ceremonial sash (*vesa*), as the artifactual reference point. However, the configuration of the turtle fishing itself cannot be restored without the reestablishment of the sacredness of the net and the monopoly.

The second ignores the ceremonial complex entirely, and seeks to rehabilitate the turtle supply for the sake of an individualistic society. The ways of yesterday differ from those of today—the way of taboo and the way of law—one protecting the group and the other the individual. In its own day the way of taboo was effective, as was also its concomitant monopoly.

Case Study of Houses

House building in Fiji is the most stable of the four contexts we have had before us. This springs from more abiding needs. All the main types of dwelling house, service quarters, and temporary facilities for exchanges and festivals, continue to be built with very little modification. However, there have been areas of change which reflect the history of the last century.

The Tongan influence in house building has been slowly spreading in the Group, having long taken possession of Lau and reaching to Kadavu and Vanua Levu. Even so, two things need to be noted; even where it has become the regular type of house building, the resultant edifice is still called a *vale Vakatoga*, a Tongan house, and in each area the house that carries prestige and pride is always an indigenous type in preference to the Tongan.

New types of building appear with each new need: shops, schools, churches, offices, jails, hospitals. These reflect their different functional requirements and also the changing social life and outlook of the people, the passage from war to peace, and new patterns of authority. The form is usually determined by the function.

Changes in religion are reflected in house building. In pre-Christian times religion was the integrator of society. It has become more compartmentalised. The old Fijian said, "*Nai vau ni Vanua na veiqaraqaravi vakalou*" ("The bond (holder-together or integrator) of the Land is the service of the gods"). The Fijian of today says, "*Rau sola vata na Vanua kei na Lotu e na nodraui dui tavi*" ("The Land and the Church journey together in their different responsibilities"). This shift is in indigenous thinking. It is demonstrated in house building. Certain houses could never be built without a series of human sacrifices, the posts had to be supported by human beings, and religious rituals were called for at each stage of the construction. Today the ceremonies are social and economic and concern food and labour also, but, except in the cases of church buildings, there are no religious rites. In the case of the church at Bau, we had a functional substitute for a god house, but the Christian dedication was much modified. The morphology of this building reflected the social organisation and was more nearly an integrator than anywhere else in Fiji. It tends to be so in traditional chiefly centers.

The principal loss in house types is the disappearance of clubhouses and young men's quarters. This is the result of the emergence of the Christian pattern of living in nuclear families.

The character of house building depends on the degree of integration in the society itself, the reality of its symbiosis, which works itself out in reciprocal work and exchange patterns. We examined in detail a case in Kadavu, which approximated the ideal, and then a second in Vanua Levu, which reflected a breakdown of cooperation. Both of these were extremes. Present-day house-building patterns lie distributed between these two poles.

Individualism arises in house building with independent farmers and absentees who live away from their villages. These increase in numbers each year, but the great majority of Fijians still live in villages, where the Fijian house is generally a stable type. Personal relationships and institutions continue and maintain the village working units. The continuity of house type is assured as long as the context is stable. Changes require group, not individual, consideration and decision. Capacity to make changes of a structural nature lies with the head carpenter, provided he can carry the group with him. Fijian house types therefore have shown less individualism and more stability than any other artifact we have examined.

In spite of the removal of much of the adult male labour force to industrial areas and towns, so that house building is neglected in some areas, the housebuilding contexts are stable. The following reasons are suggested: (1) The needs or functions have changed less. (2) Houses have been less influenced by changes in belief and values. People still must have cooking facilities, shelter, sleep, and so on. (3) It was possible for Christians to remove human sacrifice in this case without destroying basic patterns. Ceremony, though secularised, continued. (4) It was possible to introduce new types of houses without destroying the old. (5) House building was a total village project, not a monopolist service of a craft group. It has still remained a village or regional project. Where the house-building program has broken down, it will be found that the village organisation itself is not working.

General Findings

As anticipated, the study has shown changes owing to whalers, sandalwooders, and *beche-de-mer* traders, Christianity, and colonial government. However, one striking fact emerges that is a contribution of anthropology to history. The Tongan influence, usually located in the middle of the last century, is seen as a major disintegrator of social organisation before European times. We see this Tongan influence on clubs, houses, and nets, in the breakdown of Fijian craft group monopoly, and in the rivalry of the myths.

War-oriented Fijian society was stimulated by sandalwood and *beche-de-mer* traders and also by Tongan adventurers to a point of self-destruction, as evidenced by the hundreds of village foundations that lie in ruin still. Christianity resisted this orientation and undermined it, but it remained ultimately for colonial action to conquer it. The diffusion of foreign artifacts of war—Tongan clubs along the coasts, Western muskets into the interior—indicates the spread of these self-destructive tendencies. These factors permit a diachronic analysis of change.

Some ceremonial contexts have disappeared, some have continued with modification. When a need vanishes, the artifact ceases to be made. When conditions change, artifacts have to be adapted to the new needs. An old form may be retained with a new function. A new form may be taken over as a functional substitute. Form and function may reflect each other, but either must fit the context and requires the context to interpret it. The following processes apply in the Fijian situation as far as it can be appraised from the four case studies:

1. When a craft monopoly is lost, competition (either foreign, local group, or individual) tends to destroy the context altogether. The competition is suicidal.
2. In areas of deep change involving belief and value systems, the context is most likely to disintegrate, but there is always the possibility of survival by

means of functional substitutes, such as the cutter for the sacred canoe and the church for the god house.

3. Change in Fiji has been marked by secularisation, and religion has become compartmentalised. Sacred objects are now confined to religious or personal life. The secularisation is manifest in the loss of *mana*, in the disappearance of religious overtones in ceremonial, in reduction of taboo, and in termination of divination and human sacrifices. In ceremonial exchanges highly valued sacred objects have given way to foreign utility goods.

4. Some contexts disintegrate communally but continue on an individual basis. Builders and owners of expensive, complex communal artifacts may now be individuals. Usually these artifacts are reduced a little in size.

This has been a reconstruction of contexts achieved by taking the artifact in question as a point of reference and asking the questions: What is its function? What was it, say, in the war context of 1839? What is it now? What did it mean to the men who used it or those who made it? Why was it necessary for this man to modify it? Such a re-creation had to be functionally orientated. It had to explore the indigenous opinion rather than construct an extraneous one. Therefore I refrained from abstracting a typology of my own, but sought what I could find in the lexical data, and it always led away from isolated artifacts to functioning units or contexts. Our descriptions draw much from documentary material, always with a leaning toward the vernacular report or the report of indigenes. The range has been limited to four types of artifacts. I believe the method warrants wider application, both in the same locality and for comparative purposes over a wider area.

REFERENCES

Gladwin, Thomas. 1958. Canoe travel in the Truk area: Technology and its psychological correlates. *American Anthropologist* 60: 893–99.

24

"THE END OF THE AGE! ALAS!"[159]

I

I cannot tell you the year of this tale, though one who knows the stars might help to find the answer. I only know that it was the year in which the comet with three tails appeared in the heavens and when people awaited its meaning with fear; did it spell tragedy or some amazing achievement? They were not kept in suspense for long, for it was also the year the first white man's ship appeared in those parts. It might have been the *Pandora* (1791), the *Providence* (1792), or the *Arthur* (1794), or it may have been some other vessel. I do not know. I only know that three events are told together in the songs of the minstrels—the comet with three tails, the first white man's ship, and the wasting sickness.

A strange disease indeed was this legacy of the white sailor whom they took ashore from the white man's ship.

> "Our fathers," *so say the storytellers of the tribe,*
>
> felt their legs go from under them, and as they walked they swayed and fell, and where they fell they lay. Not many of them died of the disease—but their friends had need to strangle them because of their weakness. They became such a burden to everyone. Prior to that, few but widows were strangled, and that to accompany their dead husbands into the next world. But from this time there began our custom of strangling the sick. Both customs we retained until Christianity came.

Another song tells of havoc caused in Naitasiri, until a plant from which a potent medicine was made, was found and gave relief and eventually cure. Its name, *Vueti Naitasiri*, is remembered to this day.

Two old women, captured in the wars half a century later, brought with them from their village an ancient lament, and as they performed their rhythmic body movements they chanted these words:

---

159   Taken from *Road to Bau: The Life and Work of John Hunt of Viwa, Fiji* (Pasadena: William Carey Library, 2013), 5–13. Originally written in 1955.

Great is the sickness lying at the masthead,
Swollen like food baskets their heads,
And hoarse indeed their voices;
They fall, and helpless and pitiable they lie.
Degei[160] is put to shame.

A noble thing indeed is the strangling rope.

So ran the story of Vunivasa. At Vunivia it was the same:

What is this sickness that smites them?
  I remember!

The wasting sickness, that spreads far and wide.
  I remember!

And again at Kura the doleful melody is heard:

The old men are listless,
  I remember!

Terrifying indeed the sickness,
  I remember!

We do not die. We do not live.
  I remember!

Our stomachs ache. Our heads ache.
  I remember!

The strangling cords creak.
  I remember!

Spirits flow away like running water.
  I remember!

Everywhere throughout the country the same miserable tale is told and sung of the wasting sickness which came with the first white man's ship and the comet with the three tails:

Have we fallen upon a new age? Alas!
We lie down. We grow torpid. Alas!
Many die. A few live on. Alas!
Many die indeed only by the rope. Alas!
Their girdles rot around their waists. Alas!
The women despair. Alas!
Their grass skirts unloosed. Alas!
And we wonder at it all.

---

160 Degei: the name of their god.

What can it mean?
Is it a sign of death to the chiefs?
Is it the end of the age? Alas!

II

Maybe ten years later. Again I cannot tell the date with certainty. One thing only I know—
that the tale is told together with that of an eclipse of the sun and a tidal wave. It is said
that Chief Naulivou was installed into office as chief warlord of Bau on the day of the
eclipse (some say it was 7 September 1802), and he had followed Chief Banuve, who had
died a victim of another white man's disease. The eclipse, the tidal wave, a second white
man's ship, and death.

Slowly once more the graceful brown bodies begin to sway, and arms move to the
rhythmic beat of another dirge.

> Loudly roar the waves of the trade winds,
> Breakers chase each other in quick succession,
> To burst over the end of the canoe shed
> Shaking a shower of berries from the *vetau*
> Into the open doorway.
> Mother of No'wester collects them
>
> Bringing them within the house to me
> To be my playthings.
>
> Quickly run out the neap tides
> New is the tale we hear
> As a ship comes up from the ocean.
> They launch the *Word of the Chief*
> And sail out of the Kabara Sea.
> Where they lower the sail at the stern.
> O, You, who travel the ocean.
> There is Rotuma and Galagala.
> On Distant Reef the surf boils
> This is the place where canoes anchor.
>
> The foreigners have returned
> And anchor at Blowing Sand.
>
> *   *   *   *   *
>
> The sickness has come among us
> Empty is every district.
>
> Our warriors by it are bound
> Their heads droop and wither

As the *diaga* plant droops at sunset,
And are buried in the place of the dead.

The foreigners have sailed away.
Our men are swept away.
Our women are swept away.
They are as withering plantains.

There is a story told in Nakelo that the epidemic of dysentery was eventually cleared away only by a great flood, a higher flood than ever before or since, when whole villages were swept out to sea and the mangroves were buried in silt. Much of the Lower Rewa delta is said to have been built up at the time. The Bauans have a similar tale.

III

10 September 1808: Valevatu, a petty chief, entertains a party of visitors led by the paramount chief of the district. There has been a conference of the old men. They have promised to set their defences in order and to aid their overlord in war. They have feasted together on yams and breadfruit, and the remainder of the night is spent in dancing in the moonlight.

The ancient faith of their fathers has ordained that they dance while the moon shines, the men and the women in separate groups, to the tune of the bamboo nose flute. The visitors are armed with the ancient weapons of war, manufactured according to the traditional arts handed down from their ancestors. Indeed, is it not from their great ancestor, whose famous exploits are sung in the tribal ballads, and whom they have since deified, to whom they now give worship very similar to that given to the ancestor spirit himself?

Yet there is one among them who seems a little less at ease than the rest, and his weapons are new and strange—a musket on his back, and a pair of pistols at hand. Beneath the black paint that covers his body lies a white skin.

He is now asked to demonstrate the magic of his instruments of war, and having previously taken care to place more than one ball in each, he proceeds to sink some into nearby trees, and cause damage which truly astonishes his hosts. Though the paramount chief knows the secret, no other person can be induced to even touch a pistol.

For the time being the support of this tribe is assured, though later they found it favourable to aid the enemy, for which double dealings they paid dearly by a punishment inflicted by the white man's weapons.

IV

The date is about a month later. A fleet of canoes prepares to attack an island, and the island canoes come out to meet their invaders. There is a preliminary skirmish with bows and arrows and stone slinging and, as they draw closer, with spears and clubs. The spears are pointed with guard-fish bills, and many finding their marks are surgically extracted by the victims themselves by means of sharp pieces of shell or bamboo. A prisoner is taken. It is said his wounds will be dressed in the morning (but actually he will be clubbed and eaten). One hundred and fifty war canoes surround the island. The attack lasts three days and leaves the island devastated. Hogs, plantains, yams, mats, baskets, and fishing nets are plundered, and every house is burnt and the food trees are cut down. The hideout of the old men and women and children is discovered, and these are lashed to poles like pigs and carried away among the plunder. Some die of the treatment. Others are clubbed. No one is shown any respect, save a grotesque, deformed boy, who is respected only because his malformed body indicated him to be spirit possessed.

In the intense excitement the cries of the dying are hardly distinguishable from the bloodthirsty yelling of the victors. A war cry rings out with every new victim, the war songs begin and the war dances follow—filthy and lewd.

On one canoe stands a white man; beside him, forty-two bodies. All night the wild rejoicing continues. Then another day—a day spent in cutting up and cooking bodies. There is dexterity in it.

White men, clad and painted as the natives, find their participation in native war takes them further than they want to go. There are no food supplies from the quartermaster in native war. For four days there has been no prepared meal, which possibly explains the disgusting gluttony which follows plunder and massacre.

One of the white men has the initiative to say that the eating of human flesh is forbidden by his God, and this alone saves him, but his only food is yam cooked in the same pots as human bodies.

V

It is another month later.

A white man bargains with a native chief. He offers many costly presents, presents much better than he usually gives away. But the chief drives a hard bargain. He may not fully understand what lies behind the China sandalwood trade, but he does know the white man will do almost anything to get this timber.

So the white man accepts the terms and agrees to fight a native war, and accordingly a native army of some 1,800 is joined by a white man's launch, with sixteen white men armed with muskets and cutlasses, and another with a twelve-pound carronade and a swivel and fourteen men. It is an attack on an island fortress, and ammunition supplies are sent from the white man's ship. The fortress falls before the firearms, but it has been desperately defended, and the capture reveals some two hundred corpses within—among them the body of the chief.

Though the chief for whom the white men fight promised to save the women and children, he can do nothing about it. War, as they know it, is savage war. There is no mercy.

The next day sees a Christian burial—the body of a white man killed in action. Afterwards white men stand and watch the preparations for cannibal feasting.

Within a few days they have their sandalwood—one hundred tons of it—which reached Port Jackson on 14 February 1809.

VI

20 June 1808, 11 p.m. S. Lat. 17.40, E. Long. 179: The *Eliza* is fast on the reef near Nairai, Fiji.

White men escaping to the shore are met by natives with bows and arrows, spears and war clubs. Is it not their tradition that saltwater bodies are theirs by gift from their gods? The white men are relieved of their clothing and goods and left naked, but no life has yet been taken—the shipwrecked are not often so fortunate.

One of these is taken by the chief of Batiki to his island, where in a miserable state of health he lies up for a long time, almost at death's door. Nor are the natives helpful to his depressed spirit. They come and look at the poor wretch, almost blind with ophthalmia, the use of one leg gone, and internal pains from who knows what. Then they feel his legs and say, "White man, you are good to eat."

Whereupon the now long-repentant sailor becomes a preacher—perhaps the first in Fiji if the truth be known.

He tells them of his great God, who disapproves of people eating human flesh, and adds that if they would only desist from the practise and open their land to the white men, their God would surely send cattle, which are far better to eat. They say they want no cattle. If they are as big as he says, they would be afraid of them anyway.

The women see him lying there and ask him when he will die, for certainly were they so sick they would die right away. He answers that he will die when his God sees fit to take him out of the world. And they ask him about his land. Are there any women there? They will not believe him for are not the white men chiefs from the sun?

He tells them of God again. He convinces them of the greatness of God. They compare this God with theirs. He turns opportunity to his own ends and warns them to do nothing that will rouse the anger of his God—certainly nothing so rash as killing a white man.

The women are kind to him. He keeps a record of time by making knots in a spear of grass. He keeps Sunday and remembers Christmas. At times the white man feels he will die, and then he blames the devil for these feelings, and he prays:

> O Lord, spare my unprofitable life and enable me to get off this savage island,
> and protect me once more over the boisterous ocean to my native country, and
> I will try by Thy assistance to seek religion and become what Thou wouldst have
> me to be.

(The prayer was eventually answered and he lived to see America again.)

Sometime later, back in Nairai again, he sees a man clubbed and about to be eaten. Again he tells how wrong it is and how God must certainly be angry with them if they eat their fellows. They gratify him by taking the body away for burial, but they eat it just the same. They listen to his preaching but go their own way.

VII

A child of four years, half-caste daughter of a white man who has made himself the power and fear of Fiji, lies on her bed watching him go through his sea chest. He too comes from the *Eliza*, but his record is very different. A desperate adventurer, by guile and good shooting he has established himself as a Fijian hero and enjoys the privileges which go with the title. Two great ladies are given him for wives. For miles around he has brought tribes under the heel of Bau. His main business is war. In the winter months he follows the sandalwood ships, for wherever these ships go there is action, danger, and opportunity for good shooting.

Maraia lies watching her father, and is attracted by the glittering contents of the chest. She startles her father who has thought her asleep. He is going away for a long time he tells her, and must hide her property in a safe place. So he poles over to some spot on the mainland, and next morning she discovers the Bauan canoes have sailed for Bua.

Here this adventurer, whose good marksmanship has consigned so many to the ovens, ends his own bodily existence in the same form of internment. Years later Maraia is forced to marry the captain of a Manilla ship, and her father's treasure of South American dollars still lies buried within the vicinity of Bau.

VIII

Things have gone wrong somehow with the plans of the white sea captain. The death of a chief, with whom he had made a business deal, threatens to rob him of his sandalwood cargo, and he goes ashore. The principal wife of the dead chief is to be strangled. She does not want to die, and the captain determines to try to save the lady purely because he sees a way of obtaining his cargo of sandalwood thereby, even though by doing this the woman also becomes his.

So taking his largest whale's tooth he goes to plead for her life, but the priest, his enemy, and the enemy of all white people, who has repeatedly pointed out how intercourse with whites always brings trouble, hastens on the ceremony—for the rite means profit to him. The sea captain is too late. The fatal cord is drawn.

Somewhat sanctimoniously the priest explains that it is necessary. It is the law. He alone, as priest, knows the reason. Sacrifices will follow.

The captain is fifteen minutes late, and greatly agitated turns on the priest and upbraids him, but the priest is calm for has he not won the encounter. "It is the law," he says.

Even so the captain finds a trick by means of which he gets his sandalwood.

IX

One thing leads to another.

The year is 1838 and this tale concerns a certain French brig *L'Aimable Josephine*, whose captain, like so many others of his kind, has been partaking in native politics and wars.

His craft is at Viwa. His business relationships with the native people seem good. The Viwa chief is persuaded to allow his nephew to attack the vessel. He does so most efficiently, massacres the crew, steals the vessel, and thereby earns for himself the name Varani, after the Frenchman.

This sort of thing inevitably brings reprisals. Shortly afterwards there appears in these waters one M. Dumont d'Urville to avenge the death of Captain Bureau and the crew of his brig. The town of Viwa is bombarded from the sea and completely destroyed.

  *   *   *   *   *

This sequence of vignettes of pre-Christian Fiji is a kind of filmstrip and introduces us to the main basic problems created in Fiji in the few decades immediately prior to the coming of Christianity. In the episodes I have sketched, I have purposely refrained from the use of any missionary sources or documents. Much has been said to the effect that the missionaries overpainted the picture, to avoid such criticism I have confined myself to native traditions and the written records of the seamen who witnessed these events.

We may now sum up the problems introduced:

1. White man's disease and its social and psychological effect.
2. Introduction of firearms, and political importance of marksmanship.
3. Interference of white men in native wars.
4. Massacres of white men and reprisals.
5. Taking of native wives by white sailors and disputes arising thereupon.

All these are apparent on the surface, but there were other factors less apparent to the casual observer. There was a growing realisation that these "men from the sun" had behind them some great power, be it a kingdom or a god; they seemed to have an unlimited supply of munitions and landships.

Again the Fijian was mystified by a dim idea that this power, whatever it was, disapproved of many of his own traditional rites; in particular, widow strangling and cannibalism—even when men of war shrank from eating human flesh and interfered with their sacred burial rites—and this before any missionary appeared. The episode of the French reprisals introduces another element which was a bitter issue in midcentury—

French Pacific policy. This had a violent effect on the Protestant missionaries, and a native chief must have often wondered at the quarrels among the white men themselves.

At the same time it must have been hard for a friendly trader who had established good trade relationships with a tribe to return and find them openly hostile. One captain's greed for sandalwood might spoil intercourse for all strangers to follow.

There was no such thing as unity in Fiji in those days. Fiji was the world, with Tonga on the edge of it, and the white men came from beyond, from another world. The chiefs of Fiji were fighting among themselves, the stronger swallowing the others one by one. The greatest of these were Bau, Rewa, and Somosomo, at the time the missionaries came, but there were five or six others that had not yet been completely accounted for, and of the interior very little was known, even by the coastal Fijians. These chiefs were fighting for paramouncy, and if the white man could be persuaded to fight their battles, that was good, but otherwise they were best left alone. Kill a white man and something always seemed to go wrong. Perhaps it was the white man's God. Perhaps a landship would come and blast their village from the coast. Or perhaps some strange disease for which no forest cure was known. Was it not in their laments and songs?

Of course the white man brought other things—axes, knives, fishhooks, and many useful articles. And above all they would sell muskets. A musket could be obtained for as small a price as a slave woman.

And then there came the strangest white men of all—no doubt the priests of the white man's God. Fearless men who put no trust in firearms, but made new things called books, and taught new arts like reading and writing and sewing, and administered medicine to the sick, and set new words to their old melodies—new, strange words of a teaching they had not met before. They brought their wives and raised white families in their midst.

They were new days—strange and terrible. They chanted:

> What can it mean?
> Is it a sign of death to the chiefs?

Is it the end of the age? Alas!—as their graceful bodies swayed to and fro in unison to the rhythm.

25

ORAL TRADITION AND ETHNOHISTORY:
The Transformation of Information and Social Values in Early Christian Fiji (1835–1905)[161]

Theoretical Preamble

Contextualisation and Indigeneity

There has been much talk in the theory of mission about planting the indigenous church, but I think we have by now come to realise that Western type of ecclesiastical structures, even though run by indigenous people, and standing on their own feet financially, and autonomous in their decision making, are not necessarily indigenous churches at all. A native church and native pastors who are merely little replicas of our own selves are not indigenous.

An indigenous church, defined anthropologically, must be the relevant integrator (Malinowski 1961, 48) or governor (Wallace 1966, 4)[162] of the integral systems or institutions (Malinowski 1960, 38–39) which, combined, make up the whole society. Certainly this is so for a communal society like that of Fiji, which provides the case study for this paper. An indigenous church, defined theologically, must have the self-awareness that enables it to see itself as the body of Christ communicating the word, the mind, and the love of Christ to the society that it holds together; and to do this in a culturally accepted manner. A church that is not contextualised is foreign and not indigenous.

But, someone may ask, is this possible? Let me use an analogy from linguistics. The ethnolinguist Edward Sapir used to discuss what he called "linguistic drift and phonetic law" and showed how changes take place in language. He found changes taking place within the basic pattern without destroying it—a "sort of shifting about without loss of pattern, or with a minimum loss of it" (Sapir 1949, 182).

When we speak of an indigenous church, we are dealing with a self-activating organism—a dynamic phenomenon—not a static system. An indigenous church must also have

---

161 Alan Tippett's inaugural lecture at St. Mark's Theological College, Canberra, Australia, 1979

(Tippett 1980) [now St. Mark's National Theological Centre—Ed.].

162 "Religion functions as a kind of governor of society, stabilizing its members and correcting the tendency of institutions to wobble or drift" (Wallace 1966, 4).

a contextualised gospel or it cannot relate to the world which is its field of ministry. Internally and externally we must have dynamic relationships.

Take, for example, the scientific principles worked out by John Hunt and Richard Lyth in the 1840s for the Fijianization of Hebrew and Greek names in Scripture translation which so thoroughly fitted the Fijian linguistic pattern that the terms were quite acceptable and euphonious to the Fijian people, and probably 99 percent of them are still in use today after a century and a quarter.[163] Similarly Hunt's grasp of Fijian grammar, syntax, and word construction gave us a vital translation which breathed with a Fijian heart. Furthermore, from this there developed a theology, recognisably Fijian but quite Christian, and demonstrating the natural capacity of the language which hitherto had articulated only a theology and eschatology of cannibalism. The early missionaries and their Fijian linguistic assistants demonstrated what Ulfilas had done in early church history, that, against official opinion, the holy gospel could be put into the vulgar tongue of the Goths (Edman 1949, 90–93), a lesson each generation of missionaries ever since has had to learn to be effective evangelists.

Twenty years ago I called this "the culturalization of the gospel." Today in missiology we say "contextualisation." We regard the gospel as supracultural, but it has to be encapsulated or incarnated to become relevant in any given situation. This is as true for the written Word and the preached Word as it was for the Living Word Himself. The Word has to be made flesh and dwell among us. It has to acquire a meaningful form if its impact is to be dynamic.

Now I hope to describe for you some of the cultural forms which came out of cannibal society and were sanctified for the glory of God in order that the message of the gospel could be contextualised and an indigenous *koinonia* might emerge.[164]

I want to start with the appraisal of a well-known secular anthropologist who has specialised on studies of the southwest Pacific, Cyril S. Belshaw, and who spoke of the church in Fiji thus:

---

163 I have written this up in my biography of Hunt (1955, 93–95), but the linguistic researcher should bring together the primary roles of the two men.

164 A good deal of research on culture, form, and value stability through, and in spite of, change by the use of functional substitutes has been done using Fijian data. Much of this is housed in my collection at St Mark's. [St. Mark's National Theological Centre, Canberra, Australia, houses the Tippett library and archives. Ed.] In a paper entitled "Functional Substitutes in Fijian Christianity" (1977b) I posed the question to a conference of applied anthropologists: when basic religious beliefs change, do all the old forms and values have to be discarded with them? To that question I answered no! They may be modified and Christianized without depriving them of their unique indigenous character. I then discussed the cultural mechanism of the "functional substitute" which makes this possible and leaves, not the advocate of change, but the indigenous people the real innovators. In a further paper on "Personal Interplay in Intercommunity Ceremonial in Fiji," the finding of the research was:

Cultural borrowing, or acculturation, or the entry of a foreigner into custom situations, need not be destructive to the culture, provided one (1) plays the game according to the rules, and does so (2) with due respect, and (3) demonstrates this by learning to use the ceremonial language, and (4) shows that he is sharing the experience, not being a scientist studying a number of guinea pigs. (Tippett 1977b, 119)

[It] provides a relaxing and organizing principle in Fijian life. It governs Sunday, the day of rest, which is broken into only in the direst of emergencies. It provides a focus for singing, one of the greatest joys of the people. It provides for local initiative in church government and the arrangement of visits and festivities for church purposes. Its moral code is still strong in determining the puritanical mode of dress which has become associated with Fijian tradition and in securing adherence to the overt forms of ritual behaviour . . . It is tolerant of Fijian custom . . . One has the impression that after the 19th Century battle of conversion, the Church has settled down, become a Fijian-orientated institution, and is guided by a spirit of tolerance, rather than one of reformist zeal. (1964, 14)

In the following paragraph he discusses "the value of ceremonial and ritual in Fijian eyes" and the ceremonial recognition of one social group and another, which is as true in the church as in the Provincial Council. Elsewhere in the book Belshaw says that the study of the church in Fiji "is shot through with questions of fascinating interest . . . How widespread are the innovations in church ritual, for example, the chanting of the Psalms . . . according to ancient musical forms, or the sharing of the service between lay preachers?" (ibid., 250). "A feature of the organization," he says, "is that the European missionary has withdrawn as far as possible into the background" (251).

Although this is the way Belshaw saw the society, to be fair to him I should add that this is not the goal of his study, which is rather to consider the economics of that society's future and to redraw the picture within a wider parameter. Nevertheless, as I am to look at the whole question of the reality (or otherwise) of the church's indigeneity, I am using his observation as a "springboard" for this presentation. I agree that a contained, indigenous church can become an end in itself. The church's mission is in the world. Even an ideally indigenous church has to relate with the outside, and I know that would really require a quite different presentation with an outward rather than an inward look. So having anticipated that obvious shortcoming of my presentation, I now want to ask, what does the history of the first Christian century in Fiji say to the frequent criticism that the mission destroyed the culture? And this historical question I probe anthropologically, more particularly with respect to the field techniques of communication rather than the message or ethic communicated, which is another subject.

That means that the concern of my research has been a question, not a hypothesis. I wanted to know if the changes in the message and morals which came with Christianity necessarily meant changes in the cultural forms through which the message had to be communicated. Could Fijian Christianity assume a cultural garment different from that of Galilee or of Australia? Having worked on the data for some time, I have concluded that the garment of an indigenous Fijian church could be neither Galilean nor Australian; it had to be Fijian. And only now that this is accomplished can the church look out in its own self-hood and relate in mission and ministry to a wider world.

Now we must move from theory into history. Many of the pre-Christian military performances disappeared with the coming of Christianity, or at least their pagan associations disappeared. Christianity stood as a way of peace. Yet Christians displayed remarkable bravery in the face of persecution and death. They died in thousands but never retaliated. When they took refuge in the mountain fortresses, they were never subdued, as if empowered by a remarkable protecting force. When their time came, and the heathen were converted, the associations of war were cast aside—the excesses and ceremonials of victory; the dances vulgar in their extreme, like the *wate* and *dele*; the songs, dances, and gestures of sexual significance aimed at taunting the captives, which the missionaries could not bring themselves to describe except by saying "too disgusting to mention" (we have to go to sailors for our description). Christianity did dispose of all this.[165] But except for the *wate* and *dele*, dancing went on. The spear dances, club dances, dances for graduating chiefs all may be seen still today as entertainment at church gatherings, the host villages providing dances for the enjoyment of the visitors. Many of the finest accompanying chants are performed to a dance format known as a *Vakamalolo*, the performers of the dance (*na matana*) being in a seated posture, movements being confined to the upper part of the body—arms, shoulders, heads, faces, and hands. Many of the epics are performed in this manner, especially indoors at night. The art and skill of all these dance formations were never lost, nor the rhythmic chanting for preserving narrative and description, although in Christian times the word content may be quite new. Even this was truly Fijian as these chants are a record of historical events resulting from experiences lived by the people.

One of the most common presentations for the visit of Europeans or church dignitaries is known as *"Na Meke ni Yabaki Drau"* ("The Chant of the Hundred Years"). It was composed in 1935 to mark the centenary of the coming of the gospel to Fiji from Tonga. It is modelled on the genealogy of a Fijian lineage and lists the names of the missionary leaders from

---

165   The young women went out to meet the victorious cannibal warriors as the women greeted the victorious David in Scripture, but with a very different song.

The words of the women's song may not be translated; nor are the obscene gestures of the dance . . . or the foul insults offered to the corpses of the slain, fit to be described . . . ordinary social restrictions are destroyed and the unbridled and indiscriminate indulgence of every evil lust and passion completes the scene of abomination. (Williams 1884, 42–43)

The songs suggested the hero in war was to be a hero in sex, heroes were addressed in terms of their sex organs, and the sex organs of living captives were abused by the dancing women—lest the reader think the "too disgusting to mention" is mere missionary bias. See Hunt, *Journal*, 14 September 1840; Jackson's "Narrative" in Erskine (1853, 438); Hocart (1929, 143); Fison (1871).

In a manuscript life of John Hunt, I devoted several pages to a discussion of those types of invitation songs (invitation to sex) in pre-Christian Fijian life to which the missionaries took exception. As usual it is metaphoric communication (1955, 109–13).

Cross and Cargill down to the centenary celebrations. It is used in two ways: either as a chant by the women in church or as a *vakamalolo* before an assembly of visitors on the village green.

I have written up the epic of chant and dance at greater length in *Fijian Material Culture* as they relate to war and house building. The house-building chants are still performed (Tippett 1968, 146–52), even for the building of a church edifice. The point I am making here, however, is that conversion to Christianity did not "destroy the culture"; if anything it "preserved it by reform." What was good, clean, entertaining, or educational has survived. Now we must move from theory into history.

Many of the old songs and dance chants of Fiji are still to be found in the historical documents where they were recorded by early missionaries and settlers who had interest in them. Some were recaptured from old Fijians who died in the 1870s and 1880s. A resident, G. Beauclerc, translated the traditions of the pre-Christian "Path of the Soul to the After-World," which had been written down years before by a Fijian using the *nom de plume* "*Ueuelala kei Nailatinicolo.*"[166] Mr. George Barker (1925a) also produced from his research somewhere in Fiji poetic material about Conua, a town of Nakauvadra. The epic poem of Koroitamana is well known in its Fijian form, and was translated by Waterhouse in still cannibal times and later by George Barker (1925b). The Nakauvadra fable of Turukurawa, the bird associated with the diffusion of the Fijian tribes over the Group, was translated into a popular English epic rhythm by John Hunt before 1848 (1925). Some very old children's game songs have also been preserved (Toganivalu 1911, Rougier 1915).

In addition to this we have dirges that came down orally from the precontact period (or very first contact of the 1780s and 1790s), which have been preserved in the Report of the Royal Commission to investigate the decline of Fijian population in the 1890s.[167] And there are songs which explain customs, like the use of the whale's teeth in securing spouses (Toganivalu 1917, 9). The point of all this is to indicate that we have enough precontact and contact material to know the character of pre-Christian oral forms, their techniques and values—the epics, the dirges, the dance chants, the ceremonial liturgies, the children's songs, the proverbs, riddles, legal sayings, work songs, and so on. My presentation is to show that Christianity did not interfere with those forms and poetic values, however much it changed the ethics and religious truth. For over a century the Fijian church thus stood as an indigenous institution.

The Fijian mythology of the Flood was written up and published by Waterhouse in 1866 and utilised John Hunt's translation of the "Song of Turukawa," which dates to the first

---

166 Presented to The Fijian Society in 1911. The same transactions record studies of Fijian customs of precontact times, and of the 1870s—this is extremely important primary source material.

167 These are extremely informative primary sources especially in view of interdisciplinary techniques being used to fix precise dates for oral tradition (see Tippett 1973, 15–37).

decade of the century (1866, 359–60). Edouard Martin, who was a sailor wrecked on Vanua Levu in 1848, gave Waterhouse a chant in honour of Fijian tobacco in a Vanua Levu dialect (425) and the long "*Meke ni Koroitamana*" in the Rewan language. Another even longer dance chant "*A Vanua Lata*" with five movements and over eighty lines was sung at a state function before the conversion of Cakobau (429–31). It was supplied to Waterhouse by one of the women who sang it at the time, and he wrote at her dictation. Waterhouse also supplies a translation of the Epic of the Nakelo Massacre (434–35) and the Bauan "*Meke of Cakobau*" in five movements (432–33).

The pre-Christian hero tales of the Tanoa and early Cakobau period were collected by Jesse Carey, who attempted a dynamic equivalent translation in the not unsuitable rhythm of Longfellow's "Hiawatha." I myself have attempted a reconstruction of the social dynamics and ceremonial of several major aspects of Fijian technology from primary sources, so we have an abundant repository of contact and precontact material for comparative purposes (Tippett 1968). In our early Christian literature we have a diachronic sequence of Christian data.

The communal character of Fijian life provided a cooperative orientation to work, which slanted the acceptance of Christianity towards a multi-individual *koinonia* rather than Western individualism, and any indigenous Fijian theology which emerged just had to be corporate in character. The pre-Christian group values are found in the Fijian work songs.

For an example of group activity with a responsive chant, one could do no better than suggest a Fijian work song. They were used for house building, canoe construction, and other out-of-door activities. The Nadroga house required a large central post (*bou*), and after being cut and trimmed the hauling was a noisy but cooperative business. The ritual song was highly metaphoric and responsive.

> Leader: *e ----, tibi ni koli*   e ----, the dog's stern
> All: *ii ----*   ee ----
> (All hands are placed on the rope to pull or trunk to push.)
>
> Leader: *e ----, tdbotobo kadi*   e ----   catch hold of the ant
> All: *ii ----, aa ---- e ---- ee ----*   ah ---- e ----
> (Push and pull with each cry.)
>
>   *Tabotabo kadi*   Catch hold of the ant
>   *Ni vanua tani*   Of the foreign land

So they haul, push, and chant until the task is finished. This is a pre-Christian hauling song in dialect. It did not die out with the coming of Christianity. Houses still had to be built and were built of the same materials and with the same architecture. There were many regional variants. Sometimes the log was a shark (Rougier 1915). Some songs were competitive, alternating cries from those fore and aft [see Quain 1948]. I have encountered the same kind of alternating competition from rowers in a storm at sea. It was a Christian missionary itineration, and the pre-Christian pattern of expending energy to beat in unison had survived for a century.

There can be no possible room for doubt that the form of early Fijian Christianity was highly acceptable to the first Fijian converts, which may account for the hostility of pagan opposition to it. The liturgy and rituals for morning and evening worship, the formal statements—Ten Commandments, the Psalms, the Creed, the Prayers, the Catechisms—were all memorised and used for corporate worship in antiphonal response as the people had used their pagan chants at their festive occasions in the cycle of the seasons, at temple building and restoration, before and after war, in military reviews, welcomes and farewells, seasons of planting, house building, canoe launching, marriage, and so on, ad infinitum. All these social functions had their formalised religious rituals and liturgy which tied the society together and gave it cohesion in peace and war, in work, in enculturation, in entertainment. The entire daily life was ritually structured, with approved persons to administer each operation, and the people were participant. Thus from the chanted catechism before the worship service to the benediction, the congregation was involved and enthusiastic.

Thus, for example, there was the congregational chanting of the *Te Deum*, which became a feature of worship services when any heathen fell under spiritual conviction and "bowed his knee to the Lord"—which was itself a ritual act. The whole congregation spontaneously burst into the *Te Deum*.

There is a report of Joeli Bulu (1845) from a remote area, new for evangelism where no white missionary had yet been. Joeli wrote of Muanaicake:

> We had a regular service here, consisting of singing, prayer, chanting, chanting
> the Confession and Lord's Prayer, a lesson—and chanting the *Te Deum*.[168]

He goes on to describe thirty-seven converts whom he baptised. They had memorised the Creed and chanted it together. One can find dozens of records like this in the mission sources. But let me cite one from an English sea captain who attended a Fijian service at Bua in 1853:

> Some parts of the service, such as the *Te Deum* were chanted in the regular Fijian
> manner, a most judicious arrangement, not only as assimilating the worship
> to their old customs, but as attracting many heathen listeners, who, standing
> outside the door, seemed with respect and attention to enjoy the music going on
> within. (Erskine 1853, 223–24)

I particularly mention the *Te Deum* as something which could be easily clothed in a Fijian form and style. In Fiji it has survived. In my own time when I had a successful drama

---

168   See also John Hunt, *Wesleyan Methodist Magazine*, 1846, 936.0

group which travelled about Fiji with biblical plays, I sometimes had them use the *Te Deum* for the "grand finale," bringing the whole company on the stage and reciting it in unison with uniform gestures. The effect was terrific—the audience was completely empathetic. For these moments my team of activist young people and the conservative grey heads of the audience were completely one in quite intense Fijian worship.

From what I have written it should be plain that oral tradition, on which I intend to focus from this point onwards, is not a cultural element in isolation nor has it a scope for generalisation. There is always a precise context in which the particular form of oral communication is appropriate. One cannot simply analyse a chant, a dirge, or a legal saying as an artifact. It is an artifact within a context (i.e., a human situation involving personal interplay). The occasion is as much part of the act of communication as the structure of the oral form. Therefore, to avoid the danger of a paper which breaks itself down into a catalogue of forms of oral tradition, I have included brief sections on ceremonial context, formal procedure, and mediatorial function, which are all part of the picture.

The question may also arise when we speak of the indigenisation of the Christian religion with an Oceanic people of how effectively we may expect the Christian sacraments to be indigenised. This I may answer from my own experience a century after the transforming event. The current hymnbook used by the congregation contains an abbreviated form of the Ten Commandments for congregational use, responsively or in unison, together with a concluding prayer. There are also Fijian translations of the General Confession, the Apostle's Creed, an alternative creedal statement, and the *Te Deum* arranged for liturgical use. The Baptismal Service in its entirety is in the hymnbook to facilitate congregational participation, including the "address" to the congregation and the congregational response. Two alternative forms of the Holy Communion are included with a list of appropriate Scripture passages, together with optional prayers and the various devotional units of the ritual structure of the Holy Communion, with congregational responses specified. Similar orders of worship are included also for reception of full members (confirmation), Christian marriage, ordination, and burial. These are quite familiar to the congregation, which is always quite participant. They cover some fifty pages of vernacular text.

Another sixty pages are devoted to the Catechism, which is basic theology for the congregation—the theology of God, Christ, the Holy Spirit, man, salvation, the kingdom of God, the church and sacraments, the Christian life, the inspiration of Scripture, and the life to come. These are in question and answer form suitable for chanting, the questions being asked by the class leader appointed for the day, and the congregation responding in a chant after the old pre-Christian style. The responses are all Scripture passages. They are used for the spiritual preparation of the congregation immediately prior to the entry of the preacher and on other occasions, like a postservice class meeting when the leader may expound those passages. When I first went to Fiji I bought a copy of the vernacular *A*

Vakatusa ni Lotu,[169] a volume of some 280 pages of fine print, tying the Scripture into the congregational confession of faith. Thus were the pastors and class leaders equipped to expand the basic theological confession in application.

This whole configuration was possible—sacraments and other ritual performances of the church—because the forms were indigenous in rhythm and congregational participation, and thus was a non-Oceanic religion with all its basic ritual symbolism indigenised. In other words, Christianity was contextualised.

The Eschatology of the 1840s, 1850s, and 1860s, and Fijian Ethnotheology

Henderson's evaluation of Fijian eschatology (1931) was controlled by his own personal religious attitude, monoculturalism, and his historical misconceptions, because of an unsatisfactory anthropological perception of the Fijian worldview. I fail to see how a historian can write ethnotheology without a refined knowledge of the religious language and its semantic change over the first century after the conversion movements. This requires the use of translations of the Bible, the hymnbook revisions, catechisms and liturgies, and sermon outlines of native preachers. There is an abundance of this kind of vernacular documentation, and the researcher will soon find himself preparing his own vocabulary at various time depths.

Despite Henderson's training in history, he wrote in the theological frame of reference of his own day. His judgments were Western in character, and he missed the vital positive components of Fijian early theology, which he would not have done had he mastered the theological terminology, hymnology, liturgy, and indigenous preaching. Thus, for instance, he missed the ethnotheological holism of early Fijian faith and worship. And again he was so personally convinced against late Victorian hell-fire eschatology that he projected it back as the major theme into a period of history which was far more significant for its heaven preaching. He failed to see how this heaven preaching "dovetailed" into the theology of the sovereignty of God in a period of intense persecution during the 1840s, 1850s, and 1860s. I shall illustrate this in a moment, but meantime let me point out that the ethnopsychology of this is not at all dissimilar to that of the apocalyptic of Daniel and the Revelation in biblical times and the triumphalism of the Christian martyrs during the Roman imperial persecutions. It is quite wrong to interpret the positive religious dynamics of those decades in Fiji in terms of the negative hell-fire evangelism of the late Victorian Age in the Western world. If one is to seek a modern frame of reference more near to this kind of historical reconstruction for comparative purposes, one might suggest

---

169 Twenty-nine of the studies in this work were prepared by John Hunt before he died (1848), and the work was enlarged by William Moore. An edition edited by James Calvert was published in London in 1868, and another in 1884. The last reprinting of this particular edition was in the late 1930s. Thus we may say that this work was used as a basic tool by Fijian pastors and preachers for over a century.

the eschatology of "walking the heavenly streets in dem golden slippers," which came out of slavery in the New World. And where, I might ask, does one go for the ethnotheological documentation of this? Surely to the eschatologically charged hymns of slavery.

To the anthropologist, one is to some extent in the same dynamics of messianism and millenarianism when he analyses the people-movement conversions and the emergence of indigenous churches. It is a world of power encounter, and it cannot be understood or reconstructed historically without the recognition of this fact. The historian has to enter the worldview of *mana* if he is, as Hanson put it, "to get into the act." And no historian to my knowledge has yet written a history of Fiji between 1835 and Cession from that essential orientation. I do not know a truly emic history of the emergence of the indigenous church in Fiji. Etic reports with no knowledge of emic systems can be extremely confusing. This is why the methodology of ethnohistory (or ethnohistoriography) is so important. Emic study works within a language and culture as a whole ordered system, and only thus can the anthropologist, historian, or missionary understand the reactions, decision making, motivation, and values of the native actors in the drama (Harris 1970, 571). A historical reconstruction of conversion movements and *koinonia* formation has to be meaningful within its own worldview, not ours. The capacity for this orientation is important to the historian reconstructing the record, to the anthropologist researching the dynamics of culture change, and to the missionary involved in the dynamic process itself. These three streams have their confluence in what is known as missiology, and this has considerable significance for postcolonial mission.

I have made the point that an emic database for this kind of research may be found in the pre-Christian cultural mechanisms of oral tradition, which demonstrated their capacity for continuity through, and in spite of, the religious changes that came with conversion to Christianity, and will return to this from various angles through this presentation.

The pre-Christian Fijian had numerous ritual performances which were responsive exchanges between individuals and groups and the chorus. Epigrammatic couplets for group response were abundant, both for ceremonial and entertainment. Many of the dance chants made use of antiphonal dialogue. I have included a number of examples from pre-Christian times, enough to demonstrate their indigeneity and to suggest their antiquity.

As to the "continuity of the forms," Lorimer Fison (1868), travelling in the interior of Viti Levu not far from the region where Thomas Baker had been murdered twelve months before, was on the edge of the area of Christian witness and was present at the opening of a little chapel in the danger zone. The new Christians had composed a ceremonial liturgy which retained the form which might have been used for the dedication of a pagan temple. Fison translated the chant:

> 2 Voices: Jesus the path of faith!　[Affirmation]
>
> 　　　　　Where is the path?　　　[Question]

Chorus:	A silver path, an emerald path	[Expectation]
	A path of pearls	
	All within the city is fine gold—	
	Where is the path?	[Question repeated]
2 Voices:	John tells us about it:	[Expectation]
	Wonderful is the city!	
Chorus:	Its streets are pure crystal:	
	Wonderful is the fine gold:	
	Where is the path?	[Question repeated]
2 Voices:	The New Jerusalem above—	[Expectation]
	Where is the path?	[Question repeated]
Chorus:	Jesus is the path of faith!	[Affirmation][170]

This is an interesting chant. Its substance is slight, and its indigenous symmetry is lost in the translation, but it demonstrates several points. It uses the Fijian catechetical method of question and dialogue. The key question is, "Where is the path?" The city, its mineral wealth, precious stones, and its glory are not meaningful. They are wonderful things reported but not found in Fiji. They are triumphal honorifics which heighten the impression of other worldliness, of the heavenly expectation. There is a manifest influence of the New Testament Apocalypse. There is persecution and danger for any Christian confession in this part of Fiji at this date (1868). The answer is clear and direct as in the Apocalypse. Christ is Himself the way to heaven, whose glory exceeds anything on earth.

About the same time, Frederick Langham was at Viwa where Christian converts had gathered in strength and the church was better established, but the area of Viwan influence stretched away to the region where the Christian fringe faded into heathenism. The Ba area was 50/50 Christian/pagan at the time. Here Langham picked up a similar indigenous chant, which had the formal structure of a temple dedication chant and which he translated thus:

A house for the Lord we have built
Now let us make haste to prepare,
The new robe of righteousness seek
The new robe that each must wear,
To be by our Saviour approved
And by Him received into Heaven,
There ever to dwell with our God,
And the New Jerusalem fill.[171]

---

170 Fison account from Rewa, 20 November 1868.
171 Langham/Missionary Committee, 11 July 1868.

This chant, which the translator has attempted to scan, like the former one, is eschatological. Heaven is a glorious place of abode. The robe of righteousness is concomitant with that glory, like the "golden streets" of the heaven of the American slaves.

The greatest indigenous autobiography of Oceanic mission history reveals the highly significant place of Joeli Bulu's vision of the "beautiful land," his heavenly goal. His spiritual quest on earth, the thing he feared most to lose, his strength in face of danger, his ultimate hope at the end of the road was in terms of heaven. As long as there was physical danger and persecution, the Fijian Christian had a heaven-centred eschatology. The journey of Christian [*Pilgrim's Progress*] to the Celestial City most appropriately appeared in print in the same year (Moore 1867) as the murder of Thomas Baker and his party in the mountains. Not until the persecution was virtually over, the colony was established, and acculturation that followed Cession—together with the death of forty thousand Fijians in the measles epidemic had brought a temporary state of anomie—was it possible for another breed of late Victorian missionaries to shift the emphasis from the positive heaven orientation to the threat of hell fire.

This is a good example of the importance of establishing levels of time depth in reconstructing a cultural continuum of ethnotheology. To work back from the present by the ethnohistorical research method of upstreaming shows a very sharp line of demarcation between these two eschatologies very soon after Cession, and any historian or anthropologist interpreting the history of Fijian theological development had better be sure which side of that line his data falls.

The Data

The Oral Artifacts

The oral tradition of pre-Christian Fiji was transmitted or shared by means of a number of oral artifacts, among them epic chants, stories and tales, riddles, fables, proverbs, legal sayings, dirges, and responsive rituals. The contexts in which they were used were institutionalised, and the liturgy or ritual was followed with precision. Frequently a specific practitioner was set aside to attend to this, that no evil *mana* might befall them through erroneous performance.

I shall arrange these in five classifications so as to follow the passage from the precontact pagan performance to the Christian counterpart, keeping in mind the question I have been investigating—can the pagan form be Christianised? Or to put it the other way—can a Christian message be communicated or shared by means of a Fijian form that comes down from precontact times? What new innovations are made? Where do the Christian hymn, the *polotu*, and catechism come into the picture? How much oral tradition persists as the people become literate?

EPIC CHANTS AND CHRISTIAN HYMNS

In the precontact period Fijian poetry covered a wide range of themes and styles. They came from a social organisation of intertribal war, by land and sea; of cannibal feasting; giant canoe building; the construction of great temples from forest materials; of fishing, hunting, and agriculture; of trade exchanges; of the cycle of the seasons; of storms at sea. Not only did their songs come from these social systems, but they reinforced them. Their gods, like the people, were aggressive, suspicious, jealous, and warlike. There were gods of the sea and the forest, of fishing and war. They were gods who ate human flesh. These were the heroes of their songs and chants. Their epic chants included tribal origin myths, exploits of heroes—heroes in war, in magic, and in sex. Their chants reflected and idealized these supposed "virtues."

Missionaries the wide world over have never been in complete agreement on what should be done with these cultural artifacts when the people became Christian. Some have said they are demonic and have to go. Others have said the demonic value has to go but the physical form can be sanctified, and indeed must not be discarded but transformed if the church which is to emerge is to be indigenous. Mostly the missionaries to Fiji belonged to the latter type. They believed in what, in missiology today, we call "the contextualisation of the gospel."

Thus in the oral epic style reserved for tales of war, patricide, and murder,

> I stand ready: I creep softly:
> I hold my breath: I pause:
> I raise my club to the head of the chief:
> I strike once: I strike again:
> The chief we have hitherto served falls!

They committed themselves to communicate the gospel. Could it be done? Need I describe the bloody launching of a war canoe on human rollers that the canoe be bathed in sacrificial blood and the launching song that went with the wild screams of the cannibal way of life, while the death drumbeats its gruesome accompaniment.

Is it possible for that same canoe to transport preachers of the gospel, for the chant to communicate a passage of Scripture, and the drumbeat of war to call believers to a Christian worship service? Could the material artifacts of the old way of life be sanctified for a new way? Or did everything associated with the old way have to be destroyed because the things themselves were evil.

This is not a missionary talk. I am an anthropologist or an ethnohistorian investigating a case of religious change, and I am asking what it meant in Fiji for the gospel to be *contextualised*.

Here and there the pre-Christian hero epics have been secularised and preserved as entertainment. There has probably been nothing new added to that repertoire. However, there are new songs and dances for secular entertainment, some borrowed from other parts of the Pacific, others new compositions. And, of course, there has been a continuing stream of religious material, although this requires some skill in dating.

In some cases the rudimentary character of the theology of the chants indicates a very early date. One I have from the Heighway collection. Heighway was in Fiji in 1887, but speaks of this chant as from "olden times." I would translate the Fijian text thus:

> Heaven is our land
> Our land prepared for us,
> Chief Jesus has taken up the challenge [of Satan]
> You remain here [on earth] my friends
> I dance for joy to Heaven
> The world is overcome
> And is now a subject state to Heaven
> Satan is truly in difficulties.

Here again is the heaven theology of the persecution period, but the Fijian terminology has the pre-Christian war atmosphere about it. It is based on John 14:1–3, and it is a remarkable piece of exegesis. It has power encounter orientation. Chief Jesus (*Hatu* Jesus) is involved in the challenge (*ai bolebole* or the boast of a military review) against Satan. "Dance for joy" is a secondary meaning of Christian times for a pagan term, *cibicibi*, which meant originally to joyfully bring in the body for the cannibal oven—a good example of semantic change under Christian impact. The world is overcome and becomes a "subject state" to heaven. Thus Chief Jesus of heaven deprives Satan of his kingdom and assumes overlordship of his domain. The dance for joy follows this reduction of the kingdom of Satan. This type of Christian usage of these terms dates back to the 1835–55 period and is not found later than that date. It belongs to the first converts who were ex-warriors of pagan war.

It belongs to the same rudimentary Christology as the early Christian of Namara (a village of ferocious warriors famous for clubbing their enemy so violently that they were completely decapitated) who prayed at Viwa, "O Lord, deal effectively with Satan. Club him Namara-fashion" (*Me saku Vakanamara*). He was speaking the language of his own world of power encounter between "us and the enemy"—Christ/Satan. It was a generation before such terms disappeared from use.

To set these references over against the more refined educational chants should inform us how important it is to discover the levels of time depth in vernacular data, which is why historiography, if it is to deal with cross-cultural data, has to be ethnohistoriographical.

On the other hand, the first educational songs in Fiji were prepared by John Watsford and John Malvern for use by children, and many were work songs, like "the song for beating bark cloth." Others were action songs translating English models like "This is the way we wash our hands," etc. I have a collection of these that were used in Lau and date back to the 1840s.

One Christian innovation has been the school, and the techniques of poetry and dance have been slowly transferred from the mythological to the educational. I have a small selection of educational chants used as dance accompaniments for older children. One is a story of the steam engine, which appeared in Fiji after the establishment of the Colonial Sugar Refinery, and suggested a moral analogy to the poet. Its contents require a date of 1880s or 1890s. Another is a piece of moral teaching against stealing. Still another is about the physiology of the human body. These educational chants all date about the turn of the century but still employ the tricks for rhythm and metre and contain some dialect words.

Thomas Williams provides us with a literal translation of a long Fijian Christian poem used in his time in Fiji (i.e., before the mid 1850s), in which the Fijian poet describes the detail of the burial of Jesus in the tomb, the resurrection after three days, the role of the angels, and the humiliation of the Roman guards. This Fijian paraphrase of the biblical record was in epic style with a brief chorus for congregational participation at the end of each line of the epic. This poem is modeled on the indigenous hero song of pre-Christian times.

These pre-Christian songs all had this feature. Hazlewood calls it *na kenai kau*, and that is the term I have met and used myself. Williams in the 1850s and Fison a decade later speak of a *dulena*, which Hazlewood does not appear to have known, and is not in any Fijian dictionary. If the two are different, it would be that the latter was often longer, and probably either subtle and suggestive or openly vulgar. But both served the same function (viz., separating the units or episodes of a long epic) and were performed as a chorus like the "Daughters of Jerusalem" couplets in the Song of Solomon. The converts to Christianity rejected the vulgarity of the *dulena*, and many of the actual pre-Christian epics dropped out of use, for which disappearance the missionaries have been criticised. Yet they did not reject the cultural form, and Williams gives his Christian epic of the drama of the burial and resurrection of Christ with its repeating chorus as an example of the superior Christian counterpart of a continuing cultural form—in anthropology we would say the Christian "functional substitute."

Williams makes no attempt to translate the chorus which is metaphoric and does not relate to the epic itself, unless it means the Christian is building up his fortification in the truth of the death and resurrection of the Lord. One would have rather expected something like "Hallelujah! Amen!" or "Praise the Lord!" But the epic and its performance is both truly Christian and truly Fijian.

Fijian poetry as an art captured for Christianity was widely utilised in the Christian schools from the beginning as we have seen. The work songs made it relevant to their "doing" program in class. They were also utilised to widen the concept of the whole Fijian church, which was bigger than the tribes which represented the old-time war divisions of

Fiji. The translation of the New Testament created a Fijian *lingua franca* and standardised it. Poetry extended the concept of mission over all Fiji and into the islands over the horizon. For example, the Fijian church had sent a team of missionaries to the Solomon Islands. They had settled in New Georgia at Roviana, and the first reports had come home. The appeal for workers, the response to the call, and the journey to New Georgia are all described in a dance chant written by Joveni Vatunitu and performed by the schoolchildren of Nadroga. From this song we learn the name of the ship, the white missionaries involved in the course of the journey, and the name of the location in the Solomons where they landed. It is a valuable informational primary source and utilises the poetic license even in making the missionary name Runi (Rooney) into Runia. [See Tippett Collection, St. Mark's National Theological Centre, Fijian Files, "Solomon Island Letters 1902–1905" File.]

The really new innovation, of course, was the Christian hymn which utilised the traditional forms of Fijian poetry. The first collection of hymns was composed in Somosomoan by Hunt and Lyth and followed the form of native lyrics. For the first forty years Fijian hymns, mostly missionary compositions, followed this form. Only the missionaries of the later Victorian Age wanted to standardise the music and translation form of the well-known hymns. Missionary skill at dynamic equivalent hymn writing was varied. One of the more successful of them was W. A. Heighway, who translated eighty-seven hymns into Fijian and collected over thirty Fijian *meke* chants of the earlier Christian period which were compositions for school use mostly based on scriptural themes. One in the collection is a dirge mourning the missionary Waterhouse. Another (the only signed one) is a chant about Alepate Vola's great school discovery—mathematics. Most of these chants I have seen preserved nowhere else but in the Heighway collection.

Probably the capture of Fijian poetry and chants for Christ was largely the work of Hunt who demonstrated that a Christian idea could be put into a poetic dynamic equivalent. Hazlewood, who had a remarkable grasp of the language, always had trouble, for example, putting an English iambic hymn into the trochaic Fijian rhythm. (There is a trick whereby it can be done even so.) But Hunt did not try to retain the English rhythm; he put them into Fijian lyrical form. There is a whole area here which calls for the research of an ethnomusicologist. One remembers how E. G. Parrinder (1946), "influenced by the clash of rising inflections and descending notes" in his African experience, raised the question of whether African hymns were tonal like the language and advocated the use of native lyrics and instruments in Christian public worship.

Hunt also saw that musical communication techniques in Fiji were not confined to songs, but that the regular epic chant offered unlimited potential for evangelism and Christian education. His own Scripture translation was wonderfully rhythmic, and many of the descriptive or epic passages were superbly suitable for chanting. When he found Fijian converts disposed to chant Scripture in the form of cultural expression they knew, he opened the door and allowed them freedom to express themselves in their own way. In so doing he achieved two things—first, he popularized the Scriptures as a repository of material for chanting, and second, he demonstrated that a pagan cultural institution could be sanctified for the service of Christ. Thus the Christian movement began with such momentum that its direction was established for two generations.

More than this, Hunt not only opened the door for the use of cultural forms, but he sought out among his converts persons with the leadership qualities to use them. He translated simple scripture catechisms and liturgies, knowing that they would be chanted Fijian style corporately by the congregation as the catechism is to this day.

POLOTU: INDIGENISED CHRISTIAN CHANTS

Words beginning with *p* are not truly Bauan but have been introduced by culture contact. *Polotu* came from Tonga. However, the cultural borrowing was spontaneous and appropriate because the themes of the *polotu* were Christian, and Christianity came to Fiji from Tonga at the same time as the *Lotu* itself (which name for Christianity was itself a Polynesian word). However, the *polotu* was quite Fijian in form and rhythm and utilised Fijian poetic devices for achieving rhythm; for example, appending a meaningless *ya* at the end of the line—*ko vuravura ya* in the *polotu* of the storm on Galilee.

The *polotu* of the selling of Joseph into bondage is a typical Fijian dirge in its subject matter, its atmosphere and structure: a narrative verse with a lament chorus. It contains poetic rhythmic constructions not used in normal speech, a terminal *-a*, so that *yani* and *wai* become *yania* and *waia* [cf. *ya*] and an infixed *-ta-* in *vuvutakina* and *viritakina*. Here we have something more than mere translation. We are dealing with thought rhythm foreign to English—a significant configuration of cultural poetic pattern. Likewise in the *polotu* of Rahab we meet the word *yamatari*. The terminal *-ri* is purely poetical for the sake of rhythm and metre, not of rhyme.

These were devices of Fijian poetic tradition, and I have no doubt that many of the early Christian *polotu* used in Fiji were actually composed by converted Fijians. This was especially so in Lau where the conversion movements first began. Even so the *polotu* was so Fijian in character and poetic structure, lending itself to either Polynesian singing or Melanesian chanting, that it is only the word *polotu* itself and the fact that they are normally sung rather than chanted, which betray the origin.

Naturally enough, the *polotu* was an essential institution in the Polynesian areas of Fiji. However, although known and used in the Melanesian areas, it did not manifest the same vitality there. The Melanesian preferred to take the lyrical passages of Scripture itself for chanting—the descriptions of "The New Jerusalem," "The Creation," "The Ten Commandments," "The Beatitudes," and "The Psalms," for example, to which I shall return in a moment.

Meantime the *polotu* was an educational tool, a poetic restatement of scriptural information, for the transmission of the historical tradition of the faith rather than an act of worship like the Fijian use of the Psalms, for instance.

I have the text of a number of *polotu* chants. They deal with "The Creation," "Joseph Sold into Egypt," "Famine in Canaan," "Jesus as the Way," "The Death of Christ on Calvary," and "The Conversion of Paul." Many others I have heard were widely used, and still are, by Lauan people.

Another list could be prepared of *mekes* out of the Melanesian rather than Polynesian stream, among them "The Dream of Pharoah" and "Bethsaida the Pool," both of which use tricks of poetic license to secure rhythm and metre.

As an example of a *polotu* let me cite the Creation *Polotu* together with a rather free translation required because of the poetic license of the chant's construction.

Kalou bula mai liu sara	God alive from the beginning
Sa ia tiko Nona cakacaka	Performs His work
Vakarautaki vuravura lala	The empty world is prepared
E butobuto tu na wasawasa	And the seas are in darkness
Yavalaga e na dela ni wasa	He moves over the surface of the waters
Rai na Kalou ka sa vinaka	And God sees that it is good
Ka sa yakavi ka sa bogibogi	And the evening and the morning
Matakatai ni siga koya	Are the [first] day

This brief eight-line paraphrase is not concerned with all the detail of the Scripture account but with the simple fact of God as Creator. The *polotu* now changes rhythm and function:

Eda bula ga emuri	We who come later
Koi keda na tamata	We the people
Qai soli mai na bula	Are given our life
Tawa mate rawa.	And eternal [souls],
Vei rau noda qase	To our ancestors
Ko Ivi kei Atama	Eve and Adam
Were mai Iteni ka sa yalataka	The garden of Eden is promised
Sa tei tu kina na kedrau kakana:	Food is planted for them to eat:
Dua bau ga na kau e ca	The only evil tree
A yacana ga na tabu tara	Was named "Touch Not."

This second unit provides a simple biblical anthropology. Man is provided for; his environment, the earth, is productive; he has an eternal condition and is under the requirement of obedience to God. With this basic oral tradition he can subsequently, in literate times, read the Scriptures. Meantime he has a rudimentary theology of God and man.

Most of the *polotu* chants I have heard have a chorus in which the rhythm changes. The theme also of the *polotu* may change, as the *kenai kau* of a Fijian *meke*. Thus, for example, in the *polotu*, the theme of which is a historical description of the event of the death of our Lord on Calvary, the chorus is an affirmation of heaven and not specifically related to the main poem, *lewena*, by the poet. The chorus runs:

E Isa le! ko Lomalagi	Ah! Heaven
E na vunautaki	It will be proclaimed
Tukuni mai ni koro lagilagi	And told that it is a glorious habitation.[172]

Once again the heaven preaching of many of the *polotu* chants lines up with that of the more truly Fijian chants, and certainly the eschatological emphasis in the vernacular primary sources demands consideration in the rewriting of Fijian church history from an emic perspective—which task I hope will someday be undertaken by a Fijian rather than a Western scholar.

The *polotu* differs also from the chants of Melanesian Fiji in its musical accompaniment. In these days of intra-Fijian pluralism, in a church which still reveals tribal diversity within its Christian unity, at an annual *vakomisonari* celebration in a city, industrial, or institutional location, this diversity does not imperil the essential unity. The singing and chanting, their rhythm and instrumental accompaniments are manifestly either Polynesian or Melanesian. Furthermore, the Polynesian components will approach slowly from a distance, the music getting louder and louder as they draw near the assembly, with a non-Melanesian tinkling of metal and an unbroken continuity of performance like "It's a Small Small World" at Disneyland.

The Fijian church had no difficulty incorporating the Polynesian elements, probably because of the role Tonga was playing in Fiji at the time. Tongans visited Fiji regularly for trade and social functions. Many Fijian chiefs had Tongan wives. Tongan arts and crafts were practised in Fiji; settlements of Tongan canoe builders and craftsmen were attached to the chiefly localities in Bau, Rewa, Lakeba, Somosomo, and Bua. Tongan craft techniques and their accompanying mythology and folklore of the immediately pre-Christian period demonstrate the rise of Fijian/Tongan craft competition. Christianity came to Fiji in a day of considerable culture change, the agents of change being not Westerners but Tongans. Many Tongan values had been accepted in Fiji. Tonga had prestige and status there before the gospel came.

When Tonga became Christian in a great people movement in the early 1830s, it had a profound effect on Fiji. When Fiji first heard the gospel many Tongan church words were already known. The fact that a language could have a written form was not unheard of

---

172   "*Koro*," of course, is "village." The idea of a "heavenly city" is Western urbanism. Two hundred was a large village in Fiji. At the height of its power Bau had no more than three thousand persons.

(though the reality of it was astonishing), and the practice of Christian worship was already identified in a religious category and vocabulary.

The Fijians were very discriminating in religious expression and behaviour. They borrowed from both Tonga and the West, but they adapted everything to their own lifestyle. Thus in the windward islands the *polotu* became quite indigenised and is now regarded as Lauan (i.e., Fijian). In mainland Viti Levu the functional equivalents are more essentially pre-Christian Melanesian, but in central places of multitribal assembly and at united conferences the diversity within national unity is recognised and appreciated.

It was the reduction of the Fijian language to written form (a Western achievement, Hunt and Hazlewood both having been particularly gifted in this respect and both empathetic) in which the unification of Fiji and its church was achieved. Hunt, in particular, appreciated the contact points between Fijian cultural mechanisms of communication and the church's liturgy. Hunt gave them not only the Fijian New Testament but the interpretive aids, the hymns and liturgies which opened the door for the contextualisation of the gospel within Fijian forms. Hunt's (and Lyth's) hymns were not set to English rhyme and form but to Fijian lyrics and rhythm, and were spontaneously accepted as indigenous. The worship of the young church developed within its own musical and communicative structures.

It wasn't until 1877 that a later breed of missionaries wanted to standardise the Fijian hymns formally with their English counterparts, that they were reduced to rhyme and metre to be used with an English organ. It was the older generation who had come out of paganism and had learned to sing the gospel "Fijian style" in rhythm and harmony that would not fit the octave of the organ who reacted against the new hymnbook, and did so on the score that the hymns of Hunt and Lyth were utterly their own in style and feeling— and they were quite right.

Possibly as a concession to the elders the advocates of hymn standardisation into rhymed long, short, and common metre form agreed to include a number of *polotu* chants in the 1877 hymnbook. That hymnbook survived only until 1913, by which time a whole army of hymn writers had emerged, most notable in my opinion W. A. Heighway, who found in the Sankey collection a rhythm more approximating the Fijian.

The *polotu* were mostly composed by Fijians themselves. Even the new hymnbook of 1936—a century after the commencement of the mission, when the emphasis on hymnology (as distinct from chanting) was for the use of Western tunes—did not prevent a number of indigenous composers from producing hymns which passed the missionary test. The importance of these was their indigenous theological content as they came from the heart and were not translations of English models. The best known of these Fijian hymn writers was Inoke Buadromo, but hymns by I. Raseisei, Etonia Radrodro, J. Raitilava, E. P. Tatawaqa, Loata Ratu, and T. T. Waqairawai were all included in the 1936 selection.

The hymn and the *polutu* were both thus new innovations, but the verbal and rhythmic forms were indigenised, and the literary tricks of composition in Fijian dance chants were utilised and the Fijian church had a new artifact of terrific educational value within its own natural lifestyle.

PROVERBS, STORYTELLING, AND RIDDLING

Fijian speech is filled with proverbial sayings. There are 160 of them in Raiwalui's list (1954), and he admits that there are enough for another similar book. Another list was prepared by Bulicokocoko. This collection comprises about five hundred proverbial sayings collected by an organising teacher from a wide contemporary Fijian audience about the time of World War II. Many of these are phrases about the behaviour of land animals, birds, and sea creatures for comparison with that of human beings. Some are founded on customs, stories, or events. They embody an implied ethic and value system of certain aspects of daily life, such as feasting, house building, canoe building, not forgetting the life of the church and school. Each has its own set of proverbial ways of saying things, asking questions, and in all these aspects of life many things have metaphoric names. Thus, for example, the chairman of the church district was "the Old Man" (*Na Qase Levu*), although in some cases he was relatively young, achieving the "quality of age" from the "dignity of his status," not from his physical years. In my time one was so elected because in reality he was *drokadroka*, "a strong pliable twig" (*drokadroka*, literally "green").

In 1960 I prepared a study of Fijian metaphoric phrases for the Fiji Society, arranging them on a basis of the social structure, and I segregated the old proverbs from the new. What I believe I demonstrated was (1) the continuity of use of the proverbial form for expressing social values even in our own day, (2) the continuing vitality of the art of proverb making (and riddling), (3) the continuing circumlocution of proverbial instead of direct speech as a courteous form of rebuke, (4) the appropriation of foreign proverbs which fitted the Fijian lifestyle—or modification if required. The Fijian church itself also has preserved the art of proverbial circumlocution and continually creates new sayings to press its points.

Let me give you just one pre-Christian example and then a couple from Christian times, not mentioned in the published lists, to show how the creation of proverbial phrases is a continuing art.

In pre-Christian times it might be said of so-and-so:

> Sa la 'ki Naicobacoba me tei tarawau
> [He has gone to Naicobacoba to plant *tarawau*]

This means that so-and-so is dead. In pre-Christian eschatology the immediately dead went to the waiting place where the spirit company, according to their myths, would plant *tarawau* trees, which grew in great abundance on this particular headland. As long as the

Fijians believed in the spirit land of waiting before going to *Bulu*, the afterlife, this proverbial circumlocution was a way of speaking less harshly of the death of a respected person. When the people became Christian this particular metaphorical circumlocution dropped out of use, but the art continued. So much for heathen times.

Now, in the Christian period, there came a time when the Fijian preachers/teachers arrived at the village where they were to preach and were treated to a cup of tea before the service (not a proper meal, which was delayed until after the service). This cup of tea was spoken of as *nai sere ni kava*, meaning literally "the untying of the tin." Because of the frequent rain every preacher/teacher sought for himself an empty kerosene tin which he so cut that it closed like a container. In this he carried his dry shirt (*sulu*), hymnbook, and Bible. Arriving at the village, no matter how heavy the rain, he clad himself for church in dry clothes and drank the refreshing tea—"the untying of the tin." Significantly enough with acculturation the kerosene tin gave place to the small briefcase, and by the time of World War II the proverbial term began to drop out of use, and with it the picturesque period of Fijian church history.

I need hardly point out that this poetic imagery was so widely used in Scripture itself that the Fijian had no trouble recognising it at as a "Holy Book." Furthermore, many of the Fijian metaphoric sayings have actually been culled from Scripture. The Bible, like the gospel itself, has been contextualised.

A Fijian has no trouble at all, for example, with the psalmist "taking the cup of salvation and calling on the Lord," or "taking the wings of the morning," and so on. For him every phase of the dawn and dusk had its metaphoric phrase.

The point I am making is again that the pre-Christian craft of metaphoric speech did not perish with the acceptance of Christianity. It remained vital and dynamic, and Christianity was clad in an indigenous garment not a foreign one. The proverb often reflects the social condition of its period of origin.

There is a complex of Fijian words deriving from the verb, *talanoa* (to tell stories). We have *ai talanoa*, the noun, and *veitalanoa*, the reciprocal form. The expert (*na kena dau*) of any craft is a standard grammatical structure: *dau vunau* (preacher), *dau ni vucu* (expert of the dance), *dau vosa* (orator), or just *na kena dau* (the expert of the craft under discussion).

The object of the storyteller's activity had numerous forms which go back to pre-Christian times. There were hero stories of cannibal wars; origin stories of the tribal ancestors, their journeying and the establishment of custom; stories of the activities of the gods; forest tales with animal characters to whom were attributed human qualities for purpose of establishing moral values—fables, if you like. In such cases characters were often ascribed names which led the listeners to anticipate their moral qualities—*Daulawaki* (craftiness), say, for example, or *Yaloqaqa* (courageous).

Now what happened when these people accepted the gospel? The old stories had articulated the values of a system based on widow strangling, live burial, and cannibalism, and of course Christianity rejected these. But although it rejected some (not all) of the morals, it did not reject the techniques. The missionaries were quick to realise the value of this form of communication. A. J. Small translated the *Fables of Aesop* around the turn of the century and stimulated a revived Fijian interest in Fijian fables, and some of the Fijian people, literate by this time, wrote down a number of them for publication in the church paper. W. A. Heighway did the same with a few parables. But the most successful missionary effort of all was William Moore's translation of Bunyan's *Pilgrim's Progress* (1867), which was used by Fijian preachers for sermon illustration down to my own days in Fiji. In most of my own published and radio sermons in the Fijian language I used at least one illustration from this source. I doubt if there is any book, outside the Bible, so influential as *Pilgrim's Progress* for communicating the Christian value system in Third World contexts.

The institution of storytelling (*veitalanoa*) opened the door for any missionary who acquired fluency in the language to fraternize with the Fijians of all social levels. None was better at this than Lorimer Fison who, from his early ministry in the 1860s and 1870s in Lau, drew the tales from Fijian and Tongan tradition from indigenous tellers whose names he records—Inoke Waqaqele, Ratu Taliai Tupou, Roko Sokotukivei, the Tui Oneata, and Ma'afu of Tonga. His relatives at home tried to get them published, but there was no English interest in them at the time. Thirty years later, the attitude to folklore changed in anthropology due to men like George Laurence Gomme.[173] Fison, now a fellow of the Royal Anthropological Institute himself, published a collection of these stories from Lau and named his informants of thirty years before. In the meantime, of course, Fison had written in the field of communication on the corporate level through the group institution of riddling and demonstrated the structure of the corporate pastime, or team game, and the rules of the game. The riddle (*vatavatairalago*, or *vakasiridrodrolagi* in Eastern Fiji) is like a rainbow (*drodrolagi*), beginning in the middle it descends in two different directions, so a riddle has two different meanings according to a Fijian interpretation in the 1880s. We could spend a long time on this highly institutionalised pastime in which each structural element of its performance had a metaphoric name. [See Fison 1882, 1–5; Tippett 1960, 91–93.]

Fison narrated a Fijian fable of the swamphen and the rat, and gave a Fijian application which equated the bird with Dives and the rat with Lazarus in the biblical parable and related their respective fates in terms of eternity. Fison argued that riddle making was still

---

173   See George Gomme, *Ethnology in Folklore*, wherein he sets forth principles for the analysis and classification of folklore. He pointed out that history would use philology, archaeology, and even craniology, but steer clear of folklore. "If folklore, then, does contain ethnological facts, it is time that they should be disclosed, and that the method of discovering them should be placed before scholars" (1892, vi).

an ongoing art in Fiji fifty years after the arrival of the gospel, and thus gospel values had been incorporated into the indigenous social and entertainment system.

In passing, this very validation of the Fijian morals of the swamphen and rat fable by equation with the Holy Bible was true Fijian procedure where oral law was validated, if possible, by attributing it to one of their deities and thereby giving it divine authority.

Fison wrote out nine Fijian dance chants from pre-Christian Fiji which were used for entertainment purposes at this time in different dialects. They came out of the legends and war period. The significance of their words, on which he wrote a commentary, is not my point, however. They survived because of the suitability of their rhythm and tune for the dance. As the war barriers went down under the influence of Christianity, the tunes were diffused by exchange for entertainment purposes. The words in one dialect were not always understood by the dancers of another tribe, but the dance itself and the rhythm were entertaining and survived.

Fison also wrote out the fable of the swamphen and rat in seven different dialects with a commentary for each, but his concern here was comparative linguistics. He did the work for Dr. A. S. Gatschet, linguist at the Smithsonian Institution at the time. Fison's correspondence to Gatschet is now at the Turnbull Library, Wellington; his inward correspondence from Gatschet together with the basic data as published by Gatschet in Germany (1885) is in my collection at St. Mark's (see Fison Papers).

Storytelling and, perhaps less frequently, riddling, are still major pastimes in Fiji. Storytelling opens the door to the willing stranger, but becomes immediately competitive and will go on all night until dawn unless either the stranger or local storyteller bows out. Stories alternate according to unwritten rules. All the visitor needs is a fund of anecdotes, a fluency in the language, and a cast-iron constitution. The company in the house will keep the *yaqona* bowl full and the coconut cup circulating. The game is played by the rules and is one way in which a missionary can integrate with general approval and win the designation of being "one of us."

PROVERBIAL LEGAL SAYINGS

I need to distinguish between a proverb and a proverbial legal saying.

A proverb, *vosa vakaibalebale* (word with a meaning), is a metaphoric term, a "signification" or term which suggests an "interpretation," an explanation of something observed; e.g., *A vuna a qaitete*, from the root then spread throughout the branches—or:

E dua nomu waqa levu	If you have a big canoe
E dua nomu vusi tevu	Your labour also will be great

The man who uses it ascribes the meaning of the explanation (i.e., an interpretation), hidden in a metaphor or simile.

A *bole* (legal saying) is a *validation*, not an interpretation. A person in a predicament puts it forward as his authority. (*Sa tauva nai bole* or *Sa taurivaka nai bole*; i.e., he takes up [or resorts to] a legal saying.) So too he will *tura nai bole* (find the legal saying valid). As a legal saying which one "resorts to," the phrase has divine authority, as a proverb does not—*Sa vakaibole na Kalou* (the gods have their legal sayings). These distinctions were made from the beginning of culture contact, but we find that under culture contact an old *bole* may acquire a new meaning, so the changing use of a *bole* should reflect developing historical cultural values.

I have a dozen or so such legal sayings from pre-Christian cultural complexes that were subsequently used for Christian purposes. Not only is there a transfer of use, but also of divine authority to the Christian God.

Originally Cakobau, for example, would cite a legal saying against the idea of being converted. Subsequently, after his conversion and baptism he would find a legal saying to validate the new religion. The mechanism and the technique of "resorting to a legal saying" remained basic in the system of Fijian logical reasoning.

A parabolic legal saying (*bole*) was frequently used to justify a viewpoint or course of action. The usage was still very active at the turn of the century in Wesleyan circles when their work was encroached upon by a new rival mission, whose advocates argued that they had more spiritual light than the Wesleyans. The Wesleyan rejoinder was to use an old *bole* in this new predicament. Let me give a few examples, all of which come from Wesleyan Fijian informants of the period.

(A) *E sega e dua na vulagi*   There is no stranger
    me hau dau na kena davuke madrai   who has his bread pit.

It means that a newcomer should not express his opinion of the affairs of the village; Fijian bread made of old, from yams, breadfruit, or cooking bananas by the young women of the locality, was buried to mature in earth bread pits. Strangers have no land rights and therefore no pits and no local resources. So with the Christian life. The preachers of the gospel are local people, and have established their church over many years. They have plenty of bread and spiritual resources. Now strangers challenge their spiritual correctness and authority. They should be put in their place with a legal rebuke—"There is no stranger who has his bread pit" (i.e., the right to interfere in local affairs).

(B) An interesting letter signed J. Ratabua (1905) cites the legal saying, *a ca ni taumada* (the trouble of getting in first), with the same intention. Ratabua discusses at length the village preparations for a feast day. The ovens are full and the baked food is taken up for the feast, and the villagers have eaten with the guests and are satisfied. Then some latecomers arrive and are served hospitably. These latecomers however want the hosts to eat with them. The hosts have to excuse themselves—"they have already eaten" and are satisfied. They need no more. Ratabua says the newcomers have just arrived. The church has been there for seventy years. They have eaten well and are satisfied. He recommends the newcomers take their message to one of the unevangelised fields in the Pacific, like the Solomons. Ratabua put it, "When you meet the pressure of latecomers you excuse yourselves with the *bole*. You are satisfied having already eaten."

(C) Two years earlier a Fijian, signing himself TWM, used a *bole* he had received from the makers of Fijian puddings resident at Naqarani, Rewa.

E tutu na wai ka vulavula (The water [is tested] and is white). He explains the picture. The gear has been prepared and the puddings made correctly, the coconut grated and the water added, the concoction has been judged excellent. Many have eaten and been pleased with the pudding. Some latecomers have arrived and begun to complain that the concoction is not milky enough—too watery. In this event the Naqarani pudding maker will rebuke them, "The water is tested and it is white"—the coconut mixture is approved. Like Pilate's definiteness, "What is written is written"; this is a legal saying to throw at critics who find fault with the existing religious system as insipid. The process of conversion and nurture has been attended to and approved. And TWM adds a reference to Matthew 7:15—"Beware of false prophets, etc."

(D) Etonia Radrodro (1901) supplied a *bole* from the interior.

> *Sa vakalutu aliva*[174] *li eke ko tarnaqu*   Did my father expel the snake from here
> *Se dua na norm qase?*   Or was it one of your ancestors?

Etonia depicts the laborious clearing of a strip of forest land, and planting trees and gardens which grow under his father's care. Some years later a stranger comes and brings his own tree to plant on Etonia's cleared land. Etonia throws the legal question at him. He has the sole right of occupancy because he has already cleared the land, planted, and expelled the dangerous creatures. By planting the Christian religion and expelling demonism the church has the legal right of occupancy. He argues against those who want to plant other teaching. They should not steal occupancy but go to other forests and clear them and eliminate the *aliva* for themselves. He also mentions the Solomons.

These examples of a *bole* show how it differs from a proverb. You throw it at an offender or adversary as a legal right by which you stand. They illustrate very well the Wesleyan resentment against their rivals in this period of history, and demonstrate how a cluster of legal sayings can have evidential value for ethnohistorical reconstruction. This is how the indigenous Fijians, not the missionaries, dealt with the problem by means of a pre-Christian legal mechanism.

---

174 *Aliva* today is "millipede." Originally it was a poisonous creature, probably the *bola*, a small venemous snake, *Ogmodon Vitiensis.*

(E) Let me mention one more. It came from a Fijian, Jopeni Vatunitu (July 1902), in the same period and predicament.

A qase bula duadua   The liveliest of old men

This is said of a boastful old man who exaggerates about his exploits of the early days to the young men, while it is well known that when other old men are present he will remain silent because they will deny what he claims. Jopeni likened that "lively old man" to false teachers who reinterpret the gospel, and try to draw the young people away from the church when there is no catechist or native minister present who can expose him. He then equated them with Satan, who deceived Eve, citing 2 Corinthians 11:3 to "*taura nai bole.*" Beware of these "lively old men" who, in reality, might be young persons manipulating the truth when there is no one present to expose them.

It is interesting to note that at this period the white missionaries tried to deal with this proselytizing by publishing tracts which denied the truth of the doctrine, but Fijian protagonists resorted to their own cultural technique by resorting to a "legal saying" which validated their position. This counted more with the rank and file of the Fijian congregation.[175]

Other *bole* I have which are not related to a predicament like this. Some come from Fijian animal tales or fables, and advocate a set of values, urging a child to take every advantage offered by school, church, Bible, and so on [see letters of Sefanaia Navuda, Josefa Qoro, Etonia Radrodro, Eliesa Tagicakibau]. They are still "validating sayings." Some of them in the first Christian generation came out of cannibalism, but under the usage of a later generation changed their orientation (e.g., a shift from cannibal food to garden food).[176] In other cases where the lifestyle did not change so dramatically (e.g., marriage pattern), the saying continued with only a new application. From Josua Mateinaniu II, a catechist missionary in Papua, we have this saying from his home, Vutia, on the great Rewa River:

Ena yati, mai na Colo.   The journey into the mountains is a very slow one.

The scene depicts a young man who has sought a girl in marriage and has been confronted with a task to prove his manhood. He has to pole the company upstream to the marriage ceremonies. The Rewa River is navigable thus for ninety miles, and the current

---

175 It is significant that few Fijians were drawn away by personal conviction to this rival mission. Where they succeeded in planting a rival church, it was done by affiliating with a factional group within the social structure.

176 From cannibal customs and theology we have *Caoa vakabokota droka* (Talking about the uncooked body). The dead man killed in battle was charged with *mana* and a fearful thing. Many were afraid to touch the body. When cooked the fear was gone, and the food was greatly desired, and the hunger satisfied. The implication is that the man who wants to eat should have the courage to handle and prepare it. The saying was transferred to any desirable thing which needed to be prepared for. Even "education" and "Bible study" were "uncooked bodies." Only after working at them did one enjoy the benefit of the feast. After a generation of Christianity the cannibal idea gave way to garden food.

is strong and the progress very slow. The *bole* justifies the expenditure of great effort and energy on a desirable project and calls the person carrying the burden to endure hardness that the goal may be achieved.

Josua Mateinaniu's usage is interesting. He is a missionary in Papua. The burden is heavy, but it is not to be avoided, even if the pole is heavy and the current against them is strong. The journey into the mountains is a slow one, but the goal is worthwhile.

Thus a *bole* is a specifically applied proverbial saying—a legal validation or justification or (as in this last case) a saying of encouragement. We can understand the intellectual frame of reference from the traditional lifestyle in which Fijian indigenous sermons were reasoned.

DIRGES

One significant form of Fijian oral tradition is the dirge (*lele*),[177] which accompanies the "dance" performed from a seated posture, similar to but quite distinct from the *vakamololo*, which I have described elsewhere. The normal *meke* is a *meke tausara*, a continuous performance. The distinguishing feature of a *lele* is the broken chant with meditation pauses. Sudden pauses are made here and there in the theme song and dance.[178] This is the mark of a dirge. My authority for this is dated 1850 (Hazlewood 1850). This was a regular feature of cannibal times. Most heroes were honoured at death with a dirge: sometimes an account of their military exploits, sometimes the narrative of their demise. They were normally honorific performances and reflected the sorrow of the bereaved. We have two pre-Christian (eighteenth century) dirges of major significance in the records: one a translation from the last century when the Fijian dirge was extant, and the other we have in the vernacular text. These mourn the dead in two pre-Christian epidemics.

I have a small collection of Fijian dirges of the Christian period, though others were composed, I know, and still others I have heard chanted. Among the more notable, which are preserved in my collection, are those mourning Paula Vea, faithful Tongan pastor who evangelised Kadavu and died there shortly afterwards (December 1865); John Hunt, translator of the Fijian New Testament, successful evangelist of Viwa, founder of the Viwa Plan and chairman (d. 1848)[179]; John Polglaise, first full-time missionary for Fijian theological training (d. 1860); Thomas Baker, first missionary to the interior, killed and eaten by cannibal mountaineers (d. 1867); William W. Lindsay, principal of Navuloa and chairman (d. 1900); Federick Langham, chairman for almost three decades, revised the Old Testament translation, died in London in 1903.

---

177   The verbal form, transitive, is *lelevaka*. It takes the person mourned as its object.

178   *Na meke e dua tani na kenai drokudroku*, a dance with a different kind of chant. *Sa droku mudumudu*, it is chanted with repeated interruptions.

179   In my biography of Hunt (1955, 174–75) I have translated the long dirge in which he was mourned. It is a typical dirge describing in detail all the events of his death and burial and naming all the people and places. These oral dirges are very good primary sources for both the historian and anthropologist.

Hunt's dirge was composed by Inoke Bakoso of Viwa. The others are anonymous. They are all typical, using poetic aids for the sake of rhythm as already described of the *polotu* chants. Some have dialect words.

The dirge has thus become a factual "document" in Fijian church history, providing information about the sickness and death of these people, friends, and colleagues who were associated with them at the time. They run all through the Christian history of the church in Fiji, and always the pre-Christian form has survived.

Let me mention briefly two of my own experiences. At the end of World War II, I witnessed the presentation of a dirge by the young people of a village in South Kadavu. They were mourning one of their comrades, the first Fijian casualty in the Solomons Campaign. It was in every way a true dirge, honorific in regarding this war death in terms of sacrifice, performed with all the mediation pauses as from the pre-Christian times. It was a very moving experience for both performers and audience.

The other experience took place at Lomanikoro, Rewa, at an annual meeting where this very large church was crowded to capacity. The preacher, an old Fijian, preached his last sermon before retirement on David's lament over Absalom. He had the women's chanting group prepare the scriptural lament as a dirge. At the end of his sermon he signed to them to chant and they did so. It was the high point of the service and sermon appeal and left me utterly convinced of the effectiveness of oral tradition techniques for communication of the gospel to people in this kind of cultural context. The message was indeed contextualised. The church was indeed indigenous. The pre-Christian mechanism was still in use in that village after 120 years.

More common perhaps than the dirge is the Chant of Farewell (*Meke ni Tatau, Meke ni, Veitalatala*), some of which (like the *meke* for John Watsford) are very long. This one has eleven stanzas of eight lines each. They contain the same grammatical features and are performed in the same manner, but the performance does not have the meditation pauses, which from precontact times were the form of respect shown for the dead. This was the distinctive feature of the dirge, and distinguishes it from an honorific *vakamalolo*.

The Institutional Contexts

I have already pointed out that an oral artifact like a chant, dirge, or responsive ritual is not an artifact in isolation, but always has a precise context, and is always performed "according to the rules" for the occasion, and performed by the competent authority. Very briefly I must recognise this—at least, and press that point.

I shall consider briefly the cycle of the seasons and the ritual performance of planting and harvest. This I take as one type of context only, of a number of possibilities. It might have been the cycle of festivities and exchanges involved in a significant marriage; or the network of social, agricultural, or economic performances relating to a trade exchange (*solevu*) between two islands; or the ceremonial entertainment of a great visiting chief; or a program of communal house building—but I can only find time and space for one as representative.[180]

Mediatorial roles are involved in them all, so I have paid some attention in this paper to "mediating." Likewise I have discussed ceremonial presentations. There are literally scores of such occasions, but there are only a limited number of ways of giving and receiving. Things must be done with proper decorum or the *mana* may work in the wrong way. In any case I have already written much on this and it need not be repeated (Tippett 1958b, 1976, 1977b).

THE CYCLE OF SEASONS AND HARVESTS

Among the features of pre-Christian Fijian social life which was retained, or only slightly adapted, was the cycle of the seasons—living close to the soil, clearing the land, planting, irrigating, presenting the firstfruits, the pattern of the ingathering or harvests; and, of course, including the religious ritual it all engendered. All this I have written up at greater length than I can do here (Tippett 1958a, 96–106).[181] Let me merely reiterate that the importance of winning this integral system for Christianity became apparent when biblical translation had to deal with the Hebrew calendar and festivities. The Hebrew and the Fijian had much in common. It was a very simple transition from the Hebrew cycles of wheat, barley, wine, and oil to the Fijian yam harvest, from which the Fijian word for "year" (*yabak'i*) was taken. A religion without a festival of firstfruits or of ingathering would have been meaningless. Thus in Fiji the *Lotu ni Sevu* is significant to this day. My first encounter with a Fijian church district conference in the mountains of Nadroga in 1941 carried me physically into a perfect reenactment of the Feast of Tabernacles when the people lived in booths and where all the vocabulary for explaining the Hebrew festival was available. In discussing the matter with an old Fijian he affirmed my point saying "*Keimami qarava Data na Kalou ke-i nai teitei.*" "We (exclusive) 'serve' together both God and the garden." The word *qarava* can mean both "worship" and "cultivate." It means "to serve," or "to take care of in the proper manner." The old man was saying that to him religion and agriculture were part of a single conceptual network. He was far closer to the Old Testament world of Canaan than the Greco-Roman world of the New Testament. There was a healthy holism here which we of the urban West have lost. It generates a whole set of values which is strong in the preaching of Fijian pastors.

A later generation of missionaries, not properly trained in the Old Testament value system, often made confusing innovations or lost sight of essential Old Testament values,

---

180   Several of these have been described in detail in *Fijian Material Culture* (Tippett 1968).

181   See also sources in the vernacular, not always in agreement and thus suggesting two basic patterns in different parts of Fiji. Rokowaqa n.d.; Dreketirua n.d.

so that a younger generation of Fijians has also lost them, but I remember with great pleasure the preaching of the Fijian pastors who were old men in the 1940s. They lived close to the soil and God was to them the God of all life, of the seasons and harvests, the Creator and Provider—the ongoing Creator, not confined to the first few chapters of Genesis. Now as I look back I rejoice at what was preserved, although I lament the scope for potential functional substitutes which were not exploited as they might have been.

I found the Fijians very responsive to any kind of service for dedication, investiture, or induction. The idea of a tree-planting dedication service was regarded as quite appropriate. People coming out of a ritual paganism will feel the need for Christian substitutes. I recall once passing a rice field utterly overgrown with poisonous, sensitive grass and almost impossible to harvest. I commented on it to my Fijian companion whose spontaneous response was, "What else was to be expected because the cultivators made oblations to their ancestor at the time of planting?" Obviously the essential harmony of life required sympathy in cultivating and the worship of the creating and providing God. The church provided no functional substitute for the felt need, and the rice cultivators had gone back to an old animist ritual. However a Western scientist might have met the problem, for my Fijian companion at least the problem was a felt need for harmony that was not met by an appropriate ritual. Here was a value which had survived for a century and did not conflict with the Christian faith, so a Christian institution should have been tried.

If we can transform a pagan nature festival associated with the return of the sun after winter to commemorate the advent of the Redeemer so that it is now symbolic of the historic event of the Incarnation and its redemptive character (Welch 1953, 92), why should not the whole network of festivals relating to seedtime and harvest, planting and firstfruits, be transformed into Christian counterparts?—the point being that the felt need is continuous. The people still depend on the harvest, and still believe that divine factors operate in the ripening of the harvest, and should be thankfully recognised. The production of food, the environment, the lifestyle determined by the natural and cultural context continues, and the new religion has to meet the same felt needs as its predecessor supposedly did.

This precise problem was presented to missionary John Mackenzie in Africa by a newly converted Bechuana chief in the planting season. They never had planted a crop without a ritual ceremony and still felt the need. Mackenzie recognised that the *letsemma* ceremony had a social and theological value and should not be discarded. He seized the opportunity of working out a Christian functional substitute, which the chief memorised. Mackenzie retained the ceremonial form and purpose, stripped it of its pagan elements, and produced a new rubric based on the Old Testament festivals and the Psalms as he had no New Testament model.

This is how a worshipping community on the mission field retains its indigeneity. It belongs to the context, confronts the felt needs of the people, refuses to leave a void by Christianisation, and makes a positive attempt to meet those felt needs. The ritual had to be memorised for an oral tradition people, and the socioreligious role of the chief was maintained. Here is Christianisation with a minimum of cultural dislocation. The church which emerges is a truly Bechuana institution, Christianity being superimposed on the physical form of an African pagan cult. At the same time, it is no longer ancestral or animistic, but Christian.

In passing, it has been argued that Hosea's use of marriage allegory was actually the chief element of the Canaanite fertility cult, restructured in the interests of Yahweh worship to transform a popular religious form by giving a sanctified meaning to its central theme. This is not the only case of significant questions for Old Testament exegesis being raised in missionary experience (Snaith 1944, 111).

Meantime the Fijian *Lotu ni Sevu* is a good example of the kind of functional substitute I am speaking about. I have also participated in dedication services when land is opened up for cultivation or a section of timber trees is planted.

MEDIATING

Every missionary has to consider the forms of mediation accepted and utilised in the community where he takes the gospel. If the gospel is to be contextualised, it must employ the mediation mechanisms of the context—both the institutions and the personnel.

Mediation is intercommunication which takes place between an authority and a person under authority, or between two authorities or persons. It operates on two levels—between persons or groups, and between man and his God or gods. A special class of persons may be segregated for this functional activity: in the former a representative, agent, spokesman, go-between, ambassador, or herald; in the latter a priest, prophet, or in Christian times, a minister. Not only do these special persons stand out as mediators but they understand the ceremonial performances and know the oral formulae as ordinary people do not. The coming of Christianity to the islands created specific issues in this respect.

A quantity of research has been done on the nature of mediation in Fiji, especially on the role of the Fijian herald (*mata ni vanua*), whom Opetaia Dreketirua (n.d.) called "the cords of the land" (*wa ni vanua*), who bind the people and chiefs together in an integrated system. He deals with their rights, privileges, and responsibilities in mediatorial ceremonies. Much that he says about heralds on the secular level applies also for the priests on the spiritual level. In each case the responsibility for safeguarding the cohesion of society is considerable. It all depends on knowing how, when, and where to act; the appropriate language of respect; the correct and respectable formula of approach and departure, request, acceptance or rejection, and thanks. To perform or speak in a clumsy ("left-handed") manner will make the assembly "cold" (*ena qai batabata na soqoni*) and endanger the mediation.

In Fijian social anthropology the structure of the system of mediation is one of the most complex of all the social organisations, but this research has been done and is too long for me to recapitulate it here (Tippett 1976; 1977b). One point however must be made: viz., that the functional role of the herald and priest have been taken over by the Fijian church; the former, through its system of structural organisation including the stewards of the local congregations, the church districts, and the lay representatives to conference, and the latter through the Fijian ministry and the church's circuit organisation. The stewards and lay representatives utilise the entire secular mediatorial system and serve as advisors on how things ought to be done so that the church may always stand well with the land and the nation. These are the three constant subjects of Fijian prayers—"*na Lotu, na Vanua kei, na Matanitu.*"

With respect to the ministry, I remember a word of the Rev. S. A. Tuilovoni, the Fijian Secretary of Synod in 1957. He was addressing the synod Fijian ministerial delegates on their mediatorial responsibility. He called them "inhabitants of the ladder" (*lewe ni kabakaba*), which he based on Jacob's dream of the angels ascending and descending between heaven and earth. He said something like this:

> In spite of sin and separation the ladder was there, and there was contact
> between heaven and earth, and the angels symbolized the restoring of the
> broken fellowship. You are responsible, like those angels, for going up and
> down in between the holy God and the sinful world, taking up the cries of
> needy men and women, bringing them the blessing from above. This is your
> ministry as mediators.

This was not a commentary exposition but a Fijian perception. It was a pre-Christian Fijian value which had survived in the social organisation of a Christian church which had taken over from a pagan religious system. This was indeed an indigenous church.

Nor is this the only case I met of a senior Fijian minister addressing his colleagues in this manner at synod with respect to the ministerial mediatorial office. Rev. Iliesa Vatanitawake described them as "a certain type of person who operates between God and men." His model was Moses functioning between God and Israel, and he saw the role as both priestly and prophetic.

The mediatorial office was so utterly Fijian that we do not wonder that the mediatorial work of Christ Himself is possibly the most highly developed aspect of Fijian Christology. It occupies a preeminent place in Fijian prayers and preaching, in the hymnology, the Confession of Faith, and in the expositions in the class meetings. Furthermore the terminology of mediatorship both on the civil and sacrificial levels proved to be more lexically refined than that of the New Testament Greek itself when it came to a matter of translation [see Tippett 1958a, 107–17].

CEREMONIAL PROCEDURES AND PRESENTATIONS

Pre-Christian Fijian social life was intensely institutionalised with ceremonial procedure. There was a correct way of doing everything. Although this would vary from one region to another, there was always a correct way to act. I remember once on a journey in an area where I was a stranger receiving a welcome ceremony and making my formal responses as I had learned them in an area under the authority of Rewa. An old man nearby whispered loudly enough for me to hear, "He did it in the Rewan pattern." Subsequently he laughed at me. "You are a stranger. Had you been a Fijian there would have been a penalty."

Ceremonials covered welcomes and farewells, discussions over *yaqona*, preparation for war and victory afterwards, cannibal feasting, visiting a chiefly village, showing respect before the chiefly house, making requests and reports, preparing food and presenting the feast to visitors, initiations, dedications, courtship, marriage, burials, trade exchanges, and so on, *ad infinitum*. Everything had its procedure. Customs relating to patricide, infanticide, cannibalism, widow strangling, and heathen war disappeared when Christianity came, but all the events of normal village life, of agriculture, of trade, of civil negotiations and the rites of passage continued. The only things which changed were the substitution of a Christian phrase (often "May the church grow") for the phrase which related the ceremony to a deity or ancestral cult. Most of the custom continued—the agriculture, the hunting, the fishing, the trade exchanges, and most of the rites of passage were merely given a Christian phrase or prayer. The church which emerged had to be still Fijian, so Christianity had to be contextualised.

From the beginning the Fijian village churches were self-supporting, and this they achieved by an annual offering or "temple day" which reflected the pre-Christian ceremonial offering before a heathen temple, for its rebuilding or repair; or in return for priestly assurances that the gods would give them victory in war.

In the 1850s Thomas Williams described a ceremonial presentation of this type with whale's teeth, turtles, *yaqona* roots, yams, native puddings, *dalo* (taro), bananas, and craft goods like bark cloth and fans.

Christian offerings were similar. The people assembled in the same way and brought forward their offerings in a long line moving from one end of the village to the other. The goods were the same produce and artifacts, offered in the same way and received with the same formulae by the approved persons and according to indigenous protocol. The only modification was that the prayers and blessings were in the name of the Good Lord. These ceremonial presentations had functional names to distinguish one from the other—a military review before war, the ceremonies for the burial of a chief; and each had its distinctive exercise according to its function and the reason for which it required the blessing of the gods. The Christian offering would have its distinctiveness by a competitive hearing of memorised Scripture or catechism or singing from each kin group as it made its family offering.

In the church archives in Fiji are some of the records of these gifts tabulated on printed forms used for seventy years in proper accounting, and showing the number of yams, baskets of sweet potatoes, lengths of bark cloth, bunches of bananas, containers of oil, etc., given by the various family groups. Not for quite a number of years was there in the last column a record of cash gifts—a sign of slow acculturation.

This utterly Fijian system of giving, known as *vakamisoneri*, has continued to this day. The changes that have come are in the dress of the people, the shift from giving goods to cash, and some new types of music, but the basic structure remains; the system of ceremonial giving has continued from pre-Christian times. The view that each kinship group has its obligation to God, and the willing manner in which they give cheerfully in a festival of joy and draw from the absent members of their extended families, is an abiding integral system. It is indeed an indigenous church that has emerged. The cultural importance of this institution (which, in the case of the same thing in Tonga, Lorimer Fison called "tribal offerings") is that they were coordinated communal efforts, and they harnessed the church machinery to the culture and social organisation.

Not all of these presentations were for purposes of support. Some were for welcome and farewell of the delegates at a synod gathering, for example. They were expressions of fellowship, food from the hosts for the visitors, gifts of thanks for the hosts from the visitors. Sometimes these reflected local industry.

I once was present at a ceremony where the hosts gave the visitors an entire presentation of Fijian salt. This was at Lomawai famous for this commodity. At Sigatoka it was clay pots, at Nasaucoko a special kind of sleeping mat, *yo haha* (Bauan *ibe kuta*). But normally there would be a variety of gifts. When the annual meeting of the Rewa Division was held in the island of Kadavu, the visitors included urban wage-earning Fijians from Suva. They took trade goods, not so easy for the subsistence farming hosts to buy. They heaped up tins of biscuits, drums of kerosene, and bars of soap—evidence of their own acculturation, but the procedure throughout was entirely indigenous.

Here is a reference from the archives about Vanua Levu:

> As soon as the ceremony was completed the dancers took off their mats and upper cloth dresses and petticoats and threw them into a heap for the hosts. The missionaries added wedge axes.

The date is October 1848. Just a century later I saw precisely the same thing in Nadroga. Then the leading layman visitor took off his new coat and threw it on the heap, then his necktie, his *sulu*, his shirt and singlet, leaving him in nothing but his underpants. This part features a good deal of fun and innovation—but the innovations are within fixed limits. I added some trade goods and a Fijian Bible, which I found in the pulpit when next I itinerated through that village and preached there.

Thus was the courtesy of giving and receiving, of hospitality and appreciation, all essential in the Fijian value system perpetuated in the contextualisation of Christianity, and with it approved procedure whereby it is demonstrated. It also reflects the sheer joy of giving, even to the degree of giving more than can reasonably be expected—sacrificial giving—which has made more meaningful to them their theology of the self-giving Lord, even Him who gave His life for sinful men [see Tippett 1958a, 124–25].

Some Concluding Observations

In concluding this ethnohistorical study of oral tradition in Fiji over a century and a half of history, I must recapitulate my feelings on four distinct levels.

(1) On the level of *ethnohistory* I have argued that the data in the Fijian documents has revealed a cultural stability of oral tradition forms and artifacts; that even when the Christian Fijians became literate they still operated with the aid of their familiar pre-Christian tools for communicating and sharing experiences. They preserved the prescriptions for ceremonial occasions and used the same kind of practitioners—or at least their functionally identical counterparts. Christianity "wore" Fijian not Western "garments." The gospel was communicated in a Fijian manner, and worship and ritual was recognisably their own. I have not hesitated to call this gospel *contextualised* and their church *indigenous*. Furthermore I would offer the case of the Fijian church as a model for any investigation of what is meant by the term "contextualisation of the gospel" in missiology.

(2) On the level of *historiography* I have raised the thorny question of the value of oral tradition, and its techniques as a legitimate field for research in cross-cultural situations with time depth. Many researchers have rejected oral tradition as having no real value or documentation. This I would question. Oral tradition emerges in the processes of real life. It operates within strict prescriptions and evaluative criteria. If the ethnohistorian gets into the worldview, the language, and the system, then he will find the evidential value quite considerable. Furthermore a period of early literacy after conversion from paganism requires a knowledge of the oral system to evaluate the early documentary records.

(3) On the level of *anthropology* I have raised the question of "levels of time depth" reflecting "changes of worldview," and would advocate more serious use of the methodology of "culture continuum"—the research of synchronic levels in a diachronic sequence (Dark 1957) as one most likely of being fruitful. This will call for the study of semantic change at different levels of time depth and the researcher's own preparation of time-depth vocabularies. I fail to see how vernacular documents or oral tradition can be reliably assessed without a lexical tool of this kind.

The study also reveals the stability of indigenous values in spite of changes by conversion or acculturation, and throws light on cultural mechanisms that make for smooth transitions in times of dramatic change, permit the acceptance of such change, and make the changes reasonably permanent.

(4) On the level of *missiology* I have identified conversion as a process of culture change and shown the role of the indigenous acceptors in fixing the permanent forms of communication, sharing, and worship of the indigenous church which will emerge. We have seen these forms of communication and worship as belonging to a corporate complex, and we have found a configuration of Christian *koinonia* which is both indigenous and abiding. We have looked at "the fact of indigeneity" anthropologically and have found that the cultural contextualisation of the gospel is an essential requirement of indigenous Christianity.

It would appear that conversion to Christianity requires a *koinonia* held together by appropriate forms for transmitting the faith, practising corporate worship, sharing feelings, and sustaining values (including prayer, Bible study, hymn singing, etc.). In the great time depth of prehistory the precontact Fijians developed their oral artifacts for corporate communication, personal sharing, and group integration. It only stands to reason that the mechanisms which must hold together the new indigenous *koinonia* will need to have similar structures and forms to those the people have cultivated themselves.

I believe that by focusing on the oral tradition value system—artistic and aesthetic values of rhythm, imagery, response, liturgy, poetic legalisms, and dirges—we have moved a step nearer to the meaning of indigeneity. Furthermore we understand why the Fijian church is the kind of church it is, how and why it differs from our church here in the West, and what a cross-cultural worker will need to adjust himself to if he joins that church and is to empathise there.

REFERENCES

Barker, George T. 1925–1926a. Conua, a town on the Nakauvadra; and Nakauvadra tales. *Transactions of the Fijian Society.*

———. 1925–1926b. A lay of Koroitamana a Rewa chief. *Transactions of the Fijian Society.*

Belshaw, Cyril S. 1964. *Under the Ivi tree: Society and economic growth in rural Fiji.* Berkeley: University of California Press.

Bulicokocoko, S. T. n.d. *Fijian idioms, colloquialisms, customs.* Suva: Colony of Fiji, Education Department.

Bulu, Joeli. 1845. *Joeli Bulu: Autobiography of a native minister in the South Seas.* Trans. Lorimer Fison. London: Wesleyan Mission Office.

Bunyan, John. 1867. *Ai Tukutuku kei Vulagi Lako* [Pilgrim's progress].Trans. William Moore. London: W. W. Watts.

Colony of Fiji. 1897. *Report of the commission appointed to inquire into the decrease of native population.* Suva: E. J. March, Government Printer.

Dark, Philip. 1957. Methods of synthesis in ethnohistory. *Ethnohistory* 4: 231–78.

Dreketirua, Opetaia. n.d. *Ai Vola Tetegei.* 2 vols. Unpublished manuscript.

Edman, V. Raymond. 1949. *The light in the dark ages.* Wheaton: Van Kampan.

Erskine, John E. 1853. *Journal of a cruise among the islands of the Western Pacific.* London: John Murray.

Fison, Lorimer. 1865–70. Correspondence in *The Wesleyan missionary notices relating to missions.* Sydney: Wesleyan Methodist Conference.

———. 1871. The Fijian judged by his own words. Manuscript notebook in Fison papers.

———. 1882. *On Fijian riddles.* London: Harrison.

Gatschet, A. S. 1885. Specimens of Fijian dialects: Edited from manuscripts of Rev. Lorimer Fison. Leipzig, Germany: *Internationale Zeitschrift für Allgemeine Sprachwissenschraft.*

Gomme, George L. 1892. *Ethnology in folklore.* London: Kegan Paul, Trench, Trübner & Co.

Harris, Marvin. 1970. *The rise of anthropological theory.* New York: Crowell.Hazlewood, David. 1850. *A Feejeean and English dictionary.* Viwa, Fiji: Wesleyan Mission Press.

Heighway, W. A. 1897–1901. *Manuscripts of hymns and mekes in Fijian.* In Tippett manuscript Collection.

Henderson, G. C. 1931. *Fiji and the Fijians: 1835-1856.* Sydney: Angus & Robertson.

Hocart, A. M. 1929. *Lau Islands, Fiji.* Honolulu: Bishop Museum Press.

Hunt, John. 1838–48. *Journals.*

———. 1846. Correspondence with the London Committee. Wesleyan Mission Society.

———. 1850. *A Vakatusa ni Lotu.* Viwa, Fiji: Wesleyan Mission Press.

Langham, Frederick. 1865–70. Correspondence in *The Wesleyan missionary notices relating to missions.* Sydney: Wesleyan Methodist Conference.

Malinowski, Bronislaw. 1960. *A scientific theory of culture.* New York: Oxford University Press.

———. 1961. *The dynamics of culture change.* New Haven: Yale University Press.

Parrinder, Geoffrey. 1946. Worship in Protestant missions. *International Review of Missions* 35: 187–93.

Quain, Buell. 1948. *Fijian village.* Chicago: University of Chicago Press.

Raiwalui, Anare K. 1954. *Nai Vosavosa Vakaviti e So.* Melbourne: Oxford University Press.

Rokowaqa, Epeli. n.d. *Ai Tukutuku kei Viti.* Suva: Methodist Mission Press.

Rougier, E. 1915. Fijian dances and games. *Transactions of the Fijian Society.*

Sapir, Edward. 1949. *Language.* New York: Harcourt Brace.

Snaith, Norman H. 1944. *The distinctive ideas of the Old Testament.* London: Epworth.

Tippett, Alan R. 1955. *Road to Bau: The life and work of John Hunt of Viwa, Fiji.* Unpublished manuscript.

——. 1958a. *The integrating gospel.* Unpublished manuscript.

——. 1958b. Shifting foci in Methodist witness in Fiji: 1835–1900. Unpublished manuscript.

——. 1960. Fijian proverbs, metaphoric idioms and riddles: An ethnolinguistic study. *Transactions and Proceedings of the Fiji Society* 8: 65–93.

——. 1968. *Fijian material culture: A study of culture context, function and change.* Honolulu: Bishop Museum Press.

——. 1973. *Aspects of Pacific ethnohistory.* South Pasadena: William Carey Library.

——. 1976. The role of the Fijian herald in negotiations between persons and parties at different status levels. Unpublished manuscript.

——. 1977a. Functional substitutes in Fijian Christianity. Unpublished manuscript.

——. 1977b. Personal interplay in intercommunity ceremonial in Fiji. Unpublished manuscript.

——. 1980. *Oral tradition and ethnohistory: The transmission of information and social values in early Christian Fiji, 1835–1905.* Canberra: St. Mark's Library.

Tippett Collection. 1896–1905. Fijiana files. Solomon Islands letters to Fiji.

Toganivalu, Deve. 1911. The customs of Bau before the advent of Christianity. *Transactions of the Fijian Society.*

——. 1917. Ai Yau kei nai Yaya Vakaviti. *Transactions of the Fijian Society*, 1–18.

Wallace, A. F. C. 1966. *Religion: An anthropological view.* New York: Random House.

Waterhouse, Joseph. 1866. *The king and people of Fiji.* London: Wesleyan Conference Office.

Welch, Adam C. 1953. *Prophet and priest in old Israel.* Oxford: Basil Blackwell, 1953.

Williams, Thomas. 1884. *Fiji and the Fijians.* Vol. 1, *The island and its inhabitants.* London: Alexander Heylin.

PART FIVE

Case Studies

26

THE PROCESS OF RELIGIOUS CHANGE (WALLEGA GALLA, ETHIOPIA)[182]

How does a people change from its traditional religion to another? What happens when two or three "great" religions are contesting for the soul of that people?

I had been able to do research in both the "primitive" and "sophisticated" Galla areas. This permitted interesting comparisons. Our study of religious change should be set in the same localities. In the northern locations around Kirimu and Tosse, the more "primitive" part, we observe the early stages of the changing religious experience: the stage of *awareness of religious options*, of initial *decision making* and *encounter*, and of confrontation with *persecution*. These are the well-known marks of periods of religious conversion and of church planting.

In the south, in and around Dembi Dollo, the "great" religions have established themselves with a kind of religious equilibrium and accepted coexistence; witchdoctors have disappeared within a generation or so; the people are Orthodox, evangelical, or Moslem, mainly by birth, and with any threats to their religion coming from the danger of nominality rather than from persecution. The initial enthusiasm, especially for the evangelicals, has already passed into oral tradition, and current tensions are internal rather than from external confrontations.

Religious Change in the Southern Area

According to my informant, Kes Letta [a priest named Letta], the Galla were almost all animists about the beginning of the century, and the countryside was dotted with witchdoctors. They held a powerful control over the whole district. The possibility of any change in religion came when a Galla governor at Gidami proclaimed a law: "Let all witchdoctors perish!" Thereafter any witchdoctor had to pay a bribe in order to operate, and religious change was possible among the Galla without any serious obstruction. Kes Letta dates the spread of the Orthodox Church in this area within his own lifetime and in this century.

---

182   Taken from *Peoples of Southwest Ethiopia* (Pasadena: William Carey Library, 1970), 244–52. Used by permission.

The Christian mission entered Galla country as a medical venture. The occasion was the typhus epidemic of 1911 (Ethiopian calendar),[183] a year after the appointment of a certain British consul at Gambela, which was then in the Anglo-Egyptian Sudan. This individual knew of the American mission work in the Sudan, established the necessary connections, obtained the permission of the Ethiopian queen, and thus Dr. Lambie was able to commence work in 1912 (Ethiopian calendar), which means the evangelicals have been in the area for about forty years.

Islam is said to have begun spreading among the Galla under Ahmed Grand [sic Ahmed Grāñ] in the sixteenth century, but it reached Jimma, which is now the Islamic stronghold of the southwest, according to tradition, in 1830. However it did not penetrate into the area I am discussing until about seventy years ago. So the century began with a confrontation of Orthodox Christianity and Islam. The people were pagan with a strong animistic sacrificial religion and, before they had rejected this for either option, an evangelical missionary doctor arrived and he met a specific felt need after a severe epidemic. Orthodoxy, Islam, and evangelical Christianity were contemporary live options for this very unsettled animistic people. These three advocates were in competition from the end of World War I down to Italian times. Therefore any evaluation of the current religious distribution must be set against this factual background.

A glimpse of the acceptance of Islam in Jimma may throw light on their methods. We have two foreign sources (Massaja and Soleillet), and one in English (Lewis 1965) who uses them both. A merchant from Gondar, Abdul Hakim, established himself at Jiren near the ruler, Abba Jifar, with the express purpose of winning the latter to his faith. This took place, the tradition has it, in 1830. After his conversion Massaja says that Abba Jifar called a number of Mohammedan saints to disciple the Galla people. Soleillet speaks of a number of Mohammedan traders who were also accepted as teachers of the faith. Many were elevated to official positions, and they played a formative role in establishing the Islamic law, especially at the domestic level.

Lewis' comment that "by 1862 most of the people of Jimma were Muslim" rather suggests to me that the program of incorporation of converts into Islam occupied the best part of two generations. If this was so, it was not rapid for the size of the territory. It was certainly not a people movement which carried the rank and file. The people appear to have been educated into Islam in two generations, influenced by the conversion of the king, the realisation that economic advance and prestige went with the king's religion, and the religio-legal teaching program of the traders. This speculation of mine fits the known facts and would explain the slow advance of Islam in regions where the Orthodox Church is strong, some Galla areas among them. Both religions reinforced the political systems to

---

183   My informant gave the dates in the Ethiopian calendar and was able to associate events with dates. I understand this
        puts the operation described as between 1918 and 1920 in our calendar.

which they were affiliated. Meantime Abdul Hakim, the agent of conversion of Abba Jifar, is much glorified to this day, and his shrine is still there to be respected by those who follow in the process he originated.

A missionary informant in Dembi Dollo described the current evangelical community as about fifteen thousand persons, with three to four thousand of them adult communicants. On the surface this may look like a church of some strength. However the area involved has perhaps 500,000 persons, and most of them (or their fathers) have changed their religion in the last forty years. The Moslems live a little to the north and would probably only number about the same as the evangelicals, according to my informant; and there are a few Roman Catholics, but they are a station church. The rank and file are largely Orthodox Christians, although my friend added, "Many of them still seem to be pagan at heart." Nevertheless, when the choice had to be made, they chose the Orthodox rather than the evangelical option. It may be that the Orthodox Church was less foreign. Or maybe it offered more social and political advantages. But the fact remains that fifteen thousand constituents with four thousand of them full communicants, in a population of half a million, is not great growth for forty years among a people showing a disposition towards religious change.

In any case the evangelical church does not appear to have grown out of the medical work, but to have been a spontaneous growth among the indigenous people themselves. Although the mission provided the initial facilities and training that made an evangelical church possible, the main outbursts of growth came while the missionaries were absent.

I was taken out from Dembi Dollo to an eminence on the road from which I looked over the Ano area. My informant pointed out the location of three evangelical congregations; one was close, the second two hours walk beyond, and the more distant one five hours away. Here was a community which had developed during the wartime absence of the missionaries. Originally these groups had a connection with the mission compound, where the ministry was *in-taking* rather than *out-reaching*. The war ended this. The Italians occupied the mission station and eventually gave the town evangelicals a block of land where the Bethel Church now stands. Those from further distance began to worship on their own, and their congregations began to grow. At first their meetings were simple enough— morning prayers at *injera* (bread) and coffee, neighborly and without dressing up. In the evenings they met for songs and prayers, Bible reading or recitation of Scripture passages.

Somewhere in the story, I'm not sure just when, some Swedish missionaries took a Galla man overseas and educated him to the seminary level. This man translated the Bible into Gallinya and a Swiss group printed it. The Galla Christians accepted it and a few copies are currently in circulation. They were passed around from one group to another and played a significant part in building up these rural congregations as they broke away from the station complex and became indigenous congregational entities. There are five of these entities in the area now and they are a relevant witness.

Kes Gadada was a good informant who responded well to questioning and did not object to my taking notes. As I obtained his testimony almost verbatim, I record it here in full:

> The church grew by the hearing of the gospel and by coming near to the Lord. It began before Italian times when Dr. Lambie came, forty-nine years ago. Some things were hard for me in changing from the old religion, but I believed first and learned to read afterwards. I believed within a few days after hearing the word of the gospel and in time I became an evangelist.
>
> At the time I first heard the gospel I was a sick and tired man and exhausted with going to the witchdoctor. I found no help or comfort in him. When I believed, my family was opposed to the decision and the witchdoctor was angry, but they could not persuade me to give up my new faith. The witchdoctor said, "I will kill Gadada. He will die within one year." When one year had passed many people laughed at the witchdoctor and he began to lose his supporters.
>
> Then came the war time and the Christians began to increase. The last missionary was Mr. West, and when he left we had about 120 members.
>
> The next Sunday I preached to a full church. There was an Amhara there who had been attending and after church he came and shook hands and said, "Let us be together and warm up the church." This is just what I had been thinking myself. We determined to meet regularly (even without any missionary). We did this and our meetings were good.
>
> About a month later the Italians came and they took over the mission compound and our church building. The Italian (R.C.) priest said to me, "Who is the leader of your church?" I said that it is Jesus Christ. He said, "I know that, but what man is leading you?" Again I answered as before that Christ is our leader. He said, "How you talk. *We* are his instruments and we are taking your church building. Tell your people to come and worship with us." I said, "I will tell them what you say, but I cannot force them to come and worship with you." Again he asked, "Are you coming to worship with us?" I said, "I will go to my house and pray."
>
> I prayed to the Lord, "Are you not the true God? Did you not send the missionaries to teach us in the first place? Was not this the true word?" Then I kept quiet for a minute and I prayed again, "Yes, Lord I believe. These people who have come to take us by force have some other power. Will you show me the right way?" Then I felt He came to me in strength and I thanked God.
>
> I gathered our people together and told them what the priest had said. We decided not to worship with them, but that if we lost our building we would meet

in the open air under a tree. So after the Italian worship had been conducted in the church, I subsequently entered the church and took our Bibles and hymn-books and we went to the *kiltu* tree[184] and there we had our own worship service and we agreed to gather together continually. This was the real beginning of our work.

After a few months we built a church in one place and we began to worship also in other places. After four years we had churches at Bethel, Ana, Gamba, Tirini, Fana, and Chanka and our 120 members had grown to maybe two thousand.

Some people who used to come in to the mission station now had churches in their own areas. Some who had been students at the mission now worked in the rural churches. Some had been in the hospital and told what they had heard when they returned home, and because of what they told at home people came to the Lord in whole families.

We used the Galla Bible. These are hard to get today. The people are crying out for the book. We still worship in Gallinya, and visitors who speak in Amharic or English are interpreted.

This is a valuable testimony. It shows many aspects of the movement. It shows the way in which an in-taking, centralised, station church operates against good growth, is foreign in pattern and control, is comprised of individuals, students, medical workers, and so forth. It shows how, when circumstances break this pattern and scatter the individuals so they can testify to their families, the church grows by the formation of many local centers and the winning of family groups. The rejection of the Roman Catholic offer, and the possibility of favour with the Italians, is significant. It shows how these people set a high value on free, indigenous worship and the vernacular Bible. Here was a value preference the priest found hard to understand.

On another day I visited a location known as Samati, south of the mission, a half-hour journey by Land Rover. Here Ato Negri [Mr. Negri] is in charge of an evangelical congregation. I had a long interview with him. They are in the process of a rebuilding program. The old church building was made of split eucalyptus saplings and roofed with grass. A new and larger church is being built beside it, split eucalyptus frame with mud-plaster walls and an iron roof—symbol of the improving economic position of the congregation. A wooden cross stands in front of the building indicating not merely that the building is a church, but also that it has a full status and that the sacraments are administered there. Ato Negri told me the following story:

My father was the important witchdoctor of this area. The people from miles around used to come to him. Just before his death he called our family together.

---

184 *Ficus brachypoda*, where sacrificial stones are often found.

He had contracted some disease and he knew he would not recover. There was a missionary named Buchanan at the mission station over there. My father said that from now on there should be no more witchdoctors in this locality. If any person should set up in business as a witchdoctor, my father said, we were not to patronize him, for the hand of the Lord is on this land.

I never forgot those words of my father. It is still our hearts today. I went to that mission school when it was in the hospital building. When we became adults we began visiting the mission compound because we remembered the word of my father. There we studied the Bible.

I was twenty-one years of age and Mr. Buchanan advised me to go further with my schooling. We had only two evangelical churches. I attended the one at the mission station and eventually became a member.

Many of the people who lived on our land before the Italian times went away when the Italians arrived and much of the land returned to bush. After some years I returned myself and began to work the land again. I saw that the mission and the town church were far away, and I wondered what I could do about it. I met with three or four other people and we prayed in my house. Time went on and more and more were added to our group and we considered a suitable place for prayer. Before long we were about thirty in number and by working together we built this house (indicating the one with the grass roof). Those who did this work were all people with the yeast of faith, and when we had a building then others joined us.

Then we wrote to the Presbytery and asked to be allowed to operate as a church, and now we are growing spiritually and also numerically. The cross stands in front of our church, showing the Holy Communion is celebrated here. Before that cross was there, if anyone died the body had to be taken to town and that was difficult. Now we have our own graveyard and the Lord truly blesses us.

This congregation has been autonomous for five years now and over a hundred people worship here on Sundays. They come from an area of from three to five square miles and some take as long as fifteen or twenty minutes.

We now have the help of a teacher from our central training program but the congregation supports him. The school receives children up to the third grade. After this they go to the mission at Dembi Dollo.

The Roman Catholics have moved into our area and have built a school. Some Catholic Gallas have visited many of our people. Their school is only thirty minutes away. They are jealous of our growth and success and have canvassed our area to get our people to go to them. Maybe there are now more Catholics than evangelicals in the area, but from this location to the mission is solidly evangelical. The witchdoctors have all disappeared. I do not know where you could find one in this vicinity now. There has been some strong interdenominational struggle but even this is decreasing and the people understand each other better.

The congregation at Samati has four of us who do the preaching. We preach [in] Gallinya but when we have visitors we have a translation into Amharic. We use the Galla Bible and the people progress in their faith and are happy in God.

Our material life has also progressed, especially in our farming and our use of the land. There is no migration from our area to the town, but rather some come to us from the town, because there is still suitable farming land here which is uncultivated. The owners want to let their land and will help the newcomer to get settled. The settler has to pay rent and the owner pays the tax from the rent.

If you walk about one hour and a half you will come to the next rural evangelical location.

Ato Negri's account differs from that of Kes Gadada in that it is more recent and covers a different locality, but both reveal the *significance of the group* in religious change. They show the social group as a *multi-individual organism*, and they also pinpoint the role of *the leader* in the group. Both informants stressed the high value set by the people on the availability of a Galla Bible and their freedom to worship in that language.

Perhaps we have now recorded enough of the story of the change over from animism to evangelical Christianity in the southern part of the Wallega Galla area for the picture to be fairly clear. Religious change has come by the spontaneous operation of small corporate groups, frequently with a family structure and always with a strong sense of ethnic entity. They tend to form up into Christian congregations with some regional or geographical definition. Where the evangelical church has become rooted in the soil, this has been the pattern. The issues between the mission and the second-generation church are quite a different matter and concern church growth rather than church planting.

REFERENCES

Lewis, Herbert S. 1965. *A Galla Monarchy: Jimma Abba Jifar, Ethiopia, 1830–1932*. Madison: University of Wisconsin Press.

Massaja, G. 1885–95. *I Miei Trentacinque Anni di Missione nell'- Alta Ethiopia*. 12 vols. Milan: Pontifica S. Guiseppe.

Soleillet, P. 1886. *Voyages en Ethiopie*. Rouen, France: Espérance Cagniard.

27

THE HEAD-HUNTING AND SLAVERY COMPLEX AND SOCIORELIGIOUS CHANGE[185]

In this chapter I wish to take one cultural configuration and show its social, political, economic, and religious ramifications in pre-Christian times, and then trace the changes caused by acculturation and Christian contact. I shall also deal with those aspects of this configuration that left the way open for the acceptance of Christianity.

Head-hunting and slaving raids were a dominant feature of Solomon Islands life both for perpetrators and for victims. One of the most vicious of these networks operated in the Western Solomons from Roviana, in New Georgia, and Simbo a little to the south.[186] The outreaches were so widespread that other communities borrowed Roviana patterns, although often to satisfy different needs and purposes.[187] Raids were for heads, or for slaves, or for both, depending on the needs at Roviana. Usually the raids were accompanied by cannibalism, frequently but not always ceremonial.

The wide area covered by Roviana and Simbo raiding led to the emergence of many protective innovations among the potential victims, especially architectural and defence mechanisms. Penny, who had personal experience of these raids, claims that the Ysabel tree houses were devised for this purpose. They were comfortable and thoroughly effective and one of the best architectural achievements in these islands (Penny 1888, 46–50).[188] Life continually formed its patterns about the reality of raiding. It was a period of innovation. There was nothing static about this way of life. On the one hand it was open for the introduction of destructive Western features, like the use of tomahawk heads and

---

185 Taken from *Solomon Islands Christianity* (Pasadena: William Carey Library, 1967), 147–59. Used by permission.

186 Some slavery patterns had quite different motivation from that discussed in this chapter, as for instance the Ugi purchases of slaves from San Cristoval for purposes of adoption as a corrective to their custom of infanticide (Guppy 1887, 35).

187 Ysabel learned to hunt for heads from the experience of Roviana invasions. Gao and Bugotu extended the practice in the 1850s and 1860s of the last century. The Roviana people mounted tomahawk heads on long handles, using the term *kilakila*, the diffusion of which can be traced as far as Sa'a and Ulawa. Gao extended raiding to the artificial islands of Malaita by carrying off forty heads during a "friendly" entertainment (Ivens 1930, 186–87). The Bugotu people began collecting heads for canoe houses after the Roviana pattern, but drank the blood of the victim to acquire his strength or *mana* (Bogesi 1948, 224).

188 Penny climbed up into one of these houses, 150 feet above the ground, lower branches removed to eighty feet, well supplied with water, food, sandtray for fire, space of 450 square feet, and accommodation for forty people. Ascent was by means of a vine ladder.

firearms, and on the other to protective devices like forts and tree houses. The fact that the whole complex was open to innovation and not static had important consequences for traders and missionaries. It will therefore be necessary for us first to reconstruct the configuration as it was before culture contact.

Roviana-Simbo Head-hunting and Slavery as a Working Process

The influence of this pattern was felt for three hundred miles from the centre—Choiseul, Ysabel, Florida, Guadalcanal, and Buin were in the regular orbit. On occasions the raiders travelled as far as New Britain. Large-scale raiding goes back as far as our records permit investigation. The slaving system was noted by Surville's expedition in 1769 (Guppy 1887, 33). In 1844 Captain Cheyne met with an expedition returning to Roviana with ninety-three heads (ibid., 16). Woodford described another about 1886 with thirty-one heads (1890, 153). Every village had its heap of skulls for which special houses were built. In Simbo in 1901, Brown recorded twenty to thirty skulls at each repository.[189] According to Knibbs the Roviana headhunters caught so many victims that they decapitated them, for the sake of a cargo of heads, which they eventually stripped, cleaned, and ornamented before hanging them in the taboo house or the men's meetinghouse (Knibbs 1929, 38). The procedure was well established and ritualized for a multitude of ceremonial occasions.

It is frequently supposed that one of the features of political change during the last century was the emergence of master tribes. Each of the major island Groups seems to have had one or two groups fighting for the hegemony of the area. The Roviana people, with their Simbo allies, had certainly established some such paramountcy and were well on the way to establishing it in other regions. Even where they had not established direct rule they were universally feared, and they had done some colonizing. This widespread prestige of Roviana and the fear of her head-hunting propensity was reinforced further by her slaving patterns.

Psychologically the slaving established a distinction between the Roviana people and others. The slaves were captured from other islands whenever needed. They were often high-born persons taken in infancy or adolescence, so that they were usually detribalized and lived in sodalities rather than kin units. Servitude in the slave community was not oppressive, but there was never any doubt about their lowly status. They had to eat their food among themselves, or at least segregated from the Roviana people (Guppy 1887, 34). Their life was uncertain, for they might be called on at any time for some sacrificial purposes (16, 33). Nevertheless they had some degree of security, in that an economic role was assigned to them, and proficiency in craftsmanship was a reasonable guarantee against a slave's becoming a sacrificial victim. The slave community had little cohesion because the

---

189   Letter, 8 October 1901.

members came from widely scattered localities, spoke different languages and had no ties of kinship. They had to acquire the language of their masters and had no escape from the slave status. A slave's hope of survival depended on his personal capacity to make himself a useful member of society. Furthermore they were, as Guppy pointed out, "marketable commodities."

Slave traffic and head-hunting were thus both "recognised systems" and raids might be for either one or both purposes. The political and military status of Roviana and her prestige among the tribes depended on the effectiveness and regularity of these raids. Her economic stability and religious ceremonial also depended on the availability of heads and slaves for many occasions. The presence of so many slaves in Roviana and their exemption from kin involvements had important consequences for the introduction of Christianity, which certainly infiltrated through this slave community of detribalised persons.

The main business of life in Roviana was war—that is, raiding. Craftwork centred in the manufacture of those magnificent sewn-plank war canoes. Effective raiding required huge flotillas, with a force of warriors capable of dealing with whole villages.[190] However, raiding and canoe building accounted for so great a percentage of Roviana time and labour that it was imperative other economic connections be established. Roviana was by no means self-sufficient. The same applied to Simbo. In this way there evolved a system of symbiotic relationships between Roviana and a number of communities of little political consequence. Trade with Roviana gave them some recognition, but more important it freed them from the danger of head-hunting and enslavement.

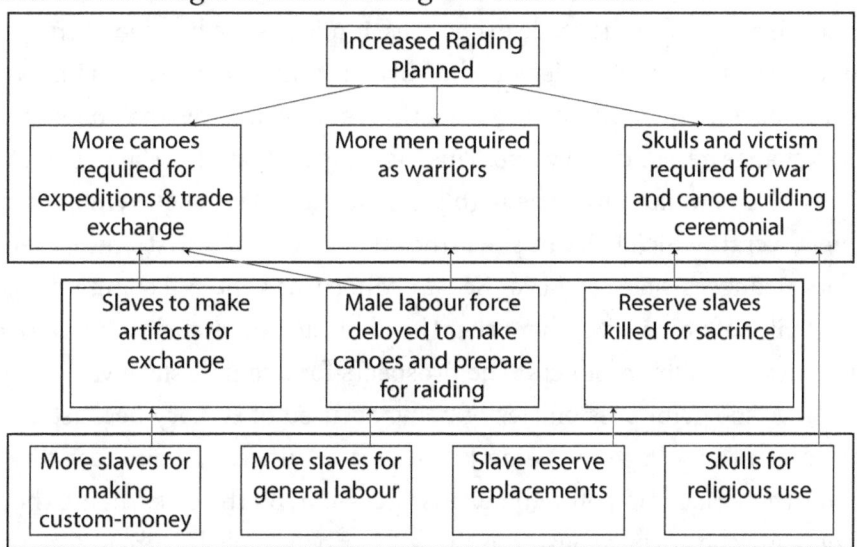

How an Increase of Head-Hunting and Slave-Raiding Maintains Its Own Equilibrium

Although Roviana engaged in plunder and raiding in Choiseul (and one informant told me of two hundred taken there in one raid), there were localities where the Roviana

---

190   Penny describes one (1888, 46).

people went for trade—for gold-lipped shells, pigs, *ngali* nuts, and turtles. Sometimes they exchanged canoes. Roviana also sought certain ornaments from Choiseul. These were not coastal productions, so that Choiseul trade networks were involved. Some of the Roviana symbiotic trade was with New Georgia communities—shell ornaments from the island of Bili, basket shields from Pondokono (which held a monopoly of this), black dye from the head of the Omba River, which shows Roviana also had inland contacts, to mention a few. Other items, like the red and yellow plaited work on combs, spears, and other artifacts, though common in Roviana, were not of New Georgia manufacture (Sommerville 1897, 374–75).

The inclusion of *ngali* nuts in the above list raises the matter of trade in food. Roviana acquired further supplies from Simbo via Wanawana.[191] They were a highly desirable exchange commodity. Simbo, however, had to supplement her food supplies with taro, which she needed for her ceremonial feasting patterns (Rivers 1922a, 109).

Like Roviana, Simbo needed a regular supply of artifacts, especially weapons. She obtained her war bows from Alu, her wicker-work shields from Kusage, via Roviana, and her reed shields and turtles from Choiseul. Later on when head-hunting was prohibited by the government, Simbo tried to maintain her slavery configuration by trading for slaves with Choiseul (Hocart 1931, 303).

Although Roviana had to maintain these trade connections, the slave community was organised to serve as a corrective to her economic vulnerability. A good deal of craftwork and the manufacture of domestic artifacts was assigned to the slaves. Any surplus they produced was disposed of in the trade exchanges. It might even be used in the purchase of more slaves from some friendly chief who had been recently successful in his own raiding. But the most important of all the slave productions at Roviana was shell money, which had a universal exchange demand and value. This task was delegated to slaves from Ysabel and Choiseul. They also manufactured the highly ornamental clam-shell symbols worn by the Roviana chiefs, a craft which has vanished since the coming of Christianity. Every Roviana village had its strangers' house, where the war canoe was kept and communal gatherings were held. In times of peace it was here that the Choiseul and Ysabel slaves were employed in making money and shell products. The prospects for a female slave varied. On the one hand, there were the grim possibilities of being accused of sorcery because of the death of some person in the village, or being killed as a sacrifice, or being used by the male population for the satisfaction of their sex instincts; but, on the other hand, there was the possibility of being chosen by a master as his wife, or being sold by him to some other man for this purpose. In such a case she had good hope of escaping a sacrificial death as long as she was faithful and obedient (Goldie 1908, 27).

---

191   Rooney, letter, 4 July 1904.

To turn from the socioeconomic to the religious aspect of slavery, slaves were held, as we have seen, against the requirement of human sacrifice. Death might come without warning at any moment. Sometimes a body was required, or a skull, or a live sacrifice. Some of these ceremonial deaths were extremely gruesome—live sacrifices buried in postholes of sacred houses, launching of great canoes over the bodies of human beings, to mention two.[192] In all these things ceremonial requirements had to be met (Woodford 1890, 155).[193] Skulls were required for sacred places and taboo houses, for funerary rites, for atonements, and for retaliation in feuds. Certain types of accident demanded human sacrifice to correct the misfortune (Brown 1910, 208).[194]

As we have already seen, behind all sacrifices was the concept of ghost worship. The ancestor had to be satisfied, in order that atonements and restitutions should be effective. For sacred houses and war canoes to be effective the sacrifices had to be adequate. The more blood spilt, the more potent the offering. This was the grim reality confronting every slave, no matter how he might have won his way into the affections of his master. His best security was to be an industrious and skilled technician.

The other religious feature of head-hunting was the acquisition of *mana*. Heads, as we have already seen, were repositories of *mana*. The number of heads held, said Penny, were "the measure of a chief's power" (1888, 46). We have also seen that any conversion required some practical demonstration such as the burial of one's accumulation of skulls. Wherever I went in Malaita, when looking at the burial grounds I was always shown the tomb without a cross where the pre-Christian skulls were buried.

Human sacrifice and skull collection represented two forms of heathen worship, two different approaches to the ghosts. The interinvolvements were so complex and the slave's fortunes were so uncertain, that his competence as a craftsman might save him one day to decorate a new war canoe, and the launching of the canoe claim him as a sacrifice on the next, or perhaps claim his head to adorn the canoe house. He may have been the son of a chief back in Choiseul or Ysabel, or he may have been bought by means of shell money made by other slaves from among his own kinsmen. By such patterns the ghosts of Roviana preserved prestige, solidarity, and superiority for the living members of the tribe and kept the lesser people in subjection. Then the white man came.

Changes Brought by the White Man

White men entered the scene seeking *beche-de-mer* and sandalwood, and later kidnapping islanders. They bought what they required with tomahawk heads, arms, and ammunition.

---

192   Both of these are also Fijian customs. For full descriptions see Knibbs (1929, 37–38) and Penny (1888, 46).
193   For example, if a pig and a human being were being offered together, they had to be of opposite sex.
194   If a workman died during the construction of a canoe, all work stopped until a human sacrifice had been offered, and the weapon used to kill the victim was placed in the bow of the canoe.

They found it most satisfactory to establish their trade connections through the regional chiefs who controlled the slaving circuits. Thus quite often these chiefs had to open new exchange contacts of their own to acquire stocks of material for the white trader, otherwise the tomahawks and arms would have fallen into the hands of lesser men. Thus the headhunters of Simbo had to procure supplies of *beche-de-mer*, ginger, and sandalwood from New Georgia for the white traders or lose the trade in arms (Angas 1865, 365). The same pattern was reported from Buin (Thurnwald 1934). Alu and Mono obtained smoke-dried copra from Siwai to supply to white traders for calico, axes, and adzes (Oliver 1955, 295–96). It is interesting to note that this new trade, which developed after 1880, followed the lines of the earlier trade in slaves. Alu and Mono obtained men and women captured by Siwai people to serve as working slaves, prostitutes, and sacrifices.

Even after controls were established to restrict the trade in arms, they were circumvented by showing arms on the ships' manifests as axes (Knibbs 1929, 44–45). Under the influence of this trade the character of raiding changed. Men could be killed from under cover and from a safe distance, and heads were easier to obtain. With the increase of firearms the manufacture of island weapons began to decline, and some of the symbiotic contacts became dispensable. Hitherto protected localities were now exposed to raiding, and some of these places near to Roviana were completely depopulated when symbiosis was no longer required by Roviana and Simbo. Wanawana, Kiso, Tetipari, and much of Kolobagara and Marova were laid waste by the headhunters of Roviana, Simbo, and Redova. Some eastern headhunters had penetrated into the mountains of Vangunu with the aid of Western arms, and the slaves exported from Siwai to the Shortlands were increasing in great numbers. The emerging master tribes were achieving their prowess by means of Western arms.

In 1891 Commander Davis of H.M.S. *Royalist* sacked and burned Roviana and destroyed the accumulation of skulls. As a result Ingava spent the next decade replenishing his stock. He exhausted his regular slaving grounds and launched a large-scale invasion on Ysabel. He used two English-built boats, hunted with five hundred men, between three hundred and four hundred of whom had rifles, and nine thousand rounds of ammunition. The fruit of this expedition was seen by the writer of my primary source—rows and rows of skulls, newly decorated and stacked round the leading canoe of the expedition (Sommerville 1897, 398–99). The captain of the *Royalist* not only failed in his purpose but stimulated an increase of the very thing he sought to correct.

This type of punitive action only made things more dangerous for the honest trader and missionary. Skulls of white men were very much in demand. Over sixty were obtained in Roviana within a few years of the arrival of the missionaries (Brown 1908, 517). In discussing *mana* I have already shown the *mana* scale of skulls that emerged in this period: a pig, a woman, a man, a warrior, a chief, a white man (Hopkins 1928, 201). Thus was the white man himself incorporated into the structure of the configuration. It also explains why certain traders were able to exert so obstructive an influence against the Missions.

Effect of the Suppression of Head-hunting by the Administration

The pattern of punitive action employed by the naval commanders was continued by the administration after the establishment of the Protectorate. Periodically a naval vessel visited the islands and accounts were "settled." The abolition of the institution of head-hunting was effected by government decree because it offended the ideals of civilised people. Traders, planters, officials, and missionaries alike were glad enough to see it go for humane and social reasons. Having said that, however, one must add that it left a void in life because of the countless social, economic, and religious involvements that were disorganised by its prohibition.

The anthropologist Rivers related the depopulation of the area to the termination of head-hunting, because it led to a loss of interest in life. In a careful analysis of this he took specific cases of head-hunting to illustrate his argument. Dealing with the factors influencing the death and birth rates at Simbo, where he worked out a number of genealogies over three generations, he found a decreasing number of marriages, a decreasing birthrate, a smaller number of children per marriage, and an increase of childless marriages, as well as an increasing death rate. Tabulating his statistics, he compared them with another Solomon Islands locality with somewhat similar general characteristics. In these localities the usually admitted reasons for depopulation were absent. There were no severe epidemics, no white residents, no missionaries, no changes of native dress or structural changes in dwelling houses, alcohol was hardly known, and there had been no kidnapping or exodus of labour force for indenture.[195]

Rivers attributed their dying out to this psychological factor, the loss of interest or zest in life. He argued that the basic cause was the suppression of head-hunting, because the whole pattern of organised life surrounded this. The Simbo and Roviana patterns were very similar. The sacrificial system, acquisition of *mana*, serving the ancestral ghosts, the ceremonials of house building, a whole year's activities round the building of war canoes, feasts, trade exchanges, funerary rites, and many craft activities were all involved. Although head-hunting expeditions lasted only a few weeks, with but a few hours of actual fighting, these were the culmination of a long period of communal activity. The canoes for the expedition had to be new and involved elaborate labour and craft organisation and a series of ceremonial feasts, which as social occasions with specific patterns stimulated horticulture, pig breeding, and the acquisition of important food through trade circuits and travel. So the abolition of head-hunting also meant the abolition of a great many social

---

195   Chapter 8 in Rivers (1922b).

functions, economic activities, and the disappearance of various crafts. These were social, religious, and ceremonial, and did represent a great deal of interest in life.[196]

There is a good deal to be said for the case presented by Rivers. All these multitudinous activities were undoubtedly tied together in a configuration, and the loss of the central feature did cause disintegration of the way of life. Undoubtedly this left what I have elsewhere called a *void*. The problem of the void arises when reformers—administrators, missionaries, teachers, doctors, or agriculturalists—remove or prohibit cultural institutions without considering the total context. Of course, head-hunting had to go. The problem was how to dispose of a bad custom without injuring the whole structure of labour, craftwork, horticulture, animal husbandry, and trade, together with their communal values and social occasions.

From this point Rivers became more theoretical, and considered the *functional substitutes* (as they are now called) that might have been tried to provide motives for the manufacture of new canoes, craft industry, and festival occasions. It is true of course, that the construction of the splendid sewn-plank canoes did die out with head-hunting. He imagined a pattern of canoe racing linked with ceremonial, fishing, and trade. He was aware that the European boat ought to replace the island canoe, and hoped that indigenous craftsmanship and labour could be attached to this trade. The essential thing was for changes to grow naturally out of native institutions and to maintain interest (Rivers 1922b, 108). In this his reasoning was good. Among the ex-Roviana people now living at Rarumana on the island of Wanawana, this is what has happened by the initiative of the people themselves. Canoe building, though greatly modified, has survived. The canoes are smaller domestic craft, dugouts not plank-sewn, but suitable to the new needs of the community. I counted seventy canoes in this spread-out village. Every household has one or more. Six households had outboard motors for use with them. The craft were built locally with tools structured as of old (i.e., adzes) but with plane blades replacing the stone heads. Local labour was used and was often available for hire. The modifications fitted the social changes of the area. Gizo has developed as a trading centre twenty miles off. Copra and other produce may be sold there for cash and trade goods bought. The small canoe with the outboard motor meets this requirement. In this village family individualism has replaced the extensive communal activity and trade exchanges. There is still an interest in life, though it has shifted from the community to the family. The modifications have come of their own accord from within the situation itself.

---

196 Ibid., 98–102. It has also been maintained that much the same situation has arisen in Choiseul because of the loss of the feuding pattern, a similar network of relationships involving economic exchanges of shell wealth, of feasting, and of facilities for the selection and development of local leadership:

It was never simply the feasting and gift exchange as such that made big men, but rather the activities which gave rise to the exchanges. Many exchanges were terminal points in series of transactions, which often began in contractual alliances between groups united in part by their support of a big man. (Scheffler 1964a, 793; 1964b, 400)

It may be difficult at first to see individuals making small domestic dugout canoes as a functional substitute for the communally organised production of a magnificent sewn-plank war canoe. Yet it may be claimed to be so because it keeps alive many of the same elements—a round of craftwork, the building of canoes that facilitate the exchange of goods, planned labour with some ceremonial affiliations—and above all it retains an interest in life and gives some satisfaction for its creativity. The foreign innovations—outboard motor, plane-blade adze, trade goods from the store—are not impositions but have been naturally incorporated into the pattern. All is within the range of practicability and meets the needs of the new situation. In this community the current tendency is for communal activity to give way to family activity. It is therefore natural for the communal ownership of two or three large canoes to give way to the private ownership of seventy. It shows that change need not necessarily upset satisfactions and create voids. Even a major cultural institution like head-hunting can be discarded without leaving a void. This can be so, as Rarumana shows, but unfortunately this is by no means typical. Furthermore the head-hunting configuration was so complex that it was possible to meet the economic needs and yet leave voids on the religious level.

Roviana Colonizing

Any study of these political outreaches of Roviana in the other islands of the Solomons would be incomplete without reference to her colonizing. To examine this we shall take the case of colonizing in Buin, because this has been carefully investigated and recorded by an anthropologist who visited the area twice and was able to observe the changes that took place in the interim. We are also interested in Buin because of its proximity to another strong trade and slaving circuit centred in the Shortlands. It says something for Roviana military strength and prestige that it could establish this colony 160 miles from home.

Connections between Roviana and Buin were social, economic, and political; they involved head-hunting and slaving, the Roviana shell-money trade, and colonization mechanisms.

The tall, black element in the Buin racial stratification can be traced to Roviana, whose pirate headhunters settled in this area, taking local women for wives like the Spanish in Latin America, and introduced many cultural features quite different from those of the Aboriginal people. Those colonizers who married local women of rank became the aristocrats of Buin society. They were spoken of as *mumira* with awe. Others married the daughters of bondsmen and were known as *minei*. They retained some status by claiming succession by patrilineal descent and also because their capacity for trade made them rich. The bondsmen were known as *kitere*. This stratification was quite stable when the white man arrived, and it was still so when Thurnwald made his first observations in 1908 (Thurnwald 1934; 1936b).

Roviana influence was evident in many features of the life of this colony, especially in their ceremonial feasting and its excesses, in the head-hunting patterns and the slave raiding and trading, and in the ritual of sacrificing to ghosts. Much of this is reflected in the secular songs of the period (Thurnwald 1936a, 14). One chief might sell a bondsman to another for one hundred fathoms of ordinary shell money, knowing that he made a worthy sacrifice. The victim would be killed after the Roviana manner, so that his head might adorn the chief's house. The ghosts of these victims were said to be ghost slaves, to serve the chief's personal war demon (Thurnwald 1936b, 349). The personal war demon (as distinct from the ghost of one's ancestor) is a Bougainville concept, so we see here a capacity for syncretism before the coming of the white man.

Among the more valuable trade brought into Buin from Roviana through this colony was that in precious necklaces, *mimici*, made of red *spondylus* shell. The shell was dived for, and the necklaces manufactured by the slave community at Roviana. The value was much higher in Buin than at Roviana, one fathom being worth twenty fathoms of ordinary shell money. These items were not used for ordinary trade or passed about in light flirtations but were reserved for marriage patterns (Thurnwald 1936a, 12). Even ordinary shell money was of economic importance in Buin, especially as exchange for pigs, which were required for feasts, which in turn were essential for the maintenance of prestige. In Buin one could enjoy the luxuries of life if he could exchange one form of wealth for another—shell money for pigs, for example (Thurnwald 1934).

When the anthropologist returned to the area twenty-five years later, he found that the administration had effected major interferences in the status pattern. A new class of chief, *kukurai*, had appeared, appointed by the government, on the basis of supposed merit, usually from the *minei*, but some even from the *kitere*. The old hamlets where the people dwelt before had been replaced largely by "lines," to simplify tax collection. This had been destructive to social taboos and made it possible for the *kitere* to look on the wife and daughter of the *mumira*. Head-hunting had been suppressed, ceremonial feasting had ceased as the aristocracy no longer had incentive to provide it—the "spice" had gone out of life in many ways. In 1920 some police "boys" had been sent in to enforce the new patterns and had been killed by the aristocrats for their interference with the established way of life. The administration executed some of the aristocrats and those who remained saw the futility of resisting the white man.

This social upheaval terminated the old head-hunting and slaving patterns and the rule of the Roviana aristocracy, and set an international political barrier between Roviana and Buin. It also permitted the rise of a new class comprising any who could exploit the situation. It was a time propitious for innovation. The mental set of the people changed. Thurnwald detected the changes in the popular songs he collected at the time—a shift from the wonders of nature, life, men, and women, to the miracles of the white man's devices and an accompanying disbelief in the old way, which now became criminal (Thurnwald 1936a, 15; 1936b, 354).

Although their tendency was now to follow the white man's way and seek his prosperity, even by using *imitative magic* to this end, this new mental set provided a readiness at least to hear the message the missionaries brought. The church became one means of access to the white man's devices. Doors for evangelism opened.

Effect on the Planting and Growth of the Church

Social factors within the head-hunting and slavery configuration influenced the character of the conversion growth of the church at several points, both aiding and obstructing it.

(1) As inhuman and unchristian customs, the missionaries were opposed to both head-hunting and slavery. This put the chiefs, priests, and warriors against them. We have already seen that the doors were not open in the Western Solomons when the mission began work there. The Methodists selected Roviana deliberately, and the Anglican bishop was surprised at the selection. The missionaries set out to undermine these customs and their supporting religion. All this was against the likelihood of conversions. The place was not interested in the gospel. The missionary faith was in terms of the challenge of the greatest needs, not the existence of open doors. Their motive was high. Their courage was great. Their faith was strong. But their strategy is to be questioned. It is to be questioned, in that the field was far from ripe unto harvest. They were correct in the assumption that Roviana was the key to a larger area—although Roviana was not loved over that area. Socially and religiously Roviana was a dominant influence over the whole of the Western Solomons, where the ghost worship and skull cults were remarkably similar.

(2) Roviana was the key to a wide area because of the head-hunting and slavery configuration. Her men were good navigators and knew their way about the islands. Having enslaved folk from all parts, they had some familiarity with many dialects and customs. Because of their symbiotic trade connections they had friendly contacts with many remote places, and ways and means of communicating. In their slave community they had many bilingual people who were available for service as interpreters. Many of the Roviana people were themselves bilingual. Roviana was certainly a key for communication. Even so, capacity to communicate does not necessarily mean acceptance. The widespread fear of Roviana was against their becoming good advocates for the new religion.

(3) We have already seen that people movements within the kin structure were slow in coming. Even after the chiefs had become resigned to the presence of the missionaries in their land, and had become superficially friendly, the regular patterns of Melanesian conversion were still slow in coming. The story is vastly different from that of Ysabel and Florida twenty years earlier. We have seen that when the conversions began to come in Roviana and the islands under Roviana influence, they were of sodalities on the mission

compounds, of persons separated from the village structure, whose conversion well-nigh wrecked the whole Christian enterprise because of the offence it gave to the tribal elders. Though these converts rendered great service thereafter, we have seen that a large percentage of them were detribalised persons, orphans, refugees, and slaves. This fact undoubtedly influenced the slave community at Roviana, though it slowed down the conversion of kin groups. There were no people movements among the slaves, because they had no family or lineage cohesion, and furthermore conversion of a village slave was a quick way of asking to be selected for the next sacrifice.

(4) However once Roviana did become Christian, the slave community immediately became a significant group for the wide communication of Christianity. Many converts returned to their own localities after manumission. Their very deliverance was itself a remarkable tale to tell.

(5) With the breakdown of the authority of the Roviana aristocracy in Buin, and the general readiness there to experiment in the new ways of the white man, the church had her opportunity. Methodist influence certainly spread in South Bougainville during this period. The first enquiries from the area led to an inspection by an island teacher, and preaching began there in 1917. There were some young men from this area among the converts at Roviana, so the mission was able to pioneer the place with its own people. They were mostly *kitere*, but the decline of the aristocrats and the rise of men of merit, regardless of status, provided an opening. One of these men pioneered church planting in twenty villages, and by 1933 almost three thousand people were at Methodist worship regularly, and education was being provided at forty-four day schools staffed by men trained at Roviana. Although the Roviana aristocracy had lost its status in Buin, the Roviana-Buin connections still provided both the men and the opportunities for planting the church.

(6) One question remains to be asked and answered. How do we account for the fact that slaves were able to introduce a new religion into animistic society, especially a dominant society with a head-hunting configuration? How were they able to act as individuals? When this angered the elders, how were they able to escape with their lives? This is really one question, which I shall try to answer from the case of Simbo, since it can be documented well. In such areas the chiefs and elders were disposed to leave much of the specifically religious activity to selected slaves, because it saved them from the risk of breaking taboos. A slave who showed signs of magical or religious capacity was more likely to be assigned to magical responsibilities than to be used as a sacrificial victim. Both Munda and Simbo were centres for the distribution of incantations, charms, and other magical devices. Ysabel charms and medicines were in great demand and also divination processes. When Hocart recorded a medicine he appended a note on its origin and purchase price, thus:

> Suna of Karivara taught Nina a headache prayer for a fee of four arm-rings.

Njukili paid Matemata of Ranonga one large ring and one arm-ring for the treatment and prayer to cure a stomach complaint, *tagosoro*.

Taravai bought a Vella Lavella cure for this same complaint for one arm-ring.
(Hocart 1925, 231–53)

Panda paid twelve rings for a war-charm. (Hocart 1931, 308)

This desirable market was not without considerable risk, and it suited the elders to keep suitable slaves to take these risks and to treat them well. The capture of slaves from a Christianised area would, to the animist headhunters, present possibilities in this direction. The elders would proceed at least with caution and would regard any Christian worship patterns with respect. Christian hymns were treated as *mana* repositories.

In his study of the Cult of the Dead at Simbo, Hocart discussed the role of the mortuary priests of the skull houses. They built and consecrated these structures on behalf of the chiefs. Although the mortuary priest belonged to the chief, the latter was very much dependent on the priest, whose post was remunerative. Of the four principal mortuaries in Simbo at the time, it is noteworthy that three were tended by foreigners. Nubui and Soge at Narovo, and Lepo at Karivara were men of Ysabel, and Rona at Ove was a native of Vella Lavella. Pero and Maro, famous Simbo magic men, were both Ysabel slaves. This shows how captive slaves who demonstrated religious propensity could establish themselves as individuals. These men brought *mana* and magical methods from Ysabel and Vella Lavella. If they did anything wrong in their rituals, they themselves ran the risk rather than the elders. To escape the dangers of foreign magic the elders were prepared to grant them status and wealth. At the same time they hoped to draw benefit from the magic. The mortuary priest wore a special protective girdle, handled the taboo skulls and other taboo paraphernalia. Any ordinary slave with knowledge of magical formulae could market these at Simbo and thereby derive enough respect to ensure his own survival. Pepele of Ysabel established himself thus, and it was from him that the Simbo magic man, Erovo, learned his arts (Hocart 1922, 105–12).

This readiness for cultural borrowing and innovation within the dimension of Roviana-Simbo magico-religion, the respect for religious foreigners, and the tendency to assign roles of religious risk to slaves, enabled the Christians to escape from the wrath of the elders and warriors. Because one more deity might even bring more *mana* to the community, which was polytheistic in any case, it was possible for individual Christians to worship and survive the period of persecution. It was Christian exclusiveness and the rejection of traditional religion which involved them in the greatest danger. But even then as religious persons they were treated with some respect. It is clear that the slaving patterns did contribute towards the eventual spread of Christianity. Unfortunately we have no way of measuring the influence of the Christian slaves, of whom there were a great many from Ysabel.

REFERENCES

Angas, G. F. 1865. *Polynesia: A popular description . . . of the islands of the Pacific.* London: Society for Promoting Christian Knowledge.

Bogesi, George. 1948. Santa Isabel, Solomon Islands. *Oceania* 18, nos. 3–4: 208–32, 327–57.

Brown, George. 1901. The Solomon Islands. Correspondence in *Australasian Methodist Missionary Review.*

———. 1908. *George Brown: Pioneer, missionary and explorer; An autobiography.* London: Hodder & Stoughton.

———. 1910. *Melanesians and Polynesians.* London: Macmillan.

Goldie, John F. 1908. The people of New Georgia: Their manners and customs, and religious beliefs. *Proceedings of the Royal Society of Queensland* 22, no. 1: 23–30.

Guppy, H. B. 1887. *The Solomon Islands and their natives.* London: Swan Sonnenschein Lowrey.

Hocart, A. M. 1922. The Cult of the Dead in Eddystone of the Solomons. *Journal of the Royal Anthropological Institute of Great Britain and Ireland* 52: 71–112, 259–305.

———. 1925. Medicine and witchcraft in Eddystone of the Solomons. *Journal of the Royal Anthropological Institute of Great Britain and Ireland* 55: 29–270.

———. 1931. Warfare in Eddystone of the Solomons. *Journal of the Royal Anthropological Institute of Great Britain and Ireland* 61: 301–24.

Hopkins, A. I. 1928. *In the isles of King Solomon.* London: Seeley, Service & Co.

Ivens, W. G. 1930. *The island builders of the Pacific.* London: Seeley, Service & Co.

Knibbs, S. G. C. 1929. *The savage Solomons as they were.* London: Seeley, Service & Co.

Oliver, Douglas L. 1955. *A Solomon Islands society: The Siuai of Bougainville.* Cambridge: Harvard University Press.

Penney, Alfred. 1888. *Ten years in Melanesia.* London: Wells Gardner, Darton & Co.

Rivers, W. H. R. 1922a. *The history of Melanesian society.* 2 vols. Cambridge: University Press.

———. 1922b. The psychological factor. In *Essays on the depopulation of Melanesia,* ed. W. H. R. Rivers, 84–113. Cambridge: University Press.

Rooney, S. R. 1904. Correspondence in *Australasian Methodist Missionary Review.*

Scheffler, Harold W. 1964a. The genesis and repression of conflict: Chiseul Island. *American Anthropologist* 66, no. 4: 789–804.

———. 1964b. The social consequences of peace on Choiseul Island. *Ethnology* 3, no. 4: 398–403.

Somerville, H. Boyle T. 1897. Ethnological notes on New Georgia. *Journal of the Royal Anthropological Institute of Great Britain and Ireland* 26: 357–412.

Thurnwald, R. C. 1934. Pigs and currency in Buin. *Oceania* 5, no. 2: 119–41.

———. 1936a. The price of the white man's peace. *Pacific Affairs* 9, no. 3: 347–57.

———. 1936b. *Profane literature of Buin, Solomon Islands.* New Haven: Yale University Press.

Woodford, Charles M. 1890. *A naturalist among the head-hunters.* London: George Phillip.

28

THE FIJI INDIAN COMMUNITY AND ITS CHURCH:
An Open Door[197]

The first Indians came to Fiji towards the end of the period of evangelisation, when only the hill tribes remained to be won and but five years after the measles epidemic which robbed the church of hundreds of its best indigenous workers. They came as labour for the cotton and sugar fields, more particularly the latter, and were not regarded as of ethnic significance at first. It was quite some time before it became apparent that a new race had been introduced into the colony. It was a bad trade and thoroughly open to abuse. The best we can say of it is that it did help develop Fiji and that it was some improvement on its predecessor. There are some who would try to "whitewash" it, but the documentation is as damning as it is considerable.[198] It is not so much our requirement to investigate this; I accept it as historically proven. Its relevance to us is to indicate that the people from whom the Indian church grew were, to a large extent, people who had been deeply wronged. Besides these, however, there were a little later a number of free Indians. During the 1860s and 1870s a constant flow of New Hebrideans, Solomon and Line Islanders (and many others) entered the country. They had mostly been kidnapped. After Cession the trade was more controlled and repatriation was taken more seriously. These foreign labour groups were scattered about the Group, sometimes in little colonies of three or four hundred.[199] When the first Indians arrived, there were still some 8,500 of these Melanesians encamped on Fijian plantations (Burton 1910, 28). Nor was the church unmindful of them, and those scattered about the Lau plantations had regular worship services provided for them by the Fijians.[200] Where they were more scattered or in smaller groups the Fijians opened their own worship services to them. At Levuka many of them, mostly from Santo, but also other strangers from Polynesian islands, joined in Fijian worship up to 1883,[201] and somewhere between there and 1886 special provisions were made for the Santo islanders and a Fijian

---

197   Taken from "The Fiji Indian Community and Its Church" (unpublished manuscript, 1962), 1–15.
198   Andrews (1937), Garnham (1918), Burton (1910), all primary sources and critical appraisals of actual facts.
199   Mago figures (Cooper's plantation).
200   Annual Report, Lau/Lomaloma 1883.
201   Annual Report, Ovalau 1883.

catechist was appointed to care for them in the interests of the Presbyterian Church.[202] The missions took comity seriously. By the next report the Fijian had a school organised for them.[203] By 1890 it had become more interracial. There had been clear conversions and one Santo man had become a preacher, another and also a Pentecost Islander had become preachers on trial.[204] A planter named Storck, living on an island in the Rewa River, had opened his plantation to religious services for the labour (Pritchard 1886), and islanders from New Britain in Rewa were sufficiently numerous to warrant the appointment of a Fijian minister, who had done service in New Britain for nine years and had just returned.[205]

The first Indian indentured labourers were cast into this scene—498 of them in 1879 from all over north and central India (Gillion 1956, 46). Outnumbered by more than seventeen to one, they were absorbed without much notice into the already heterogeneous foreign labour community. Nine hundred and twenty-two arrived in 1882–1833; 1,514 in the statistical year 1883–1884; and in the year following 2,316. Thus by 1885, a larger portion of the last number had been absorbed in the Rewa plantations, where the Colonial Sugar Refining Company opening with overseas capital.[206] Bromilow, the resident missionary, pressed the claim of the Indians for a full-time missionary, to work in their language.[207] At least he obtained a full-time Fijian appointment by 1887, but the response was up and down. Bromilow travelled about visiting the mills and sugar estates and tried preaching to the Indians in English. Lindsay, from Navuloa, gave some assistance in this (Reed 1888, 63), and the missionary at Viwa kept in touch with the three mills along the north coast of Viti Levu as far as Ba. He held services both in English and Fijian and reported to his home church that this was ineffective—a full-time man was needed for Indian work in one of their languages.[208] The Bau Circuit also reported in that year (1887) that eighty-nine persons (mostly Indians) were worshipping with the Fijian people on Sundays.[209]

These archival references show that the missionaries were now aware of the truth that the Indian had become a permanent element in the Fijian mosaic, and that he represented both a danger to the Fijian work itself and an opportunity for evangelism. This had been recognised and discussed in 1885 at the jubilee celebrations of the Fijian Mission, and the missionaries pressed their claims with the church leaders who visited Fiji for the celebrations. Nothing eventuated. They had asked for a worker to learn the Hindustani language or an agent from India. A year later James Calvert, the old missionary warrior, visited Fiji and was commissioned by Langham, the chairman in Fiji, to negotiate with the chairman

---

202   Annual Report, Ovalau 1886.
203   Annual Report, Ovalau 1887.
204   Annual Report, Ovalau 1890.
205   Annual Report, Rewa 1885.
206   Opened 18 August 1882.
207   Annual Report, Rewa l887.
208   Annual Report, Viwa 1887.
209   Annual Report, Bau 1887.

of the Lucknow and Benares District for the appointment of an Indian catechist to Fiji.[210] This was done with the approval of the Fiji government,[211] and John Williams, a Methodist catechist from Dilkusha, Lucknow, left in April 1892,[212] and was received by Beauclerc, a Methodist layman, in Suva, 8 July, and introduced to the Indian work there. He was then taken by Worral, the Rewa missionary, and they travelled round the Rewa and Nausori areas visiting the Indian settlements. He preached in the lines, and sometimes in Fijian churches and in the gaol, and a short time after his arrival he had twenty-five persons ready for baptism.[213] His contract was for three years, and after its completion he returned to India.[214]

The experiment had been successful in as much as he came to the area, visited the "homes" of the people, and conversed with them in their own language, and preached in public buildings and on plantations as far as Ba and Labasa.[215] On the other hand his wife was ill and returned leaving him alone to complete his contract, and he had considerable trouble in making himself understood in English. There were misunderstandings, but no one can read the letters he wrote without feeling that the man had more than the missionaries who came a decade later acknowledged. He won converts and brought them to baptism. He was not replaced. The district renewed its efforts for a full-time missionary for Indian work. The local church, not the home church, had carried the responsibility of the catechist experiment.

In Fiji a change came about 1890 when the time-expired labourers were becoming a problem. Some turned out to be good settlers, others were a public nuisance and their presence was felt in some of the Fijian communities. Some of the missionaries became alarmed. The synod of 1891 urged the home church to do something about the situation. It has been stated that John Williams was appointed in response to this resolution, but this is a misunderstanding—the Fijian church itself acted on its own in that respect. All the time Williams was at work, they were still pressing the board for action. In May 1893 *The Spectator*, the Australian Methodist paper in Melbourne, then enjoying its heyday under the editorship of Dr. Lorimer Fison, printed an article on the Fijian Indians by Henry Worral. It spoke of bands of "indolent and dissolute" time-expired labourers wandering along the coasts getting into trouble, and of complications caused through the arrival of so many indentured labourers, and pointed out that the only way of saving the young converts of Fiji from this "subcutaneous injection of old-world heathenism" was by converting them. Fison's editorial comment was, "More than one of our friends in Fiji, laymen as well

---

210   Agreement, Methodist Overseas Mission Archives, 18 March 1892.
211   Colonial Secretary, Methodist Overseas Missions Archives, 4 December 1888.
212   Parsons/Broadhead, 26 April 1892.
213   Williams' Report, 1892.
214   Agreement, 18 March 1892.
215   Williams/Langham, 23 November 1893.

as missionaries, have written to us privately on this matter. It is evidently a very serious question" (*The Spectator*, 19 May 1893).

In 1894 at the general conference in Adelaide the missionary administration drew attention to reports on the Indian question, whereupon Rev. A. J. Webb moved:

> That in view of the fact that 10,000 Coolies are in Fiji and are exercising a serious influence on the Fijians the Mission Board be directed to take what steps are possible for the evangelization of the Coolies in Fiji, and that it places itself in communication with the British Conference with a view to securing a suitable agent to labour among the people.

This was carried.[216] It had taken three years for the 1891 resolution to get this far. Meantime the missionaries went on carrying the load as an adjunct as far as possible. As a result of the general conference resolution Worral prepared a special report with the necessary data for promotional purposes. Nothing happened.

A person named Joseph Jacobs worked with the Indians. I imagine from indirect comments that he was a worker found locally, but there is no direct evidence. By April 1896 Worral wrote with some impatience to the board: "You have never said a word about our Indian Mission, neither have you printed the Annual Report I wrote of it for 1894. We have an adult and a children's school now for them."[217]

Five months later he wrote again:

> Joseph Jacobs still pegs away at the Indians but nothing much is being done. The General Conference was going to communicate with the authorities of the Indian Mission on this subject. What has been done? We shall accomplish nothing in this Indian work till we have a European who will take it up. It can be done but not in the way we are fooling with it. We must turn the steam on, for it is madness to try to work the engines by turning the cranks with our hands. (Underlining his)[218]

A year later the board appointed Miss Dudley, the first full-time European to work among the Indian people (1897). She was followed by Messrs. Bavin (1901) and Burton (1902).

The first phase lasted about two decades. It was a decade of open doors and lost opportunities. The statement made by Bavin that the Indian people were "20 years in Fiji before any definite effort was made to win them to Christ" is neither true nor fair (Bavin 1914, 190). Worral, Burns, Bromilow, Small, and Langham had made what efforts could be made in English and Fijian. Fijians Bunoa, Soqo, and Seru had been segregated for work among them together with other labourers; Beauclerc, a layman, had organised a night school in Suva; catechist Williams had been introduced from India at local expense, and

---

216   *Worral's Notebook*, Methodist Overseas Mission Archives (Sydney, 1896), 295.
217   Worral/Brown, 23 May 1896, Methodist Overseas Mission Archives (Sydney), 165, 36.
218   Worral/Brown, 22 September 1896, Methodist Overseas Mission Archives (Sydney), 165, 36.

Jacobs had carried on after him. The missionaries had certainly called out for help from the home church.

We know that there had been converts. Williams had converts, quite a number of them[219]; and some of the Fijian workers also had had converts from among the Indians (Langham 1885, 21).

There is no doubt that a great door was open and not greatly used. The Indian labourers were, I believe, more winnable at that time than they have ever been since. By crossing over the sea they had lost their caste. By the mode of transport, their being herded together, the food distribution, the mixing of language and caste, and the tasks they had been forced to perform, and the general disillusionment which accompanied the breakdown of custom and the bitterness of the trickery behind their indenture, their broken homes and virtue, and the disgrace which led to so many suicides even during the voyage before they reached Fiji, certainly made them receptive to any line of hope (Andrews 1937).[220]

Had the opening been taken up with vigour, undoubtedly there was great growth that might have been won. The failure of the mission board to take up the challenge, and when they did nothing, the failure of the district to set aside one of its own European staff for the project calls for comment.

For some reason or other the board of missions seems to have been most reluctant to start work among the Indians of Fiji. Unfortunately I have been unable to locate any statement or document that says why. From indirect references I am led to believe that the focus of the Church in Australia was on two great issues which rather left the Fiji Indian question as a matter of lesser count. In 1891 the new mission to Papua was commenced. It was the largest scale project the Wesleyans had yet attempted, and with the Congregationalists, Anglicans, and Roman Catholics, and government support it was started on the basis of comity. To make the effort demanded by Sir William MacGregor put a tremendous load on the home church and the older island fields. It was the major appeal of the decade

---

219   For example, see Williams' Report, 1892, where twenty-five of his converts were prepared for baptism. He preached to a congregation of four hundred in Suva, who came of their own volition, and whose representatives eventually urged the chairman to leave him stationed there as their pastor (letter, 11 July 1892). These represented eight of the four hundred who were already Christians. His house congregations varied from ten to thirty. He reported nine converts in gaol, eleven at Suva, and five at Nausori on another occasion. He disposed of religious literature and was often given donations for the work.

220   Even as late as 1912, when things were under tighter control because of public criticisms, of the 3,428 emigrants, twenty-seven either died or were listed as missing on the voyage, twenty-two died in the Suva depot, and nine in the hospital, and eighteen suicides (pp. 26–27, 56); children of eleven and twelve were imported as "adults" and forced to become indentured (p. 5); 80 percent of cases investigated revealed deceit on the part of the recruiting agent, who was paid at so much per head, and often represented himself as a government official (p. 10); a Hindu, a Musalman, and a Kabir Panthi set to work together in a butchery cutting up meat (p. 15); the Sardars arranged the location of the women in the lines according to payment (p. 20); abandoned and honourable women were thrown together (p. 26); the prostitute class was considered necessary to make the indenture system work (p. 29); and the women were regulated per male to this end. Suicides in Fiji were twenty times greater per million than in India, and murder eighty times.

and the full force of promotional effort was directed towards it. New Britain and New Ireland had been commenced in the 1870s, now Papua, and considerable pressure was being exerted by the Solomon Islanders for another mission in that group. The latter was ruled out because of comity agreement. Whatever criticism may be made against the missionary administration for failing to take up the Indian call from Fiji, it cannot be put down to lack of interest or fear of a new project. The church was missionary minded and expanding—but her mind was on the thrust into Melanesia and in particular, New Guinea.

Politically, New Guinea was heavy thunder in Australia during those years. For many years Australia pressed for annexation, and her major fear was Germany. Repeated attempts were made to break down the opposition of the British government to intervention in New Guinea. Sir Arthur Gordon, British high commissioner, stationed in Fiji, sought a reserve power to annex New Guinea, should events make it necessary. Public meetings were held in New South Wales, and Queensland was even more outspoken. Faced by prolonged inaction on the part of the colonial office, Queensland took possession of Port Moresby in 1883; Great Britain refused to ratify the action, though the other Australian Colonies sided with Queensland. These were tense days in Australia, when Britain's "minimum intervention policy" was the most unpopular public issue. When Germany's assurances proved valueless and the *Neu-Guinea Kompagnia* raised the German flag over New Britain and Northern New Guinea, the British government had to face a blaze of fiery criticism from Australia.[221] At this moment Bromilow was, for the first time, pressing for a full-time European for Indian work in Fiji. It was a faint cry. The eyes and ears of Australia were on New Guinea. The power adjustments of 1885 and 1886 left Australia with specific responsibilities in Papua, and for the next fifteen years she was more inclined to look in that direction than towards Fiji.

New Guinea was considered the area of immediate concern, and whether history should determine this to have been a sound or unsound appraisal, it certainly thrust the Indian problem of Fiji into the background.

There was another matter which also occupied the concern of Australian Methodists during that last decade of the century; namely, that of Church Union. The new century brought the Methodist Church of Australasia into being. The *Lotu* Web came from the Wesleyan Methodist Church. Union brought in the Primitive Methodists, Free Methodist, and Bible Christian communities. The movement for union had occupied a prominent place for a number of years, with negotiations and ironing out of obstructions—more particularly from the church trustees than the people—with referenda and other focal points of interest. It all tended to the view that it was not time for establishing a new mission. New Guinea was being attended to, there was a strong Fijian church in Fiji, which could keep

---

221 For a concise but thoroughly documented statement of these relationships see Ward (1848, 311–23).

its eye on the situation, until such time as union was organically effected, and the church would be able to go into the matter of a mission to the Fiji Indians. If this kind of feeling was abroad in the home church, we can understand the reluctance of the board to begin still another venture in the 1890s.

Furthermore, if we can take the general development of the mind of Dr. George Brown, the board secretary, as reflected in the various activities in which he engaged over his long career, he most probably felt rather strongly that the Fijian church itself ought to be caring for this matter. It was Brown who pushed outside evangelism on the Fijians in the 1870s, and increased the pressure again in 1891, and after the turn of the century literally forced lay representation on the Fijian church—an issue which completely divided the European missionary company in Fiji. For thirty years Brown's attitude towards Fiji was to make the local church carry more responsibility. Based on what we know of his mind over the period, I think it likely that Brown would have replied to those appeals by throwing the load back on the local church. Not until the number of Indians in Fiji was over ten thousand is there any indication that he brought the matter before conference. Now in the light of this, and in the knowledge of the strength of the European staff in Fiji, and the strength of the indigenous ministry, I cannot see why they could not have set aside one of those Europeans as a full-time man for Indian work. The Bau, Rewa, Navuloa, and Viwa stations were all occupied and sufficiently close to permit the appointment of a first Fijian circuit superintendent. An opening for constitutional development was lost, which would also have freed a European for full-time Indian work. However, these were days when status counted as much for the European as indigene, when standards were perfectionist and puritan, when severe discipline was applied for very minor matters. The character of the late Victorian Age imposed itself on Fiji, heaven preaching gave way to hell-fire, church forms changed from the cultural pattern in a number of cases to the forms of the puritanical West, and many of the missionaries just did not believe the Fijian leaders were capable of carrying superintendent positions—the paternalistic attitude still existed in Fiji when I arrived many years later. If ever a case of urgent need for strategic restationing of staff existed in Fiji, it was in the 1890s; and because it was allowed to pass, an open door was allowed to close.

Blacket says that the Indian church in Fiji sprang from the ancient church in India itself and that many of the earlier accounts of the mission suffer by the failure of the writers to recognise this, by presenting Miss Dudley as the founder and ignoring that she built on a foundation which she found awaiting her (Blacket 1960, 3).[222] Those who came out from India as Christians were indeed few. It is doubtful if they numbered a score by Williams'

---

222 Blacket points out that the immigration statistics from Calcutta 1879–1916 shows a small percentage as already Christian. The percentage was 0.1 percent (Gillion 1956, 152) and, if related to Table 1 (ibid., 143), this represents only about sixty persons over thirty-seven years and widely distributed in Fiji. The Indian roots seem to have been rather slight. This does not allow for South Indian connections.

day, nor is there any evidence of leadership or Christian community among them. Williams travelled round making contacts in the "world" and getting his converts there. It is, however, quite true that Miss Dudley did have something, however small, to start work on. However her work was more sedentary, and her arrival did not solve the problem of handling the openings on the labour fields and at the milling centres. It wasn't until the arrival of Bavin that any serious attack was possible on this. In these places also some previous contact, however slight, had been made. Of the four hundred Indians who came to hear Williams in Suva upon his arrival, eight had some Christian affiliation. Some of the free Indians had been Christians in India, and were to play important parts in the young church, but on the whole very little came from India itself.

Another point made by Blacket is that the failure of the early efforts to produce much growth was due to the initial policy of building a mission on the work of catechists. In the case of Williams, he says the conditions were not properly explained to him, and he found Fiji very different from India, he faced frustrations because of his poor English and his misunderstandings with his superintendent—all of which is quite true. Then Blacket adds—short-term contracts with provisions for return to India were unsettling. In the years that followed, this became a typical pattern; men found it difficult to settle down and adapt themselves to a situation so different from that at home (1960, 8). Blacket knows Indians and he knows Fiji, so we are bound to note his feeling at this point. On the other hand, many Indian catechists, of less educational standing than Williams, have proved good church builders,[223] and we remember the point Blacket is pressing is not concerning Williams himself, but the policy of mission—or church building on the work of catechists, which remained a policy of the mission until as late as 1925, and perhaps some of the feelings of later days have been projected out of historic context at this point. Clearly Williams did not have an easy time, he was misunderstood and frustrated, but he was a good evangelist with a good knowledge of the non-Christian religions, who by discussions, hymn singing, preaching, and prayer, did win converts.[224] His work was mobile, and as he went he sold Christian literature. In his first year he was pressing the missionary to come and perform marriages, and had asked for baptismal, burial, and school registers[225]; he explored new work in hospitals and other public places,[226] acquired a pass for entrance into plantations where Indians were at work,[227] and no one can read his 1894 report without feeling that under his broken English lay a real experience and sense of mission.[228] When one digests this correspondence whole, one feels that whatever the cause of failure, it wasn't

---

223   For example, the movement among the Garas in Orissa came from the efforts of a catechist (McGavran, 1956, 14).
224   Williams' Report, 1894.
225   Williams/Langham, 3 August 1892.
226   Williams/Langham, 8 February 1893.
227   Williams/Langham, 1 March 1893.
228   Williams' Report, 1894.

the catechist. Had the Fijian church assigned one of its best Europeans to full-time work among the Indians about 1885, when Bromilow was first pressing for such an appointment, there probably would have been a Christian church of some thousands among the Fiji Indians by the end of the century. The records from which I have formed this opinion are widely scattered in Fiji, in Sydney, in libraries, missionary journals, and private collections, and in documents relative to indenture. For about a decade and a half from 1885 the door was wide open, and the Indian mental set was receptive.

As a result of Worral's efforts, Miss Dudley was appointed. She established herself in Suva under the chairman of the district. Beauclerc, the layman, had been working there before with his night school. Synod, 1899, pressed for a male appointment, and a lay missionary Bavin was appointed to Rewa, under the chairman, not under the Rewa superintendent. Burton, the first ministerial appointment, came the following year to Davuilevu, also under the chairman.

It will have been noticed that the above appointments were all placed under the chairman of the district. There was apparently a fixed intention that this should be a separate work and not tied up with that of the Fijian church. During 1902 the organisation had taken definite shape with Burton at Nausori, an orphanage at Suva, and a sister at Ba. By 1903 Burton was superintendent and was employing an evangelist, Daniel Nisamuddin. By 1905 the work had expanded into two circuits—Nausori and Lautoka.

REFERENCES

Andrews, C. F. 1937. *India and the Pacific*. London: George Allen and Unwin.

——, and W. W. Pearson. 1918. *Indian labour in Fiji*. Perth: Colourtype.

Annual Reports. 1833–90. Various circuits. Sydney: Methodist Overseas Missions Archives.

Bavin, C. 1914. The Indian in Fiji. In *A century in the Pacific*, ed. J. Colwell, 175–97. London: Charles H. Kelly.

Blacket, Arthur H. 1960. *The growth of the Indian church in Fiji within the mission of the Methodist Church of Australasia*. Multigraphed publication.

Burton, John W. 1910. *The Fiji of today*. London: Charles H. Kelly.

——. 1944. *Brown and white in the Pacific*. Sydney: Australian Institute of International Affairs.

Colonial Secretary. 1888. Correspondence. Sydney: Methodist Overseas Missions Archives.

Garnham, F. E. 1918. *Report on the social and moral conditions of Indians in Fiji*. Sydney: Kingston.

Gillion, K. L. 1956. The sources of Indian emigration to Fiji. *Population Studies* 10, no. 2: 139–57.

Langham, F. 1885. *Ai Tukutuku ni Lotu e Viti*. Jubliee volume. Viwa, Fiji: Methodist Missionary Press.

McGavran, Donald A. 1956. *Church growth in West Utkal*. Indianapolis: United Christian Missionary Society.

Methodist Overseas Missions Archives. 1892. Agreement. Sydney: Methodist Overseas Missions Archives. Item 238.

———. 1892–94a. Williams' correspondence. Sydney: Methodist Overseas Missions Archives.

———. 1892–94b. Williams' report. Sydney: Methodist Overseas Missions Archives.

———. 1896a. Worral's correspondence. Sydney: Methodist Overseas Missions Archives.

———. 1896b. Worral's notebook. Sydney: Methodist Overseas Missions Archives.

Pritchard, W. T. 1866. *Polynesian reminiscences*. London: Chapman and Hall.

Reed, William. 1888. *Wanderings in Fiji*. London: Woolmer.

The Spectator. 1893. Melbourne.

Ward, J. M. 1848. *British policy in the South Pacific (1786–1893)*. Sydney: Australian Publishing.

29
PIONEER MISSIONARIES AMONG THE AUSTRALIAN ABORIGINES[229]

It is often suggested that the church neglected the Australian Aborigines[230] until it was too late. The world certainly says so, and perhaps the judgment is just. The purpose of this paper is not to defend the Australian Conferences, but to investigate what had been done in this respect prior to their separation from the British Conference, a matter which I think has not been written up by any historian over the last forty years and is therefore in danger of being forgotten altogether.

It seems to the writer that we owe this in fairness to the pioneers, to clear them of this criticism which we must undoubtedly take unto ourselves.

It would have been a remarkable thing if all the pioneer missionaries to Australia, appointed by the British Conference, had "passed by on the other side," because so many of them had come from other mission fields and had already served races other than their own. They were men of very wide experience plucked from fruitful labours In Ceylon, South Africa, Newfoundland, Sierra Leone, and other places.

When the Australian staff at work among both settlers and convicts was but three (Leigh, Lawry, and Carvosso), these men had all pressed the claim of the Aborigines. Let me quote Leigh on the matter:

> If the Methodist Conference should think it right to send a zealous, holy, patient and persevering missionary to be devoted entirely to the native tribes, I have no doubt that he would be gladly received and well supported by the inhabitants of the colony.

Furthermore the British church rose to the occasion and appointed the Rev. William Walker as a full-time missionary to the Australian Aborigines. By 1821 the station sheet read:

> Sydney, Parramatta & Windsor—Erskine, Mansfield and Horton, also William Walker, who is to devote his labours entirely to the black natives.

---

229 Taken from "Miscellanea: 1950–1960" (unpublished manuscript, 1961).
230 [We have used a consistent spelling for the term "Aborigine" through this article with the exception of direct quotations.—Ed.]

Van Diemen's Land—Carvosso
New Zealand—Leigh, White
Friendly Islands: Lawry, One to be sent.

The New South Wales Mission

William Walker arrived at Sydney Cove on 16 September 1821—a Sunday. Within a few days he had made contacts with the natives and his real work had begun. By 19 October Leigh was able to write that they were "encouraged to hope that his mission would succeed."

The tribe with whom he began work had quite a smattering of English, and conversation was thus made easier. Sometimes, however, there were misunderstandings, which ended in laughter; whereupon the patriarch of the tribe would rebuke them:

> You no laugh when Mr. Walker speaks to you . . .You mind what he speaks . . . Mr. Walker come to do black man good . . . Mr. Walker our parson . . . We must be good, no get drunk, no swear; you young people mind book, old people no like book, very good young people learn the good book.

So, Leigh, who gives us this episode adds:

> The serious people of the colony are much pleased with commencement of our mission among this race of heathens, and some, have already come forward with their subscription towards its support.

Benilong, an Australian, who had some time before been taken to England, was a native of this tribe, but had since died. Leigh showed them his portrait, which they recognised and over which they wept much. Walker did not miss the opportunity to contact. No doubt, in their own way, they respected him and wanted to follow, but the greatest hindrance we have already observed in the words of their old chief. The thing which absolutely ruined them was the white man's liquor. Let us hear Walker himself on the subject:

> They are very idle and vagrant; and the colonists too often encourage their vices. If they cut wood or do any other trifling work, they are rewarded with what they call "bull," sometimes this is composed of a mixture of spirituous liquors, and at others it is the washing of liquor-puncheons. When they are permitted, they take a bucket of boiling water, and put it in the puncheon, where they agitate it until it has drawn out the strength of the liquor. They then surround the puncheon, drinking until they are intoxicated. Quarrelling ensues, and if ever incarnate devils appeared in this world, surely the natives are at such times their representatives.

He goes on to tell how on one occasion when returning to Sydney from the Native Institution, which was at Paramatta, he fell in with a tribe of these revellers and was recognised by them. Fearing they would meet a band of convicts and there would be a general fight, he led them off into the bush:

So much wanton barbarity I never witnessed. The men would take their wad-
dies, which are made of hard wood, about three feet long, and four or five inches
in circumference at the end, and strike the heads of their women with such
violence that I expected nothing less than the death of some of them, as the
husbands stood up to defend their wives. When one man lifted up his waddy to
strike another, I stepped in between them. I then turned round and found another bleeding most profusely. Before I had wiped away the blood from the head
of one, another would be in danger. I declared I would not live with so quarrel-
some a people. This produced a clamour, which made the woods ring, and all
vociferated, "Parson do stay," a hundred times repeated.

All the men who worked among the Aborigines met with this same problem, but few
have left a better picture of the issues involved than that just quoted. It shows how liquor
craving took hold of them, and how the facilities were provided by the white people, and
what a hopeless wreck it made of Christian work. With the possible exception of their nomadic habits, there was no greater cause of failure in the early pioneering days.

We have also had reference to the Native Institution at Paramatta. Now though I have
not seen it so stated in black and white, I believe that institution must have been in existence before the arrival of William Walker. This is implied by certain references he makes
to it in his early correspondence, and that being so we must assume that Leigh did more
than just appeal for a man to work among the blacks—he actually started the work. That
may be open to dispute as the government had a native institution, and this may be responsible for confusion in references. If this be the explanation, then the missionaries did
work in the government institution.

Girls from the Paramatta institution had married into a rather wild tribe which lived
in the vicinity of South Creek, some twenty-eight miles from Sydney. Walker found their
small settlement of poor huts and made his contacts explaining the reason for his visit.
He distributed a number of presents he had taken—garments—and asked the women, who
had learned to read in the institution, to produce their Bibles. They read together from the
fourth Gospel, and he attempted to catechise them, addressing himself first always to the
chief. He then gave general advice and prayed with them.

So the work began, and so it went on. But the tribes were small, and they were widely
scattered, and furthermore they were too nomadic. There were cases of conversions and
they were generally well received, but true identification was impossible because of these
nomadic habits. Walker at one stage seriously contemplated going and living with the
South Creek natives. We cannot wonder that results were few.

Shortly there was a move by the LMS [London Missionary Society] to open up the
Moreton Bay area on the Brisbane River, and a missionary with South Sea Island experience was designated for the project. This was approved by the Press, which also pointed

out that the Wellington Valley also called out for similar attention. A young man who had been an instructor of the natives in the institution was sent by the governor to seek information about the tribes there, and after doing this in a most satisfactory manner, knowing something of their language, he was appointed as an assistant missionary and sent back to them. A native school that had been established at Black Town was doing good work. The native teacher worked his way down to Jervis Bay, and forty miles beyond, and contacted new tribes whose language he did not know—a cleaner, healthier, and kindlier people than those who lived within range of civilisation.

It is essential for us to realise that about this time there was a deep sense of responsibility towards the native, and regrets for the miry record of the past. This was as early as 1827. Threlkeld took his job seriously and did much very good research and attempted translations. This was the LMS man, but his work, like our own, crashed because of its mobile requirements, wide areas, and no great concentration of native peoples. Neither the LMS nor the WMS [Wesleyan Missionary Society] could finance this. Government and settlers' help, though good, was not enough. Then in 1828, the New South Wales Mission to the black people terminated, or as the committee resolution expressed it, "suspended," assigning the reasons:

> the numerous obstacles opposed to its efficient operation by the habits and circumstances of the natives themselves, and the very great expense that would be incurred by the adoption of any vigorous or extensive plan for localizing the tribes and bringing them under constant and regular instruction.

The government spent thousands of pounds and likewise got nowhere. The native nomadic character was ingrained. They did not like institutional life. The things of the white man they absorbed most readily were his evil forces. Even the native teacher had no more success than his white friends.

Let us glance then at Van Diemen's land.

In Van Diemen's Land

The white man's record in Van Diemen's Land is grim as far as dealing with the Aborigines is concerned. The Tasmanian race has long been extinct. Very little is known about it. Here is a brief description left by Leigh:

> The Aborigines have a better appearance than the natives of New South Wales. They are black, with wooly hair; their limbs are small; their bodies are exceedingly thin, arising no doubt, from the poverty of their diet. They live by hunting, and have no knowledge of the arts. They decorate their fleecy locks with the teeth of kangaroo, pieces of wood, or the feathers of birds. They draw a circle around each eye, and waved lines down each arm, thigh, and leg, which give them a most savage appearance. In summer they wear no clothing; in winter

males and females dress themselves in the skings of the kangaroo. They believe in the existence of two spirits; the one good, the other bad. When they are on a journey, they sing in honour of the good spirit, for the purposeof securing his protection. Their voices are sweet, and their melody simple and expressive.

Leigh wrote that in 1821—a most important statement, which throws light on several points not at all well known. For our immediate purpose we learn from other comments that there had already been converts among the Aborigines in Van Diemen's Land, and also that the first missionaries had set out to get some idea of the religious notions of the natives as a starting point for their own labour.

During that year there were increases in the Wesleyan Society: some thirty-four members and a congregation of three hundred and a Sunday School opened that year in May, at the Argyle Street Wesleyan Chapel in Hobart Town, beginning with twenty-three scholars. Services were also held at New Norfolk. By August Leigh made a survey of the state of affairs in Van Diemen's Land, and his report shows, among other things, the sympathy and support of Lieutenant Governor Sorell, and lists the white settlements throughout the island. Clearly the work was in its infancy. Two missionaries were at work there, stationed 120 miles apart, contacting thirty-five settlements and other outposts, but except at Hobart Town, there was not any point of great concentration.

An interesting letter written by one of them a year later shows the roving nature of their work, which was done on horseback. I read of their attempts at establishing adult classes for teaching reading and writing and am impressed with the similarities of the early work in the Australian outback with that in the Pacific Islands. Among the more literate, tracts were freely used, and Horton began fortnightly services in the hospital and gaol. Small services were held in scattered farmhouses as he travelled from place to place. The moral state of the place may be judged by Horton's statement:

> In the District of New Norfolk, inferior in population only to Hobart Town, there
> have been but two natural deaths, since it was first inhabited! The rest have
> been killed by accidents or hard drinking. Indeed, deaths by drunkenness are
> numerous to an awful and alarming degree, throughout the country.

The records clearly establish that fact that two itinerant preachers could do very little against the specious forces released by the white man in the island. The amazing thing is that they accomplished what they did. Horton appealed for assistance, but for the time it was not available.

Though appointed to work among the white settlers and townships, he did not ignore the Aborigines. In another communication he writes,

> They are in every respect the most destitute and wretched portion of the hu-
> man family . . . Miserable, then, as is their present condition, we know that it
> is capable of improvement, and humanity and religion require the strenuous

efforts of our benevolence to raise these degraded beings into men: yea, justice
itself demands that we who have taken possession of their native soil, and driv-
en them from its most fertile districts, should now extend to them our fostering
care, to preserve their race from extinction, and to impart to them the blessings
of civilization and religion.

That appeal to humanity, religion, and justice was printed in Britain. It is illuminating
in several respects. It is an appeal for more labourers for the work, but more than this it
shows the mind of the early ministers regarding humanity, however degraded in terms of
brotherhood and family. Men of this mind did not bypass the Aborigines. It is also illuminating in respect to what was happening to the natives—dispossessed of their coastal and
river-flat hunting grounds, they were migrating further inland and further away from the
missionary.

Horton himself made contacts with the natives living in the vicinity of Pitt-Water.
Settlers spoke of them as the Tame Gang, because of their inoffensive habits, in contrast
with the hostility of those who came down from time to time from the bush. This tribe
comprised between twenty and thirty of each sex, and of varying ages. They were not a
normal tribe but a collection of natives who had absconded from other tribes for various
reasons. Their leader was actually a Port Jackson native, named Muskitoo, who had been
transported some years earlier from Sydney to Van Diemen's Land for murder. Horton
throws more light on their habits:

> This party, like the rest of their race, never work, nor have any settled place of
> abode, but wander about from one part to another, subsisting on what is given
> to them by the benevolent and on kangaroos, opossums, oysters, etc., which
> they procure for themselves. They lodge in all seasons around their fires in the
> open air. Though they have now been accustomed for several years to behold
> the superior comforts and pursuits of civilized man, they have not advanced
> one step from their original barbarism. All that they have imbibed from us is a
> smattering of our language, and a fondness for tobacco and spirituous liquors.

That is a perfectly typical missionary reference, and many others could be found to
quote. As in New South Wales, so in Van Diemen's Land, here were the problems of working
among the early Aborigines—no fixed place of abode and no desire for one, and a great love
only for liquor and tobacco among the things the white man brought.

Horton gives us further details of the Tame Gang (valuable to the anthropologist)—
they smeared their bodies with red gum and fat, some were tattooed on the shoulders,
many were infected with a form of scurvy. He describes some of their hunting and cooking
habits, and episodes which throw light on their reasoning; he questioned them on many
points of religion, but got little information in this respect—possibly because they were a
new and composite tribe, held together by the power of Muskitoo rather than tribal rites.

On the issue of settling down to a fixed place of abode and cultivating the land, Horton pressed Muskitoo, who said he himself wouldn't mind trying it, but he felt none of the tribe would support him in such a project.

Again Horton appealed to England for a full-time missionary for the Van Diemen's Land natives, and the lieutenant governor promised assistance. Horton felt Muskitoo's tribe would make a good starting place and that through them access might be had to the interior. But no full-time missionary was ever appointed to work among them, though Horton's appeal was published for the Wesleyan people of Britain to read, and Horton's prophecy was eventually fulfilled—the race became extinct. But let it not be overlooked that the few missionaries appointed to the settlers did what they could for the Aborigines.

Wanton outrages and the governor's policy not only militated against the work of Christianising the natives, but made friendly relations between white and black extremely difficult and speeded up their extermination. This was soundly evaluated by Fison in the Tasmanian sections of *Methodist History* (c. 1902). On the other side of the account the name of Robinson "The Conciliator" must be remembered. He was a bricklayer by trade and a Wesleyan by faith.

Aborigine Work in Early Victoria

As Horton had observed the needs of the natives in Van Diemen's Land, so did Orton in Victoria. He preached to them on Batman's station, and it was in response to his appeal on their behalf that the names of Benjamin Hurst and Francis Tuckfield appeared on the 1839 station sheet against "Port Philip." Orton describes his hopes for them in his journal, and Governor Gipps of New South Wales supported him in his efforts to establish a proper station.

In the same year Rev. William Simpson of Launceston had been sent to Port Philip to investigate possibilities of the work and make a report. In his interesting report he makes an appeal on behalf of the Aborigines, whom he described as "miserable specimens of human nature":

> Their long matted locks, coal-black skin, lank and wasted limbs, and disgustingly filthy habits, render them truly pitiable objects. I, this evening, visited their encampment, a short distance out of town, where several tribes, amounting altogether to two or three hundred persons, pass the night. The spot selected for this purpose is the crown of a low hill near to the river. Each family seemed to have a separate break-wind, with a fire in front; and under this break-wind the whole family, including several dogs, were crowded; men, women and children, in many instances without the smallest covering . . . The Missionaries who are called to labour among them will have much to discourage them; but it is the Gospel of grace they have to preach.

Eventually the land for the station was procured some forty miles west of Geelong on the Barwon, and for twelve years the missionaries stationed here did good work and much translation work. About three years before the midcentury year we read the following reference to it:

> The aboriginal mission is rising above its pecuniary difficulties, while it is extending its limits and influence. Hitherto the expenses of the establishment, have, for the most part, been met by the Wesleyan Society, the colonial government and local donations and contributions; but at present it is expected that the mission is in a position to defray the expenses of one missionary and one tribe of natives, independently of the three sources from which supplies have hitherto been drawn. The flock of sheep which was formed by the generous donations of friends of the mission, amounts at present to about 2000; and the proceeds of the herd of cattle, which have been taken on terms, have already been laid out on cattle to form a mission herd, which amounts to about 120 head. 3000 sheep have also been taken on terms, to graze on a portion of the reserve for the benefit of the blacks the proceeds of . . . the agricultural department, will supply, with economy, the temporal wants of the scattered tribes in the vicinity of the mission, and afford to the young the means of education.

An extensive plan had been worked out by the district meeting to cover the following points: (1) a good school to draw youths and children from forty to sixty miles, (2) application for establishment of suitable buildings, and (3) employment of a qualified schoolmaster.

The Lord Bishop of Adelaide had shown considerable interest in the Wesleyan work in the area, and in particular this Aboriginal station at Gallillelup, riding out on horseback to inspect it and examining the boys and girls in reading, writing, Scripture knowledge, and belief. He summed up his visit thus:

> You have proceeded upon right principles, pursued right plans, and I now witness the efficiency of your operations: you want only one thing more, namely good and suitable land, to make this a self-supporting system. Your present situation is not good: I advise you to fix upon some other, and state your wishes to the government.

Yet the Gallillelup Institution had triumphs of another type during its lifetime. There were conversions, baptisms, Christian marriages, and some death-bed testimonies of good faith, and even long after the abandonment of the station there is evidence of individual nomads who still carried and read their Bibles and catechisms. From time to time they appeared near some missionary's station, shared greetings and worship and went on their way. Such references are scattered throughout the literary works of the period, and probably if gathered together in one study they would make a formidable answer to the critic who says the Aborigine was wholly neglected. Nor can it be said the authorities ignored the problem. Wherever we find reference to native institutions, we find some form of government aid. In the case of the institution near Geelong, the land itself was a government grant for the purpose. Missionaries were always encouraged in such projects, and sometimes financial assistance was also given.

In spite of this, however, there were difficulties. In New South Wales, under the "Squatter's Act," settlers could establish themselves anywhere, and this act did not recognise the existence of the natives nor make provision for them. They suffered much through this act, which indirectly led to starvation, pilfering, and all forms of human misery, and even extermination: an opinion expressed at the time.

Furthermore the early missionaries had engaged in several extremely perilous expeditions in their attempt to ascertain the whereabouts of various tribes in the hope they could report home to British Wesleyans the needs of the field. Were it possible to gather together all the early journals and correspondence in one place, it would probably provide a most valuable library of exploration and anthropological data.

Yet in Victoria, as in New South Wales and in Van Diemen's Land, the work broke down, and all the missionary historian can claim with real certainty is that it was not neglected, nor were those appointed unfaithful to their task.

As the time came for the handing of the Australian and Pacific work over to an independent conference, the staffing needs became more and more urgent, and the men were simply taken away from the less fruitful labour among the natives.

Melbourne in fifteen years had jumped from a cluster of huts to a town of eighty thousand people, and there were twenty-two thousand in Geelong, and the Conference deputation discovered that, in the previous seven months, sixty-three thousand persons had entered Victoria through Melbourne, and the shanty towns of the gold fields had come up almost overnight. With practically no established social services or police force, the church had a major problem on its hands—and before these pressing claims those of the Aborigines took a secondary place.

Yet we must not pass the work of Messrs. Hurst and Tuckfield without acknowledging their work both as explorers and as pioneers in language study among the Victorian natives. Some day their story must be told, and then the biographer will bring out the facts—facts like this, for instance:

> "Colonization counteracted our labours and prevented our success," said Hurst, and went on to expound the statement—negligence of religion by whites, often their hostile opposition, prostitution of native women, employment of the men for liquor.

> Within three years from the commencement of the Mission, the three tribes with which we were more immediately connected, had decreased fully one half,

and the progress of annihilation was still going on with fearful rapidity
... A few were killed clandestinely by their countrymen, or fell in war; but fatal
disease introduced by licentious Europeans, committed the most fearful rav-
ages, and brought multitudes to a premature grave ... Within the limits of the
three tribes already mentioned, there were only two really Aboriginal children
born after our arrival at Port Phillip. (Statement made 1854—ART.) It is true that
there were many children born, but they were "half-caste" and were invariably
destroyed. (Because of tribal law probably—ART.)

As early as 1840 Hurst reported to the colonial government on the decrease of native
population and said, "Unless prompt and decided measures are taken to preserve these
degraded and deeply injured tribes, in a few years they will be entirely extinct."

Hurst saw his work as promoting the social and physical welfare of the Aborigines in
terms of preventing "collision both amongst themselves and the Europeans."

The government established an institution also at Mount Franklin in the midlands,
and this establishment they put in the capable hands of a Mr. Carvosso, who was himself the son of one of the early missionaries already mentioned in this paper. He ran his
institution very much along missionary lines. He considered the Aboriginal mind much
higher than usually rated, but found little response among the adults, concentrated on
early teenagers, and hoped to graft them into agricultural pursuits as they grew. He had a
few on the station with little farms and found these to rise higher both socially and mor-
ally than the others. Their religious knowledge was limited, but again it was better among
those living on the station.

We observe also the reasons he gives for the decrease of native population: (1) the introduction of European vices, especially liquor; (2) the slight regard they pay to health; and
(3) their indifference towards marriage, and love of celibacy.

Before leaving Victoria, we owe a paragraph to Tuckfield, who

travelled about with the blacks and camped in their *miamias* in order to understand their manners and customs and learn their language in its various dialects.
He soon compiled a vocabulary and a grammar and became a proficient speaker. It
was his joy to preach to them "in their own tongue wherein they were born" and
declare unto them "the wonderful works of God." He translated portions of the
Bible, hymns, catechisms &c., which were read and learnt by the natives, whose
memories though quick, were not retentive. Various useful arts were taught, such
as the cultivation of the soil, and how to build cottages for themselves, though
they did not appreciate them but preferred their own *miamias*.

So wrote his son, for Fison's *Methodist History* (c. 1902), and of his mother he added that
she "remained on the station for weeks when her husband was away. She taught them to
sew, read and sing ... She also gave them medicine and bound up their wounds."

In reminiscing on the days of his younger life he also confirms our finding based on other sources that the most serious difficulty was the nomadic habit of the people, and the habits they learned from the white man: "Their numbers decreased chiefly through the evil habits of civilized people."

Another finding expressed above is supported by the same source, that the interests of the black were more or less crowded out by the increasing claims of the white population, growing out of all proportion or expectation, and with no corresponding increase of staff. He puts it thus:

> The missionary committee was unable to continue the mission, and in view of the pressing claims of the large and still increasing English population in Geelong, where for ten years Mr. Tuckfield had periodically conducted services, he was appointed to reside there as its superintendent minister.

Actually many natives still visited him there, and Tuckfield himself still had contact with natives who had been converted at Buntingdale, as the station was known among the white people.

Fison, recording the foundations of the church in Colac and Birragurra area, says of Buntingdale that it "had an appreciable influence in moulding the destiny of the Church," and also points out that the early residents of that district who remembered the place claimed that its presence "had a softening and subduing influence on whites and blacks alike."

So it would seem that when Joseph Orton appealed to his fellow countrymen on behalf of the Aborigines in his first sermon at Port Philip, and subsequently toured the areas frequented by blacks under the guidance of Buckley, the "wild white man," he set in motion a train of events, which, though they failed in their immediate ends, did contribute much to the fabric of the church to come.

South Australia

William Longbottom was appointed to Western Australia in 1838, but after a delay of five months at Van Diemen's Land he was wrecked off South Australia, and there he established himself and laboured until his death. I know nothing of his work among the natives, but as he had been transferred from India, they would hardly have escaped his attention. He certainly communicated with the mission authorities in London on their needs and pressed their case. Eggleston supported his appeal in 1840, but I am not aware of anything having come of it.

Swan River Settlement

Missionary notices published in 1840 reported the departure of Rev. John Smithies and family on the *Prima Donna* for the Swan River Settlement in Western Australia. He was designated for specific work among the blacks, and work among the settlers was to be where possible only. He had previously served for nine years in Newfoundland, and the native work immediately won his sympathy. At first he had the use of an experienced interpreter and made rapid progress. He was an observant man and wrote much of their beliefs, weapons, and customs, and had good opinion of their mental capacity. He established schools, and taught letters, spelling, counting, and did some translating, including the Lord's Prayer and a number of hymns, and appealed to London for two additional workers.

Smithies turned on a first-class display of schoolwork and a public examination of his black and white children that left the colonial officials staggered, and there is no room for doubt that under John Smithies the mission was a great success—especially so among the children. And by 1846 there were converts in the real sense of the term and baptisms among the natives—eighteen native youths were baptised that year.

His biggest trial was that he had the whole of West Australia to handle—black and white. Year after year he appealed for help. A stout heart was John Smithies.

Bishop Augustus Short of South Australia visited his native institution in 1849, approving its plans and principles and discussing its problems with the missionary. Governor Fitzgerald also now took an interest in the project.

Eventually after eleven years of asking, Smithies got the help he wanted—at least, he got one additional missionary, William Lowe. This was possible because the colonial government offered to pay the stipend of one of the men.

As a result of the advice and interest of the bishop, the station was now transferred to a better site, where good land was available and the station had hope of becoming self-supporting—or as it was reported in the annual meeting of the Wesleyan Missionary Society that year: "The Native Institution has been removed to a more healthy site and one better adapted to the agricultural operations, which constitute so important an auxiliary in the work of reclaiming that degraded race."

Thus the Wannaroo Station was removed to York, and Lowe took over the work at Perth and Fremantle.

In the establishment of the station the government appropriated "one hundred and eight acres of good cornland, forever, for the Native Institution; and two acres I secured in fee simple for the erection of buildings; so that the property would be perfectly secure to the Society," wrote Smithies.

He also secured bullocks, carts, provisions, and so on, and the work of clearing went ahead. Upon the arrival of Lowe he and his family now moved to York and gave full time to native work. Smithies cleared the land and established substantial buildings, and by the end of the year he had

> a substantial school-house, 40 feet x 20, a good dwelling house for the manager,
> in which we now live, 50 feet x 15; and two more buildings as dormitory and
> cook-house. We have also cleared about 30 acres of good land; and have fenced

and under crop about 12 acres. The buildings have cost about the amount of the sale of Wannaroo; and thus by the transfer of our property into this, we have now a Mission, with suitable appliances, amid a populous district of colonists and natives, and every chance of doing something temporally and spiritually.

Yet even with the station so well established there were disappointments, and after a time some of the Perth natives who had removed to York absconded, and Smithies' own saying about the Australian wanderer, "A native is never at rest out of his own locality," throws light again on the difficulty of ministering to a nomadic people. This was partly behind Smithies' new plan to bring in half-castes and bush natives from as low as four to eight years of age, and try bringing them up under earlier Christian influence, and within the educational process, "thereby hoping to raise a Church."

At the same time it must not be supposed that the natives who absconded rejected the church. One, who died soon afterwards in Perth, left a sound testimony and profession of faith.

The government presented a further eight acres for the erection of a chapel at York, where services were held at first in the courthouse, which, however, proved too small.

When the Australasian Conference was approved in 1854, there were four circuits in Western Australia and the native work—and still only two ministers. The deputation only called at Perth on the way home for an hour or so, and likewise on the way out, but the missionaries had made use of the call for an appeal for increased staff. The deputation did not see the York Institution.

Eventually in 1855 Smithies was transferred to Van Diemen's Land, where he laboured for a further nine years, before retiring, a physical breakdown.

Some Observations and Conclusions

Although Robert Young was unable to go out to York to see the Native Institution at work, there is plenty of evidence in his report of his interest in the problem of the Australian Aborigine, of whom he speaks as "the dark pagans of Australia." He says, however, bringing settlers and natives together,

> The Society, in sending missionaries to scattered and neglected emigrants, as well as to dark pagans, has in Australia realized a great reward. It has established a cause in that island continent which is Christianity in aggressive action going everywhere through the land.

My reading of early printed and written documents would support that judgment.

As to whether or not the work among the Aborigine section was a failure is not the point at issue. What matters and what this paper purports to substantiate is that Wesleyanism provided Christianity an aggressive action in going everywhere throughout the land. No one will argue that more could not have been done with a bigger staff—but with the staff that was sent, it is hard to see how much more could have been done than was done. It is therefore unfair to the pioneers to say that the Aboriginal work was neglected. They gave of their best—Leigh, Walker, Horton, Hurst, Tuckfield, Smithies, and others. Let their names be well remembered in this respect. I do not know of one who gave up the task of his own accord, but only by Committee decisions.

As to whether or not the London Committee should have heard the repeated cries for more staff for work among the Australian Aborigines, I am not prepared to debate at this juncture. That requires more documents than I have access to at present, but I must confess that, to a reader of the sources that have come my way, there does not seem to be a proportionate balance between the place of the needs of the Australian Aborigine in the missionary propaganda of British Wesleyanism at the time and the staff supplied to work among them. The disproportionately small staff sent to work among the Aborigines is surely accentuated further by the fact that even this would not have been possible without extensive government aid. No—in my own heart of hearts I feel that if Wesleyanism is to be held responsible for the neglect of the Aborigine in that early and vicious period, the blame must not fall on the missionary or on the generous subscribers of Britain, but on the authorities who assessed the distribution of mission funds and staff.

Again, although the colonial governments did do something, clearly it wasn't enough. Far too often, it seems to me, they were ready to push a mission into a project with a grant of land or money and satisfy themselves thereby that the job was being attended to. This was very good, but not enough.

Some blame also must fall on the Christian people of Australia. At the time when the native institution in Victoria was struggling for its existence and trying to establish itself by self-support, there were eighty thousand in Melbourne, twenty-two thousand in Geelong, and twenty thousand in Ballarat. Chapels everywhere were full, and being enlarged. New places of worship and schools were going up like mushrooms—at three- and four-figure sums. Various charity institutions were being established; £3,500 for one in Melbourne, with £1,000 grant from the government. In the light of these figures, should the church have allowed the Aboriginal work to have been snuffed out. Is not this a case of where two of our favourite sayings are at variance?

"Duty begins at home" and,

"Go always, not only to those who want you, but to those who want you most."

Undoubtedly one of the major factors in native depopulation in Australia and in the failure of missionary work among them, is what some missionaries called "colonization"— i.e., its introduction of liquor, its spread of disease, its hunger for native lands, and its determination to force the native into the labour demands of its commerce and trade establishments. The missionaries were not alone in this belief. An eloquent statement on the subject was made in Melbourne itself, where it was particularly relevant at the time, at the Mechanic's Hall in a public meeting in 1854, by Edward Stone Parker, a Victorian M.L.A., who had actually been the person to establish the Mount Franklin Institution.

Of the effect of ardent spirits on the Aborigines, he says, "a dire evil doing its work of death among them . . . before which our population are falling almost as thickly as the slain in battle."

He also spoke of the increase of white man's diseases. The lecture was published in Australia, London, and Edinburgh, and reprinted in the *Wesleyan Magazine* for British Methodists to read.

To what extent the causes of the failure of missionary work in the early period lay within the ways and habits of the natives themselves is open to debate. Clearly their no-madic habits were against the form of organised religion we know best. Manifestly also their ingrained dislike for work and discipline made things difficult, as did also their love for the bottle and their natural proneness to fight among themselves.

Yet despite these difficulties there were conversions and enough successes in the early period to have warranted a more concentrated and persistent effort. We are unhappy that the projects were discontinued after such short terms of trial. They had very much more to show for the time than many other Pacific missions. It is hoped that some student in Australia will take up this study after the year 1855—the year with which this work ter-minates.

Now in conclusion one question remains to be raised and answered if possible. To what extend did the failure of missionary work among the Australian Aborigines arise from the form of religion the church attempted to give them? This is an anthropological question. It is relevant today, and will continue to be so as long as the church seeks to evangelise nomadic peoples.

The natives who tied themselves to the Buntingdale station in Victoria became known as the Mission Tribe. The Perth natives, we have seen, did not stay very long in their new and greatly improved settlement at York. To what extent should missions try to break the nomadic habits of a people and bind them to a station? Now the answer to that question in Australia today may be very different from what it should have been a century ago. Today it is a case of saving a perishing people, and giving them a stability without which they cannot hope to exist in the face of competition. I am not dealing with that question. We are dealing with beginnings. All the missionaries felt lost in the face of nomadism. Yet there were moments for Walker and Tuckfield and others when they got close to the peo-ple—they were moments when they too became nomads. I have yet to be convinced that the God who called the nomadic Abraham could not call the wanderers of the Australian continent also. I can well imagine what an obstruction our institutional religion would be to a nomadic people. No doubt the time has come now for these people to settle down, but a century ago they were absolutely nomadic—and would have been more quickly won by a nomadic ministry.

In Victoria, for instance, although the natives were cannibals, they were well disposed towards the white man, for good reasons. They believed in the transmigration of souls, each stage passing through a change until they eventually turned from black to white. When the white man arrived they took them to be their ancestors returned to life again, they welcomed them with respect, they allowed them to claim their ancient lands, they emulated their habits. This attitude of mind gave them receptivity potential, which could have been turned to good, but was unfortunately more often turned to evil. Yet the church failed to avail itself fully of that potential. It is, of course, not fair to make judgments save in the historic sense. It is all very well for us who follow. Our wisdom or otherwise will be judged in turn, and we must needs ask ourselves whether or not our methods and worship and general religious organisation is in sympathy with or at variance with the primitive or semiprimitive people among whom we are engaged as missionaries. Or are we trying to force a white man's church upon them? This is a question for every modern missionary to ask himself and answer.

And for those who maintain missions, the point of this paper is the tragedy of putting the hand on the plough and taking it off again.

REFERENCES

(This study is mainly compiled from early records, reports, articles, and correspondence forwarded to England by the missionaries and mostly published in *The Wesleyan Magazine* over the years 1820–1855. Other sources used [are noted below]—ART.)

Blacket, John. 1914. *Missionary triumphs among the settlers in Australia*. London: Charles H. Kelly, 1914.

Blamires, W. L., and J. B. Smith. 1886. *The early story of the Methodist church in Victoria: A jubilee volume*. Melbourne: Wesleyan Book Depot.

Fison, Lorimer, ed. [1902?] *Methodist history of Victoria and Tasmania*. Vol. 1. Melbourne: Spectator Publishing.

Strachan, Alexander. 1870. *The life of the Rev. Samuel Leigh*. London: Wesleyan Mission House.

Young, Robert. 1854. *The southern world*. London: Hamilton, Adams and Co.

30
PERSONAL INTERPLAY IN INTERCOMMUNITY CEREMONIAL IN FIJI[231]

This paper focuses on the institutionalised forms and personal interplay of intercommunity ceremonial in Fiji in the face of culture change. By intercommunity ceremonial I mean ceremonies by means of which one regional, political, linguistic, or kinship community interrelates with another, whether it be for trade, or marriage, or maybe military alliance.

In pre-Christian times Fiji comprised seven or eight native kingdoms aligned in a balance of power. Each kingdom had many subject states; some subject because of conquest and contributing tribute, others voluntarily so for the sake of military protection and contributing support in war. All these relationships involved intercommunity ceremonial. Each of these homogeneous communities had some skill, or natural resource, or craft production which it supplied to others through ceremonial exchanges at intercommunity assemblies. Some of these gatherings related to political events in the wider world of Greater Fiji, or they might provide for intergroup discussions or marriage proposals, which in Fiji involved kin groups rather than individuals.

This paper is a diachronic study, inasmuch as it speaks of custom at widely separated levels of time depth, permitting us to identify the degree of stability and change in ceremonial structures over the period. Thus we are comparing and contrasting pre-Christian and recent times.

For the earlier period the paper is informed by archival documents and published sources of the contact period, reports of sea captains, shipwrecked sailors who lived with the native people, missionaries, early Tongan evangelists, and the first generation of Fijian indigenous preachers. Some of this material is in the Fijian language. I also used a number of written notes compiled by Fijian heralds, and many elderly informants well grounded in tradition were consulted by me some thirty odd years ago.

Against these earlier accounts I have thrown my own personal experiences over twenty years living with the Fijian people, sharing their ceremonial life and custom as a participant observer. This, of course, was mostly done in the Fijian language (Bauan, which became the *lingua franca* under missionary influence), but it exposed me to much Fijian

---

231   Paper presented at the annual meeting of the Southwestern Anthropological Association, San Diego, California, 1977.

dialect, for the ceremonial life of the people is the one public manifestation of the survival of dialect. This, more or less, makes this presentation a study of reminiscences rather than of documentation.

However the more I reflect on these matters the more I am convinced of the basic stability of Fijian cultural ceremonial and the traditional interplay of persons and parties involved. Even when a colonial administration and the acceptance of Christianity render many customs obsolete, and demand the creation of new functional ceremonials, the structure and the personal interplay remain essentially Fijian in character and are not at all foreign. Because of the popular disfavour of the word "survival," some anthropologists have spoken of this formal continuity of cultural forms as functionally vital as cultural tarriance.

Someday a whole book will need to be written on this subject, and then some kind of typology will be needed. It seems to me that such a typology should be functional, and that the ceremonial might fall naturally into four categories in the following manner:

1. Economic ceremonial would include the rituals of trade exchanges, canoe construction, house building, etc. These are both community and intercommunity, involving whole villages in a cycle of work and social activities, and subsequently distribution.

2. Politico-religious ceremonial is performed at decision-making assemblies of church and state (either on the district or national levels) and concern the making of requests, their acceptance or rejection, and the plans for communicating the assembly decisions to the community at large. Since World War II this has been extended to an international level.

3. Honorific ceremonial includes the rituals of welcome and farewell, recognition of achievement, ceremonial entertainment of visitors, rituals associated with mourning the honored dead, and so forth.

4. Ceremonial related to rites of passage are not confined to communal occasions. Many are intercommunity—investitures, significant marriage, and funerary rites, for example.

This would be a suitable typology for further study of the subject. They are, of course, abstractions for purpose of analysis. In reality two or three of them will be found together. For example, almost any of the others will also have honorific ceremonial associated with it.

The Tarriance of the Fijian Characteristics

All these mechanisms and institutions were developed long before the contact period. In some cases and in some locations they have been modified in the course of time to fit the changes which have come with acculturation, modern government, and Christianity, but structurally and functionally they still exist today. Although in some cases old roles have become defunct (e.g., those associated with cannibalism), and because of government, educational, medical, commercial, and missionary influences, there has been considerable new role creation, nevertheless the ceremonial structures, their occasions, and their personal interplay have remained stable throughout.

One of the features of Fijian ceremonial is that in spite of change, no matter how many foreign borrowings or innovations are included, it nevertheless remains essentially a Fijian ceremony. The thing is done "in the Fijian way," *yakaviti*, and the participants behave and interact with the same traditional Fijian interplay—the seating arrangement; the protocol; the responsibilities of host chief, visiting chief, heralds, and subordinates; the honorifics; and the ritual formula remain the same. The two parties are spatially set in their respective "territories," each with its herald, through whom they interact. The ceremonial paraphernalia— *yaqona* bowl, *tanoa*, and cup, *bilo*, also the whale's tooth *kamunaga*, *tabua*, etc., are always present, and those participating are knowledgeable in the correctness of sequence and symbolism of every act of the total performance. A ceremonial blunder is still to this day a "thing of shame," *ka ni madua*, for those in key roles are expected to know better. If things are not done properly, a Fijian told me, "the ceremonial assembly will be cold," *ena qai batabata na soqoni*.

Fijian Exchanges

I am saying, then, that change due to acculturation and tarriance of the customary decorum are both manifest at the same time. A ceremony may change in a material way so that it is relevant to the society's degree of acculturation or Westernisation, but the "way it is done" remains virtually unchanged, as also the personal interplay of the functional participants.

For example, I have been present at many Fijian traditional exchanges—usually those associated with political or religious assemblies, *bose*, rather than trade exchanges, *solevu*. On these occasions one observed the participants seated on mats in the council house, *vale ni bose* or *vale levu*, or on the village green, *rara*, according to their respective status as residents, *taukei*, or visitors, *vulagi*, and the presentations will be made in the open space between them. A farewell ceremony, for example, *veitalatala* or *veitatau*, may include, in addition to the ceremonial drinking together, *sova yaqona*, an exchange of presentations. The visitors have the freedom to present their own kind of gifts, the commodity itself being determined by their home resources and craftwork. In ancient times this might include wooden bowls, clay pots, and lamps, carved war clubs, woven mats, stenciled bark cloth, or "whatever" according to the skills for which they were renowned. They were extremely proud of their workmanship, and the whole village would have been preparing for this for months. Their prestige is scaled by the quality of this workmanship. The hosts then would make a return presentation of their produce, maybe of turtles, monster yams, and perhaps a canoe. Their food presentations, of course, would be made every day throughout the assembly, which might last for a week. In farewell ceremonies the entire presentation may be limited to one kind of commodity. I have seen clay bowls and pots, *dari* and *kuro ni Viti*, at Sigatoka and in the Yasawas where the best clay for pottery is found. At Nasaucoko in the mountains it was a presentation of soft reed sleeping mats, *ibe kuta*, and at Lomawai it was Fijian salt. Subsequently our approved officials divided the salt among the visitors. The whole *rara* was dotted in small heaps of baskets on a basis of the social divisions represented in our party.

I remember when I was on the host aide of the ceremonies in Kadavu and we were entertaining people from Suva, a community of townsmen wage earners. They were not freed from their traditional obligation but made a presentation of large bars of soap, bags of sugar, tins of cabin biscuits, drums of kerosene, and lengths of dress material. The soap, sugar, and biscuits were Fiji produce, but all of it had been bought for money—were they not wage earners? To this extent, traditional ceremony had accommodated itself to industrialization. Here was a shift from subsistence to money economy, from cultivation and fishing to wage earning.

However, were it possible to recall an old cannibal from the grave, he might well ask, "What are soap and clothing?" As he saw the host serving-men carry in the carcass of a bullock for the feast, he might be astonished at a creature of such size and want to know where the cannibal bodies, *bokola*, were. But in spite of the strange items in the presentation, he would have no trouble with the procedure being enacted. He would recognise the exchange presentations of a farewell ceremony and the ritual formulae of the various officiants, where they came from, and what their responsibilities were. Even if the semantics were changing, he would still know what was going on and recognise it as his own traditional custom.

The Ceremonial of the Intercommunal Dance

Let us notice also the changing ceremonial of the communal or intercommunal dance—i.e., a dance performed by one homogeneous group for the entertainment or honoring of another. (I am not speaking of Western-type dancing or folk dancing which the Fijians have borrowed. These are based on the male-female pair, which never occurs in traditional Fijian dancing. He never confuses a *taralala* with a *meke*.)

The Fijian traditional dance is performed by a homogeneous group—warriors, youths, maidens, or matrons as the case may be; the rhythmic accompaniment being provided from the remainder of the village. The theme was developed by the dancing master, *dau ni vucu*, who also trained the dancing party itself, *mata ni meke* or *matana*. The dancing party performed in front of the visiting party which was seated ceremonially for the occasion, with the chanting party inconspicuous in the background. Sometimes the dancing party has a central song leader who sings a kind of descant, which might provide a cue for the rhythm. The movements of the dance, however, are varied by an additional note in the drumbeat. All this is the same today as it was in cannibal times. Even some of the hero songs and tribal epics are still used.

In ancient times this form of entertainment was performed before honored visitors, for meeting the warriors returning from successful war with bodies for the oven, for the mourning of the dead, for the investiture of young warriors (*bulivaca*—name giving, after the killing of the first victim), and other similar occasions. From the functional need of dancing for such occasions a variety of dancing styles emerged in pre-Christian times. They were performed by specific groups and each dance had its name, which might relate to its function or its style: a slow dance by chiefly matrons was highly honorific, *seasea*; a war dance, *meke ni valu*, was performed by young warriors with clubs, *meke wau*, or spears, *meke moto*. A fan dance, *meke iri*, has a number of forms and may be male or female according to the chant which goes with it.

Some villages near chiefly centers were entirely comprised of entertainers and had a number of performing groups always at call in the chief's service. This was their contribution to any assembly, and they were "paid" with food and exchanges commodities from the presentations. Some dances were purely aesthetic; some dramatised the hunt, the battle, or the waves falling over the reefs. Some recalled the exploits of ancestral heroes; others were laments or dirges which mourned the dead in some epidemic or defeat in war. Some were humorous. The only sexy [sexually oriented] dances I ever found trace of were all associated with victory in war. They concerned the sexual abuse of the victims before their being baked in the cannibal ovens. The conquering heroes were welcomed home by the women with sexy [sexually oriented] dances which praised their capacity for sex and gave them vulgar titles. These dances, *wate* and *dele*, were foreplay for the warriors who depended on war for sex, they being not polygamists like the chiefs. These dances should be distinguished from the dance performed when the bodies were brought to the ovens, *cibi*.

With the disappearance of internal war and cannibalism under Christianity and colonial government, the *wate* and *dele* have become obsolete, and the name *cibi* has been transferred to another dance, a fun dance, after certain kinds of athletic victory, especially *veitiqa*. Apart from these changes due to Christianity and the establishment of law and order, all the other dances are still performed with the approval of both church and state, and used for purposes of entertainment at religious and civil assemblies.

The performance is the same: the exits and entrances, the behavior of the dancing master, the interjections from the audience, and many of the chants themselves, the movements of the dance themes, the rhythmic nuances, and the criteria for appraising a dance well performed. All these are utterly Fijian. Perhaps it may be that the deep, thumping beat is obtained by a unit of a commercial water pipe rather than a large bamboo, and maybe some of the trimmings worn by the dancers were colored by dyes obtained commercially from a Chinese store, and perhaps the reality at least of the war dances has gone, but nobody could call them anything but Fijian. The "rules of the game" remain the same, and the "players" seek the same ancient forms of excellence.

The Ceremonial of House Building

Or let us take the matter of house building. I have in one of my notebooks a long description of the construction of a Fijian house. It was a beautiful house built under the chiefly arrangement. I recorded every piece of material used and how it was used. I noted the superb social organisation. It was built by the people of a district. Each group of workmen had been assigned specific tasks of preparing material and bringing it to the site. Everybody was there at the right time and place, and everyone knew his precise role and responsibility. The house was actually built in a single day. Every task had been assigned on a basis of social structure, and one by one the units took shape according to plan. As the thatch began to rise towards the ridge, one group detached itself from the others and commenced the house-builders' chant, which continued until the waterproofing vines were woven over the ridge. This house was constructed in an absolutely Fijian manner, with the correct timber used for each component, with all the architectural units which had been developed before their ancestors ever saw a white man. Not a nail was used in the construction, not a piece of metal or a sawn plank, although these were available at a nearby store. The procedure of the building performance, the organisation of labour on a basis of kinship structure, the architecture, and the social festivities were all recognisably Fijian, although these people knew how to use coral lime for house construction and galvanised irons a century before.

This particular house was to be occupied by a schoolteacher. It was built in the chiefly way, *vakaturaga*. It was not contracted for in the white man's way of business, but rather by farming out responsibility through a community whom the teacher was to serve, and by the expectation of perfect workmanship without pay—except the house-builders' feast. You can always tell a chiefly house, or a school or a church which has been built in this way, by the perfection of the workmanship. The principal is of course expected to behave as a chief with due generosity. This will be manifest in the house-builders' feast which he provides. The principal's generosity or otherwise, of course, is manifest. He can be shamed if he fails. I remember once noticing a figure four woven into the ceiling of a Fijian house and asked its significance. My companion said it represented the number of pigs the house owner had given the workmen for the house-builders' feast.

Today a house may be built by contract or in the chiefly way. The former puts us in the world of commercial bargaining. The latter expects perfection regardless of cost—but perfection warrants generosity in return. The system still operates for those who want to use it. The church in Fiji, being indigenous, has utilised the chiefly system. Possibly this accounts for the cultural tarriance.

The Investiture Ceremony

I lived for a period on the chiefly island of Bau, where ceremonial is still very much alive, and where I was given a fairly respectable place in the social structure. This meant that I had to know the system and to act within the requirements of my assigned status. It assured me of a place in all ceremonials, and thus I was able to participate in an investiture ceremony known as *Na Veibuli ni Tu-ni-dau ni Bau.*

This ceremony had not been performed for forty years and was largely remembered through tradition. I asked my herald for information about it beforehand. He gave me a full account of the performance together with much of the rhythm of the liturgies involved. Subsequently I discovered that it followed very much the line he had expected, with one interesting exception. The paramount chief whose duty it was to invest the *Tu-ni-dau* into office had spent much of his life away from Bau. He had been overseas to school. I had first met him on the cricket field. Under the colonial government he has assumed a civil role, and this had kept him away from Bau. In many ways he had accommodated himself to the Western lifestyle, although he clung to Fijian forms for dealing with his own people. When it came to the key moment in the investiture in the liturgy of loyalty, accompanied by his tying a sash on the arm of the *Tu-ni-dau*, he declared the investiture with a typical Western official pronouncement, instead of using the traditional rhythmic couplet. The shift was not unnoticed by the Fijian elders, whom I heard discussing the matter a few days later. (The full detail of this event has been written up [Tippett 1968, 129–39]). Even after forty years the Fijian elders were quick to notice a variation—this is indeed a mental set for cultural tarriance.

Pagan Temple to Christian Church

I recall also the restoration of the church building at Bau in the ceremonial of the chiefly pattern. The church had been damaged by both hurricane and earthquake, and although the money for its restoration was in the bank the work was delayed because of an argument about who was to do the work. Ultimately it was determined that it should be done "in the chiefly way." The Bau chiefs made their presentation to the people of Daku requesting them to undertake the assignment. This in itself was a ceremonial in its own right—a whale's tooth of request. With its acceptance a whole set of formal obligations come into play. In ancient times the Daku people performed the role of restoring pagan temples. Now, after a century of Christianity, they were still performing this role in the religion of the land. They undertook the task and did a superb job. It is a long story but contains some significant points. It was done as a religious service with numerous religious taboos. The chief of Daku first selected his team of workmen. He eliminated everyone with any doubt about his character. Only workmen in good church standing were used, and none who indulged in drink or tobacco. Such taboos had always been imposed on Daku temple builders, and this was an obvious functional substitute. The tools for the job and the workmen gathered at the site and were dedicated to the Lord before the task was begun. The restoration was entirely done without pay, but the Daku workmen were feasted daily by the Bauan chiefs and people. The Daku builders had the right to demand the best materials from the Bau chiefs, and to reject any piece of timber regarded as inferior. The timber was to be without blemish. Eventually the task was finished and the church was dedicated for use. Here again the old ritual of pre-Christian times was followed, the Fijian pastor taking the place of the pre-Christian priest. The Daku village church choir prepared and presented a ceremonial chant telling the story of the project, especially composed for the occasion by the choir-master. The basic roots of these ceremonies, the structure, and the parties in interplay were the same as would have been used in pre-Christian times tor the restoration of hea-then temples. The individuals and parties involved were descendants of former cannibals, who had turned to Christianity a century before. True, the Bible was read by the Christian pastor, and prayers were offered to the Christian God, but the forms, the protocol, and the personal interplay of the ceremonies had come down from pagan days.

The Ceremonials of Fijian War

One must grant, of course, that some intercommunity ceremonial has passed out of use with the acceptance of Christianity and internal law and order. The most picturesque of these was the military review, *taqa*, and the pledge and boast of loyalty, *bolebole*. One of the best descriptions of these was left by the missionary Thomas Williams, in 1846, when an army of three thousand, armed with clubs, spears, battle-axes, and muskets boasted loy-alty to Bau at Somosomo. The accompanying food presentation included forty thousand large yams (*uvi*) and a wall of ceremonial *yaqona* (seven feet high and thirty-five feet in length) and twenty huge bales of native cloth. The *taqa* was a mass maneuver with multi-individual pledging of loyalty made by the forces of a subordinate chief who was allying himself with another in some military effort. The food was providing support for the Bau-an forces who were now the allies of Somosomo. The boasting was to assure the Bauan chief of the personal loyalty of each warrior among the allies. Should the war be effective, the women would celebrate with the *wate* and *dele*, and the men with the *cibi*.

This whole complex, which is well described in several of the early missionary jour-nals, has disappeared with the coming of Christianity and central government. To some extent the place has been taken by the Fiji Military Forces, but Fiji is now a united country and the old felt needs have gone, and these customs with them. In their place we have the F.M.F. [Fijian Military Forces] with their colorful uniform, and the army band and displays of precision marching. The pre-Christian pageantry has given way to a new form of military display which satisfies the feeling of national pride where in ancient times there was no nation. Yet through it all a good deal of the ancient value system continues and some of the structural elements. But the enemy now is not a hostile neighbor but someone away beyond the horizon in the outside world.

What local rivalry there is at home is rather transferred to the football field, where the traditional enemies sometimes work off the old hostility in a supposedly more Christian fashion.

Meantime the principle of organisation behind the *taqa* and *bolebole* in which the company advanced down the center of the village green to the principal chief in front of the chiefly house, is structurally the same as that used by the Fijian churches for their annual offerings, *vakamisoneri*, and for all communal contributions to public causes, service projects, and charities. Once again the procedure, the responsibilities on a basis of kin structure, and the interplay of officiants is recognisably old Fijian.

Ceremonies of Welcome and Farewell

Ceremonies of welcome and farewell are really sequences of several ritual units of performance. Many of them include the presentation of a whale's tooth, *tabua* (ceremonially termed *kamunaga, vatu makawa, bati ni ika* according to the locality), the presentation of a *kava* root, *vu-ni-yaqona* (*sevusevu*), a welcome or farewell beverage ceremonially mixed, poured, presented, and drunk, *sova yaqona*, and a presentation feast, *magiti*—the actual feast is *tuku ni laca* or *nai kele ni toko*, according to location (terms which really presuppose arrival by sea)—and so on.

Depending on the occasion and the dignitary being welcomed, there may be ceremonies at sea, at the waterfront, and/or when entering the village. The visitor's boat anchors in deep water. When the anchor is raised to come in closer to the shore, we have *cavuikele-kele*. Also on board, the ceremony *ai qaloqalovi* was originally performed by swimmers who went out to the boat and presented a whale's tooth. If the swimmers were ranking women, the ceremony is *qalowaqa*. These vary in different parts of Fiji, but always there is an approved sequence of events for receiving the visitor into the community. The ceremonial formulae remain virtually unchanged from generation to generation, and the persons who perform the various responsibilities are determined by their social rank. Originally it was correct to offer a human body to the visitor upon arrival. The flesh for eating is *bokola*, and the name of the feast *ai luva ni tawake*. This was the first act on shore. In Christian times the human body was replaced by a turtle or the presentation of a whale's tooth, but the title is retained. The ceremony is otherwise identical. These terms comes from Lau and Cakaudrove, not from Bau. In Nadroga it is *matakarawa*, even when the ceremony is presented in the mountains. A welcome feast for the visiting crew is *magiti ni mua*, and their farewell feast is *magiti ni bili ni mua*. Their institutionalisation remains stable to this day in the island communities.

In the course of time as the Christian gospel spread inland, diffused by native evangelists, these preachers carried a dry shirt and *sulu* in a case made from a kerosene tin. When the evangelist arrived at the village he changed from his wet clothes and was given a light meal before he preached to the villagers. This snack was presented ceremonially as "the loosening (untying) of the tin," *ai sere ni kava*—cf. the setting free of the turtle, *ai luva ni tawake*—and again the procedure stands firm. Today modern preachers cannot obtain kerosene tins, and the term but not the custom has dropped from use. A more substantial feast is served after the church service (the feast for preaching, *magiti ni vunau*). A portion of this will be packed in a basket and sent home with the preacher afterwards. This is called the *talevunau*, the return from preaching. The preacher is worthy of his hire, but traditionally it is the old Fijian value of mutual responsibility. These offerings of food are always ceremonially presented. Prayer or grace follows this. If the women of the village have prepared a meal for a visitor, even if he is just a casual passerby, they will look about for a male of the proper status to present it. The personal interplay is preserved at all times.

The End of Mourning

I was present in Suva, the capital of Fiji, at the time of the lifting of the mourning after the death of King George VI. Mourning ceremonies may be held on the fourth, tenth, and/or one-hundredth night (*bogiva*, *bogitini*, and *bogidrau*). Full mourning of one hundred days is given only to persons of the highest rank, and the final feast is called *ai burua*. In this case this was a national event with a whole day of ceremonial at government expense. All the chiefly houses and the leaders of the church received their portions in the ceremonial division. Colonial officials were usually on the receiving end of these presentations. This time the roles were reversed as they were the officials in the service of the king.

The Ceremonial Footrace

Ceremonial is not always confined to persons of rank. The rules apply at any level. A good example of this is the honorific ceremonial footrace, *cere*, given as a gesture of goodwill by the young people of the host village where the chief's vessel put in for the night his crew. The crew recognises the situation when a young man comes out into the water blowing a conch shell, *davui*, daring them to capture him. The women on the beach are all waving pieces of stencilled bark cloth. The crew bounds overboard and pursues the locals trying to capture the young man and the women. If they do so they claim the bark cloth as their prize. To catch the trumpeter means a more valuable prize—maybe even a whale's tooth. The purpose of the *cere* is to relieve the tensions of protocol and formality, and to welcome the crew into the village community. It is accompanied by a good deal of levity. It is not as common today as it used to be, but is still used in the outer islands for parties who visit with government and church dignitaries. I once jumped overboard and ran in a *cere* and secured a nice piece of bark cloth for doing so. I found myself in another Fijian world of jesting, quite different from the formality of the chiefly superstructure.

This could go on and on, but my space is used up. The ceremonials of the *buliyaca* (mentioned above) and the whole ritual of canoe building are written up in *Fijian Material Culture* (Tippett 1968) for anyone who wishes to study these matters further, but having gotten myself involved in the *cere* I will leave the matter there. I always found that involvement in Fijian ceremonial helped my rapport, but it is important that one learns first what to do and how to do it.

The point of this paper is that cultural borrowing, or acculturation or the entry of a foreigner into custom situations, need not be destructive to the culture provided one (1) plays the game according to the rules, and does so (2) with due respect, and (3) demonstrates this by learning to use the ceremonial language, and (4) shows that he is sharing the experience, not being a scientist studying a number of guinea pigs.

REFERENCES

Tippett, Alan R. 1968. *Fijian material culture.* Honolulu: Bishop Museum Press.

CONCLUSION
The Anthropological and Ethnohistorical Pilgrimage of a Missiologist[232]

I did not sit down to write this paper with a well-thought-out outline or even with a specific title. The title is an afterthought. The subject matter, however, covers a number of diverse elements which have been formulated in my mind over these recent years when I have been trying to apply anthropology to the study of missiology. They concern several aspects of missiology as a research field—methodology, data collecting, strategy of missions, and rapport in working with people of other cultures. From the old pre–World War II world in which I was supposedly trained to go to the mission field, we had two streams or disciplines—one was theology and the other the philosophy of religion—which the church has frequently assumed were adequate for the training of missionaries, as long as they had an accompanying knowledge of the Bible. I believe this assumption to be erroneous.

As I study the history of mission over the last 180 years—that is, since the time of William Carey—I perceive that some missionaries were naturally equipped anthropologically, whereas many of their colleagues were responsible for all kinds of cross-cultural indiscretions that interfered with their work. I do not believe that the difference between the two types of missionary can be put down just to piety, or faith, or faithfulness to the Scriptures, on the one hand, or to capriciousness on the part of the Holy Spirit, on the other. I believe that God is constant, and that these shortcomings may be counted against the missionaries concerned. This conviction has come upon me by some thirty years of studying the documents in missionary archives. Both the letters written by the missionaries, and their journals, reflect their anthropological orientation. Sometimes the same event has been described by two different men clearly enough to show how those two men must have stood very differently in the eyes of the people to whom they tried to communicate the gospel.

Having contact here with some hundreds of students like you, from all branches of the Christian church and from all countries of the world, I have had the opportunity to look beyond my own self and my own mission field at others who are engaged in the same

---

232 Presented to the faculty and doctoral students of the School of World Mission, Fuller Theological Seminary, Pasadena, CA, 1974.

ministry of communicating Christ to the nations. Sometimes this has brought home to me our common feelings and strengths, and at other times it has indicated the peculiarities of my own church and my own mission field.

What I hope to do in this paper, then, is to sketch briefly a number of anthropological insights that have come to me since that point about seven years along in my missionary career, when I realised that my missionary training was quite inadequate for the task the Lord had called me to do. Thus, this presentation has something of an autobiographical character. But rather, will you please consider it the pilgrimage of a missionary, and look at it objectively, asking yourself if the new ideas that came to me as I was confronted by the insights of the great anthropologists, and as their literature unfolded before me, say anything to your own missionary life.

I should like to feel that someone from among you will take up serious anthropological research as a dimension of your missiology. Scientific research of the kind that we undertake here requires not only the collection of clear data and the writing of case studies, but a body of sound theory to go with it. Theory without data is mere speculation. Data without a theoretical frame of reference is unapplied. Some of you will write descriptive accounts and collect data, but unless others produce a theoretical base then our total program will only be partly effective. My days here are numbered, but I would certainly like to feel that among those who graduate in my time, some at least will learn to explore the riches of anthropological theory, apply its methods, and give a truly scientific dimension to the missiological analyses which will henceforth be associated with the name of the School of World Mission.

Missionary Training

Now let me backtrack to my training as a missionary. My interest in Christian missions goes back to the days of my boyhood, when, I think, the seed was probably planted by my father, then a country minister in the state of Victoria, in Australia. Unfortunately, when Australia was hit by the great economic depression that followed World War I, my schooling was cut off at the junior high school level with what was known as the Intermediate Certificate, and I went to work to help with the family budget. Employed as a clerk in the Orient Line of Steamers, I worked every day until 5 p.m. The evenings were the only time I had for study, and I attended a night school, doing a number of subjects, concentrating in history, for which I had had a passion from my earliest childhood.

In 1935 I went out into the world, into a pastorate. In my church, the theological student of those days served for three years in the pastorate on probation before he was ordained, all this time doing further examinations in four subjects each calendar year. In addition to this I completed the diploma of theology with the Melbourne College of Divinity.

In spite of the fact that training as a minister (or missionary) in my country included six years of examination work, there was not a single course on Christian mission, either its history or its strategy. At the college, where we had tutorials, and at the university, where we were free to do degree classes if we so desired, we had nothing at all in the subject of anthropology. All that I could do for myself in this direction was to find an elective which occupied me for twelve months of course work in the field of comparative religion. This covered one term on the religions in general, another on primitive religion, and on one select religion, which, in my case, was Hinduism.

After serving the home church in rural appointments for six years, I was sent out to a mission field with no further preparation. By exam, by course work, and by practical experience, I had been trained for the ministry of the home church, except for that one course in comparative religion. We did have a missionary training college in Sydney, where our missionaries normally were sent for three to six months special preparation for the mission field, but the circumstances associated with the activities of Adolf Hitler in Europe denied me this opportunity, and I was sent out into the islands to be there in the event of anything happening; as you all know, it certainly did, for we were well at war in Fiji long before Pearl Harbor. During 1941–42, when Fiji was occupied, first by New Zealand troops, and then later by Americans who had survived the Guadalcanal experience, we missionaries passed through a traumatic experience, as indeed did the Fijians themselves.

In 1942 I wrote a long paper called "Fijian Shadowline," which, fortunately, I never published. As I look back on it now, I think it shows, not so much a picture of Fiji under army occupation in 1942, as my own *self*—my own *culture shock*. Because of the war, our first furlough did not come to us for six and a half years, by which time the war was over, and the Fijian people were now alarmed because they had discovered that, according to the vital statistics, they were now quantitatively only the second race in their own country.

However, the postwar period brought a new spirit and a new readiness on the part of the Fijian people to move ahead. We had faced up to the problem of missionary domination in the local church, and had established a new constitution which gave the Fijians autonomy over their own church and its affairs, and made us Europeans just servants of the church, colleagues, but with no more voting power for any one of us than any Fijian had. We had over 160 Fijian ministers who outnumbered us by about twenty to one. These were tremendous years to me because I took my place under Fijian leadership, and anthropologically, it made a world of difference to me. After many years in the backwaters, the church commenced to grow again, both organically and qualitatively.

[Here follows a section of twenty pages in which Tippett enumerates the various anthropologists he studied and the ideas that he borrowed from them in his missiology. We resume with sections on applied anthropology and ethnohistory.—Ed.]

Applied Anthropology

I ought also to say, now that I have moved into the subject of applied anthropology, that my old friend Homer Barnett really introduced me to this as an aspect or field of the discipline. We got on very well together because I knew I needed his theory, and he was glad to draw from my field experience. We were both Oceania men, and I did a culture area analysis of Indonesia under him, and a reading course on French Oceania. [Homer Barnett was one of Tippett's instructors in his doctoral studies in anthropology at the University of Oregon in the early 1960s.—Ed.]

Another applied anthropologist who stimulated my thinking a good deal with Charles Erasmus, who wrote the book *Man Takes Control*. When I began teaching anthropology at the Institute of Church Growth, I made use of material derived from Erasmus on the American Point Four Program to help me show how an advocate ought to choose the area of the greatest potential for his advocacy. [The Institute of Church Growth was located on the campus of Northwest Christian College in Eugene, Oregon. The Institute was subsequently moved in 1965 to Fuller Theological Seminary in Pasadena, California, to become the School of World Mission and the Institute of Church Growth.—Ed.]

I am convinced that there is a great deal in the writings on applied anthropology which yet remains for us to explore in the sense of discovering its applicability to the Christian mission. I never specialised in this field for comprehensives, and so my reading was only superficial in it at that time. Since I graduated, and indeed, since I have come to Fuller, I have been trying to fill in some of the gaps. The 1960s were productive years in applied anthropology. I read Lucy Mair, George Foster, Conrad Arensberg, and Arthur Niehoff, because I believe that in this kind of writing there is an almost inexhaustible gold mine of material.

A year or so ago, I had a class in the theory of anthropology in which five or six men in the class had carried anthropology to a fairly advanced degree. Several had done their masters' degrees under well-known anthropologists. One was a Hoebel man, another's professor was a graduate of Graebner (whose writing I knew from his battles with Boas), another was a graduate of George Foster, and still another had a bias against the writings of Malinowski, which he had inherited from his own professor. I found I got quite different reactions from the class that year, so much so that I devoted about three class periods to the writings of Malinowski, not because he was my favourite anthropologist, but because I think he is probably one of the most misunderstood, and if understood properly his writing is highly suggestive for us in missiology.

Bronislaw Malinowski

For some reason or other, I do not really know why, I am often identified with the writings of this anthropologist. When I had defended my dissertation and my advisor was trying to make a genial compliment of some kind to me, he said very generously, "Malinowski would be proud of you." Now honestly, this really surprised me, because I was not very widely read at the time in the writings of Malinowski, and there were only three references to Malinowski in my dissertation. But it seemed to me that if my mentor saw similarities, I should read more of his writings to see why. And so, since my graduation I have made myself more familiar with this man's work. If in my lectures and later writings I have often quoted from Malinowski, it is not because he influenced me greatly, but because in reading him I have found many things which I had already discovered in my missionary experience. Whether I had cogitated very much on the various theories of functionalism does not really matter, I was methodologically a functionalist, so Malinowski rang the proverbial bell with me.

I do not want to enter into a debate about Malinowski's place in the history of anthropology, except to say that I think he was one of the greatest anthropologists of history. In both anthropological theory and methodology he was responsible for the most urgently needed correctives in his day, and he has to be evaluated in that context. His applied anthropology was directed to the colonial situation with the presupposition that it was going to survive. That context is now obsolete, but he had very many fine insights, which are still true although the context is changed dramatically. He saw the colonial situation as dynamic; there was nothing static or irrelevant in Malinowski's colonialism. Although he did not anticipate its demise, nevertheless, he saw that its survival through cultural change demanded adaptation and accommodation to new situations and new relationships among the participants. His concept of the *new autonomous entity*, in which the administration, the missionary, and the indigenous people had to interrelate with each other in order to survive, was a brilliant concept. Possibly there is no other concept in all theoretical and applied anthropology which says more to the "mission-church relationship" situation that we face on so many of our old mission fields. The tendency of many of his critics to dismiss him as a figure of the colonial age is not fair to him, for every man should be judged in the context in which he operates.

Some recent writings in applied anthropology have taken up this very theme for the new age, but without recognising that the concept itself was enunciated in the colonial period. Furthermore, some functionalists have gone to ridiculous theoretical extremes, but I do not hold Malinowski responsible for them. I know of no theoretical concept which has been more fruitful for the study of culture in the process of change than the notion of things being functional and surviving because they continually function in their formal adaptation to change. Please note that this is a dynamic not a static view of function in society. To us, in missiology, it has been methodologically tremendously important, because it has demonstrated to us that felt needs continue and must be met, that in all change some new things survive, and that without this continuity of function we run into cultural voids.

I think that probably the most profitable notion which I have developed myself is the place of the *functional substitute* in church planting and the incorporation of converts into the fellowship of believers. In developing my ideas of the functional substitute in church planting, I used a frame of reference based on Malinowski's *integral institutions* of a tribe. It is Malinowski who impressed upon us the complicated, interrelated character of an ethnic community or multi-individual group. He tells the missionary that if he changes one tribal institution dramatically, this will affect other institutions as well.

And Many Others

There is something endless about this catalogue of names of anthropologists from every one of whom I have learned something that may be applied to missiology.

Although I found Nadel a bit heavy, nevertheless, I learned from him the methodological distinction between *diachronic* and *synchronic* research, which has become so basic in my own research. J. H. Steward also used the same terms, though in a slightly different sense, and I read Steward about the same time. From Steward also, in his exchange with Ford on typology I derived some insights which I used in my dissertation and which I think we could use as a model for church growth studies. Several other exchanges interested me greatly and helped to warn me to be more careful with my interpretations of data—there was the exchange between White and Bidney about God, and that between Boas and Graebner on diffusion and convergence. From Hallowell, the ethnopsychologist, and Dobzhansky, the physical anthropologist, I was led to think of the notion of *self-awareness*, which I "collectivised" for use in my study of indigeneity.

I have no time to mention Oscar Lewis, Melville Herskovits, E. E. Evans-Pritchard, Robert Redfield, and many others from whom I picked up points somewhere along the line; and anthropologists like Baldwin Spencer, A. W. Howitt, and Lorimer Fison, who were databases for me; but let me just mention one I do not know how to classify unless I call him an anthropological philosopher like David Bidney. I speak of V. F. Calverton, who wrote on the title of my own article, "Cultural Compulsives," and deals with the problem of cultural conditioning which prevents people from admitting the truth. It seems to me that one of the first essentials of being able to make an objective, or reasonably objective, analysis of a church growth situation, is to recognise the cultural conditioning which will tend to force us to the conclusions we want to reach.

Archivists and Ethnohistorians

One of the rich qualities in the discipline of anthropology has been the infusion of ideas from other disciplines. Many of the great anthropologists came into anthropology from other disciplines. Nadel was a psychologist, White was from physical science, Bidney came from philosophy, Boas from geography, Morgan from law, Frazer from the classics; and of the much lesser breed, I came out of history. It was therefore natural that my anthropology should have a historical flavor to it. I think that perhaps *Aspects of Pacific Ethnohistory* is the nearest of all my writings to the real "me"; you might call it my hobby, or the fruit of my "leisure." It is the result of a combination of factors such as go to make up the methodology of ethnohistory, which I believe has tremendous potential for the development of missiology. I firmly believe we should have a course in *ethnohistorical method* in this institution, but I have not yet been able to sell this idea to my colleagues. [Within a year Tippett was teaching a course on ethnohistory. I took the course in 1975 and sat through it again in 1976.—Ed.] I think this little book on the Pacific is the most important methodological thing I have done. Each chapter is based on a different kind of documentary source. If in missiology we are to provide case studies of church planting and church growth, and begin with their roots in the culture in the contact period, we have to take the methodology of ethnohistory more seriously.

The point I have made in that book is that this is not just a combination of history and anthropology, it is *a maturation process of the interaction of the methodologies of the two from which arises a new methodology of its own.* It is essential for the reconstruction of the dynamics of the power encounter between the Aboriginal religion and Christianity. The people movements of our own lifetime have reopened the importance of the subject of the pioneering people movements of the last century, and indeed of the European people movements of the Middle Ages. I once presented a paper to this forum arguing that the present-day people movements demanded the reopening of critical studies on those of the Middle Ages, and this method is not without some support among historians.

It would be difficult to specify the people who have influenced me most in this direction. History was my first love in grade school, and I owe that love to my early history teacher, and to the other history teachers along the way. But it was Dr. Ernst Posner, professor of archives in Washington DC, who opened up to me the fascination and the methodology of archival studies. Posner had escaped from Germany at the beginning of the Hitler regime, and was an expert in medieval German documents. He could identify a document as pre-Luther or post-Luther by reading a few pages of it. I wrote my first paper on Pacific archives under his direction.

Of the many significant concepts he gave me, I think the most important was what is known as archival *provenance*, or the context from which documents come, and the relationship of documents to each other within that context—the French *fonds d'archives*. Thus at the same time both in history and in anthropology the significance of *context* was bearing down on me. I saw that neither documents nor individuals are isolates, that they derive meaning from their contexts.

Now I learned the difference between archival and library classifications. I learned the dangers of subject matter classifications, which pulled things out of their context to simplify the system of finding aids. This has made me cautious of what I consider one of the most frightening weaknesses of church growth case studies; namely, that we state some theoretical principle or speculation, and then search for evidence to prove it, quite often extracting our evidence from its context. I now saw how every context is *a total interacting thing*, that a file of assorted papers, which the creator of the file had put together, had some principle of cohesion in his mind, and that once those documents were separated into their subject files, the unifying element, or set of relationships, was lost.

While I was in Washington I did an in-service project at the National Archives, and worked on the American Consular Records of the Samoa Post, 1853–1927, after which the consular office was transferred to Fiji. This was a tremendous experience, worked out for one full day each week, behind the security bars of the National Archives. It revolutionised my ideas of historical method and of historiography. It opened up to me by a practical demonstration the significance of context in documentation, and the importance of the creating agency. From that day to this I never really enjoy an undocumented historical manuscript.

Before going to Washington, while I had been engaged in historical writing in Fiji, I had attempted a heavily documented monograph on the early Fijian Christians. It concerned two or three critical problems about which I disagreed with the generally accepted historians, so that probably I went to Washington with some expectation of improving my methodology along these lines, but what I discovered was far beyond my expectations. I did my master's thesis on the South Pacific labor trade, and I am now convinced that the documentation of this thesis was adequate for a doctoral dissertation. Later on, at Oregon, Homer Barnett borrowed this thesis, and when he eventually returned it after eighteen months, commented on its documentation.

The weakness of most of our church growth case studies lies in their inadequate documentation from primary sources. Our bibliographies are overweighted with secondary sources, which means another person has come between the documents and our writing; another interpretation, another bias. We do not know if these references are related to, or extracted from their archival context. Probably this is because we write our studies in too short a period of time. Historical, and especially ethnohistorical research, is a time-consuming matter. In the footnotes, or endnotes, of a book we can discover whether or not the research is from secondary sources, or if it is a genuine ethnohistorical reconstruction.

This conviction which I owe to my archives and history teachers in Washington, DC, especially Posner and Schellenberg, may perhaps be reflected in the endnotes of *People Movements of Southern Polynesia*, which was written while I was at Oregon, and *Solomon Islands Christianity*, which was written between my Oregon and Pasadena periods. In each case the endnotes are in small type, but they occupy forty-two pages in the former, and twenty-five in the latter. Most of these are additional factual information; references to official mission, government, and other documents; and comments on critical histo-riographical problems, which would make the text of the book dull, but are essential to validate the whole account.

Now the interesting thing about ethnohistory, which, by the way, is a methodology and not a discipline, is that it has developed, not in the discipline of history, but in the dis-cipline of anthropology, and mostly among the anthropologists who have been working on the study of American Indians. In more recent times it has been penetrating into African studies but only very slightly in Oceania.

When I did my PhD dissertation, I found myself working in the ethnohistory of Fiji, and this drove me back to the journal *Ethnohistory* and its methodological articles. Here I met a number of new anthropological writers—Fenton, Sturtevant, and others—and I saw a new set of values and a new approach to ethnological reconstruction. Some of these men I have since met, and once I was able to go to the American Ethnohistory Association annual meeting at the University of Georgia and present a paper I had worked out on the encounter of Fijian and Papuan values. My documentary base for this had been a collection of Fijian letters of the early evangelists working in Papua at the turn of the century and a little before it. The presentation was well received, and the discussion centered in the methodology I was using.

I am convinced, therefore, that if we are diligent in SWM [School of World Mission, Fuller Theological Seminary] in digging up the documentary material of the early mission-aries who date back to the culture contact period, that we have a reservoir of information in which we can develop a *missiological methodology* that will be acceptable to ethnohisto-rians at large. I see no problem why some of the basic research done by our graduates and alumni should not find its way into the anthropological textbooks on methodology that will be produced in the next so-many years. We have, in point of fact, an advantage over the secular anthropologist in that we have a priority in the use of missionary archives.

Currently there is in the world a readiness to collect material for preservation. In my country an organisation known as the Pacific Manuscripts Bureau, a small body main-tained by four or five of the big libraries in the Pacific, operates for this purpose. The function of the PMB is to locate all kinds of documents, journals, correspondence, reports, and unpublished manuscripts, which belong to the contact period, but have been forgot-ten in attics and store rooms, where they are held by the descendants of earlier planters, traders, missionaries, and sea captains. Then, having located them, they seek permission to microfilm them, the microfilm being made available to libraries or to private persons who wish to buy them. I myself have procured microfilms of five or six missionary journals this way. I have now spent my last two sabbatical terms hunting out this kind of material from my mission field and working on it, with very great profit to myself.

Many of the old problems of interpretation have now proved solvable, as they were not before. The point I want to make is that the validity of our case study church planting reconstructions of the early periods depends on the availability and recovery of the basic documents—I mean the letters and the journals which give us the real feelings of the missionaries, not the reports they wrote for the boards, societies, or sending churches back home. And study of the dynamics of church planting in the contact period requires this kind of documentation; likewise, any reconstruction of the pre-Christian religion. This is only possible when the researchers are prepared to spend time and effort in the recovery of these documents. It is far too easy for us to say they just do not exist. How do we know that? We should be like collectors, seeking the rare specimen, learning to know the likely place for some treasures to turn up, and *this is part of anthropology, and it is part of missiology.* It is part of the methodology of case study reconstruction in our discipline.

I started off some years ago with a basic collection of the writing and notebooks of Lorimer Fison, given to me by his daughter, then over ninety years of age. The story of how I heard about her, searched her out, and eventually how she asked me to carry on her father's work, handing me his papers, is an exciting adventure in itself. But the point I want to make is that for twenty years I have been seeking the documents I know to have been alienated from that collection. Each year I update my typed manuscript of his bibliography and manuscripts. Each year I write at the top of the checklist the date of the new redaction. When I first began this, it had about fifty or sixty entries in it. The one I have just finished now, as a result of my last sabbatical, has well over 150 entries. Here is an archival repository large enough for five or six volumes covering the man's work as an anthropologist, a missionary, and journalist, of which he, in each respect, was an exceptional figure. Twenty years ago I could have said I had it all, and I might have believed that. I now know I can never say that, because each year something turns up, in Australia, in Fiji, in New Zealand, and now in the University of Rochester, New York.

[We have included as Appendix B of this volume Tippett's 1973 redaction of the Fison materials. Its inclusion serves a double value; first, noting the scope of the Fison materials, and second, as a model in ethnohistorical documentation.—Ed.]

Nothing in our work is ever final. We never know when some treasure still remains awaiting our discovery. It was this belief that delayed the publication of *People Movements in Southern Polynesia* from 1963 to 1971, because I could not find a certain document which I needed. Eventually I found it, and my hunch was correct. The book, when it did come out, was far more accurate than it would have been at one very critical point. This is why so much of my published work is marked "Research in Progress." The danger of publishing a book or an article is the danger of *giving the impression of finality.* We seldom go back to it again once it is finished and in print. The phrase "Research in Progress" in an article or a book is not only a safeguard against another critic, it is a continual reminder that the research is unfinished. You will not stay long enough with us in this institution to be definitive or final in anything you write. What really counts is what you will do with all this when you go out, how thorough you will be in your future digging. Both historiography and anthropological research have taught me the truth that we never really reach finality in a subject, even our own potential is not exhausted, "not on this side of the tomb," as the poet said.

[The concluding section of Tippet's presentation, "Current Trends," has not been included.]

APPENDIX A
Outline for a Proposed Book on Ethnohistory in Missiology[233]

The Ethnohistorical Approach to Church Growth Case Study Research and Church Self Studies (Cross-cultural)

Introduction: The Nature of Ethnohistorical Reconstruction in Missiology, and Its Contribution to Contemporary Scientific Research on Human Communities.

Part One: PERSPECTIVE

1. Missiology as Applied Science:
   a. The need for church growth case studies.
   b. The role of the researcher, as the church being studied sees him.
   c. The church as the subject for research as seen by the researcher.
2. When Is an Institution "Indigenous" and What Do We Mean by "Contextualisation"?
3. Cultural Perspectives Across Time (Synchronics) and Through Time (Diachronics).
4. Self Studies and Periodic Reviews. Second-generation Analyses and Perfection Growth.
5. Relating Academic Research and Data Banks to Field Situations: A Two-way Process.
6. Awareness and Synthesis of Parallaxes.
7. Worldviews, Morals, and Cultural Values.
8. Beyond Measurement and Documentation: Meta-history and Meta-anthropology; Documents and Traces.
9. Experiment, Discovery, and Revelation in Scientific and Missiological Research.
10. Conversion as a Dynamic Process Described with Scientific Models.

In Summary (Part One): The Significance of Ideas in Developing Research.

---

233 [Alan Tippett felt the pressing need for a textbook on ethnohistory to be made available to students and practitioners of missiology. He had typed his ideas for the contents of the book, and had spoken to former student Darrell Whiteman about the two of them collaborating on the book. Whiteman planned his sabbatical for spring semester 1989 to go to Australia and write the book with Tippett. Shortly after his letter in September 1988 Tippett passed away. Whiteman went on to become professor of cultural anthropology and dean of the E. Stanley Jones School of World Mission and Evangelism at Asbury Seminary as well as editor of the journal *Missiology* (1989–2002), a role Tippett had earlier filled (1973–75). The table of contents for the book Tippett envisioned are reproduced here.—Ed.]

Part Two: METHODOLOGY

11. Setting One's Course: Paradigms and Models. The selection of and requirements in a Paradigm.

12. The Function of a Model and Its Appropriateness.

13. The Case Study of a Church in Mission: What, Why, and How?

14. Identifying Dynamic Cultural Themes in a Cross-cultural Church. Learning to research in cross-cultural situations and patterns.

15. "Getting into the Act": Rapport and Empathy. Harmonizing the purposes of the people being researched, and out-group researchers doing the job. How to develop their good relations.

16. The Function of Cultural Institutions in Changing Society (especially relating to religion).

RESEARCH ADJUSTMENTS.

17. Selection and Responsibility. How to be practical and responsible in terms of the paradigm, to the end that those being researched will benefit from it.

In Summary (Part Two): How to bring research skills to serve the felt needs of the field situation being researched, meeting the needs with abiding results that are both progressive and yet indigenous.

Part Three: INTERPRETATION

18. The Ethnohistorical View of Context.

19. The Complex Nature of an "Event."

20. Ethnohistorical Light on the Meaning of Meaning.

21. The Complexity of Historical Causation.

22. The Need for Clear Awareness of Anthropological Diversity.

23. How Westernised Can Tribal Society Become without Ceasing to Be Tribal?

24. How Pagan Can a Western City Be?

25. The Essentiality of Equilibrium in Synthesis.

In Summary (Part Three): No research procedure can be truly performed or interpreted in a vacuum; and likewise it needs to be applied in its own context, and to the felt needs and expectations of communities in that context. No findings are valid in the abstract.

Part Four: DATA COLLECTING

26. Persons, Institutions, and Structures : The importance of being aware of, and familiar with, previous research, the models that have been used, and the data-collecting techniques, etc.

27. The Basic Arts of Field Data Collecting:

     a.   Art of observation

    b.   Art of interviewing

    c.   Participant observation (when and where)

    d.   Basic data-collecting tools—questionnaire, schedule, sampling, etc. When and where. How reliable? Using the best tools for each specific situation.

    e.   Validation of research.

    f.   Researcher and research assistant relations.

28. The Library as a Resource Centre: Mastering the Classification System, Discovering Resource Strengths, Special Collections, Copying Facilities.

29. Archival Repositories: Understanding Their Principles of Arrangement, Provenance of Documents, etc. How and why they differ from library arrangements, and what this signifies for research.

30. Observing and Measuring Institutions and Processes Experiencing Social and Religious Change, and Especially How These Apply to Church Planting and Growth. Why do they change, when, and how?

31. Identifying and Measuring Processes and Institutions that Are Continuous in Spite of Surrounding Change. How to identify cultural clusters involved. Why and when is change resisted by a society, and what does all this say to functional substitutions in church or religious transition?

In Summary (Part Four): The importance of drawing one's tools for research from an ever-widening range of interdisciplinary methods, both for data collecting and checking (validating) our own research in every possible way. Why must this be done? Discuss ethnoscience, ethnopsychology, ethnomusicology, relating to missiology.

Part Five: APPLICATION

32. Relevance and Responsibility in Science: "Science for Science Sake" or "Applied Science." What moral values underlie science in our new era? What is the responsibility that goes with special knowledge and special skills for its application to needy humanity? How does this relate to postcolonial mission?

33. Relevance and Responsibility in History. What is the value of history in an age of atomic technology and computers? Under what conditions can history justify its own existence as an academic discipline in our day and generation? Proceed to ask the same question of the history of mission and church history. Does the colonial era speak, negatively or positively, to postcolonial church growth studies?

34. Relevance and Responsibility of Ethnohistory. What new research methods have been developed in the last two to three decades? What research structures, models, values, etc., come from its interdisciplinary experience? What does this do to church growth analyses and church self studies?

35. Relevance and Responsibility in Postcolonial Missiology. How does the synthesis of its component disciplines speak to the postcolonial idea of Christian mission?

36. Relevance and Responsibility of the Biblical Mandate for Mission. What has changed since colonial times? What remains firm?

   a. Does the biblical base remain the same? Do we have a better understanding of context in the Bible. How does it speak to modern mission?

   b. Is theology a thing of the cloister, or is it to be applied in the world— relevant and responsible?

   c. What does this imply for missiological research case studies, and church self studies? What does it say to the basic purposes and functions of such studies?

In Summary (Part Five): Where is postcolonial missiology heading? What research projects need to be done? Ethnohistory, ethnopsychology, ethnolinguistics, ethnotheology, ethnomedicine: what do we incorporate by introducing them to missiology, and what do we do to missiology by ignoring them? When the resources of interdisciplinary fields are available, are we relevant and responsible by ignoring them and following still the old colonial paths, be it under new names?

APPENDIX B

Lorimer Fison: Checklist of Material Known to Exist
Redaction March 1973[234]

1. 1858   Poetry published in *The Wyndham Journal* under the pen name VIATOR. Fison travelled to Australia in 1857 on the ship *General Wyndham*. See letter at the Mitchell Library dated 25 February 1871.

2. 1861–75   (mostly 1871–74) *Fison's Cuttings Book of Published Articles*. See Item 9, which includes material to which these articles were replies.

3. 1861–63   Poems: "Visions of a Dying Saint" (1861)
    "Consolation" (1863), which seems to have been written after the death of his father, mother, and little brother.

4. 1862   "Recollections," *Wesleyan Chronicle*

5. 1863–64   Copies of correspondence in Fison's hand, relating to the missionary ownership of lands, together with regulations and minutes of official committee resolutions.

6. 1865–70   Fison Letters from Fiji, published in *Wesleyan Missionary Notices*. 13 long letters from Viwa, Lakeba, and Rewa. Most of these were published as "From a Missionary in Fiji" (see card file).

7. 1865   Letters published under the *nom-de-plume* FILIUS.
    "Fijian Words," *Christian Advocate*
    "Cannibalism in Fiji," *Watchman*
    "Letter from Viwa," Missionary Notices
    "Letter from Lakeba," *Christian Advocate*
    "Fiji Correspondence," *Christian Advocate*

8. 1865–68   Miscellaneous Papers, microfilmed by Pacific Manuscript Bureau, Australian National University.

---

234 [Tippett did not prepare this document for publication. It was updated annually as new items were located, which explains differences in bibliographical style and the inclusion of occasional personal comments. For Tippett, this record represents "Research in Progress."—Ed.]

9.   1865–94   "Extracts"—a book of reading notes and newspaper clippings, every item numbered, and an index of Fison's tastes. Many of the cuttings inspired articles in Item 2. They cover, among other things, material on the Pacific in general, Fiji, the Melanesian Mission, the Labour Trade (including the Carl Case), Bishop Patteson, Fiji population figures, notes on Fijian culture and riddles, the Naga rites, references to the Samoan Civil War. This is specially important material through the seventies.

10.   1867–69   Fison's duplicate Letter Book. Letters written from Rewa, July 1868 – July 1869, and Lakeba Report 1867.

11.   1867–73   Letters and articles about the Fijians, sermons. Manuscripts currently at the Mitchell Library, Sydney.

12.   1869–70   Correspondence to Goldwin Smith—4 letters. In the Rare Manuscripts Collection, University of Rochester.

13.   1870–71   Small Notebook. Rough notes on shipping, and Fison's experiences in Tonga and Samoa.

14.   1870–81   Correspondence from Lewis Henry Morgan and others. Transcript of 41 items, 35 of them addressed to Fison. The others refer to his work (2 are to Howitt) and its publication. At the La Trobe Library, Melbourne.

15.   1870–81   Correspondence from Lewis Henry Morgan—37 letters. In Rare Manuscripts Collection, University of Rochester.

16.   1870–87   Correspondence received from missionaries and other informants regarding Australian Aborigines, especially concerning the marriage pattern and kinship terminology. 36 items, including 8 from Taplin.

17.   1871   "The Murder of Judge Norman" on the methods of Islam. *Advocate*. *Nom-de-plume* NEMO.

18.   1871   "The True Hope of the Christian Church," *Christian Advocate*.

19.   1871   "Westward Ho!" A series of articles in the *Advocate* through November and December, under the *nom-de-plume* OUTIS.

20.   1871   "Volunteers for Fiji," *The Herald*, 18 December.

21.   1871   Review of Joseph Bush's *What to Preach and How*. Wesleyan Conference Office, *Advocate*. December.

22.   1871   "Interchange of Pulpits," *Advocate*, 30 December under the pseudonym MEDEIS.

23.   1871   "United Communion," *Advocate*, 1 December.

24.   1871   "Intolerance of the High Church Party," *Advocate*. November. Under the pseudonym OUTIS.

25.   1871   "Tahombau, King of Fiji," *Town and Country Journal*. 25 November.

26.   1871   "Speech on the Late Bishop Patteson," *Advocate*. December.

27.   1871   "The Murder of Bishop Patteson," *Sydney Morning Herald*.

28. 1871   "Letter on the Labour Traffic" written 25 November, published *Sydney Morning Herald*, 4 December. Copy in Cuttings Book has marginal comments by Fison.

29. 1871   "The Fijian Judged by His Own Words." Written in August 1871. Manuscript. Some of this was subsequently used in Item #129.

30. 1871   *Joel Bulu: The Autobiography of a Native Minister in the South Seas*, Wesleyan Mission House, London. Translated from the Fijian by Fison.

31. c. 1871   Notebook. Apparently this notebook had been supplied to James Havea, who recorded his autobiography in Fijian. Then follows the account of the death of Sailasa Yaba in the same handwriting. At the other end Fison filled up the book with his own rough notes on political affairs of the period of the British consulate, and some reading notes, as, for example,his notes for writing Item #21.

32. 1871–72   Controversy with "Master Mariner" about missionaries, in the Sydney Empire.

33. 1871–81   Correspondence to Lewis Henry Morgan—56 letters. In Rare Manuscripts Collection, University of Rochester.

34. 1871   Two Fison Letters, one to Joseph Henry and the other to Andrew Mackenzie. In the Rare Manuscripts Collection at the University of Rochester.

35. 1872   Data Collecting Form for Samoa, filled in by George Brown in the Fison/Morgan papers in the Rare Manuscripts Collection, University of Rochester.

36. 1872   "To Melbourne," *Christian Advocate*, February.

37. 1872   "Politics," *Christian Advocate*, 1 March, under the *nom-de-plume* MEDEIS.

38. 1872   "Our Melbourne Letter," written for the *Advocate*, in Sydney.

39. 1872   "The Classificatory System of Kinship," manuscript (46 pp.) as completed by Fison and bound with the title "Systems of Consanguinity and Affinity," December. (Note: Does this relate to Smithsonian publication #xvii, 1871? Check.)

40. 1872   Fison's own printed data collecting form. Specimens with the Fison Papers include his own, filled in for Rewa, Codrington's for Mota, and Taplin's for the Narriyeri.

41. 1872   "The Classificatory System of Kinship," *Proc. Royal Society of Victoria*, 10: 154–79.

42. 1872   Letter about Dr. Murray and the "Carl" Atrocities, published in the *Argus*, 10 December, under the *nom-de-plume* VITI.

43. 1872   Communications from Moulton of Tonga on the Tongan language

44. c. 1872   "The Schools of Bullham" under the pseudonym NEMO. The text of this article is in Item #2, but the paper and date are not cited.

45. c. 1872   Controversy with John Dennis with respect to the Earl of Pembroke's book in the *Daily Telegraph*, April.

46.   c. 1872   Review of John Inglis' *The Slave Trade in the New Hebrides*, Edmonson and Douglas, Edinburgh.

47.   c. 1872   "Laws of Consanguinity and Affinity among the Australian Aborigines," letter published in *The Australasian*, written 3 June.

48.   1872–89   Correspondence received from R. H. Codrington, mostly linguistic material, some letters very long, not all dated—24 items.

49.   1873   *The South Seas Labour Traffic.* A series of eleven long articles published in the *Daily Telegraph* early in the year, with resultant correspondence and replies until November. Essential documentation for the subject. Pseudonym OUTIS used.

50.   1873   "The Present State of Fiji," *The Chronicle*, September.

51.   1873   Controversy in *The Age* over the Labour Traffic. Letters published during December.

52.   1873   Controversy with Butters in the *Daily Telegraph* (see "Published Articles," 37–39, and "Extract Book" 232, 240, 241; Item #2, #9). *Nom-de-plume* OUTIS used.

53.   c. 1873   Notebook. Rough draft of writing about the work of native agents in the Fijian church. It seems to date from Fison's Lau period—must be after 1871, but probably 1873.

54.   1873–76   Newspaper articles from various sources, collected by Fison, with respect to the Labour Traffic; *Daily Telegraph*, *Fiji Gazette*, *Fiji Times*. These also cover Labour Ordinances and material on the Planters' Society. Some of these raise issues answered in Item #2.

55.   1873–77   Fison's Letters to the General Secretary of the Australian Wesleyan Mission in Sydney. Bound in a single volume. Item #104 Methodist Overseas Missions Archives, Mitchell Library, Sydney (m/f obtained).

56.   1873–86   Fison's correspondence with Howitt, 67 letters (some long), collected notes and tables. Some material collected after the publication of their book (Item #77). Australian Aborigine polyglott vocabulary of 30 basic words in 25 Victorian languages and dialects.

57.   1874   "South Sea Cannibalism" by FIJIAN, *The Australian*. 10 October.

58.   1874   Labour Trade Controversy: Letters from the *Daily Telegraph*, which involved Frederick Langham, February.

59.   1874   "Lay Representation," *Wesleyan Chronicle*, 24 April. Pseudonym FESTINA LENTE used.

60.   1874   "The Volunteer Movement," *Christian Advocate and Wesleyan Record*, 2 June. Pseudonym used MEDAMOS.

61.   1874–75   Material concerning Fison's exposure of the *Daphne* Case. Newspaper correspondence July 1874 – January 1875, *Daily Telegraph*.

62. 1874–81 Letters from Fison and Howitt to Lewis Henry Morgan. Now at University of Rochester. See entry #135, "Stern" 1930.

63. 1875 "The Bo'obo'oi" (about a Tongan newspaper), *Sydney Morning Herald*, 4 January, pseudonym DELTA.

64. 1875 Letter on Fijian Words, *Sydney Morning Herald*, April.

65. 1875 "Correspondence from Fiji," *Daily Telegraph*, May.

66. 1875 Articles on Tubou College, Tonga, *Sydney Morning Herald*, June–July.

67. 1875–77 "The Dominion of Fiji": series of 35 long articles in the *Sydney Morning Herald*, November 1875 – December 1877. HARDY LEE was the pseudonym used.

68. 1876 Fiji Labour Ordinance, 21 April, full text from the *Fiji Times*; Fiji Ordinance, re Polynesian Immigrants, 7 July, full text from *Fiji Times*, long letter by Wilkinson on Gordon's land policy (involving Langham) and other items collected by Fison.

69. 1876 "Angels in Fiji" article in *Sydney Morning Herald* on Nativism in Lau, 10 October, Fison investigated this. See Letter Book, item #50.

70. 1876 Howitt's letter to *The Argus* on Australian Aborigines and involving Fison, 11 October.

71. 1876–77 Notebooks (6) with notes in Fijian, written by Fijians for Fison. Nos. 1–4 with respect to Fijian Vows; No. 5 accounts of the death of Taniela Kepa and Rupeni and also notes about Emosi Kau, apparently written down by Joeli Bulu; and No. 6 with *mekes* (words for dances).

72. 1876–77 Notebooks—rough notes and rough drafts of reports. 1. Church matters, 1876; 2. Land claims (n.d.); 3. Mission lands, Maafu, American claims on Cakobau, 1876–77; 4. Crown lands, notes on Cession, and 5. notes on Kinship (5 books in all).

73. 1877–78 Newspaper correspondence to the *Weekly Advocate*, July 1877 – July 1878, under the pseudonym MANSELL HALL.

74. 1878 Memorial of Fison and Langham on Levuka lands. Several items.

75. 1878 "The Origin and Development of the Turanian System of Kinship as shown in the Class Divisions of the Australian Aborigines, with their Laws of Marriage and Descent." Finely written manuscript: 89 pp. and 12 pp. app., as Fison completed it in August 1878. It was subsequently used in *Kamilaroi and Kurnai* in 1880.

76. 1878 "Theory of the Kurnai System" 22 pp. Handwritten manuscript as Fison completed it in November 1878. Used in *Kamilaroi and Kurnai* in 1880.

77. 1878–81 File of correspondence received with reference to land, native laws, 1903–5 marriage, and other customs, 7c, from Gordon, G. Brown, Thurston, Allardyce, Wake, Gatschet, Taplin, Jackson, and Fraser.

78. 1878–1906 File of letters in Fijian, some notes and Fijian tales, a *meke*, and other odd items.

79. 187? *Old Sefanaia, the Fijian Herald*, by a friend of his (Fison), London n.d., Charles H. Kelly. The Mitchell Library thinks this was published about 1895, but the data was certainly collected in the seventies, when Fison was in Lau.

80. 1879 Newspaper correspondence regarding Dr. George Brown and the Blanche Bay Case.

81. 1880 File of material on Fijian lands, including the Appeals Case and a map.

82. 1880 *Kamilaroi and Kurnai; Group Marriage and Relationship Marriage by Elopement.* Melbourne, George Robertson; written jointly with A. W. Howitt. The parts of this volume actually written by Fison were: pp. 21–176, "Kamilaroi Marriage, Descent and Relationship," and pp. 293–314, "The Kurnai System." Fison's annotated copy still extant.

83. 1880 Review of *Kamilaroi and Kurnai* from the Melbourne *Argus*, together with newspaper clippings on the Aborigines. At the Mitchell Library.

84. 1880 *A Lands Appeal Case in Fiji* by F. Langham and L. Fison, reprinted from the *Fiji Times*, 29 November. G. L. Griffiths, Levuka. Printed copy in Turnbull Library, Wellington, New Zealand. (Microfilm held.)

85. 1880 R. H. Codrington's "Notes on the Customs of Mota, Banks Islands, with remarks by L. Fison." *Trans. Royal Soc. of Victoria* 16, pp. 119–43.

86. 1880 Letter to Spencer Baird in Fison/Morgan Papers in Rare Manuscripts Collection, University of Rochester.

87. 1880–81 Documents with respect to the Niukaubi Land Appeal Case, maps and notes by Fison. Correspondence with Sir Arthur Gordon and notes on the same.

88. 1881 Review of *Kamilaroi and Kurnai* by E. B. Tylor in *The Academy*, pp. 264–66.

89. 1881 "Notes on Fijian Burial Customs" *Journal of Anthrop. Inst.* 10: 332–52.

90. 1881 "Land Tenure in Fiji." Lecture based upon item #84.

91. 1881 Articles on Polygamy and the Decrease of Fijian Population in Fijian newspapers—*Fiji Times* and *Fiji Argus*, September–October.

92. 1881–83 Newspaper correspondence to the *Sydney Morning Herald*, September 1881 – September 1883, also leading articles based on Fison's articles.

93. 1882 "On Fijian Riddles," *Journal of Anthrop. Inst.* May. Reprinted by Harrison, London.

94. 1883 "Attic Demes and Australian Hordes," manuscript, 33 pp. Fison's part of a work done in association with A. W. Howitt.

95. 1883 "The Annexation of Melanesia" Series of five articles which appeared in the *Daily Telegraph*. November–December.

96. 1882–87 Official Tonga Publications. *Koe to hi fanogonogo fakebulaaga.* Nos. 8, 11, 14, 21, 29, 44.

97. 1884 "The Naga, or Sacred Stone Enclosure of Wainimala, Fiji," *Journal of Anthrop. Inst.* xiv, pp. 14–30.

98. 1886 Correspondence with respect to language, mythology, and genealogies of Melanesia and Polynesia, from A. Carroll: 5 letters.

99. c. 1886 "Specimens of Fijian Dialects arranged by L. Fison." Bound manuscript in Turnbull Library, Wellington, New Zealand. This is the original material sent by Fison to Gastchet. (Item #94.)

100. 1886 *Specimens of Fiji Dialects*, edited by A. S. Gastchet from Fison material (Item #93). *Internat. Z. Fur Allge-meine Scrachwissenschaft.* Leipzig, pp. 193–208. Reprinted.

101. 1887 Correspondence received from Thurston with respect to the Tonga Question. Two original letters.

102. 1888 "The Gospel According to Adam Smith," lecture delivered at Wesley Church, Melbourne, published in *The Spectator* and reprinted.

103. 1888–89 "Burial Customs in Fiji," *The Centennial and the Australasian Monthly Magazine*, vol. 1, pp. 238–46, 256–463.

104. 1888–1905 *The Spectator*, under the editorship of Fison. This covered many important Pacific issues—the Tonga Affair, the establishment of Wesleyan missions in Papua and (after Methodist Union) in the Solomons, in both of which Fijian agents were used, the law case against *Vagabond* over Cakobau of Fiji.

105. 1889 "The New Norcia Marriage Laws," *Journal of Anthrop. Inst.* xviii, pp. 68–70.

106. 1890 "Beachcombers' Yarns" by John Lugg in Centennial Magazine. June, pp. 822–24 deals with Fison.

107. 1890 "Aborigines of Victoria" Section in W. B. Spencer's *Handbook of Melbourne.*

108. 1891 Letter with reference to Australian Aborigines written for Section G, *Aust. Adv. Sci.* It is at the Mitchell Library, Sydney.

109. 1891 "A Note on Perforated Stones," *American Anthropologist* (old series) 2 pp. 177–79.

110. 1892 "Group Marriage and Relationship," *Proc. Australsian Assn. Adv. Science.* Section G. Anthrop. Paper 7, pp.688–97. Hobart.

111. 1892 "The Nair Polyandry and Dieri Pirauru," *Proc. Australasian Assn. for Adv. of Science.* Section G. Paper 10. Hobart.

112. 1892 The Presidential Address, *Australian Assn. Adv. of Science*, Proceedings pp. 144–53. Hobart.

113. 1893 "The Little Woman, or the Regeneration of Taffy's Creek," Nos. 1 to 5, Manuscript. Letter of Fison's relating the narrative to fact and identifying places. Letter mentions Howitt. Pseudonym HARDY LEE used.

114. 1894 Two short stories set in England, "The Mystery of the Attic" and "Aunt Lois' Charges." Manuscripts, under the pseudonym HARDY LEE.

115. c. 1894   "The Scoth Boys' Claim," Nos. 1–2. Manuscript. An Australian story under the pseudonym HARDY LEE.

116. c. 1894   "The Two White Hats," a story of the land boom in Victoria, written under the *nom-de-plume*, HARDY LEE.

117. c. 1894   "Introduction to the Study of Ancient Society" Nos. 1 to 5. Rough drafts in manuscript. (Was this ever published?)

118. 1895   "The Classificatory System of Relationship," *Journal of Anthrop. Inst*, xxiv, pp. 360–71. Basil Thomson's material is also in the same number. Reprinted.

119. 1896   Correspondence from Langham. Small and certain Fijians on R.C. activities. A good example of how Fison built up evidence before making public statements.

120. c. 1896   File of miscelleneous letters. Mostly about Australian Aborigines.

121. 1898   "On Apparent Reminiscences of Totemism in Fiji," Annual Report of New Guinea, 1897–98, Brisbane.

122. 1902   "On Surface Similarity in Words," *Report Australasian Assn. Adv. of Science* 9th Meeting, pp. 521–24.

123. c. 1902   *The Methodist History of Victoria and Tasmania*, Spectator Publishing, Melbourne, edited by Fison. No exact date, but reprinted from *The Spectator*, special issues, nos. 1–24, 1898–1901.

124. 1903   Land Tenure in Fiji, E. J. Marsh, Government Printer, Fiji. Official edition of Item #84. It was delivered as a lecture in 1881. My copy has also a number of newspaper cuttings on Fiji lands (1908–15).

125. 1903   Official correspondence with respect to the republication of this survey of Fijian Land Tenure, published in the *Australasian Methodist Missionary Review*. November 1903.

126. 1903   Manuscript copies of narratives used in Item #123.

127. 1903   "Fijian Volunteers for Papua," manuscript in rough draft narrating their experiences in Sydney.

128. c. 1903   "From Mother-right to Father-right" by Fison and Howitt. (Where was this used?) Pages 33–46, with Fison's annotations, are with Fison's papers.

129. 1904   *Tales from Old Fiji*, De La More Press, London. Second Impression 1907 by Maring.

130. 1904   Review of *Tales from Old Fiji* in *Nature*, lxx. p. 150 by A. C. Haddon.

131. 1905   Review of *Tales from Old Fiji* in *Review of Reviews.* 20 June by W. H. Judkins. [*sic* Misnumbering; no item 132.]

132. 1905   Letter to J. G. Frazer. Fison had been ill and was unable to write in his own hand. He used an amanuensis. The letter covers two important points: Fison's attitude to white men owning Fijian lands and his appreciation of Frazer's efforts in securing him the imperial pension, and also his surprise that Stanmore had also endorsed it.

133. 1906   Correspondence from A. J. Small to Fison with respect to the Tongans in Lau, together with typescript enclosures from other parties involved.

134. 1907   Letter to John Reed, in Fison/Morgan Papers, University of Rochester.

135. 1907   Typescript copy of petition by men of science for Fison's imperial pension.

136. 1907–8   File of Fison's Obituaries (died 29 December 1907). Worall, Danks, Frazer, Spencer, Brown, *American Anthropologist*, and Australian papers—*Age, Argus, Aust. H. M. Review, Spectator, Daily Telegraph,* and *Victorian Field Naturalist.* The file also includes the funeral notices from the Melbourne papers.

137. 1908   Biographical File: Reviews of *Tales from Old Fiji* and *Kamilaroi and Kurnai.* Odd clippings, questionnaire, references to the imperial pension, Fison family obituaries, etc.

138. 1909   "Howitt and Fison," *Folk Lore,* xx. 2, pp. 144–80. Article by J. G. Frazer.

139. 1916   Letter to Fison's daughter about her father, from C. Brunsden Fletcher.

140. 1927   "Howitt and Fison." Sir J. G. Frazer's article (Item #132) was included in his book *The Gorgon's Head,* Macmillan, London, 1927, pp. 291–331.

141. 1930   "Selections from the Letters of Lorimer Fison and A. W. Howitt to L. H. Morgan" by B. Stern, *American Anthropologist* 32: pp. 257–279, 419–453.

142. 1944   "George Brown and Lorimer Fison," in Fletcher's *Black Knight of the Pacific,* pp. 123–130.

143. 1956   "Dr. Lorimer Fison: Scientist, Journalist, Missionary: A Summary of the Literature He Left." Typescript article by A. R. Tippett for a symposium on the Literature of Fiji.

144. 1957   "How the Mosquitoes Came to Oneata," in E. H. Heddle's *The Boomerang Book of Legendary Tales,* pp. 29–36.

145. 1971   "James George Frazer and Lorimer Fison." Typescript unpublished article by A. R. Tippett.

146. n.d.   File of miscellaneous correspondence and notes mostly from the later period, but unrelated and mostly undated.

147. ?   Critical Notes on John Fraser's Island Tribe and some correspondence from Fraser and some of his published material.

148. n.d.   An unpublished manuscript without a title on the nature of Fijian conversion, 5 pp. 150. n.d. Early Melbourne Newspaper Cuttings, vols. 30 (15–16), 165 (52–4), and 167 (1116)—J. M. Forde. At the Mitchell Library, Sydney.

149. Biographical Volumes listing Fison:

    a.   *Dictionary of Australian Biography* Percival Serle, ed. Angus and Robertson, Sydney, 1949. pp. 296–97.

    b.   *Dictionary of National Biography* (Volume 1901–1911), article written by Eve Im Thurn.

    c.   *The Australian Encyclopedia*, Ed. by A. W. Jose and H. J. Carter, Angus and Robertson, Sydney 1925, article by James Colwell, p. 467.

    d.   *Fred John's Notable Australians and Who is Who in Australia*, G. Robertson and Co., Melbourne 1911, pp. 132–133.

    e.   Colwell's *A Century in the Pacific*, Beale, Sydney, 1914, pp. 662–665 devoted to Fison.

    f.   C. I. Benson's *Century of Victorian Methodism*.

    g.   *Lights in the Southern Sky*, Carrothers, London, Epworth Press. p. 99 is devoted to Fison.

150. Fison Material Published in Fijian. During his period at Navuloa. Published in the eighties by the Methodist Mission Press, Viwa.

    a.   *Ai Tukutuku kei Jisu* (Life of Jesus)

    b.   *Ai Tukutuku kei Paula* (Life of Paul)

    c.   *Ai Vola ni Fika* (with F. Langhaia) (Arithmetic)

    d.   Typescript of *Ai Tukutuku kei Isireli* (*History of Israel*), dating from this period is in the M.O.M. archives in Fiji.

    e.   From the same period we have *Na Kedraui Tukutuku ko Taniela kei Esiteri* (Story of Daniel and Ester), but this was printed by Mason, Firth and McCutcheon, Melbourne, 1883.

    f.   *Ai Tukutuku kei Jisu* was enlarged by Fison and printed by Spectator Publishing, Melbourne, in 1897, and again by the M.O.M. Press, Suva, in 1932.

    g.   *Ai Tukutuku kei Paula* was enlarged by Fison before he died. Subsequently it was reprinted in Fiji in 1916 and 1933.

    h.   The book on Daniel and Esther was reprinted in 1909 in Suva with the title *Ai Tukutuku kei Taniela kei Esiteri*.

    i.   Fijian hymn known to have been the work of Fison inlcuded:
       "Jisu, au tamata cala" (original)
       "Me biu vakataki evei" (original)
       "Jisu, nai Vakabula dua bau" (translation)

    j.   One of Fison's sermon outlines is preserved in his own handwriting: Exodus 14:15.

UNLOCATED MATERIAL:

One of Fison's communications was reprinted in a British Blue Book: which one was it? (See file of obituaries: Item #130). ? Land Tenure in Fiji. Several references exist to Fison having contributed to Hasting's Dictionary of the Bible, but I cannot trace anything. Was it one of the other Hasting's Dictionaries?

INDEX

www.ingramcontent.com/pod-product-compliance
Lightning Source LLC
Chambersburg PA
CBHW081223060526
44539CB00051B/1719